INTERNATIONAL ENGLISH USAGE

LORETO TODD
& IAN HANCOCK

ROUTLEDGE

London

First published 1986
by Croom Helm
First published in paperback 1990
by Routledge
11 New Fetter Lane, London EC4P 4EE

Printed and bound in Great Britain
by Butler & Tanner Ltd, Frome and London

British Library Cataloguing in Publication Data
Todd, Loreto
International English usage.
1. English language—Usage
I. Title   II. Hancock, Ian
428   PE1460

Library of Congress Cataloging in Publication Data
Todd, Loreto.
International English usage.
Includes index.
1. English language—Usage—Handbooks, manuals,
etc.   I. Hancock, Ian F.   II. Title.
PE1460.T64   1987   428   86-28426
ISBN 0-415-05102-9
ISBN 0-709-94314-8 hb.

Contents

Introduction

In the four centuries since the time of Shakespeare, English has changed from a relatively unimportant European language with perhaps four million speakers into an international language used in every continent by approximately eight hundred million people. It is spoken natively by large sections of the population in Australia, Canada, the Caribbean, Ireland, New Zealand, the Philippines, Southern Africa, the United Kingdom and the United States of America; it is widely spoken as a second language throughout Africa and Asia; and it is the most frequently used language of international affairs.

In the past, there has been a tendency to regard the English of England as the standard for the world. In recent years, more acknowledgement has been made of North American, Australian and New Zealand varieties; but in countries such as Kenya or Malaysia, where English is used widely but is not normally a mother tongue, 'localisms' are usually considered 'mistakes'.

Over the years many handbooks of English usage have been published, but *International English Usage* differs from its predecessors in two important ways. First of all, it acknowledges that speakers of English have won some of the battles with 'prescriptivists' who, for as long as usage books have been written, have legislated against such practices as split infinitives and ending sentences with prepositions. *International English Usage* offers a balance between *description* and *prescription*, basing its insights on recent research throughout the English-speaking world. Secondly, it adopts the position that English belongs to all those who have learnt to speak it, and that established regional varieties, whether spoken natively or not, have as much legitimacy as British, American or Australian dialects of the language.

The compilers have attempted to achieve two goals in the present work: to deal objectively with English as a world-wide language with many local varieties, and to distinguish legitimate regional practices from actual errors. This has not been easy, since a nebulous international written English is everywhere in competition with local, colloquial varieties, which often differ markedly from it. It is when the latter intrudes upon the former that conflict arises, and there will always be pundits who are ready to take local usage to task in the letters-to-the-editor columns. Without a doubt, much of what we have included here will be felt by some to be out of place in a usage book, but it is precisely because the world community of

English speakers *is* so diverse, and because the language reflects this, that the need for such a book exists.

We have tried to make *International English Usage* encyclopaedic in content. It contains precise information on:

1 speech in all its manifestations: the network norms, the regionally marked, the emerging 'standards';

2 the written language, offering clear rules on abbreviations, grammar, spelling and punctuation;

3 stylistic variants, from intimate to formal;

4 the language of literature;

5 the language of linguistics;

6 the conventions established for writing dissertations, essays and letters;

7 swear-words and linguistic taboos;

8 catch phrases, clichés, idioms, proverbs and slang;

9 prejudice in language: racism and sexism.

International English Usage is designed for all users of English, whether students, teachers, editors, writers, librarians or even our fellow linguists—who, while adept at taking English to pieces, are not always so skilled at putting it together. It is designed to bridge the gaps between colloquial and written English, to illustrate regional richness and to clarify how and why words and phrases are used. It provides information on innumerable topics hitherto not discussed in a reference book of this kind. And, most important of all, perhaps, it challenges pedantry, causing the user to become aware of the English language as it is, rather than as others tell us it should be.

Loreto Todd, *University of Leeds*
Ian Hancock, *University of Texas at Austin*

Contributors

Many scholars from English-speaking communities around the world have contributed entries to *International English Usage*. We should like to record our debt and our gratitude to:

Dr Mary Penrith, Research Associate to *International English Usage*.

Professor George Cave, Department of English, University of Guyana, Georgetown, Guyana, South America.

Professor Andrew Gonzales, President, De la Salle University, Manila, Philippines.

Professor John Holm, Department of Linguistics, New York State University, New York, USA.

Mrs Margery Houghton, Sea Point, Cape Town, South Africa.

Dr R. D. Huddlestone, Department of English, University of Queensland, Brisbane, Australia.

Dr Tony Hung, Department of English, National University of Singapore, Singapore.

Dr John Ingram, Department of English, University of Queensland, Brisbane, Australia.

Dr Munzali Jibril, Department of English and European Languages, Bayero University, Kano, Nigeria.

Dr Devindra Kohli, Department of English, University of Delhi, Delhi, India.

Dr David Lee, Department of English, University of Queensland, Brisbane, Australia.

Dr Paul Mbangwana, Department of English, University of Cameroon, Yaoundé, Cameroon.

Mrs Mona McCausland, Portadown Polytechnic, Portadown, Northern Ireland.

Professor T. C. M. Milward, Department of Linguistics, Sophia University, Tokyo, Japan.

Dr Satendra Nandan, School of Education, University of the South Pacific, Fiji.

Jonathan Price, Croom Helm Publishers, Beckenham, Kent, UK.

Dr Bruce Rigsby, Department of English, University of Queensland, Brisbane, Australia.

Professor Gildas Roberts, Department of English, Memorial University of Newfoundland, St. John's, Newfoundland, Canada.

Ms Diane Sutton, Centre for British Teachers Ltd., Rabat, Morocco.

Dun Ren Zhou, Department of Foreign Languages, Fudan University, Shanghai, The People's Republic of China.

We should also like to record our thanks to the following for their help and support:

Professor F. G. Cassidy, Wisconsin, USA. Dr Moira Chimombo, Zomba, Malawi. Professor Dennis Craig, Kingston, Jamaica. Robert A. Dunbar, Dublin, Ireland. Professor Walter Edwards, Chicago, USA. Ms B. Honikman, London, UK. Dr F. C. V. Jones, Berlin, Germany. Ms Annie Lee, Kuala Lumpur, Malaysia. Mrs Katharine Mendelsohn, London, UK. Professor John Pride, Wellington, New Zealand. Mrs Aiko Reinecke, Honolulu, USA. Brother A.N. Seymour, Nashdom Abbey, UK. Dr Kashim Ibrahim Tala, Yaoundé, Cameroon. Ms Isabelle Tsang, Hong Kong.

Symbols

A limited number of symbols occur in *International English Usage*. The most frequently used of these are:

→   means *can be rewritten as*. Thus A → B + C means that A can be rewritten as B + C.

⇒   means *can be transformed into*. Thus A ⇒ B means that A can be transformed into B.

~   means *is in free variation with*. Thus A ~ B means that A and B are in free variation, just as *dreamed* and *dreamt* are for many speakers.

<   means *derives/derived from*.

>   means *becomes/became*.

∅   is the symbol for *zero*.

*   precedes a structure that is not acceptable.

These and other symbols are explained in greater detail in the entries in which they occur.

Bold print in the main text of an entry means that the word or phrase has its own entry in the book.

Pronunciation Guide

/i/	the sound of *ee* as in *green*
/ɪ/	the sound of *i* as in *lip*
/ɛ/	the sound of *e* as in *get*
/æ/	the sound of *a* as in *man*
/ɑ/	the sound of *a* as in *arm*
/ɒ/	the sound of *o* as in *got*
/ʊ/	the sound of *u* as in *put*
/ɔ/	the sound of *aw* as in *lawn*
/u/	the sound of *oo* as in *loom*
/ʌ/	the sound of *u* as in *but*
/ɜ(r)/	the sound of *ur* as in *church*
/ə/	the sound of *e* as in *the*
/eɪ/	the sound of *ay* as in *day*
/əʊ/	the sound of *o* as in *go* (UK)
/oʊ/	the sound of *o* as in *go* (USA)
/aɪ/	the sound of *y* as in *sty*
/aʊ/	the sound of *ow* as in *how*
/ɔɪ/	the sound of *oy* as in *joy*
/ɪə/	the sound of *ear* as in *hear* (UK)
/ɛə/	the sound of *air* as in *hair* (UK)
/ɔə/	the sound of *ar* as in *war* (UK)
/ʊə/	the sound of *oor* as in *poor* (UK)
/θ/	the sound of *th* as in *thin*
/ð/	the sound of *th* as in *then*
/ʃ/	the sound of *sh* as in *shot*
/ʒ/	the sound of *z* as in *azure*
/ŋ/	the sound of *ng* as in *sing*
/ɬ/	the sound of *ll* as in *full*
/l̩/	the sound of *le* as in *bottle*
/m̩/	the sound of *m* as in *rhythm*
/n̩/	the sound of *on* as in *cotton*
/ʍ/	the sound of *wh* as in the Scottish pronunciation of *which*
/ʔ/	the glottal stop that can replace *t* in the middle or end of words in some UK pronunciations, for example *metal* and *put*
ˈ	indicates primary stress
ˌ	indicates secondary stress

A number of other sounds such as /r̥/, the initial consonant in a Welsh pronunciation of *Rhondda*, are introduced and explained in individual entries.

a- words

Apart from its use as an **article,** *a* occurs frequently in English. It can mean '(for) each/every' in:

three times **a** *week* (i.e. every week)
$1 **a** *dozen* (i.e. for each dozen)

A- occurs as a **prefix** with a range of meanings. It can precede body parts and a number of common nouns to indicate direction or location:

abreast ahead aside
abed abroad aloft

A number of *a* + *body parts* are now only used figuratively in the standard language:

He was taken **aback**. (i.e. surprised)
There was something **afoot**. (i.e. going on)

It is found in a set of nautical items indicating position:

abaft aboard astern

condition:

adrift afloat aground

or a desire to establish contact:

ahoy

Prefix *a-* is also found in a number of words indicating a state or process:

ajar alive atingle

The *a-* form in these words derives from **Old English**. It is no longer productive as a prefix and although many a- words such as:

aloud aloof asleep

are commonly used, many others such as:

ablush aflame aflutter

are found mainly in literature.
There is also an *a-/an-* prefix which derives from Greek *a-/an-* meaning 'not' or 'without' and which is still productive. It occurs in such words as:

amoral asocial asymmetrical

The *an-* form is the prefix used before vowels:

anaemic anarchy anastigmatic

See: **affix, wake.**

abbreviations

Abbreviations are appropriate in scholarly articles and **footnotes** (*VP* = verb phrase, *cf.* = *confer* = compare) and in documents where their use will not cause confusion. Elsewhere, abbreviations should be used sparingly.

Many abbreviations consist of the initial letters of the significant words in a phrase, for example *BBC* (British Broadcasting Corporation), *FBI* (Federal Bureau of Investigation). In speech, the main stress normally falls on the last letter of the abbreviation. Sometimes the letters used can combine to form new words or **acronyms,** for example *NATO* (North Atlantic Treaty Organisation).

The titles *Dr, Mr, Mrs, Messrs* are always abbreviated when used with names. (*Ms* is not strictly an abbreviation but a blend of Mrs and Miss.) Other standard abbreviations are *a.m.* and *p.m.*, *BC* and *AD*, *Jr.* (e.g. *James Smith Jr.*), and those for large organisations (e.g. *CBI* = Confederation of British Industry or *TUC* = Trades Union Congress). In formal writing, titles indicating high rank are given in full (*President, Prime Minister, Reverend*) but they may be abbreviated or clipped in informal writing especially when used with initials or first names (e.g. Professor Smith, *Prof.* J.A. Smith).

Abbreviations may vary in different countries or in different institutions. A Bachelor of Arts degree, for example, is referred to as a *B.A.* in the UK and in many universities in the USA but as an *A.B.* in Harvard.

Generally, contemporary UK usage avoids the use of full stops after abbreviations unless ambiguities would occur (as with *a.m.* becoming indistinguishable from *am*). In the USA, a full stop is usual after a lower case letter (*Fr., Lat.*). Latin abbreviations (such as *c.* = *circa*, *e.g.* = *exempli gratia* and *i.e.* = *id est*) tend to take full stops throughout the English-speaking world. Only one full stop is necessary after an abbreviation which occurs at the end of a sentence:

His name was Dai Jones Jr.

The article used before an abbreviation is determined by the pronunciation of the first letter (*a UFO* = unidentified flying object, *an M.A.* = Master of Arts).

The plural forms of abbreviations are occasionally specialised (*MSS* = manuscripts, *pp* = pages, *SS* = saints), but they generally take lower case 's' (*JPs* = Justices of the Peace, *MPs* = Members of Parliament).

The description above is concerned with abbreviations in written and formal styles. Certain abbreviations can also occur in informal speech and writing. Among these are:

BFN (Bye for now)
BLT (Bacon, Lettuce and Tomato)
TCB (Taking Care of Business)
TLC (Tender Loving Care)

See: **acronym, apostrophe, Bible, clipping, footnotes.**

-able, -ible

In spoken English there is little or no difference in pronunciation between the **suffixes** *-able* and *-ible* and this fact adds to the uncertainty many people feel about **spelling**. **Etymology** is of little help. It is true that many *-able* endings derive from the Latin suffix *-abilis*, whereas *-ible* endings are from *-ibilis*. Such information only puts the problem back one language. There is, unfortunately, no easy set of rules, although the more recent the compound word the more likely is the suffix to be *-able*:

permute—permutable
televise—televisable

because *-ible* is no longer productive as a **morpheme** and because *-able* is meaningful not only as a morpheme but also as a word that allows compounds to be rephrased:

permutable—able to be permuted
televisable—able to be televised

The following information will help to prevent spelling errors.
1 *-able* can be added to many verbs to form adjectives:

laugh—laughable
interpret—interpretable
think—thinkable

and negative adjectives may be formed by prefixing *un-*:

unflappable
unsinkable
unworkable

Where the verb ends with a consonant + e, as in *like* or *shake*, the 'e' is dropped before *-able* and, incidentally, before all suffixes beginning with a vowel. A number of words such as *likable/likeable* have two acceptable forms, the former more widely used in the USA, the latter in the UK. It is probable that the form without 'e' will become accepted worldwide. Where variants are possible, however, we provide them in 6 below. The only exceptions to this rule are words whose **base forms** end in *-ce*, *-ee* or *-ge*:

> *pronounceable*
> *agreeable*
> *gaugeable*

2 Where the base form ends in a vowel + y, the 'y' is retained:

> *buyable*
> *enjoyable*
> *sayable*

and where the base form ends in a consonant + y, the 'y' is changed to 'i':

> *deny—deniable*
> *petrify—petrifiable*
> *vary—variable*

The exceptions to this rule are:

> *flyable*
> *fryable*

neither of which is widely used.

3 Where the base form of a polysyllabic word ends in *-ate*, the *-ate* was originally dropped before *-able* was added:

> *alienate—alienable*
> *calculate—calculable, incalculable*
> *demonstrate—demonstrable*

This rule does not apply to monosyllabic words:

> *date—datable*

or to disyllabic words:

> *dilate—dilatable*
> *vacate—vacatable*

In recent **coinages** and frequently in speech, *-atable* forms occur:

> *infiltrate—infiltratable*
> *inundate—inundatable*

4 Base forms ending in a single consonant usually double the consonant before adding -able:

forgettable
battable (of a ground capable of being batted on)

This rule only applies to one verb ending in -er, thus:

conferrable

All the others have -erable:

preferable
referable
transferable

5 -ible endings occur in a fixed number of words deriving from Latin, such as:

audible
destructible
tangible

It is no longer a living suffix, and often we find **dyads** occurring with -ible in the Latin-derived (and usually formal) word and -able attached to the more frequently used verb:

credible—believable
edible—eatable
risible—laughable

A useful though not infallible rule is that when we delete -able we are usually left with a recognisable verb. This is not true when we delete -ible (cf. ed-, cred-, ris-).

6 The following lists give the recommended spellings of words that people often worry about.

(a) -able

abominable	accountable	adaptable	adorable
advisable	agreeable	alienable	amiable
appreciable	approachable	arguable	assessable
available	believable	bribable	bridgeable
calculable	capable	changeable	chargeable
conceivable	conferrable	consolable	curable
datable	debatable	definable	demonstrable
desirable	despicable	dissolvable	drivable
durable	educable	equable	excitable
excusable	expendable	finable	foreseeable
forgettable	forgivable	gettable	givable
hirable	immovable	immutable	impalpable

impassable	impeccable	implacable	impressionable
indefatigable	indescribable	indispensable	inflatable
inimitable	insufferable	irreplaceable	justifiable
knowledgeable	losable	malleable	manageable
measurable	noticeable	operable	peaceable
penetrable	perishable	permeable	pleasurable
preferable	pronounceable	readable	reconcilable
regrettable	reliable	removable	reputable
serviceable	suitable	tolerable	transferable
undeniable	unexceptionable	unknowable	unmistakable

(b) *-able/eable*

likable/likeable
lovable/loveable
salable/saleable
sizable/sizeable
usable/useable

(c) *-ible*

accessible	admissible	audible	avertible
combustible	compatible	comprehensible	contemptible
contractible	controvertible	convertible	defensible
destructible	digestible	discernible	divisible
edible	eligible	fallible	feasible
flexible	forcible	gullible	illegible
incorrigible	incredible	indelible	indigestible
intangible	irascible	irresistible	legible
negligible	ostensible	perceptible	permissible
plausible	possible	responsible	reversible
risible	susceptible	tangible	unintelligible
visible			

See: **morpheme, spelling.**

abstract

An *abstract* is a summary of a thesis/**dissertation** or scholarly article. It provides essential information on the claims, the development of the **argument**, the evidence used and the conclusions reached and should be intelligible to a person who has not read the original.

Abstracts of articles generally contain no more than 200 words, and theses are usually abstracted in approximately 300 words. An abstract should be concise and specific, normally consisting of one coherent paragraph for an article and a number of paragraphs, each representing a major line of development, in a thesis. It is usual in abstracts relating to the Arts for the **active voice** to be used; abstracts relating to the Sciences often prefer the **passive voice.**

See: **précis.**

Academy

This word goes back to Greek, where it indicates the Platonic school of philosophy. It is now often used to refer to an institute of learning or to the French Academy, *l'Académie Française*. This is an association of scholars and writers concerned with maintaining the standards, purity and eloquence of the French language. It was the *Académie Française* which in the late 1970s criticised the adoption of English items such as:

> *le shopping*
> *le weekend*

The *Académie Française* has considerable prestige but there is little evidence that its pronouncements have limited the use of English words in the speech of the young.

No such academy exists for the regulation of English, although several authoritative bodies have tried to introduce formal controls. The Royal Society, for example, was established in 1660 and it encouraged its members, scientists and writers alike, to develop 'a close naked, natural way of speaking; positive expressions, clear senses, a native easiness'.

The USA too had its informal 'academicians'. Webster, for example, helped modify spelling conventions, preferring *-or* to *-our* in words such as *colour* and the simplification of endings in words such as *catalogue* and *programme*, giving *catalog* and *program*.

Today one may claim that the media, especially in the quality press and in the authoritative statements of radio and television, function like an academy in that they arbitrate on what is acceptable and they influence the entire population, encouraging a modification towards **network norms**.

See: **network norms, purist, Standard English.**

accent

An *accent* relates to a person's **pronunciation**. Everyone who speaks has an accent but people often think of the accent which approximates to the prestigious **network norms** as being 'clearest', 'most intelligible', 'best', even 'accentless'. Unlike French, which has an *Académie* to arbitrate on pronunciation, the English language has never had a single spoken standard. Nevertheless, the notion of a socially prestigious accent goes back at least as far as the sixteenth century, when grammarians began to suggest that the most acceptable form of pronunciation was that used by educated speakers in London and at the Court. (The term *accent* is often popularly confused with **dialect**. It is, however, perfectly possible to speak the standard language with a regional accent.)

As far as the UK is concerned, the most prestigious accent is RP (**Received Pronunciation**). This variety was characterised in the mid-nineteenth century by A.J. Ellis and in the twentieth century by Daniel Jones. RP was originally an educated regional accent but it became the accent of social position and privilege—the accent used by educated speakers in the southeast of England, in Oxford, Cambridge and the public schools such as Eton and Harrow. In the 1930s it was adopted by the BBC as the accent for news broadcasts. In this way, RP came to be associated with the 'right way' of speaking, and through its use in education and the media it has exerted an influence on all speech in the UK. In the early part of this century, it was impossible to hold a post of any seniority in the army, government or law unless one's speech approximated to RP. It was against this background that G.B. Shaw wrote *Pygmalion*:

> ...for the encouragement of people troubled with accents
> that cut them off from all high employment...
>   (Preface to 1912 edition)

Nowadays in the UK there is more tolerance towards regionally-marked accents, but RP continues to be the most prestigious accent and the one still used by the media for all official pronouncements.

The position is somewhat analagous in the USA, where the accents used by the regional networks exert an influence on listeners. However, there seems to be more tolerance of regionally marked accents in the USA than in the UK and it would probably be true to generalise that in the UK an accent other than RP connotes first class and then regional differences; in the USA an accent which differs from the network norms would probably connote first regional and then class or ethnic differences.

Each country in which English is a mother tongue or an official language has its own pronunciation norms which are dealt with under separate headings. The most significant difference between varieties of English, however, often relates to the pronunciation of 'r'.

See: **dialect, pronunciation, rhotic.**

accent marks

Most of the *accent marks* in English are on words or names borrowed from other languages:

Acute	— exposé
Bar (indicates long vowel)	— bēad

Breve (indicates short vowel)	—breăd
Cedilla	— façade
Circumflex	— maître d'hotel
Dieresis (indicates a syllable)	— naïve (2 syllables)
Grave	— à la mode
Tilde	— mañana
Wedge (indicates consonant change)	— Černak, Doležel
Umlaut (indicates change of vowel)	— Göttingen (Umlaut is often shown by inserting an 'e' as in Goettingen.)

Conventionally we do not indicate accent marks in French when upper case letters are used:

Ecole Normale
MAGAZIN D'ELEVES

but with German words the umlaut is required even with capitals.

Once a borrowed word becomes an accepted part of the vocabulary of English, the accent mark tends to be dropped as in *cortege* < *cortège*, *detente* < *détente*, *Haiti* (2 syllables) < *Haïti*, *role* < *rôle* and *tete-a-tete* < *tête-à-tête*.

The dieresis and the hyphen have in the past been used to mark a syllable break between vowels. Nowadays, the dieresis is rarely found and the use of the hyphen is declining:

coöperative, co-operative, cooperative
reëstablish, re-establish, reestablish

Accent marks have some special uses in verse. The grave is sometimes used to mark stress on a syllable that is normally unstressed, thus producing a regular metrical pattern:

Accursèd Faustus, where is mercy now?
Christopher Marlowe, *Doctor Faustus*

More idiosyncratically, the poet G.M. Hopkins uses accent marks to distinguish particular stressed syllables when the normal **orthography** cannot signal their status adequately:

Márgarét, áre you gríeving?
Over Goldengrove unleaving?
Leáves, líke the things of man, you
With your fresh thoughts care for, can you?
    'Spring and Fall'

See : **borrowing, -ed forms, foreign words in English.**

acquisition of language

Linguists, educationists and psychologists have all attempted to explain how it is that a normal child who is chronologically and emotionally immature, whose motor skills are relatively undeveloped and whose responses to time, space and measurements are imprecise, is capable of acquiring the language or languages of his environment. To add to the achievement, we have to acknowledge that the mother tongue is acquired without any formal teaching, in a relatively short time (most children have a good command of the language(s) of their environment by the time they are four) and, stranger still perhaps, although no two children are exposed to identical language input, all children in the same speech community emerge speaking essentially the same language.

To explain this phenomenon scholars have come up with two competing theories which, for simplicity, can be referred to as the *Behaviourist* and the *Species-Specific* schools.

The behaviourist viewpoint had its first comprehensive treatment in B.F. Skinner's *Verbal Behavior* (1957). The essential thesis here is that children acquire the language of their environments in very much the same way as dogs learn to beg for bones. The behaviour is rewarded and socially sanctioned. According to Skinnerians, children imitate the sounds, intonation patterns, words and structures that they hear around them and then by a process of 'generalisation' they create new and acceptable patterns based on the old ones. There is considerable support for Skinner's views in the evidence of children's early speech and from the fact that speakers continue to expand their use of language by means of imitation, stimulation and the promise of reward. Such views cannot, however, satisfactorily account for everything in the acquisition process.

From about the age of 18 months there is an 'explosion' in the amount of speech children use, and much of it cannot be explained in terms of imitation. With English-speakers, for example, it is not uncommon for a child to learn *see* and *saw* by imitation, but then produce forms such as *seed* and *sawed*. It is almost as if the child has worked out that many verbs change from present to past by the addition of '-ed' and so is trying to regularise *see*. In this way, the child moves from a list to a system. Similarly, irregular plurals like *men* often become *mans*. Children do not learn these forms: they create them, as they do patterns for negation and interrogation. Because such linguistic behaviour seems to come from the children and not from an outside source many scholars believe that the human ability to acquire language is species specific. This means that human beings are genetically programmed to acquire language and they will talk automatically at a certain time just as they will walk automatically at a certain time, if they are given the right environment. The last proviso is important: a child is not a miniature talker but a potential talker in the same way that an acorn is a potential oak tree. Children do not develop into language users if they are denied the right conditions and environment.

One fact which lends weight to the species-specific argument is the regularity and similarity of the onset of speech in all normal children. Eric Lenneberg called the developmental stages 'maturational milestones' and the following stages seem to be universal:

Birth to 3 months— crying, gurgling, non-speech noises
3 to 6 months   — babbling
6 to 12 months   — intonational babbling
12 to 18 months — words, set phrases
18 to 24 months — rapid increase of vocabulary, rudimentary
                   grammar
24 to 36 months — inflections, transformations
36 to 60 months — good approximation to adult norms

Although there are a number of similarities between a child's acquisition of his first language and an adult's acquisition of a second or foreign language, second-language learning does not follow an identical pattern.

See: **Behaviourism, Mentalism, pidgins and creoles.**

acronym

Abbreviations that are pronounced as if they were words are called *acronyms*, the word deriving from Greek *acr(o)* = topmost point, beginning + *onyma* = name. Thus *IATA* (International Air Transport Association) is an acronym and *the UN* (United Nations) is not. Acronyms are formed by selecting the initial letters of all words necessary to produce a pronounceable word, even if this means including a preposition:

AFASE—Association for Applied Solar Energy
ASH—Action on Smoking and Health
laser—Light Amplification by Stimulated Emission of Radiation

Occasionally, to aid pronunciation, two letters or a **syllable** will be selected:

LASSO—Laser Search and Secure Observer
radar—Radio Detecting and Ranging
quango—Quasi-autonomous non-governmental organisation

and, as *radar* and *quango* illustrate, they are written with lower case letters when they are adopted into the language as meaningful words in their own right.

A large number of acronyms, perhaps the majority, relate to the military or to national security:

NATO—North Atlantic Treaty Organisation
SAM—Surface-to-Air Missile
START—Strategic Arms Reduction Treaty

but a number are also deliberately lighthearted:

POPE—People Opposing Papal Edicts
POSSLQ—Person of opposite sex sharing living quarters

Acronyms are usually regarded as proper nouns and where they are written with upper case letters they are used without articles. The more widely used they are the more likely are they to become indistinguishable in their use from ordinary common nouns.

The distinction between acronyms and abbreviations is not clear cut. There is no infallible means of determining what is a set of letters and what is a word, although pronunciation is the most reliable guide. Often, too, an abbreviation can become an acronym. *UFO* (Unidentified Flying Object), for example, is often regarded as an abbreviation but UFO enthusiasts pronounce it 'yufo', possibly analogising from 'info', and have coined the term 'ufology' (the study of unidentified flying objects). Because most acronyms are also **coinages**, their status as words often depends on **analogy** with an existing word whose pronunciation they mimic.

See: **abbreviations, clipping, coinage, word formation.**

active voice

In traditional grammars, English **verbs** were classified according to **tense, voice** and **mood**, largely because such distinctions were relevant to Latin verbs. The sentences:

Julie arrived.

and:

Julie fed the chickens.

are described as *active* and:

The chickens were fed (by Julie).

as **passive.**

Active voice is thus the term used to categorise **sentences, clauses** and **verb phrases** where the **subject** of the sentence is the agent or instigator of the action. It is thus frequently associated with the pattern:

actor/agent NP_1 + action VP + (goal/recipient NP_2)

whereas passive sentences have the structure:

NP_2 + form of BE + past participle of V + (by + NP_1)

where 'by + NP_1' is optional.

The pattern of active constructions is closely related to the basic sentence order of English:

Subject + **Predicate** + (**Object**) + (**Complement**) + (**Adjunct**)

as in:

They elected him president yesterday.

and is most frequently found in speech and in contexts where the emphasis is on the agent. They are called *active* because the subject of the verb usually performs the action. We can contrast the different emphases in the following:

John broke the plates.
The plates were broken (by John).
The plates broke.

Although all English verbs can occur in an active construction:

John wrote that book.

and also:

John arrived.
John died.
John resembled his father.

only the first sentence can be transformed into the passive:

That book was written by John.

This is because *arrive* and *die* do not take objects and are thus barred from a **transformation** which involves transferring the object to the subject position. *Resemble* is barred for a different reason. 'John' is not an agent in the sentence:

John resembled his father.

in the sense that no action of his brought about the resemblance.

Traditional treatments of active and passive voice suggest that all **transitive** verbs (i.e. verbs which can take an object) can be passivised, but the example of *resemble* above shows that this generalisation does not always apply. It is true that *intransitive* verbs cannot occur in the passive but many transitive verbs (including *endure*, *enjoy* and *suffer*) often seem to be barred semantically from occurring in passive transformations.

The simplest generalisation we can make about *active voice* is a formal one: all sentences which are not of the form:

NP + BE + past participle of V (+ by NP)

are active.

See: **case grammar, ergative, passive voice, transformations, verb phrase.**

address and reference

The linguistic forms by which we *address* and *refer* to one another are not simply conventional but also reveal our attitudes towards the people concerned. Most **Indo-European** languages preserve second person pronominal distinctions (usually referred to as T and V from Latin *tu* = you singular and *vos* = you plural), allowing the users to imply such attitudes as respect, intimacy, formality or condescension. Such distinctions still existed in the pronouns of **Middle English**, enabling Chaucer to use *thou* and *you* in a variety of contexts. *Thou* could be used as a means of addressing:

1 one person
2 an addressee who was socially inferior
3 an intimate friend
4 a person normally addressed politely but for whom the speaker wished to indicate a loss of respect.

Complementing the T forms, *you* could be used in addressing:

1 more than one person
2 a single addressee who was socially superior
3 a fellow member of the upper classes with whom one was not intimate.

These patterns continued into the seventeenth century and were often used by dramatists to reveal the attitudes of their characters. In Shakespeare's *Othello*, for example, Emilia switches from respectful 'you' to contemptuous 'thou' when she learns that Othello has murdered Desdemona:

> *I do beseech you that I may speak with you. O good my Lord...*
> *Do thy worst!*
> *This deed of thine is no more worthy heaven*
> *Than thou wast worthy her.*
>   Act 5 Scene 2

A misused T form could be extremely insulting and this point is made explicit in *Twelfth Night* when Sir Andrew Aguecheek is given specific instructions by Sir Toby Belch on how to ensure a duel with Cesario:

> *Go, write in a martial hand ; be curst and brief...*
> *taunt him with the licence of ink: if thou thou'st*
> *him some thrice, it shall not be amiss.*
>   Act 3 Scene 2

The only Modern English pronominal remnant of the pattern is the use of *thou* in poetic, regional or religious language. The function of expressing social attitudes and role relationships has shifted from pronominal usage to address terms. This shift has occurred because modern **Standard English** has the invariable *you* to indicate singularity, plurality, intimacy and respect.

Today, in the English-speaking world, the commonest forms of address and reference are: first name (e.g. *John*), endearment(s) + first name (*my dear John*), last name (*Brown*), title + last name (*Mr Brown*) and terms of respect (*sir, ma'am*). Of these, the most frequently used are title + last name to express politeness, formality or respect (*Dr Brown*) and first name to express intimacy, equality, friendship or power. An employer, for example, might call an employee by his first name but would expect a title and last name back. It is rare for terms of address (i.e. the terms we use in person-to-person contact) to match terms of reference (i.e. the terms used in speaking *about* rather than *to* an individual).

Although the above generalisations apply to most parts of the English-speaking world, some local and national customs cut across them. For example, the term *love* is normally expected to be an endearment, but it occurs commonly in Yorkshire speech as an apparent expression of solidarity with no distinction of sex. It is not unusual to hear one Yorkshireman address another as 'love'. Expressions such as *buddy, cobber* or *flower* may be heard in other parts of the world, but they tend to be more limited in application than *love*. In the trade union movement terms such as *brother* and *comrade* are used specifically to stress solidarity. Certain terms of respect are also culturally or geographically specific. For example, in many African societies respect for one's elders is expressed in titles. Thus a woman who has children or a woman of some other special status is respectfully addressed as *Mama* or *Ma* even by those not related to her.

Newspapers have evolved a style of their own with regard to courtesy titles. In general, they advise:

1 titles should not be used for the first reference to a person. First and last names are preferred: *Hilary Adams, Michael Little*.

2 'Mr' should only be used when combined with 'Mrs': *Mr and Mrs Green*.

3 the first reference to a married woman should be first and last name: *Penelope Jones*. Subsequent references may be to *Mrs Jones*. The use of *Mrs Michael Jones* should be avoided unless it is preferred by Mrs Jones. The second reference to an unmarried woman should involve the last name prefaced by *Miss* or *Ms*, depending on the individual's preference. If a woman prefers the title *Ms*, then reference to her marital status should be avoided unless it is essential to the story.

Most newspapers follow such guidelines but may vary this style if someone specifically asks to be referred to in a different way. A Nigerian woman, for example, who prefers *Mallama* to *Mrs*, will be referred to in the way she specifies.

addresses

The conventions for writing *addresses* are designed for quick interpretation and minimal ambiguity. Practices tend to vary slightly from one country or language to another, but international communication is reducing the differences.

1 The format for an address represents a progress from personal (and small) to impersonal (and large) thus:

title + first name/initial(s) + surname
(number of office/flat/apartment + name of building)
number of building/house + name of street
name of town + post/zip code
(name of county)
(name of country)

A comma may be used at the end of each line except the last, which is given a full stop (where **punctuation** marks are used). Increasingly, the practice is to omit all unnecessary punctuation:

Mr Brian Smith   Ms Mary Smith
52 Otley Road   1234 Sunset Boulevard
Leeds LS16 4BT   Pasadena
West Yorkshire   California 91124
England   United States of America

2 On envelopes, the name and address are usually written with each line beginning at an arbitrary left-hand margin. Occasionally, although much less frequently, the lines may be indented, each starting between two and five letter spaces to the right of the line above. In **letters**, the address of the sender is given at the top right-

hand corner of the first page. The lines are usually directly below each other although they too may be indented, usually two spaces for each line. If the name and address of the recipient are given they should begin one space below the writer's details, with each new line beginning at the left-hand margin.

See: **dates, letters**.

adjective

Adjectives are descriptive words that:
1 modify nouns and pronouns:

*a **tall** man*
*He is **tall**.*

2 can have comparative and superlative forms:

big bigger biggest
hateful more hateful most hateful

3 can be modified by an adverb:

*a **very** tall man*
*He is **very** tall.*

Adjectives can occur in two positions. When they occur before a noun as in:

a lovely girl
happy children

they are called *attributive adjectives*. When they occur after a **copula** verb such as BE and SEEM as in:

*The boy was **cheerful**.*
*They seem **intelligent**.*

they are called *predicative adjectives*. Many adjectives can occur in both positions:

*a **happy** child*
*The child appeared **happy**.*

but some adjectives tend to occur in one position only. *Elder*, *mere* and *utter*, for example, are found in attributive position whereas **a-words,** *ill* and *well* are more likely to be used predicatively. It is perhaps worth stressing the flexibility of English at this point. While *ill* and *well* are frequently used predicatively they can occur in constructions such as:

> *It's an ill wind that blows nobody any good.*
> *He's not a well man.*

Adjectives normally precede the nouns they modify but in a number of fixed expressions, all of them borrowed from other languages, the adjective immediately follows the noun:

> *attorney general*
> *court martial*
> *secretary general*
> *whisky galore*

Most adjectives are regular with regard to forming comparatives and superlatives. Monosyllabic adjectives, frequently occurring disyllabic adjectives and all disyllabic adjectives ending in *-y* form the comparative by adding *-er* and the superlative by adding *-est*. When an adjective ends in one vowel + one consonant, e.g. *big*, *fat*, the consonant is doubled before *-er/-est*. All other adjectives form their comparatives and superlatives by using *more/most* before the **base form**:

> *green greener greenest*
> *yellow yellower yellowest*
> *lively livelier liveliest*
> *thin thinner thinnest*

When two nouns are compared, the comparative form of the adjective must be selected:

> *John and Bill are both strong athletes but Bill is the **stronger**.*

Often, in colloquial speech, the superlative form is incorrectly selected.

When adjectives co-occur, they tend to do so in a fixed order which usually involves such a pattern as:

> ...+ 5 + 4 + 3 + 2 + 1 + noun

In position 1 we tend to find nouns used adjectivally to indicate purpose:

> *a fish bowl*

In position 2 we often find nouns indicating materials:

> *a glass fish bowl*

In position 3 we sometimes have an indication of origin:

a Wexford glass fish bowl

In position 4 we often have colour:

a blue Wexford glass fish bowl

and in position 5 we find the possibility of adjectives of intensification, size, age, shape and temperature:

a huge blue Wexford glass fish bowl

Such adjectives also appear in a fixed order:

a great big old square building
a small round ice-cold object

We rarely find lists of more than four adjectives but when five or more co-occur they are usually in the above order and they are usually separated by commas. There is no comma between the adjective in position 1 and the noun.

Adjectives can also co-occur after copula verbs:

He was short, old and ugly.

the two final adjectives usually being linked by *and*.

Occasionally, adjectives can be used as nominals. This happens in two main ways:

1 adjectives are used with the definite article to indicate a group:

*Their aim was to help the **poor**, the **sick** and the **ignorant**.*
*The **unemployed** have the same needs as the **employed**.*

2 adjectives are often used when the noun to which they refer is contextually apparent:

*How do you like it—**white** or **black**?* (when offering coffee)
*Is it fully **automatic**?* (of a washing machine)

and when superlative forms are selected:

*I want the **cheapest** even if it isn't the **best**.*

A number of adjectives are related to **causative** verbs:

Brand X makes your whole wash white/whitens your whole wash.
Brand Y makes your skin soft/softens your skin.

Often the verbal equivalent is preferred in advertising because it can imply both the base form of the adjective and its comparative:

Brand Y softens your skin.

Here 'softens' can imply 'makes it soft' and 'makes it softer', the second being a much weaker claim than the first.

Other adjectives are related to noun phrase and preposition phrase **complements**:

> *John is cheerful.*
> *John is a cheerful person.*
> *John is in a cheerful mood.*

The **preposition** phrases in such related groups often involve such nouns as *disposition, mood* or *nature*. When adjectives are related to nouns as, for example:

> *powerful power*
> *silent silence*

then they can often be paired with preposition phrases containing the noun:

> *He became powerful. He came into power.*
> *He went silent. He lapsed into silence.*

COME is often used when the complement is positive or pleasant and GO when it is not:

> *He came into money. It went out of control.*
> *It came right/good. It went wrong/bad.*

Adjective phrases and clauses function like adjectives in that they modify nouns. With the exception of **rank-shifted** phrases and clauses used mainly for journalistic or humorous purposes:

> *an off-the-cuff remark*
> *There she was with her I-couldn't-care-less expression.*

noun phrases and clauses tend to follow the nouns they modify:

> *The man in the white suit comes from France.*
> *The man who was wearing a white suit suddenly went out.*

See: **adverb, aspect, deep structure, transformational grammar, verb.**

adjunct

This term has been used very differently by a number of linguists. Its most general definition is that an *adjunct* is the sentence unit which is not the **subject**, not the **predicate**, not the **object** and not the **complement**:

> S → (A) (Sub) Pred (Obj) (Comp) (A)

It is an optional element in a sentence, optional in that the sentence is still grammatical without it. Thus, in the sentence:

Yesterday he arrived at noon.

we have two adjuncts: 'yesterday' and 'at noon', both of which can be deleted, leaving the grammatically acceptable:

He arrived.

Adverbials are the commonest adjuncts in English but some scholars have also classified attributive adjectives and vocatives as adjuncts. It is certainly true that:

Where did you put that big red pen, John?

can function as an acceptable sentence with the adjectives and 'John' removed:

Where did you put that pen?

See: **adverb, modifier, sentence.**

adverb

Adverbs are often morphological variants of **adjectives**:

absolute absolutely
beautiful beautifully
exceptional exceptionally

but, whereas adjectives modify nominals, adverbs modify verbs:

*She sang **beautifully**.*

adjectives:

*He's a **happily** married man.*

other adverbs:

*They both ran **exceptionally** quickly.*

preposition phrases:

*We were **absolutely** out of our depth.*

and **sentences:**

***Interestingly**, I wouldn't have noticed the mistake if she hadn't drawn my attention to it.*

Like adjectives, adverbs have comparative and superlative forms:

quickly more quickly most quickly

and several words can function both as adjectives and adverbs. The most frequently occurring items in this category are: *cheap, clean, dead* (= completely), *easy, fast, fine, free* (= without paying), *hard, high, just* (= recently), *late* (= not in time), *loud, low, pretty, quick, real* (= very), *sharp* (= punctually), *slow, straight, sure* (= certainly), *well, wide* and *wrong*.

Adverbs are among the most mobile elements in a sentence and can occur in three positions:

1 at the beginning:

Suddenly *I understood what it meant.*

2 in the middle:

*He was **suddenly** aware of the difference.*

3 at the end:

*She left very **suddenly**.*

As we might expect, however, not all adverbs can occur in all positions. The adverbs that are most likely to occur in initial position are **discourse markers** such as *actually, alternatively, briefly, finally, however, perhaps, unfortunately*; adverbs of time such as *today, yesterday*; adverbs of frequency such as *occasionally, sometimes*. In literary style and for emphasis we often foreground adverbs:

Ah distinctly I remember...
Gently does it.

When adverbs occur in the middle of a sentence, they precede all verbs except auxiliaries:

*I **usually** go there after work.*
*He **invariably** thinks he's right.*
*I'm **usually** exhausted after jogging.*
*I can **usually** spot the winner.*

They can, however, precede auxiliaries, especially in speech, if extra emphasis is required:

*I **really** do try hard.*

Adverbial phrases and clauses function like adverbs with the exception that they normally occur at the beginning or the end of a sentence:

After three days I decided to forget what had happened.
When he arrived *we were all delighted.*

He visits us from time to time.
I can't make it on Tuesday.

The tendency to use adjectives as adverbs as in:

He talks real nice.

has been so frequently stigmatised that many speakers hypercorrect
by using inappropriate '-ly' forms such as:

more importantly
thusly

See: **adjective, comparison of adjectives and adverbs, foregrounding, hyper-correction, sentence.**

affinity

The term *affinity* implies a relationship between two items and collocates with the prepositions *between* and *with*:

There is a marked affinity between adjectives and adverbs.
John has a certain affinity with most people.

The use of *affinity* with *for* is limited to **scientific English** when a
substance is said to have an affinity for another if it unites easily with
it. The use of *for* in non-scientific English is regarded as incorrect.

affirmative

Sentences are often classified as being **declarative, imperative** and
interrogative with all three being capable of occurring in the *affirmative*:

I love Paris.
Go away.
Are you tired?

or **negative**:

I don't love Paris.
Don't go away.
Aren't you tired?/Are you not tired?

Occasionally, to avoid misunderstanding, the words *affirmative*
and *negative* replace *yes* and *no*:

Q. *Are the burglars still in the house?* A. *Affirmative.*
Q. *Can you see the runway?* A. *Negative.*

affix

Affix derives from Latin *affixare*, meaning 'attach to', and it comprehends **prefixes**, that is **morphemes** which are attached to the beginning of a word:

un + fair → unfair

suffixes, that is morphemes which are attached to the end of a word:

fright + ful → frightful

and infixes, that is morphemes which can be fitted into a word. In
English, prefixes and suffixes occur frequently but infixes are limited
to a number of disyllabic words, such as *bloody, blooming* (and their
more taboo equivalents) which can be slotted into polysyllabic words
directly in front of the main stress:

abso'lutely + bloody → absobloodylutely
inter'national + blooming → interbloomingnational

Prefixes are morphemes like *anti-, de-, dis-, ex-, in- (il-/im-/ir-), re-,
un-* which can precede words, modifying their meaning. The majority
are of Latin origin and they can affect the meaning of the root word
in terms of direction:

contra + flow → contraflow
retro + rockets → retrorockets

negation:

in + edible → inedible
in + legal → illegal

quality/degree:

quasi + official → quasi-official
semi + circle → semicircle

and quantity:

multi + national → multinational
poly + syllabic → polysyllabic

Suffixes are morphemes like *-en, -er, -ing, -ise/ize, -ly, -less, -ling,
-ness* which can follow words and modify their meaning:

dark + en → darken
duck + ling → duckling

The majority of suffixes in English are Anglo-Saxon in origin and
whereas prefixes tend not to change the word class:

pro + create (verb) → *procreate* (verb)
un + happy (adj) → *unhappy* (adj)

suffixes are often associated with word-class changes:

legal (adj) + *ise* → *legalise* (verb)
ugly (adj) + *ness* → *ugliness* (noun)

Words can have two or more prefixes:

unprepossessing

and two or more suffixes:

hatefulness

and occasionally two or more prefixes and suffixes as in:

antidisestablishmentarianism

See: **derivation, morpheme, prefix, suffix, word formation.**

African English

It is estimated that there are approximately five thousand languages in the world, at least half of which are found in Africa. Africa is thus the most multilingual continent and no brief summary could possibly do full justice to the variety of languages found there nor to the numerous influences to which English has been exposed.

It is possible, however, to divide the continent into six main areas, each of which has a continuum of Englishes:

1 Central Africa
2 East Africa
3 North Africa
4 South Africa
5 Southern Africa
6 West Africa

See: **Central African English, East African English, North African English, South African English, Southern African English, West African English.**

age

Generally, a person's *age* is expressed according to the conventions that apply to **numbers**. There are some differences, however. When the age is given predicatively, words are used:

She is twenty-one.
She is twenty-one years old.

the first being preferred in the UK and the second in the USA. When the age is given attributively, the elements are hyphenated and, to avoid excessive hyphenation, numbers are often preferred:

> *The **twenty-one-year-old** girl was appointed.*
> *The **21-year-old** girl was appointed.*

See: **numbers**.

agent

This term relates to the instigator of the action or the state indicated by the **predicate** in a **sentence**:

> ***John** broke the window.*
> ***The dog** ate the model plane.*
> ***The wind** tore up the trees.*

Normally the *agent* is animate, as in the first two examples, but occasionally, especially when natural phenomena like drought, hurricanes and floods are concerned, inanimate agents occur. In active sentences, the agent is often the **subject**. We can see whether or not the subject is the agent by passivising the sentence. If we look at two sentences which appear similar:

> ***John** opened the door.*
> ***The key** opened the door.*

we notice that the passive versions differ:

> *The door was opened **by John**.*
> *The door was opened **with the key**.*

revealing that 'John' was the agent whereas 'the key' was the instrument with which the door was opened.

See: **active voice, case grammar, ergative, passive voice**.

aggravate

Etymologically *aggravate* means 'increase the gravity of, make worse' as in:

> *The dismal weather **aggravated** his low spirits.*

and linguistic **purists** have argued that its colloquial meaning of 'annoy, irritate' as in:

> *The loud music really **aggravated** me.*

should be avoided.

It is difficult to assess why people who criticise the shift of *aggravate* from 'make worse' to 'annoy' do not condemn the change of meaning of *prevent* from 'come before' to 'inhibit' or the change of *regiment* from 'government' to 'troop'. Purists tend to overlook the fact that meaning changes are inevitable in a language and that no amount of dogmatic assertion will prevent them. Since few people argue that *silly* should still mean 'holy', for example, we have to look for another reason why purists insist on the fossilisation of a number of favoured words (e.g. *jejune*, *mutual*, **nice**, *presume*). Perhaps the insistence on etymology is related less to a desire for 'good English' than to the exclusion of some users from the elite circle of what the *Times* of London called 'proper users of English'.

There is a distinction to be made between natural meaning change and inaccurate or imprecise use of language.

See: **Academy, 'chestnuts', etymology, malapropism, nice, problem words, purist, semantic change, shibboleth.**

ago

Ago is a temporal marker which links a time in the past with the present:

*I first saw her five years **ago**.*
*That happened a long time **ago**.*

It thus does not usually collocate with non-past or aspectual verb forms. These tend to co-occur with **since** and *for*:

*It is five years **since** I saw her.*
*I have not seen her **for** five years.*

Ago can take a following clause:

*It was five years ago **that we met**.*

but it should not be used with *since*:

*It was/is five years ago since we met.

because *since* involves looking at the present from a point in the past:

*It is **twelve years since** we first met.*

and *ago* reverses the viewpoint:

*We first met **twelve years ago**.*

See: **since.**

agreement

Agreement involves a type of harmonisation between different parts of a language. Thus in English we have:

> *The boy sings.*
> *The boys sing.*

but never:

> **The boy sing.*
> **The boys sings.*

In French, **determiners** and **adjectives** agree with the **nouns** they modify and so we have:

> *la fermière française*
> *le fermier français*

There is comparatively little agreement left in contemporary English. With the exception of the verbs BE, HAVE and to a much lesser extent DO, we find it only in the non-past tense where a third person singular subject triggers off the use of a change in the **verb**:

> *I/you/we/they run*
> *he/she/it run + s*

Such agreement is not found in the past tense, where all **subjects** take the same verb form:

> *I/you/he/we/they ran*

Often, subject complements are in agreement with both subject and predicate:

> *John is a good boy.*
> *John and his brothers are good boys.*
> *It wasn't my dog.*
> *They weren't my dogs.*

It is, however, possible to find sentences such as:

> *His collected **papers** are now a **book**.*
> *His **feet** are his greatest **asset**.*

It is the subject which determines the agreement in the predicate.

Similarly, object complements tend to show agreement with the object:

> *He called **his son a fool**.*
> *He called **his sons fools**.*

although this does not happen when the complement is a proper noun:

> He called **the city Georgetown**.
> He called **the cities Georgetown**.

In recent grammatical analyses the term **concord** is often preferred to *agreement*.

See: **complement, concord, modality.**

ain't

Ain't is one of the most widespread nonstandard forms in the language, occurring as a regional and class variant throughout the English-speaking world. It has many roles, being used as an undifferentiated non-past **negative** form of BE:

> *I/you/he/we/they **ain't** here no more*.
> *I/you/he/we/they **ain't** saying nothing*.

as an undifferentiated **auxiliary** where the standard language requires HAVE:

> *I/you/he/we/they **ain't** got no more money*.
> *I/you/he/we/they **ain't** been out all week*.

and it is also found without an overt subject in some varieties of US speech:

> *Ain't no joke*.

Ain't occurs most frequently in the spoken medium but it has been employed by fiction writers as a stereotyping word to signal a speaker's low social status or regional origins. In *Great Expectations*, for example, Dickens uses a literary variant *an't* as a linguistic device to emphasise Joe Gargery's humble status:

> *And I **a'nt** a master-mind...*

and Mark Twain employs *ain't* as one of the characterising elements in the speech of Tom in *Tom Sawyer Abroad*:

> *Why the Holy Land—there **ain't** but one*.

Occasionally *ain't* is adopted by educated speakers as a marker of solidarity. President Reagan successfully used the slogan:

> *You **ain't** seen nothin' yet*.

in his 1984 presidential campaign.

See: **nonstandard English, speech in literature, style.**

alienable, inalienable

Many languages distinguish between **possession** which is transitory and non-essential, for example a spoon, and possession which is permanent or essential, for example a leg. Possessions of the first kind are *alienable* whereas those of the second kind are *inalienable*. Gaelic makes this distinction overt in such structures as:

> *mo chuid eadaigh* (lit. my share of clothes)
> *mo chuid gruaige* (lit. my share of hair)

and:

> *m'anam* (my soul)
> *mo chos* (my foot/leg)

where any possession that can be lost can be prefixed by the equivalent of 'share of'. Family, friends and religion are treated as inalienable.

English does not mark this type of distinction overtly except in the organisation of adjectives which co-occur to modify a noun. If we look at **noun phrases** such as:

> *poor old Joe*
> *ancient Egyptian architecture*
> *the nice little fat Corgi pup*

we see that the more permanent the characteristic/attribute the closer it comes to the noun it modifies. Poverty, for example, is more easily counteracted than age and the pup's most inalienable characteristic is its Corgi-ness.

The distinction between alienable and inalienable possession is not as clearly marked in English as in other languages although some speakers of **US English** use the variants *got* and *gotten* to mark alienability:

> *I've got two brothers.* (inalienable)
> *I've gotten two trucks.* (alienable)

See: **bring/take, location, speaker orientation.**

all, both

All and *both* can function as **determiners**:

> **All** *the children arrived late.*
> **Both** *the children arrived late.*

and as **pronouns**:

> *All is not lost.*
> *Both are useful.*

They can occur in a number of different patterns:

> All/both + (definite article)
> All/both + (possessive adjective)
> All/both + (demonstrative adjective)
> All/both + (of + possessive adjective/personal object pronoun)
> NP/pronoun + all/both

as in:

> *All/both the letters arrived late.*
> *All/both his horses were scratched before the race.*
> *All/both those words are misspelt.*
> *All/both of his children are tall.*
> *All/both of us are exhausted.*
> *The girls all/both love swimming.*
> *We all/both thought the same.*

All/both can occur as the subject (as above), object or complement:

> *It pleased **all/both of us**.*
> *It pleased **us all/both**.*

(Notice that when a personal pronoun occurs before *all/both*, then *of* is not required.)

They are also found after the first element of a complex verb phrase:

> *We have **all/both** had as much as we can take.*
> *They may **all/both** have seen the film.*

When *all/both* occur in the subject position they tend to be negated differently. Such sentences as:

> *All the letters arrived late.*

are normally negated:

> *Not **all** of the letters arrived late.*

whereas sentences such as:

> *Both the letters arrived late.*

are usually negated as follows:

> *Neither letter arrived late.*

As well as meaning 'everyone', *all* can approximate to the meaning of 'complete, entire':

> *I've done it all my life.*
> *You can't work all the time.*

In this role, *all* resembles 'whole' and not *both*:

> *He has worked hard all his life/his whole life.*

and it takes a singular noun. *All* can also function adverbially, especially in colloquial speech:

> *He's all at sea.*
> *She's all washed up.*

Both often occurs in a balanced structure with *and*:

> *They drink both tea and coffee.*

It is usual for both parts to be followed by structurally equivalent items:

> *They like both cricket and baseball.* (noun + noun)
> *He can both sing and dance.* (verb + verb)

See: **determiner, either.**

all right, alright

In UK English only the two-word spelling is acceptable:

> *It will be all right on the night.*

In the USA, *alright* is not fully accepted.

alliteration

Alliteration developed as an aid to memory and is based on the repetition of consonant sounds in closely associated words or syllables. In the following couplet from Tennyson's *Lotus Eaters*, for example, we have an interlacing pattern of r, f, l and t:

> *Ripens and fades and falls and hath no toil*
> *Fast rooted in the fruitful soil.*

A number of scholars have claimed that vowels can also alliterate but we shall use the term **assonance** in our description of vowel patterning, leaving *alliteration* for consonants.

Alliteration is a type of **sound symbolism** which can appeal to the listener's ear, evoking associations and conditioned reflexes. It also links the alliterating words, focusing attention on their interrelated meanings. In the following lines from Shakespeare's sonnet number 30, for example, alliteration helps to forge a link between the debtor's court (*sessions, summon; waste*) and emotions (*sweet, sigh; woes, wail*):

> *When to the sessions of sweet silent thought*
> *I summon up remembrance of things past,*
> *I sigh the lack of many a thing I sought,*
> *And with old woes new wail my dear time's waste.*

Alliteration is a traditional Germanic device, preceding **rhyme** in English poetry. In **Old English** verse, the lines were divided into halves, the first half line having two alliterating segments and the second half one, as in the following lines:

> *hreran mid hondum hrimcealde sae*
> *wadan wraeclastas: wyrd bith ful araed.*

When French verse began to influence literature in England, rhyme tended to replace alliteration as a metrical device:

> *Whan Zephirus eek with his sweete breath*
> *Inspired hath in every holt and heath*
> *The tendre croppes, and the yonge sonne*
> *Hath in the Ram his halve cours yronne*
>   Chaucer, Prologue to the *Canterbury Tales*

but alliteration has never been totally absent from English poetry and often when poets seek to register strongly-felt emotion or to recreate proverbial wisdom they tend to use alliteration:

> *Hurrah for revolution and more cannon-shot!*
> *A beggar upon horseback lashes a beggar on foot.*
> *Hurrah for revolution and cannon come again!*
> *The beggars have changed places, but the lash goes on.*
>   Yeats, 'The Great Day'

In **prose**, alliteration has been employed to reinforce rhetorical patterns, as in Robert Greene's 'The Carde of Fancie' (1584):

> *Nay, there was no fact so filthie, which he would*
> *not commit, no mischief so monstrous, which he would*
> *not enterprise: no daunger so desperate, which he*
> *would not advanture...*

to focus attention on details, as in Frank O'Connor's story 'In the Train':

> *The woman sat alone. Her shawl was thrown open*
> *and beneath it she wore a bright blue blouse. The*

carriage was cold, the night outside black and
cheerless, and within her something had begun to
contract...

or for the sheer enjoyment of revelling in sound patterns, as in Dylan Thomas's 'Holiday Memory':

I remember the sea telling lies in a shell held to my
ear for a whole harmonious, hollow minute by a small, wet
girl in an enormous bathing-suit marked 'Corporation Property'.

Because of its value as an aid to memory, alliteration is commonly found in proverbs:

Look before you leap.
Wilful waste makes woeful want.

in clichés:

come hell or high water
tried and true

and in advertising:

Lilt—with the totally tropical taste.

Generally speaking, it is impossible to avoid some alliterative patterns in any prose style, but this device should be used with care since it could distract attention from the argument to details of style.

See: **assonance, sound symbolism.**

allusion, delusion, illusion

These words are often confused or misused. An *allusion* is a passing, indirect reference to an unnamed person, place, time or event:

*While telling us her present problems, she made several **allusions** to her troubled past.*

A literary allusion makes a reference to a writer or his work. The allusion may be in the form of a quotation (sometimes incorrectly remembered) but assumed to be well known:

A little knowledge is a dangerous thing.
Tomorrow to fresh fields...

It may also be a **parody** of the style or content of an unnamed work, as Fielding's *Shamela* is a parody of Richardson's *Pamela*, and Pope's *Dunciad* alludes to *Paradise Lost* in both form and content.

A *delusion* is a mental condition involving a sincerely held false impression or opinion:

> *Lady Macbeth suffered from the* **delusion** *that nothing could remove Duncan's blood from her hands.*

An *illusion* is a false image or concept, a false belief often based on misleading evidence:

> *Because he always wore a beret she was under the* **illusion** *that he was French. He was, in fact, a baker from Barnsley.*

See: **malapropism.**

alphabet

Alphabet derives from the first two letters of the Greek alphabet, *alpha* and *beta*, and is a term meant to designate an inventory of letters (or signs) which correspond, often very roughly, to the sounds of a particular language. An alphabet which provided a perfect one-to-one correspondence between letters and sounds would be a 'phonemic' alphabet. No European language has a phonemic alphabet, although the Spanish alphabet is much closer to being phonemic than the English one is. In English, for example, the same sound can be represented by different letters:

> *machine sheep sugar*

and the same letter can represent different sounds as in:

> *cat ceiling*

Linguists have constructed the International Phonetic Alphabet (IPA), which offers a set of letters and diacritics (signs that can be placed above and below letters) which can represent all the sounds of every language.

See: **orthography, phoneme, pronunciation, spelling, spelling pronunciation.**

also

Also is an **adverb** which is more common in the written than in the spoken medium, where *too* or *as well* are preferred:

> *I have* **also** *got a little sister/I have a little sister* **too.**
> *She had* **also** *lived in Greece/She had lived in Greece* **as well.**

Its normal position is before the verb when the **verb phrase** is simple:

*They **also** sent some flowers.*

after the **auxiliary** in a complex verb phrase:

*They have **also** sent some flowers.*

and after **copula** BE:

*He is **also** a highly skilled mechanic.*

Occasionally in speech *also* is used as a conjunction suggesting that what follows it is an afterthought:

*Smoking is bad for your health, **also** it is expensive.*

This usage is less acceptable in writing than:

*Smoking is bad for your health—it is **also** expensive.*

where the afterthought is signalled by parentheses or a dash and where the adverb has its usual position.
Also can occur at the beginning of a sentence to offer special prominence to a phrase:

***Also** on the platform were the Prime Minister and the Chancellor.*

but the use of *also* followed by a comma in sentence initial position:

***Also**, I'd like some information on housing.*

is regarded as stylistically awkward.
Also, like *too* and *as well*, tends to occur only in affirmative sentences:

*He **also** likes peanut butter./He doesn't like peanut butter **either**.*
*Did John go **too**?/Did John **not** go **either**?*
*She tried ballet **as well**./She didn't try ballet **either**.*

alternately, alternatively

Alternately means 'first one and then the other in sequence' and refers to an ordering of two:

*She revised history and geography **alternately** so that she would not become bored with either subject.*

Alternate as a verb and adjective also implies an ordering of two:

*On Sundays we **alternated** between visiting my parents and visiting my husband's.*
*We played bridge and chess on **alternate** evenings.*

Alternatively means a choice between two mutually exclusive possibilities:

> *She may marry George.* **Alternatively**, *she may marry Herman.*

Although *alternatively* specifically referred to a choice between two, its meaning has been widened to include a choice of several possibilities. This widening of meaning applies also to *alternative* as a noun and an adjective:

> *She had so many* **alternatives** *she couldn't make up her mind.*
> *She had three* **alternative** *options with regard to her future: she could get a job, get married or go to university.*

See: **problem pairs**.

although, though

Although and *though* are closely related in form and meaning and are freely interchangeable in most contexts. The following differences should, however, be noted:

1 *Although* can only be used as a **conjunction**, that is, it can introduce a **clause**:

> **Although** *he was poor, he was honest.*

2 *Although* can be used in any style from extremely formal to intimately informal whereas *though* tends to be limited to informal usage.

3 *Though* can be used at the end of a sentence as a form of concessive emphasiser:

> *He wasn't well prepared for the test,* **though**.

Although can never be used in this context. The use of *but* in sentence-final position is characteristic of speakers in the north east of England, Northern Ireland and Australia:

> *He wasn't well prepared for the test,* **but**.

Such usage is both informal and regionally marked.

4 For emphasis, *even* may be combined with *though* (but never with *although*):

> **Even though** *I was well prepared, I found the test hard.*

5 *Though* (but not *although*) can be used as an adverbial filler:

> *The best preparation of all,* **though**, *is a good night's sleep.*

6 The clipped forms *altho* and *tho* occur in US usage but are only fully acceptable in very informal letters and notes.

See: **Australian English, clipping, fillers.**

ambiguity

The term *ambiguity* is applied to a structure that is capable of more than one interpretation. There are two main types of ambiguity: lexical and syntactic. Lexical ambiguity is a common feature of many languages and derives from the fact that many words have more than one meaning. *Spare*, for example, can mean 'extra' and 'healthily lean' and both meanings are possible (if not equally probable) in:

*His body was **spare**.*

Lexical ambiguity often goes unnoticed in speech because the **context** suggests one meaning rather than another. In the context of architecture, for example, we would interpret:

*His **designs** were unacceptable.*

as *drawings*, but in the context of personal behaviour as *intentions*.

With syntactic ambiguity we find structures capable of more than one interpretation. In English, two of the most ambiguous structures are:

1 V_{ing} + NP—V_{ing} can be either an adjective modifying the noun or a verb taking an object:

Eating apples can be good for you.

2 NP + NP—To illustrate the ambiguity of NP + NP, we only have to look at such a list as:

apple pie (a pie made from apples)
bird sanctuary (a sanctuary for birds)
field mouse (a mouse that lives in the fields)
silkworm (worm that produces silk)

A further example of NP + NP ambiguity occurs when an adjective precedes the first nominal:

young men and women

which can be interpreted as both:

young men and women of any age
young men and young women

Ambiguity is often cultivated by advertisers:

Go to work on an egg.
Let colour go to your head.

and by poets. G.M.Hopkins plays on the NP + NP ambiguity in:

Not, I'll not, carrion comfort, Despair, not feast on thee

Alliteration links 'carrion' and 'comfort' and the various possible meanings are exploited: comfort composed of carrion, comfort for carrion, comfort that lives in carrion, comfort that is carrion and comfort that produces carrion. In literature, such ambiguity extends the range of references, adding to the complexity of the work.

See: **pun, syllepsis.**

America(n)

The word *America* is used in two distinct ways:
1 to refer to the New World, including North, Central and South America
2 to refer to the United States of America, the USA.
A similar point can be made about *American*, which can refer to anyone from the Americas including Argentines, Brazilians, Canadians and inhabitants of the USA.
Occasionally, the term *Anglo* is used by American Hispanics to refer to any mother-tongue speaker of English.

See: **US English.**

Americanism

This term refers to:
1 words borrowed into **US English** from American Indian languages:

moccasin wampum

from African languages:

jamboree jazz

from Dutch, French, German, Spanish, Yiddish:

cookie prairie pretzel rodeo lox

2 words or expressions which originated in the USA:

palimony realtor
bark up the wrong tree
be between a rock and a hard place

3 words and word forms now obsolescent or obsolete in UK English:

closet   gotten

4 words which are characteristic of US (and often Canadian) usage:

condo (UK flat)
elevator (UK lift)
railroad (UK railway)

See: **UK and US words, US English.**

Amerindian influences

The languages of the Indians of both North and South America (*Amerindians*) have contributed a considerable number of words to US and world English, some directly and some through French and Spanish. Many of these are the names of New World animals:

coyote   raccoon   skunk

natural phenomena:

hurricane   pampas

food:

chilli   tomato   potato

clothing:

moccasin   poncho

cultural items:

caucus   pow-wow   totem

and a number of place names such as:

Okefenokee   Tallahassee   Yosemite

See: **Americanism, US English.**

among, amongst

There is no semantic difference between these words, but the use of one rather than the other has regional and probably age implications. *Amongst* occurs in northern and eastern parts of the UK and is regarded by young speakers as being archaic and/or literary. Many speakers use *amongst* in prayers:

> *Blessed art thou **amongst** women.*

but *among* in all other contexts and it is likely that *amongst* will gradually cease to be used.
Among/amongst must be followed by a plural noun or pronoun:

> *They divided the food **among** the poor/them.*

or by a noun which may be singular in form but is plural in meaning:

> *They divided the winnings **among** the crew/family/staff/workforce.*

Some scholars argue that *among* should be carefully distinguished from *between*:

> *They divided the cake **among** the boys (more than two).*
> *They divided the cake **between** the two.*

Current usage permits the use of *between* when more than two are indicated, especially in the spoken medium:

> *Share that equally **between** the lot of you.*

but *among* always implies 'more than two'.

See: **while.**

anacoluthon

Anacoluthon (plural *anacolutha*) from Greek *anakolouthon* meaning 'inconsistency in logic' involves a deliberate or accidental change from one syntactic structure to another within a single sentence:

> *He came over to me and—you're not listening.*
> *You should really try to—I only want what's best.*

Most people produce anacolutha in spontaneous speech and in unedited writing.

See: **dangling participle.**

analogy

Analogy has three main language-related meanings, all concerned with the comparison of different items that share some significant characteristic.

1 *Analogy* is a figure of speech by which two items are compared or equated:

She's a Greta Garbo type.

2 Analogy may be used to explain the unfamiliar in terms of the familiar. For example, an arithmetical process such as subtraction may be explained to a child by giving him four apples and taking away two, showing that $4-2 = 2$.

3 The term *analogy* is frequently used in **linguistics** to describe the tendency of all users of language to regularise and classify according to the familiar rules of their mother tongue. Thus, for example, many young children produce past tense forms like *bited*, *comed* and *seed* by analogy with the regular marking of the past time in English.

Analogising is evident at all levels of the language. In vocabulary it may be seen in the development of **back formations** such as *craze* and *laze* by analogy with *blaze* or *gaze*; in pronunciation it is found in the anglicising of non-English sounds, making *loch* rhyme with *rock* and *rouge* with *stooge*; in **morphology** it helps to account for the formation of new compounds such as *telethon* (from *television* + *marathon*) or **coinages** such as *pinx* (from *permanent* + *jinx*); and in syntax it is apparent in every speaker's ability to form unique sentences and utterances in accordance with the rules of the language. Analogy is a motivating force for both comprehensibility and change.

See: **argument, figures of speech.**

analytic

Comparative linguists have, by examining how words behave in different languages, established two main types of human language: *analytic* and **synthetic**. Synthetic languages are further subdivided into *agglutinating, inflecting* and *polysynthetic.*

1 In analytic (also called *isolating*) languages all words are composed of one invariable **morpheme** and syntactic relationships are indicated mainly by **word order**. An example of such a language is Korean.

2 In agglutinating languages the word is composed of a series of distinct morphemes where each morpheme has a specific meaning. Swahili is an agglutinating language.

3 In inflecting (also called *fusional*) languages words are composed of more than one morpheme but it is usually not possible to separate the morphemes. Welsh is an inflecting language.

4 In polysynthetic (also called *incorporating*) languages, words tend to be long and morphologically complex. Amerindian languages like Apache are examples of polysynthetic languages.

Most languages show mixtures of the above types.

The terms *analytic* and *synthetic* are also applied to the relationship between **adjectives** and semantically related **causative** verbs:

	analytic	synthetic
	make better	*improve*
	make clean/cleaner	*clean/cleanse*

and between variants such as:

	check the truth of	*verify*
	give food to	*feed*

See: **derivation, morpheme, synthetic, word formation.**

anaphora

In connected speech and writing many items refer back to others in the discourse. A sentence such as:

He has!

for example, is only comprehensible if both 'he' and the action performed have previously been mentioned as in:

John hasn't delivered the paper yet.
He has!

The term applied to backward reference is *anaphora*, a word which comes from Greek *anapherein* meaning 'to carry back'. Reference need not, however, be backward. In the following introductory sentence from a magazine story:

He was tall, dark, handsome and at twenty-eight John Smith was already a power in the city.

we can only understand 'he' by referring forward to 'John Smith'. This type of reference is called *cataphora*, and it is a device favoured by people who wish to create a sense of mystery or expectancy.

The term *anaphora* is frequently used to refer to both forward and backward reference.

See: **discourse analysis, pro-forms.**

and

And is a co-ordinating **conjunction**, that is, it joins units of equal value:

*Tom **and** Jerry*

*the good **and** the bad*
*He sang **and** danced.*
*She was kind **and** gentle.*
*I put them on the table **and** on the chairs.*

Often in colloquial speech *and* replaces *to*, especially in imperative constructions using *come, go* and *try*:

*Come **and** have a good time.*
*Go **and** see him at once.*
*Try **and** call in when you have time.*

Some scholars have criticised this usage as 'sloppy' or 'inelegant'; others have shown that there can be a semantic difference between, for example:

He came and saw me.

and:

He came to see me.

in that only in the second sentence did 'he' come for the purpose of seeing 'me'. Many speakers use the structures interchangeably.

Stylists used to condemn the use of *and*, *but* or *so* at the beginning of sentences. The practice is more acceptable today, especially in the representation of colloquial styles. It can be a useful literary device, as in the writings of Swift and Hemingway, but should be used sparingly.

And is frequently used with *so forth/so on* at the end of lists:

*He did his washing, cleaning, mending **and so forth**.*
She grows carrots, parsnips, turnips ***and so on***.

These phrases serve no useful purpose and should be avoided in writing and careful speech. Either they should be omitted:

He did his washing, cleaning and mending.

or replaced with a phrase which provides more information:

She grows carrots, parsnips, turnips and other root vegetables.

See: conjunction.

Anglicism

An *Anglicism* is a word, expression or **idiom** which is characteristic of the English language. Language-specific structures such as the method of indicating possession:

the minister's authority

can be considered Anglicisms. *Anglicism*, and its equivalent *Briticism*, is more frequently applied, however, to a usage that does not occur in the USA, for example *lecturer* (US professor).

See: **Americanism, Anglo-English, UK and US words.**

Anglo-English

The word *English* is increasingly ambiguous. It can refer to 'mother-tongue English', 'international English' or any variety of the language spoken in any part of the world. It is particularly ambiguous in England, where it is frequently used to mean both 'the English of England' and 'the English of the UK'. To avoid confusion, the term *Anglo-English* is sometimes used to refer to the varieties of English spoken in England; 'British English' has the wider connotation of 'the types of English used in Britain, that is, England, Scotland and Wales'; and 'UK English' comprehends the varieties occurring in England, Scotland, Wales, Northern Ireland, the Channel Islands and the Isle of Man.

See: **Standard English, UK English.**

Anglo-Irish

This term has been used to refer to:

1 the English gentry who were granted lands in Ireland in the late sixteenth and early seventeenth century

2 the type of English used by these people, often virtually identical in the written medium to the educated variety in England, but marked in the spoken medium by the retention of certain features of pronunciation that changed in England. The most obvious retention was the /e/ sound in words like 'receive' and 'tea'. The name of the Anglo-Irish poet Yeats rhymes with 'hates' whereas the name of the English poet Keats rhymes with 'heats'.

3 the literature written by people who were born in Ireland but were of English origin. Among such writers were Oscar Wilde and George Bernard Shaw.

4 the literature of people born in Ireland who were not of English origin but who used English as a literary medium. Among these are Sean O'Casey, James Joyce and Seamus Heaney.

5 the English used by Irish people whose ancestral mother tongue was Gaelic.

There are marked differences in the speech of people whose ancestors spoke English and those whose ancestors spoke Gaelic. The former differs only superficially from the English of their peers in other parts of the UK; the latter shows the influence of Gaelic in phonology, vocabulary, idiom and grammar. Recently, linguists have called this variety **Hiberno-English,** reserving the term 'Anglo-Irish' for the language of the English who settled in Ireland and for the literature written by their descendants.

See: **Hiberno-English, Irish English.**

Anglo-Romani

Romani, in one of its many dialects, is the mother tongue of perhaps 50% of the six to ten million Gypsies in the world. The Romanis originated, not in Egypt as **Gypsy** suggests, but in northern India and Romani (or Romnimos) is an inflected language closely related to Hindi. Below is part of the Lord's Prayer in Romnimos:

> *Amro dad, ka shan ar'o ravnos, t' avel Tiro nav parikedo.*
> Our father, who art in + the heaven, that become Thy name esteemed.
> *T' avel Tiro kralisesko them ; t' aven kede Tire lava*
> That comes Thy kingly land; that becomes done Thy words
> *ar' o them odzha-sar ar' o ravnos.*
> in the land same-as in the heaven.

In the UK for the past five hundred years some Romani people have also spoken *Anglo-Romani,* a restructured Romani also used by Romanis in the USA, Australia and South Africa. Anglo-Romani contains many English words and **morphemes,** as can be seen in the following version of part of the parable of the Prodigal Son (Luke 15):

> *But his dadrus penned: 'My chavvi, tuti's with mandi*
> But his father said: 'My son, you are with me
> *sor the cherus and tuti can have sor of my kovels...'*
> always and you can have all of my possessions...'

Anglo-Romani shares features with Lewis Carroll's 'Jabberwocky' in which the syntax is English but much of the vocabulary is new:

> *Twas brillig and the slithy toves*
> *Did gyre and gimble in the wabe.*

See: **Gypsy, pidgins and creoles.**

animal terms

All languages seem to have **similes** and **metaphors** based on the perceived or assumed similarity between human beings and animals.

In English, many everyday language uses are based on metaphor, as can be seen from a brief listing of the commonest nouns, verbs, adjectives and adverbs applied to people and deriving from animal names or characteristics.

Nouns ape, ass, baboon, badger, bear, beaver, bird, bitch, bulldog, canary, cat, chicken, clam, cock, cow, crow, cuckoo, dog, donkey, elephant, fox, goat, goose, gopher, guineapig, hen, hog, horse, kitten, lamb, lark, lion, louse, magpie, march hare, minx, mole, monkey, mouse, mule, ox, parrot, peacock, pig, pup(py), rabbit, rat, shark, sheep, squirrel, snake, stoolpigeon, toad, tortoise, turkey, turtle, viper, weasel, wolf, worm.

Verbs As well as many of the above nouns which can be used as verbs, the following animal attributes can occur as verbs: bark, bleat, bug, catnap, claw, ferret (out), flap, flounder, fly, gallop, gobble, growl, hare, hiss, lionise, paw, peck, pussyfoot, roar, rook, snap, snarl, snort, toady.

Adjectives bearish, bullish, bullnecked, catty, dog-eared, dogged, dovetailed, elephantine, fishy, flighty, foxy, hare-brained, kittenish, lousy, mousy, pig-headed, ratty, sheepish.

Adverbs Many adverbs can be formed from the adjectives above.

See: **metaphor, simile.**

-ant, -ent

A number of words have two forms: a noun form ending in *-ant* and an adjective ending in *-ent*:

   a dependant   a dependent child
   a pendant   pendent clouds
   a propellant   propellent fuel

The following nouns often cause **spelling** problems:

   attendant/ce
   independent/ce
   relevant/ce
   superintendent
   transcendent/ce

See: **spelling.**

ante-, anti-

Ante- is a **prefix** meaning 'before':

   *Before her child was born she attended an **antenatal** clinic, and after the birth she received postnatal care.*

Anti- is a prefix meaning 'against':

He manned an **anti-aircraft** *gun during the war.*

See: **affix, problem pairs.**

antecedent

This term is used of a unit to which a later unit refers. Thus, in the sentences:

The cat that John found was very small. It was also very old.

'the cat' is the antecedent of both 'that' and 'it'.
The personal **pronouns** *he, she, it, they* and the relative pronouns always have antecedents. Often, **auxiliary** verbs have antecedents:

John **loved** *cats. He really* **did**.

See: **anaphora, auxiliary, discourse analysis, pro-forms, pronoun.**

antithesis

Antithesis is the stylistic technique of juxtaposing statements that are opposite or strongly contrastive in meaning. Such statements often involve structural **parallelism**:

Marry in haste ; repent at leisure.
One small step for man ; one giant leap for mankind.

The force of the antithetical statement often depends on the semantic contrast involving words in the same position in both halves, often the first and last stressed words. As a stylistic device it has much in common with rhyming couplets, particularly the epigrammatic couplet favoured by Alexander Pope:

Sole judge of Truth, in endless Error hurled ;
The glory, jest, and riddle of the world!
    Essay on Man

See: **epigram, oxymoron, parallelism.**

antonym

Antonymy, from Greek *anti* 'against' + *onyma* 'name', is the general term applied to the sense relation involving 'oppositeness' of meaning. It is useful to distinguish three types of 'oppositeness', namely:

1 implicitly graded antonyms
2 complementarity
3 converseness

1 *Implicitly graded antonyms* are pairs of items like *big, small, good, bad*. Words like *big* and *good* can only be interpreted in terms of being 'bigger' or 'better' than something which is established as the norm for the comparison. Thus when we say that a boy is 'big' or that one boy is 'bigger' than another, we imply that 'big' is to be understood in the context of boys. This accounts for the apparent paradox of a 'big boy' being smaller than a 'small horse' because 'small' in the latter context means 'small when compared with other horses'.

In English, the larger member of the pair is the unmarked or neutral member, and so we can ask:

How **big** is it?
How **old** is he?
How **wide** is the river?

without implying that the subject is either big, old or wide. On the other hand, if we ask:

How **small** is it?

we are prejudging the answer, assuming that 'it' is small. There is nothing universal about the larger member of the pair being the neutral member: in Japanese it is the smaller member that is neutral.

2 *Complementarity* refers to the existence of such pairs as *male* and *female*. It is characteristic of such pairs that the denial of one implies the assertion of the other. Thus, if one is not male, then one is female. Notice the difference between graded antonyms of the 'good/bad' type and complementary pairs. To say:

John is **not single**.

implies:

John is **married**.

but to say:

John is **not good**.

does not imply:

John is **bad**.

In certain contexts, the following can be complementary pairs:

black and white (piano keys and coffee)
food and drink
land and sea

Related to complementary pairs are sets of terms like colours or numbers where the assertion of one member implies the negation of all the others. Thus if we have the set:

(violet, indigo, blue, green, yellow, orange, red)

to say:

This is green.

implies that it is not violet, indigo, blue, yellow, orange or red. In a two-term set such as:

(male, female)

the assertion of 'male' implies the denial of the only other member in the set. Such terms, as well as being described as 'complementary', are often referred to as 'incompatible'.

3 *Converseness* is the relationship that holds between such related pairs of sentences as:

John sold it to me.

and:

I bought it from John.

where BUY and SELL are in a converse relationship. English has a number of conversely related verbs and so sentence converseness is a common phenomenon:

John lent the money to Peter.
Peter borrowed the money from John.

The most frequently occurring converse verbs are:

borrow lend/loan
command serve
give take
lease rent
teach learn

Occasionally, the same verb can be used in a conversely related pair of sentences:

John rented the house to Peter.
Peter rented the house from John.

Sometimes we find converse nouns corresponding to converse verbs:

teach/learn   teacher/student
treat/consult   doctor/patient

See: **gradable, semantics, synonym.**

any way, anyway

Any way and *anyway* have distinct meanings. *Any way* means 'by any method':

*Organise these **any way** you like.*

Anyway is a more mobile unit and can usually be deleted without altering the grammatical acceptability of the sentence:

*There wasn't any blue paint left, and (**anyway**) I prefer green (**anyway**).*

Anyway tends to be colloquial and it usually implies a dismissal of what has preceded it:

*I don't want to see her; **anyway** I'm too busy.*

Anyways is regionally marked and regarded as nonstandard.

aphasia

Literally, this word means 'without speech' but it is often applied to the sudden or gradual loss of language as a result of age, an accident or a stroke. Most people have some experience of 'nominal aphasia', the temporary loss of nouns. This reveals itself in two ways: the inability to remember the name for something:

What's the word for that dessert I love?

and the use of the wrong word in essentially the right context, as when we use 'fridge' when we mean 'cupboard' or 'cooker'. Such slips are commonplace and are made by all speakers when they are tired or tense or getting old. The slips we make are rarely random. The three words cited above have a lot in common: they are all nouns; they can all hold food; they are all in the kitchen; and they all have large doors. Other slips, such as the use of 'bigger' when we mean 'better', suggest that we may store some vocabulary items, especially adjectives, according to sound.

See: **a- words, acquisition of language, competence and performance, dyslexia.**

aphesis

Aphesis, from Greek *aphienai* meaning 'to let go', involves the dropping of a short, unaccented vowel from the beginning of a word:

along > long
esquire > squire

Aphesis is thought to be a gradual process, whereas **clipping**:

pianoforte > piano
spectacles > specs

tends to be rapid and usually applies to the loss of more than one syllable.

Aphesis is a phenomenon of the spoken language although it can be extended to the written medium. It is frequently found in English-related **pidgins and creoles**.

See: **apocope, clipping, contraction, elision, pidgins and creoles, syncope.**

aphorism

An *aphorism*, from Greek *aphorismos* meaning 'definition', expresses an abstract truth, usually concisely and memorably. Strictly, an aphorism is based on personal experience, but the term has been widened to apply also to **maxims** and **proverbs**. Francis Bacon uses aphorisms extensively:

Histories make men wise; poets witty; the mathematics subtle; natural philosophy deep; moral grave; logic and rhetoric able to contend.

Shakespeare also uses aphorisms (sometimes taken from Bacon) as when Malvolio explains in *Twelfth Night*:

Some are born great; some achieve greatness; and some have greatness thrust upon 'em.

See: **maxim, proverb.**

apocope

Apocope, from Greek *apokoptein* meaning 'to cut off', refers to the loss of one or more sounds or letters from the end of a word. It has occurred historically in English, as when verbs such as *bindan* and *singan* became *bind* and *sing*. It also features prominently in speech:

Michael > Mike
sand > san

See: **aphesis, syncope.**

apostrophe

There is considerable confusion concerning the use of the *apostrophe* although the rules governing its usage are simple. Apostrophes must be used:

1 to indicate **possession** of a noun or noun phrase:

Mary's bag
the boy's books
the boys' books
the Wife of Bath's hat

with *'s* being used to indicate a singular possessor and *s'* indicating a plural possessor.

2 to indicate time or quantity:

in a week's time
my money's worth

3 in contractions to indicate the omission of letters:

I am > I'm
cannot > can't
influenza > 'flu' > flu

4 in the literary representation of nonstandard speech:

'My lan', ef Huck ain't got him ag'in! Huck's landed
him high en dry this time, I tell you! Hit's de
smartes' trap I ever see a body walk inter...'
    Mark Twain, *Tom Sawyer Abroad*

Apostrophes are also sometimes used to indicate the plural of numbers:

He reached his peak in the 1970's.

letters:

How many s's are there in 'Mississippi'?

abbreviations:

There are very few women MP's in the House of Commons.

and words being discussed as words:

How many the's are there in that passage?

It is, however, advisable not to overuse the apostrophe and so it is preferable to have:

the 1970s
650 MPs

There are a number of specific problems relating to the apostrophe:
1 *it's* always means 'it is'. Apostrophes are not needed with possessive pronouns:

His *is better than either* **yours** *or* **hers** *but* **theirs** *is the best.*
Whose *is that?*

2 Singular names ending in 's' add *'s* to indicate possession:

Keats's poetry
Yeats's drama

Some writers avoid using *'s* to indicate the possessive form of names
which have more than one sibilant (e.g. *s, sh*) in the last syllable:

Jesus' followers
Xerxes' ambition

The wisest rule, however, is to be consistent and treat these names
as one would 'Keats' or 'Jones'.
3 The use of *'s* to form the plural of words ending in vowels:

*avocado's
*pizza's
*potato's

is incorrect but widespread. It probably derives from the custom of
using *'s* to indicate the plural of non-English words such as:

folio's
quarto's

The correct use of the apostrophe can add to the clarity and
precision of one's writing.

See: **punctuation.**

apposition

Frequently a **noun** or **noun phrase** may be followed by an explana-
tory nominal:

Tom, **the muffin man**
Sweeney Todd, **the barber**

and the nouns or noun phrases are said to be 'in apposition'. Thus
'the muffin man' is in apposition to 'Tom'. The second nominal is
also sometimes called an *appositive.*
    The head noun and its appositive refer to the same person or thing
and agree in number:

my son, the bridegroom, and my daughters, the bridesmaids

and case:

> We, John and I, will do all we can to help.

and usually either of the nouns (or noun phrases) can be omitted without syntactic loss:

> We will do all we can to help.
> John and I will do all we can to help.

There is usually a comma before and after an appositive, except when the headword and appositive together form a title:

> They nicknamed her **Attila the Hen**.
> **William the Conqueror** won the battle of Hastings in 1066.

Arabic influences

Many words of Arabic origin have found their way into English, either directly or by way of other languages including French, Italian, Persian, Spanish and Turkish. The oldest **borrowings** date back to the Crusades and are found in almost all west European languages. Among these are:

> albatross admiral alchemy alcohol
> alkali algebra elixir zenith zero

words that emphasise the pre-eminence of Arabic scholars of the period in astronomy, mathematics, medicine, science and seafaring. Arabic **numbers**, too, were borrowed, and thus all literate speakers of European languages would recognise 1, 2, 3 although English speakers would call them 'one, two, three' and French speakers 'un, deux, trois'.

More recently, other borrowings came into the language: words for items of clothing:

> burnous

culture:

> fakir genie houri

food:

> kebab lemon sugar candy

Many of the latest borrowings were brought into the language by soldiers. Among these items are *bint* meaning 'woman' and *buckshee* meaning 'free'.

See: **North African English**.

archaic retentions

Archaic retentions are those elements in the language which derive from an earlier period and which preserve features no longer found in English. For example, *willy nilly* comes from *will he, ne + will he* and retains a type of negation common until Shakespeare's day.

Archaic retentions are most frequently found in legal language:

> *attorney general* (noun + adjective)
> *the aforementioned*

in liturgical language:

> *brethren*
> *Lady Day* (Our Lady's Day)

in some types of **letters**:

> *inst.* (this month)
> *prox.* (next month)

in trades and occupations:

> *bespoke tailoring*
> *houses to let*

and in **dialects**. Many dialects retain older past tense and past participle forms:

> *bring brung*
> *climb clumb*

multiple negation as a form of emphasis:

> *He didn't say nothing to nobody.*

and words that are no longer current in the standard language:

> *buss* (kiss)
> *thole* (endure)

See: **archaism, dialect.**

archaism

An *archaism* is a word or expression formerly in use but no longer occurring naturally in contemporary speech and writing. If a twentieth-century writer produced the sentence:

> *Forsooth, 'tis thee, thou varlet.*

he would be using archaisms, although none of these words would have been archaic to Shakespeare.

An archaism has a certain amount of prestige largely because it has antiquity value. That is probably the fundamental distinction between an 'old-fashioned' expression and an *archaism*.

Among the well-known archaisms in the language are:

anon (soon, immediately)
behest (order, request)
delve (dig with a spade)
thou (you singular)
Yuletide (Christmas)

See: **address and reference, archaic retentions.**

argot

The term *argot* has derogatory **connotations** and like **patois** tends to be used by educated speakers to describe the language of a socially inferior group. An *argot* refers to the special, sometimes secret, vocabulary and idioms of a group such as thieves and it is sometimes mistakenly confused with **jargon**.

See: **cant, jargon, patois.**

argument

An *argument* is the process by which the writer or speaker attempts to convince the reader or audience about the validity of some conclusion, principle or point of view. The term normally applies to the sequence of points through which a case is presented and may include illustrations. A related meaning of *argument* (or thesis) is the writer's or speaker's particular reason for presenting a detailed case.

Conventionally, we tend to distinguish four types of writing: argument, description, **exposition** and **narration**. Although these categories are not totally discrete (*description*, for example, may be involved in *narration*), awareness of them is useful when the writer is deciding on the objective of a particular task.

The writer who intends to present an argument needs to observe the rules of logic. It is not enough simply to express an opinion or impression, such as:

Jane Austen's humour implies social judgements.

All the reader needs to do to refute such an unsupported claim is reply:

I disagree.

Claims like that above have to be expressed precisely (What is meant by social judgement?), with explanations (What sort of humour is being referred to?), examples or **quotations**, and some analysis or explanation of how the illustrations support the initial claim. In general, a clear and persuasive argument requires the reader to:

1 be precise, eliminating ambiguous or vague words, clumsy sentences, poor organisation and irrelevant details

2 avoid unsupported generalisations

3 define terms, so that there can be no dispute about meaning or interpretation

4 progress methodically from one step to the next

5 be critical and selective in the use of emotive language.

The main procedures by which an argument is developed are **analogy**, cause and effect, deduction and induction. Each provides a means of presenting ideas, evidence and conclusions.

Analogy This is concerned with comparison, chiefly of two different things that share a particular quality. It is a means of explaining the strange or new in terms of the familiar or known. Well used, an analogy can promote concise explanation and coherent argument.

Causal statements These are used primarily to convince the reader to accept a particular interpretation of certain facts. The connections between causes and effects are indicated by words and phrases (*because, consequently, since, so that, therefore, thus*) and can, depending on the choice of **active** or **passive voice**, be overt or covert:

Thus, Joan won eighteen battles.
Thus, eighteen battles were won.

Deduction This is a method of reaching a conclusion from a premise that is accepted as true. For example, we notice that a book is arranged alphabetically and conclude that it could be a type of reference work. The basic premise, founded on existing knowledge, is that reference books are often arranged alphabetically. Deductive reasoning is often epitomised by the syllogism (A implies B, B implies C, therefore A implies C), the three stages being known as the thesis, the antithesis and the synthesis. For deductive reasoning to be valid, the premise (or thesis) must be valid:

All men are animals.
Animals have brains.
Therefore all men have brains.

and the vocabulary must be used consistently and not as in the following false syllogism:

A horse for a penny is rare.
Rare things are expensive.
Therefore a horse for a penny is expensive.

Induction This is a method of arguing from the evidence to the conclusion. For example, we may notice that more and more shop-keepers use **apostrophe** + s to indicate plurality on signs in their shops. We collect samples of the usage and can then conclude, inductively, that there is a growing tendency to use 's for plurals in shop signs.

The presentation of an argument relies ultimately on precise, concise expression as well as on common sense.

See: **analogy, discourse analysis, style.**

article

There are two *articles* in English: the definite article *the* and the indefinite article which is realised as *a* before consonants and *an* before vowels. Both 'the' and 'a' have two pronunciations, /ðə/ and /ə/ when unstressed, /ði/ and /eɪ/ when stressed.

Teachers of English as a Second Language have found it particularly difficult to explain when to use 'the', 'a' or a plural noun because native speakers can use all of the following:

The cat is a feline.
A cat is a feline.
Cats are felines.

The best simplification is that the form of the article is determined by the interplay of the features 'definite' and 'known to the listener', thus giving four possible realisations:

1 Both definite and known to the listener → the
  Look at the sun!
2 Definite but not known to the listener → a/an
  I passed through a village.
3 Indefinite but known to the listener → the/a/∅ + s
  The lion is dangerous.
  A lion is dangerous.
  Lions are dangerous.
4 Neither definite nor known to the listener → a/an
  If a person wants something...

A number of common expressions exist without articles. Among them are:

at breakfast/dinner/lunch/supper/tea
at home/sea/work
by boat/bicycle/bus/car/plane/train
in/to class/hospital
in bed/church

at/from/in/to school
on foot

In addition, *the* can sometimes replace possessives before body parts:

The stone hit him on the head.

This usage tends to be limited to sentences relating to blows, injury or pain where the body part follows a preposition:

She poked him in the eye.

It is a convention of narrative fiction that a novel, story or poem may open with *the* even though the reader cannot possibly be familiar with the character or topic. This usage is like a contract between writer and reader by which the writer undertakes to make these things familiar. A random selection of works that open with this 'promissory *the*' includes:

The suburb of Saffron Park lay on the sunset side of London...
  G.K. Chesterton, *The Man Who Was Thursday*
The Assyrian came down like a wolf on the fold
  Lord Byron, 'The Destruction of Sennacherib'
The first thing the midwife noticed about Michael K...
  J.M. Coetzee, *Life and Times of Michael K*

See: **anaphora, determiner.**

articulatory setting

Just as each language has a unique set of **phonemes** (distinct sounds), so too each group of speakers has a preferred position for the vocal organs, particularly the tongue and the lips but including also the soft palate (which allows the air from the lungs to escape through the nose, thus producing nasalisation) and the jaw. The preferred setting can, in part, account for dialectal differences. Scots and Canadians have more lip-rounding than Australians or Londoners. Irish speakers form the consonants /t,d,l,r,s,z/ with the tip of the tongue against the teeth, producing the dental quality often associated with Irish speech. Speakers in southern England form the same sounds with the tip of the tongue touching the ridge behind the upper teeth and many speakers from India pronounce these sounds with retroflexion, that is, with the tip of the tongue curling towards the hard palate. Some speakers from Liverpool and from the American Mid-West have a nasal quality in their speech, resulting from a tendency to speak with the soft palate lowered. It is rare for such articulatory differences to cause misunderstandings but they are enough to mark one group of speakers out from another.

The most frequently occurring sounds in a language and the means of their articulation help to determine the position of the mobile organs in the mouth, the jaw and possibly even the body when speaking. One will always sound foreign in one's **pronunciation** of a language if one does not adopt the articulatory setting of its native speakers.

See: **phoneme, phonetics, pronunciation, shibboleth.**

as

As is used in a variety of ways in English:
  1 in comparisons:

  I like him as a person, but as a teacher he's a disaster.
  He admires you as much as I/me.
  She is as tall as I/me.

In the second example, the choice of pronoun is significant. Selection of 'I' implies:

  He admires you as much as I admire you.

whereas 'me' implies:

  He admires you as much as he admires me.

In the third example it is stylistically but not semantically significant. Many grammarians have insisted that since Latin took the same case before and after BE, English should do the same. This reasoning overlooks the **parallelism** of such patterns as:

  He is taller than I am. He is taller than me.
  He arrived before I did. He arrived before me.

It is, however, conventional to use the nominative case after BE in formal contexts.
  2 to describe the role or function of a nominal:

  The doctor used his scarf as a rough bandage.
  I have worked as a waitress for many years.

  3 to indicate that two actions occurred simultaneously:

  We sang as we went along.

  4 to suggest a reason. In this context *as* can often be replaced by *since* or *because*:

  As he was the only person with access to the room, suspicion naturally fell on him.

5 In very formal styles *as* can be followed by inversion:

*She was a suffragette, **as** were most of her friends.*

The expressions *as if* and *as though* are also used in comparisons and are interchangeable, but *as if* is slightly less formal:

*You behaved **as if/though** you were mad.*
*It looks **as if/though** it could rain.*

Often, in formal contexts, 'were' is used in dependent clauses, particularly if the comparison is extravagant or unreal:

*He looked as if/though he **were** about to burst.*
*She looked at me as if/though I **were** a Martian.*

In less formal circumstances, 'was' is used and is perhaps gradually ousting 'were'. In colloquial speech *like* is sometimes used instead of *as if/though*:

*She looks **like** she's seen a ghost.*

but this structure should be avoided in writing.

As regards is a focusing device often used in business or legal correspondence:

***As regards** your request of July 15...*

Similar in function but indicating varying degrees of formality are the words and phrases *about, concerning, regarding, with reference to* and *with regard to*.

See: **comparison and contrast, conditional, subjunctive.**

aspect

As well as temporal distinctions which are made overt in the **verb phrase**, English makes distinctions relating to the continuity or non-continuity of an action:

*I **was walking** home when we met.* (emphasises continuity)
*I **walked** home.*

and the completion or non-completion of an action:

*I **have read** that book.* (i.e. I have finished it)
*I **read** that book last night.* (but may not have finished it)

Aspect is the term applied to these distinctions. In English, two types of aspect are clearly marked: **Progressive/Continuous Aspect**, which involves the use of BE + a present **participle**:

*I **am singing** in the rain.*
*I **was laughing** at the time.*

and **Perfect** *Aspect*, which involves HAVE + a past participle:

> *He **has painted** the whole house.*
> *He **had painted** the door by nine o'clock.*

The progressive and the perfect can be combined:

> *She **has been looking** for her dream house for ten years.*
> *She **had been looking** for a dream house for years.*

The so-called 'Historic Present' as in:

> *So I **goes** up to him, he **turns** to me and I **says** to him...*

has occasionally been described as 'narrative aspect'.

See: **verb phrase**.

aspiration

The term **aspiration** is used to describe a sound that is produced with audible breath. The symbol used to indicate this is a raised 'h' following the aspirated sound:

> /pʰɪt/

In English, /p,t,k/ are always aspirated when they occur in word-initial position:

> /pʰɪn/—pin
> /tʰɪn/—tin
> /kʰɪn/—kin

The aspiration disappears and the distinction between /p,t,k/ and /b,d,g/ is effectively lost when /p,t,k/ follow /s/:

> /spɪn/—spin

See: **pronunciation**.

assimilation

In normal speech, adjacent sounds often affect each other so that they become more alike and thus less of an effort to produce. In slow, careful speech, for example, *London Bridge* is pronounced /lʌndən brɪdʒ/ but, in casual speech, the final nasal in 'London' becomes an m, under the influence of the b in 'bridge'.

Assimilation may be *partial* as when n changes to m under the influence of b. If n had changed to b then the assimilation would have been *complete* in that adjacent sounds would have become identical. Complete assimilation of nasals often occurs when we have a cold:

> *come back* → /kʌb bæk/
> *ten dogs* → /tɛd dɒgz/

The direction of the influence can also be indicated.

1 The term *regressive* or *anticipatory* assimilation indicates that a sound changes under the influence of a following sound. Thus, when:

> *ten pence* → /tɛm pɛns/

the first sound in 'pence' has modified the last sound in 'ten'.

2 In *progressive* assimilation, a sound changes under the influence of a preceding sound. Thus when:

> *Bridge Street* → /brɪdʒ ʃtrit/

the last sound in 'bridge' influences the first sound of 'street' causing the s to be pronounced sh.

3 In *reciprocal* assimilation, two sounds influence each other. The **tags** *can't you, don't you, won't you* often involve reciprocal assimilation in casual speech when the t and the y blend into /tʃ/, thus:

> *don't you* → /doʊntʃʊ/

See: **accent, pronunciation.**

assonance

Assonance involves the repetition of vowel sounds in words or stressed syllables:

> *vine* and *hide*

It is always involved in rhyme:

> *see* and *flee*
> *seen* and *green*

although, as illustrated in the second example, rhyme can also involve the repetition of the final consonant. Assonance is a characteristic of verse and of some descriptive prose. Dylan Thomas exploits its potential in such lines as these from 'On the Marriage of a Virgin':

> Waking alone in a multitude of loves when morning's light
> Surprised in the opening of her nightlong eyes
> His golden yesterday asleep upon the iris
> And this day's sun leapt up the sky out of her thighs
> Was miraculous virginity old as loaves and fishes...

Assonantal patterns are found in *waking* and *day's*; *alone*, *opening*, *golden*, *old* and *loaves*; *multitude*, *loves* and *sun*; and *light*, *surprised*, *nightlong*, *eyes*, *iris*, *sky* and *thighs*.

Unintentional assonance can be distracting and should be avoided in ordinary prose.

See: **alliteration, sound symbolism.**

Australian English

Australia has a population of approximately 15 million, and as the majority of its mother-tongue speakers of English are of British origin, the varieties of English in Australia share many features with Britain. Many of the Aboriginal Australians live in Northern and Western Australia and speak both an Aboriginal mother tongue and an English-derived pidgin. Some have adopted a creole English as a mother tongue. Since the end of World War II, settlers have come to Australia from several Western European countries, India and the Pacific. These groups have acquired *Australian English* and their children's linguistic behaviour differs little from that of other Australian-born children.

Because of the small population, the relative classlessness of Australian society and the homogeneity of the original settlers, Australian speech is less differentiated than the speech of any other English-speaking community of comparable size. This is not to claim that there is *no* regional or class differentiation in Australia. Clearly, there is. A Queenslander can spot the difference between his own usage and that of a speaker from Perth or Adelaide; Black and White speakers are sharply differentiated; and working-class Australians are as easy to separate from their middle-class contemporaries as in any other anglophone area. Nevertheless, class and regional differences are fewer in Australia than in the UK or the USA.

Phonology

Three overlapping sound systems are recognised for Australian English, 'Cultivated', 'General' and 'Broad'. The **phonology** described below is based on 'General Australian'.

1 Australian English is non-**rhotic** and the consonant system approximates closely to **Received Pronunciation** (RP), with three exceptions: there is a tendency for the dark l in words like *milk* and *pull* to be realised as a vowel:

/mɪ^{ʊ}k/ or even /mɪʊk/

there is some aspiration on /t/ in word-final position:

/bat^{h}/—bat

and word-final /z/ is sometimes devoiced to /s/, causing 'letters' to sound the same as 'lettuce'.

2 Australian English has the same number of vowel contrasts as RP but the realisation and distribution of vowels are different. The following features are widespread:

(a) the long monophthong /i/ tends to be diphthongised so that we often hear:

/bəɪt/ for *beat*

(b) the long back monophthong /u/ is centralised and often diphthongised, producing:

/gʉs/ or /gᵊʉs/ for *goose*

(c) the vowel sound in words like *hard*, *laugh*, *pass* is realised as a long central vowel.

(d) the diphthongs in *here*, *there* and *sure* tend to be monophthongised.

(e) the diphthong /eɪ/ in words like *tail* is lowered and realised by many as /aɪ/, the vowel sound in RP *tile*. Partly because of the shift from /eɪ/ to /aɪ/, the diphthong in words like *high* often becomes /ɒɪ/:

/taɪl/—tail and /tɒɪl/—tile

(f) the short monophthongs in *get* and *hat* are closer than in RP so that the Australian vowel in *hat* is similar to the RP vowel in *get* and the Australian vowel in *get* is similar to /e/.

(g) the unaccented endings -*ed*, -*est*, -*es* and -*ness* have the schwa vowel /ə/ and not the /ɪ/ of RP. This difference is very significant and can result in such misunderstandings as Australian *patted* and *villages* sounding like RP *pattered* and *villagers*. In addition, the past participle -*n* in *flown*, *grown* and *shown* is often realised as /ən/:

/flouən/ /grouən/ /ʃouən/

Australian English sounds closer to UK than to US norms and the pronunciations that most clearly reveal an Australian's origins are those of words like *hard*, *patted*, *railway*.

Vocabulary

The vocabulary of British settlers was not adequate for the new environment and so it was extended in three main ways:

1 Words were borrowed from Aboriginal languages for animals:

kangaroo koala wallaby

birds:

budgerigar currawong kookaburra

trees and plants:

boobialla burrawang

place names:

Geelong Wollongong

and weapons:

boomerang woomera

Relatively few Aboriginal words have entered International English.
  2 New compounds were made:

backblocks (sparsely inhabited area far from the city)
bush-fire/horse/hut/lawyer
gum tree

3 Words were used with modified meanings:

brush (impenetrable thicket of shrubs)
creek (small river, as in the USA)
forest land (grass and not trees)
mob (flock, herd)
sheila (woman)

Australia has its own range of colloquial language. *G'day* (good
day) is the usual greeting and *dinkum* meaning 'genuine' is a widely-
used compliment. Australians (both men and women) tend to use a
number of *-ie/o* abbreviations: *Aussie, Brissie/Brizzie* (Brisbane),
cossie (swim suit), *metho* (Meths drinker), *nasho* (national service-
man), *Pommie* (unflattering name for someone from England), *rego*
(car registration), *shrewdie, smoke-o* (tea break) and *wharfie*
(docker/longshoreman). And like English speakers thoughout the
world, Australians have adopted many US words and expressions.

Grammar
The grammar of Australian English reflects the educational background of a speaker. The written language of an educated Australian
is indistinguishable from that of an educated English person. Working-class Australian English reflects many of the characteristics of
working-class English throughout the world:
  1 the tendency to reduce the number of verb forms:

I do	I done	I have done
I see	I seen	I have seen
I go	I went	I have went

2 the use of *them* as a plural demonstrative adjective:

*Gimme **them** boots.*

3 the tendency to distinguish between *you* (singular) and *youse* /juz/ (plural).

Many Australians also use *but* at the end of a sentence:

I like him but.
I didn't do it but.

as a sentence **modifier**, equivalent to *though*. This usage is also found in New Zealand and in northern Britain.

The description above applies to mother-tongue speakers of English and not to the majority of Aboriginal people, many of whom speak a pidginised or creolised English. Since the eighteenth century, two types of Pidgin English have been used in Australia:

1 Aboriginal Pidgin English, probably dating back to the earliest contacts between settlers and the original Australians. An 1828 sample of this is:

All gammon white fellow pai-alla cabon gunya me tumble down white fellow. (It was all lies that the whites spoke in the court house that I killed a white.)

2 South Pacific Pidgin English, confined mainly to the sugar-cane plantations of Queensland in the nineteenth and early twentieth centuries but now found also in Northern Australia and the Torres Straits. A recent sample of this pidgin is:

Im bin hitim mi long an. (He hit me with his hand.)
Pikanini i go krai. (The child will cry.)

See: **Papua New Guinean English, pidgins and creoles.**

auxiliary

An *auxiliary* (also known as an *auxiliary verb*) is a verb which is used with another to help make aspectual, modal or temporal distinctions. In a **verb phrase** such as:

may be going

'may' and 'be' are auxiliaries and 'going' is the headverb. There are several auxiliaries in English:

1 **BE** is used in the expression of progressive aspect:

is practising
were struggling

2 BE is used also in the expression of the passive:

were followed
were robbed

and in this usage BE triggers off the use of the past participle of the following verb.

3 **HAVE** is used in the expression of perfective aspect:

have finished
had disappeared

4 the modals (i.e. *can, could, may, might, must, shall, should, will, would*) which are used in the expression of ability, futurity, insistence, intention, obligation, permission, possibility and willingness:

can swim
will arrive
must go

5 There is a fifth auxiliary, **DO**, which is often called the dummy auxiliary because although it is syntactically significant it has little semantic value. When there is no other auxiliary in the verb phrase, DO is used to form **negatives** and **interrogatives**:

(he) *sings*
(he) *doesn't sing*
does (he) *sing?*
does (he) *not sing?/doesn't* (he) *sing?*

The auxiliaries BE, HAVE and DO can also occur as headverbs:

Auxiliary	Headverb
(I) *am singing*	(I) *am a steeplejack*
(I) *have sung*	(I) *have two dogs and a cat*
(I) *don't sing*	(I) *do my tax returns*

but when these verbs and the modals are used as auxiliaries they have certain characteristics:

1 they always precede the headverb
2 they are not obligatory in **affirmative**, declarative sentences:

(you) *try*

3 they can be used anaphorically:

He was trained in Switzerland.
Was he? (= Was he trained in Switzerland?)

4 they can be used for **emphasis**, especially in emphatic affirmation or denial:

*We **have** been followed.*
*You **don't** practise hard enough.*

5 they can be followed directly by 'n't':

(he) *mightn't go*
(he) *hasn't gone*
(he) *isn't trying*
(he) *doesn't go*

6 all the auxiliaries with the exception of *may*, *might* and *did* have **strong and weak forms**:

I am striving/I'm striving
he has gone/he's gone
she will go/she'll go

See: BE, DO, dummy subject, HAVE, modality, quasi-modal, strong and weak forms, verb phrase.

back formation

This process involves the formation of a new word from an assumed but imaginary root of an existing word. A change of word class always occurs. For example, the verb *televise* is a *back formation* from the noun *television* and the verb *edit* from the noun *editor*. The new word is formed by **analogy** with other existing words: *televise* is similar to *revise* (and *television* to *revision*); and *edit* to *audit* (and *editor* to *auditor*). Because back formations result from analogy with words which already exist, the new formations are readily acceptable and are indistinguishable from words with conventional roots. Thus *burgle* seems as regular as *gurgle* or *curdle*: only the historical records reveal that *burglar* existed first.

Other well-known back formations include: *automate* (automation), *craze* (crazy), *donate* (donation), *enthuse* (enthusiasm), *filibust* (filibuster), *liaise* (liaison) and *psych* (psychology).

See: **clipping, word formation.**

Bahamian English

Linguistically as well as geographically, these islands with a population of under a quarter of a million lie between the Caribbean and the southern USA. There is a spectrum of varieties in the Bahamas, ranging from standard US usage through nonstandard usages to a creolised English which shares features with US **Black English** and Caribbean **creoles.**

See: **Black English, Caribbean English, creole, West Indian English.**

Barbadian English

This island has speakers of several different varieties of English, from **Standard English** to 'Bajan', a form that shares lexical features with Caribbean **creoles**. Since 1625 Barbados has had close links with Britain and its speakers have been renowned for the excellence of their English. Increasingly, the English of the 250,000 Barbadians is being influenced by US rather than UK norms.

See: **Caribbean English, creole, West Indian English.**

barbarism

Barbarism is a term used to condemn words formed from or even **cognate** with words with the same function but of superior status. For example, *disassociate* is regarded as a barbarism because an etymologically more correct form *dissociate* exists. It is not, however, difficult to see how *dis + associate* came to be formed, nor to find analogous words (*dis + agree, dis + allow, dis + appoint*). Other so-called barbarisms are:

adaption (adaptation)	cf. adoption
educationalist (educationist)	cf. nationalist
grievious (grievous)	cf. devious
orientate (orient)	cf. meditate/meditation
preventative (preventive)	cf. tentative
pronounciation (pronunciation)	cf. pronounce
reoccur (recur)	cf. reaffirm
untactful (tactless)	cf. unhelpful

It is likely that some barbarisms will oust their more respectable counterparts. Ultimately, it is general usage, rather than etymological pedigree, that determines the survival of a word.

The term *barbarism* is sometimes used to refer disparagingly to foreign, vulgar, uneducated or impolite expressions.

See: **analogy, cognate, etymology.**

base form

The *base form*, which is also known as the *root* or the *stem*, is the unmodified word, that is, the singular form of a noun (e.g. *bird* and not *birds*), the **imperative** form of a verb (*go* and not *goes*, *going* or *gone*), and the positive form of an adjective (*big* and not *bigger* or *biggest*). **Affixes** are added to the base form:

dis + respect + ful
un + like + ly

See: **affix, derivation, inflection.**

Basic English

Many people have believed that international co-operation would improve if a universally understood language existed. Esperanto was invented to fulfil such a purpose but it has never received the attention its creator hoped for. English has, over the last two hundred years, become an international language, employed in every continent and increasingly recognised as the world's **lingua franca**. It was already a widely-used second language in the 1930s when C.K. Ogden created *Basic English*, a reduced and simplified form of English which Ogden believed would be easy to teach and learn. Basic English consisted of 850 words:

1 600 'Things', ranging from *account* to *year*

2 150 'Qualities', including *able, bad, good* and *young*

3 100 'Operators', containing 16 full verbs such as *BE* and *PUT*, two modals *may* and *will*, a number of pronouns, adverbs, determiners, conjunctions, prepositions and the words *yes, no* and *please*

The rules of Basic English were simple:

1 all plurals were formed by adding *-s*

2 adverbs were formed by adding *-ly* to **qualifiers** (some but not all of the 'Qualities')

3 comparatives and superlatives were formed by using *more* and *most*

4 questions were formed by **inversion** and the use of DO

5 verbal and pronominal 'Operators' conjugated in full

The following verses of St Luke's account of the Prodigal Son are in Basic English:

But he made answer and said to his father, See, all these
years I have been your servant, doing your orders in
everything: and you never gave me even a young goat so
that I might have a feast with my friends

Basic English was an attempt to make English easier for learners. It failed because:

1 the English produced was unnatural:

I have love for you. and not *I love you.*

2 it did not lead on to the mastery of natural English

3 the 850 words are the minimum one can use. 150 extra words were necessary for the translation of the Bible. A normal Bible uses approximately 6,400 words.

4 many words were allowed to be used both literally and metaphorically.

See: **pidgins and creoles**.

bath, bathe

These verbs cover different but overlapping semantic areas in the UK and the USA. Because their spelling differs only in the **base forms**, the distinctions between them are becoming blurred.

Bath as a verb is used in the UK. It means 'wash oneself or someone else' usually in a bathtub:

*I'll **bath** after you.*
*Shall I **bath** the baby?*

US usage would prefer *bathe* in the above examples or distinct periphrastic phrases:

*I'll **take a bath** after you.*
*Shall I **give** the baby **a bath**?*

UK speakers also use the expressions *have/take a bath.*

Bathe is used more extensively in the USA where its meanings include 'give a bath to' and 'apply a liquid to something':

*I'll **bathe** the baby.*
***Bathe** your eyes in a saline solution.*

In conservative UK usage, *bathe* tends to be confined to alleviating pain, as in the second example. Increasingly, however, US usage is spreading among the young.

BE

BE is the most irregular and also the most frequently used verb in the language. It has eight morphologically distinct forms: *am, are, be, been, being, is, was* and *were, am* and *is* being marked for **person**, *was* and *were* being marked for **number**.

BE has three main roles in English:

1 as a **copula**. In this role, *BE* introduces a **complement**:

He is a mechanic.
I am very tall.
She was out.
They are in my bad books.

When the copula introduces a nominal, it is sometimes referred to as 'equative BE' because the subject and the complement refer to the same person or thing:

Karen is a waitress. (Karen = waitress)
It's the Pacific Ocean. (It = Pacific Ocean)

2 as a marker of progressive **aspect**. Traditionally, this BE was referred to as 'continuative BE' because it was used to indicate the continuing nature of the action described:

She is training.

This **auxiliary** triggers off the use of the present **participle** of the following verb, can occur in non-finite phrases:

to be training

can exhibit past/non-past contrasts:

She is training for the marathon.
She was training for the marathon.

and can co-occur with the perfective auxiliary HAVE:

She has been training.

and the passive auxiliary BE:

She is being trained.

3 as a marker of **passive voice**. Traditionally, this has been called the 'passive auxiliary'. In this use, BE triggers off the use of the past participle of the following verb:

It is called 'Fido'.

and can exhibit past/non-past contrasts:

He was followed home.
He is often followed home.

Many languages use BE existentially, that is, with the meaning of 'exist'. This is rare in English except in translations from Hebrew:

I am who am.

or French:

I think, therefore I am.

See: **aspect, auxiliary, copula, irregular verb, prime verbs.**

Behaviourism

The Behaviourist School of Psychology has concentrated on the study of observable, measurable and predictable features of behaviour in animals and human beings. As far as language is concerned, *Behaviourism* is most clearly apparent in the works of structuralists like Leonard Bloomfield who insisted that each language should be studied in its own right by means of rigorously applied discovery procedures. The psychologist B.F. Skinner specifically applied the findings of behaviourist psychology to language in *Verbal Behavior* (1957).

Skinner's view suggests that language or 'verbal behaviour' differs in no fundamental way from any other type of stimulus-controlled activity. The underlying premise is that when a child is born, its mind is empty, that all learning is the product of environment and experience and that learning can be facilitated by stimulation, repetition and reinforcement.

Skinner's work suggests that children learn to speak just as pigeons learn to play pingpong, because certain spontaneous patterns of behaviour are elicited, conditioned, reinforced and rewarded. Gradually, according to Skinner, children learn to generalise from sound patterns they know to sound patterns they do not know as they acquire the language of their environment.

See: **acquisition of language, Mentalism, structuralism.**

better

The word *better* is surprisingly ambiguous in its popular uses. It is the comparative form of *good*:

  good **better** *best*

and can be used both adjectivally and adverbially:

  *Michael is the **better** talker (of the two).*
  *Michael is talking **better** now.*

Better is also used to signify that someone has recovered from an illness:

  *He is **better** now.*

The question 'How are you?' often elicits an answer involving *better* which may mean 'better than before but still not well' or 'completely recovered'. This type of ambiguity is normally resolved either by the context or by the addition of a word or phrase to clarify the meaning:

  I'm a lot better now but I'm still very tired.
  I'm completely better.

Better can also function as a **quasi-modal**, similar in meaning to *must*. In this function it collocates with *had* and the base form of the verb:

  *You'd **better** check the time.*

This usage does not imply a comparison but is a means of offering advice or indicating an intention. It occurs more frequently in speech than in writing and often the *had/'d* is deleted:

I better go.

See: **adjective, adverb, quasi-modal**.

Bible

When the word *Bible* applies to the Old and New Testaments it is conventionally written with a capital letter but without quotation marks, and the same rule applies to the individual books of the Bible. When its meaning is extended to an authoritative work, an initial capital letter is not required:

*That book has become the gardener's **bible**.*

The adjective *biblical* also takes lower case:

*We now know a great deal about **biblical** times.*

The same orthographic conventions apply to the sacred writings of other major religions, such as the Koran, the Talmud and the Vedas.

The usual forms of reference to parts of the Bible are: the Old Testament, the New Testament, the Ten Commandments, the Gospels, the Epistles, and references are given according to book + chapter + verse, thus Genesis 2: 8-10, II Kings 4: 34, Psalm 22, St Luke 21: 3-7. Accepted **abbreviations** of the names of the books of the Bible are:

Old Testament (OT)—Gen, Exod, Lev, Num, Deut, Josh, Judg, Ruth, I Sam, II Sam, I Kgs, II Kgs, I Chron, II Chron, Ezra, Neh, Esther, Job, Ps, Prov, Eccles, S of S, Isa, Jer, Lam, Ezek, Dan, Hos, Joel, Amos, Obad, Jonah, Micah, Nahum, Hab, Zeph, Hag, Zech, Mal.

Apocrypha—Tobit, Judith, Wisdom, Ecclesiasticus, Baruch, I Maccabees, II Maccabees.

New Testament (NT)—Matt, Mark, Luke, John, Acts, Rom, I Cor, II Cor, Gal, Eph, Phil, Col, I Thess, II Thess, I Tim, II Tim, Tit, Philem, Heb, Jas, I Pet, II Pet, I John, II John, III John, Jude, Rev/Apocalypse.

The language and **imagery** of the Bible, in Hebrew, Greek, Latin and English **translations**, have had a profound effect on literature and on popular usage. Although tradition suggests that biblical translations in Britain go back to the eighth century, complete translations date only from the sixteenth century. The translations by William Tyndale (1525) and Miles Coverdale (1536) provided the basis for all subsequent translations up to and including the Authorised King James Version of 1611, with the result that the language of the King James Version was archaic even in its own day.

References and allusions to the Bible permeate literature in English, much of which (such as Metaphysical Poetry, *Paradise Lost* or *The Scarlet Letter*) cannot be fully understood without a knowledge of the Bible. A number of expressions involving biblical names are in common usage, among them *Babel, the mark of Cain, David and Goliath, serving God and Mammon, Job's Comforter, a Judas, as wise as Solomon* and *a Philistine*. In addition, many felicitous words and expressions derive ultimately from Tyndale. Among these are *beautiful, die the death, eat, drink and be merry, the fatted calf, glad tidings, a land flowing with milk and honey, peacemaker, the powers that be* and *to see eye to eye*.

Fixed biblical phrases **calqued** from Hebrew are also now part of the English language. These include possessives such as:

man of sorrows
rock of ages

superlatives of the form:

king of kings
holy of holies

and emphatic statements involving repetition:

die the death
Eating thou shalt eat.

A number of expressions such as:

three score years and ten

are not Hebraicisms but occur in the Authorised Version and so tend to be associated with biblical language.

See: **archaism, calque.**

bibliography

A *bibliography* is a list of books or articles on a particular subject. The way in which it is organised and the items that are included depend on the purpose and scope of the compiler. The style of a bibliography should follow existing conventions, should harmonise with that of any notes or **footnotes,** and should be consistent.

For a **dissertation,** a bibliography should include not only items referred to and quoted but also any related works. Students should endeavour to show an examiner that they are familiar with other scholarship in the area including recent publications. For an article or book, items specifically related to the topic should be provided as well as any that would be of special help or interest to a reader. A Select(ed) Bibliography lists only some of the works cited in the text. Bibliographical items may be grouped into categories, such as 'Primary Sources', 'Secondary Sources', 'Original Works' or 'Translations'. As a rule, however, all items should appear in a single list, organised alphabetically according to the last name of the authors. If no author is named, the first major word of the title should be used. Each entry should begin at the left-hand margin, with subsequent lines indented five spaces.

There are two main styles of bibliographical form:

1 the author-date or Harvard system
2 the author-title system

When taken in conjunction with notes or footnotes, the first system is simpler and more economical:

1 Graham, William (1977) *The Scots Word Book*, Edinburgh, Ramsay Head Press.
2 Graham, William *The Scots Word Book*. Edinburgh: Ramsay Head Press, 1977.

· With format 2 full footnotes are necessary within a text, whereas with format 1 a reference may be contained within the main body of the text:

...Graham (1977:15) or (Graham 1977:15).

The sample entries that follow use the author-date system, and the author-title system when this differs considerably. With both, each entry should be considered a sentence, opening with a capital letter and ending with a full stop; titles of books and journals should be underlined and those of articles and short poems should be given within quotation marks.

Two or more books by one author:

Page, Norman (1972) *The Language of Jane Austen*, Oxford, Blackwell.
—— (1973) *Speech in the English Novel*, London, Longman.

For the second and subsequent books, a line rather than the author's name is normally used.

A book consisting of more than one volume:

Wells, J.C. (1982) *Accents of English*, 3 vols., Cambridge, England, Cambridge University Press.

Wells, J.C. *Accents of English*. 3 vols. Cambridge, England: Cambridge University Press, 1982.

A book by more than one author:

O'Donnell, W.R. and Loreto Todd (1980) *Variety in Contemporary English*, London, George Allen and Unwin.

The surname of the second author should not be given first.

An edited work:

Austen, Jane (1923) *Sense and Sensibility*, ed. R.W. Chapman, London, Oxford University Press.

Subsequent reprints may be indicated if used:

Austen, Jane (1923, repr.1974) *Sense and Sensibility*, ed. R.W. Chapman, London, Oxford University Press.

An edition revised by someone other than the author:

Mencken, H.L. (1977) *The American Language*, one-volume abridged edn. R.I. McDavid Jr., ed., New York, Knopf.

An edited compilation:

Ferguson, C.A. and S.B. Heath, eds. (1981) *Language in the USA*, Cambridge, England, Cambridge University Press, pp. 177–209.

A chapter or an article from a compilation:

Cassidy, F.G. (1982) 'Geographical Variation of English in the United States', *English as a World Language*, eds. R.W. Bailey and M. Görlach, Ann Arbor, University of Michigan Press.

A translation:

Pedersen, Holger (1962) *The Discovery of Language: Linguistic Science in the Nineteenth Century*, trans. J.W. Spargo, Bloomington, Indiana, Indiana University Press.

An article in a journal:

Parasher, S.V. (1983) 'Indian English: Certain Grammatical, Lexical and Stylistic Features', *English World-Wide*, IV:1, 27–42.

A book review:

Kachru, Braj B. (1983) Review of *New Englishes* ed. J.B. Pride, *English World-Wide*, IV:1, 97–99.

In this example and in the one immediately above, the volume number (IV) corresponds to the year (1983) and the second number (1) indicates that it is the first issue of the year. If the number and year do not correspond, then the month should also be indicated (April 1983).

Two books or articles by the same author in the same year:

Hancock, I.F. (1971a) 'West Africa and the Atlantic Creoles', *The English Language in West Africa*, ed. John Spencer, London, Longman, pp. 113-22.

——— (1971b) 'A survey of the pidgins and creoles of the world', *Pidginization and Creolization of Languages*, ed. Dell Hymes, Cambridge, England, Cambridge University Press, pp. 287-92.

An unpublished dissertation:

Penrith, Mary (1980) *Sub-Styles in* Emma *: The Nature and Values of Idiolects and Narrative*, unpub. M.Litt. thesis, University of Lancaster.

A person preparing a bibliography may wish to include other types of publication not listed above, such as a traditional ballad, an article in a newspaper or a reprint of an old text. The categories above should be used as guidelines. Some publishers omit the place of publication, but this habit can cause problems if a reader wishes to trace the item but does not know the country of origin. It is useful and informative to be clear, comprehensive, precise and consistent.

See: **abbreviations, dissertation, footnotes.**

billion (bn), million (m), thousand (K)

In the USA *billion* means 'one thousand million', that is, a one followed by nine zeros: 1,000,000,000. In the UK, *billion* traditionally referred to 'a million million', that is, a one followed by twelve zeros: 1,000,000,000,000. The US meaning is gradually replacing earlier UK usage, even in government documents and school books. Wherever there is even a slight risk of misunderstanding, an explanation of *billion* should be provided.

A *million* is represented by a one followed by six zeros.

In financial dealings the symbol *K* is often used to signify 'thousand', so that 2,000 pounds is referred to as £2K.

See: **numbers.**

black

The word *black* has many negative uses in English. It can suggest pessimism in:

   black comedy/despair/humour/mood

disapproval in:

   a black list/look/mark

In trade union circles a *blackleg* is synonymous with a *scab* and if any consignment is *blacked*, trade unionists will not touch it; *black* can also imply 'dirty':

   black hands

cruelty:

   blackbirding (indentured labour in the South Pacific)
   Blackshirts

illegal actions:

   blackmail
   black market

unnatural spiritual activities:

> *black magic*
> *black Mass*

pain or trouble:

> *black eye*
> *black ice*

people who do not behave as they should:

> *blackguard*
> *black sheep*

In traditional European descriptions of heaven and hell, God is white, the devil is black and sin is thought to *blacken* the soul.

Many of the words and phrases cited above are derived from the colour of the clothes worn, black shirts by Nazis, black vestments by exponents of the black Mass. Nevertheless, the equation of *black* with negative associations in so many phrases and idioms probably contributes to unconscious racism.

See: **racist language**.

Black English

Black English is a nonstandard variety spoken by the majority of the USA's 26.5 million Blacks. It is regarded by many linguists as having evolved from a **creole** once widely spoken in the USA and related to West Indian creoles and West African pidgins. The language of Blacks in South Carolina and the Sea Islands, locally called 'Gullah', is the most creole-like of all varieties of Black English and differs sharply from the speech of the upwardly mobile Blacks, especially in the North and on the West Coast. Yet, in spite of better education and conditions for US Blacks since the 1960s, most still speak a variety of English which differs from other varieties of **US English**.

Phonology
Many phonological features of Black English occur in the speech of Whites, especially poor Whites from the Southern States, but since many also occur in the creoles of the West Indies, it seems reasonable to assume an African influence on the speech patterns of US Blacks.

1 Black English is non-**rhotic**. Rhoticity is prestigious in the United States.

2 There are fewer vowel contrasts in Black English than in US **network norms**, with *sure* and *shore* being realised as /ʃo/ and *dare* and *dear* merging in /deə/.

3 The diphthong in *side* tends to be monophthongised so that *side* is realised as /sad/.

4 The vowel sound in words such as *burst*, *church*, *clerk* is realised as a long central vowel /ɜ/ or occasionally as a diphthong approximating to the *oy* sound in *toying*.

5 When /θ,ð/ occur in syllable-final position, they are often replaced by /f,v/:

/wɪf/—*with*
/smuv/—*smooth*

In word-initial position /θ/ is frequently replaced by /d/:

/dat/—*that*

6 Clusters in syllable-final position tend to be reduced, especially when the last consonant is /t/ or /d/:

yesterday > *yeserday*
tripped > *trip*

Vocabulary
The study of Black English has been hampered by scholarly disagreements regarding how much of the vocabulary is distinctively Black. Many believe that Black English gave world English such words as *banjo*, *boogie-woogie*, *bug* (annoy), *jamboree*, *jazz*, *jive* and *okay* as well as a number of items for food such as *goober* (nut), *okra* and *yam*. In some Black communities, African **calques** such as *corn stick* (cob without the ears of corn), *hard ears* (stubborn) and 'to like something *bad* (very much)' are widespread, but much of the information in this area is anecdotal since only some aspects of Black English have been studied in depth.

Grammar
It is in the area of grammar that most evidence has been presented in favour of a creole origin for Black English. Among the features frequently found in Black speech are:

1 lack of inflection in nouns for plurality or possession:

I got too many rabbit.
He on my daddy chair.

2 fewer pronominal contrasts, with the nominative form often functioning as nominative, accusative and possessive:

I ain know he lose he wife. (I didn't know he lost his wife.)

3 tendency not to use a copula:

I tired.
She sick.

4 tendency to mark the continuity rather than the tense of an action:

She readin'. = She is/was reading.

5 use of *be* with all subjects to convey habitual action:

We be lookin'. = We're usually looking.
He be dancin'. = He's usually dancing.

See: **creole, pidgins and creoles, US English**.

blend

Blending is a type of **word formation**. It is a combination of **clipping** and compounding in which new words are created by the overlap of words or fragments of existing words:

sham + amateur → *shamateur*
motor + hotel → *motel*

The fragments are not necessarily **morphemes** at the time of the blend although they may become so later if several blends are made with the same fragments:

motor + pedal → *moped*
motor + town → *Motown*

and the jocular:

motor + bike → *mobike*

Many blends are isolated, one-off creations:

manimal (man + animal)
marleyvous (Marley tiles + marvellous)

but others have become or are becoming part of the language:

Amerindian (American + Indian)
breathalyser (breath + analyser)
brunch (breakfast + lunch)
happenstance (happen + circumstance)
smog (smoke + fog)
tawdry (St Audrey)

A notable part of the word-play in James Joyce's *Finnegans Wake* involves such various forms of blending as:
1 discontinuous—*ventitillated* (ventilated + titillated)
2 enclosing—*voluntears* (volunteers + tears)
3 overlapping—*blessens* (bless + lessens)
4 punning—*handmades* (handmade + hand maids)

See: **clipping, compound, derivation, word formation**.

bombast

Originally, *bombast* was a soft material used for padding. By metaphorical extension it was applied to extravagant, insincere language.

bon mot

A *bon mot* (plural *bons mots*) is a French phrase meaning a witty or clever saying (literally 'good word'). Oscar Wilde's utterances were famous for such bons mots as:

> *I can resist everything but temptation.*
> *I have nothing to declare but my genius.*
> *The English have really everything in common with the Americans except of course language.*

A *bon mot* is sometimes confused with *le mot juste*. The latter implies the perfect word or phrase in the perfect position.

See: **diction, style.**

borrow, lend, loan

Borrow means receive something from someone on the understanding that it or its equivalent will be returned:

> *May I **borrow** your pen?*
> *Could we **borrow** some sugar?*

Lend is the converse verb to *borrow* and means give something to someone on the understanding that it or its equivalent will be returned:

> *Could you **lend** me some money until next week?*
> *I won't **lend** it to you because you never pay anything back.*

Loan is frequently used as a noun:

> *They got their **loan** in record time.*

As a verb, it is similar in meaning to *lend*:

> *Can you **loan** me some money?*

is more widespread in the USA than in other parts of the English-speaking world. Many linguistic commentators object to the verbal use of *loan* although such objections have not stopped the spread of verbal *loan* internationally.

See: **antonym.**

borrowing

The term *borrowing* is a misleading **metaphor,** in that *borrow* implies temporary use of something that is eventually returned to its owner. Linguistic 'borrowings' are different. Items are taken into one language from another without permission and with no prospect of return. Additionally, the 'borrowing' of, say, *restaurant* from French does not leave the French language without the borrowed word. 'Adoption' and 'adaptation' would be more accurate descriptions of the processes by which words and phrases from outside sources are taken into English and modified to conform to English patterns of **phonology** and **morphology**.

Strictly, *borrowing* suggests a simpler division between native and non-native vocabulary items than actually exists. Scholars use terms such as 'native English' to refer to words of Anglo-Saxon (or **Old English**) origin although these are a product of at least three Germanic tribes, the Angles, the Saxons and the Jutes, together with any *borrowings* these groups may have made before and during their settlement in Britain. The notion of the 'purity' of native English is thus based on a false interpretation of the ways in which a language develops and changes.

The chief impetus to borrowing is contact between speakers of different languages, and speakers of English have been extensively involved in such contacts. A large part of the vocabulary of contemporary English consists of borrowed rather than native elements. (An examination of the previous sentence shows that seven words [*of* occurs three times] are English in origin and seven have been borrowed from French.) **Core vocabulary** items such as *man, woman, tree,* together with function words such as auxiliaries, determiners, pronouns and prepositions, tend to be English in origin although, even here, inroads have been made by speakers of other languages (*they* and *till* were 'loans' from the Vikings and the Irish reinforced the use of *she*).

English has borrowed words from every group of people with whom English speakers have been in contact. The earliest borrowings were from the Celtic, French, Greek, Latin and the Scandinavian languages, but these have been augmented by other borrowings from Europe (e.g. *commando, pretzel*), Africa (e.g. *safari, yam*), Australia (e.g. *boomerang, kangaroo*), the Middle East (e.g. *ayatollah, sheikh*), the Far East (e.g. *shanghai, tycoon*), India (e.g. *bungalow, jodhpur*), the Americas (e.g. *jigger, moccasin, pampas*) and the South Pacific (e.g. *taboo, tattoo*).

See: **foreign words in English, word formation**.

bowdlerise/ize

This verb derives from the name of Thomas Bowdler (1745-1825), who published an expurgated edition of Shakespeare in 1818. Since the classics were often read aloud to family groups, Bowdler removed anything that he felt might cause embarrassment. He cut out large sections and modified others, causing Lady Macbeth, for example, to proclaim 'Out, crimson spot' instead of 'Out, damned spot.'

The term *bowdlerise* consequently means delete or modify written passages that are regarded as rude or offensive. The puritanical urge to 'clean up' literature is not limited to fiction. The lexicographer Noah Webster spent sixty years producing a version of the Bible from which all the rude and suggestive words and passages had been deleted.

Sometimes *bowdlerise* is mistakenly associated with bringing older texts up to date. In 1984 Arrow Books produced a series called *Shakespeare Made Easy* which has been severely criticised by people who forget how difficult some of Shakespeare's language is for people today. Admittedly, some of the poetry is lost, as when in *The Merchant of Venice* Portia's:

The quality of mercy is not strained...

becomes:

By nature, mercy is never subject to compulsion...

Such changes cannot be equated with *bowdlerisation* because they were introduced not for the sake of propriety but for comprehensibility.

bring, take

Bring and *take* are **prime verbs** that express not only **location** but also the relevance of place in relation to the speaker or the writer. *Bring* usually expresses movement towards and emphasis on the place where the speaker/writer is:

Bring *your book over here and I'll stamp it.*

Take expresses remoteness from or movement away from the speaker/writer:

*He **took** the cargo from Shanghai to Chicago.*
***Take** your book over there to the Librarian's desk.*

Bring often refers to the immediate location, whereas *take* may imply the remoteness of a specified location:

*I'll **bring** it home* (back to where one of us is now).

*I'll **bring** you home* (back to where we are now).
*I'll **take** it home* (away from where we are now).
*I'll **take** you home* (away from where we are now).

The emphasis on place extends to the past and future, so that *bring* may be used of a place where the speaker was or will be:

*I **brought** that book in last week.*
*I'll **bring** my book to the next class.*

However, the relationship between *bring* and *take* is not a simple dichotomy in that there can be considerable overlap in usage:

*I **took** that book in last week.*
*I'll **take** my book to the next class.*

The choice of *take* rather than *bring* emphasises that the speaker is not at the specified place at the time of speaking, either physically or emotionally.

All words in English depend for their meaning on the interlocking web of patterns in which they can occur. *Take* has a duality in that it contrasts with both *give* and *bring*:

*She **gave** him $10 and he **took** it.*
*She **brought** the books over and he **took** them home.*

but whenever *take* is used it tends to imply movement, physical or emotional, away from the speaker.

The best rule for using *bring* and *take* according to the canons of **Standard English** is to concentrate on the speaker. When the action involves proximity to the speaker, use *bring*; when it is remote from the speaker use *take*.

See: **alienable, prime verbs, speaker orientation.**

British

British is a very ambiguous term, particularly when problems of nationality and citizenship are involved. It can refer to residents of the British Isles (that is of the Republic of Eire as well as England, the Isle of Man, Northern Ireland, Scotland and Wales) and to citizens of ex-British colonies who are entitled to a British passport but not necessarily to residence in Great Britain (that is, England, Scotland, Wales).

English people tend to use *English* when *British* would be more accurate, often referring to 'an English passport' (there is no such thing), 'English place-names' (many of which are Celtic) and to 'English' when they mean British English.

Americans often use 'British English' to refer to varieties of English which are non-American, concentrating on such differences as spellings: US *center, check,* as opposed to *centre, cheque*; grammar: US *different than, gotten,* as opposed to *different from, got*; and different words for essentially the same thing: US *call collect, elevator* as opposed to *reverse the charges, lift.* Since these differences are found in Australia, Eire, India, parts of Africa and New Zealand as well as in Britain, a more appropriate term should be selected.

See: **Anglo-English, Anglicism, Irish English, Scottish English, spelling, UK and US words, Welsh English.**

burst, bust

Burst is unchanged in the past tense and past participle:

> *She **burst** the balloon yesterday.*
> *She has **burst** another balloon.*

In the UK, *bust* is nonstandard as a past tense or past participle but acceptable, especially in casual speech, in such fixed expressions as:

> *There's been a **bust-up**.*
> *'June is **busting** out all over.'*

In the USA, *bust* derived from *burst* and is standard. The past tense and past participle may be either *busted* or *bust.*

See: **-ed, -t forms, problem pairs.**

business and finance

Although a great deal of international trade takes place through the medium of English, there are some differences between UK and US terminology that can cause problems for the unwary. The commonest of these are:

UK	US
bank guaranteed cheque	certified check
Bank of England	Federal Reserve
bill, account	account
bill (restaurant)	check
building society	thrift bank
current account (bank)	checking account
deposit account (bank)	savings account
drapery	dry goods
Foreign Office	State Department
gilt-edged stocks	Government stocks
hire purchase	installment plan

nought, zero	zero
phone someone	call someone up
reverse (telephone) charges	call collect
shares	stocks
shop assistant	sales clerk
solicitor	lawyer, attorney
stocks	bonds
ten pound note	ten dollar bill

See: **Americanism, Anglicism, UK and US words.**

but

But is a co-ordinating **conjunction** joining contrasting units of equal grammatical rank. It can link adjectives, adverbs, phrases and sentences:

> (*She was*) *very quiet **but** remarkably efficient.* (adjectives)
> (*He worked*) *quietly **but** efficiently.* (adverbs)
> (*He didn't lecture*) *on the given topic **but** on another equally interesting one.* (phrases)
> *Harold defeated Tostig **but** William defeated Harold.* (sentences)

But has a number of other uses:
1 It can introduce a clause after such fixed negative expressions as 'nothing would do/please/satisy him/them':

> *Nothing would satisfy them **but** we should stay overnight.*

2 It can function as a preposition, usually capable of being replaced by *except*:

> *He eats nothing **but** bananas.*
> *She loves everyone **but** me.*

3 It can occur as an adverb in formal, somewhat archaic styles:

> *She had **but** one child and now he too was ill.*

Modern stylists would prefer *only* to *but*.
4 It occurs as a sentence modifier in Australian and Northern British English:

> *You have to admire him **but**.*

In the past, sentences beginning with *but* were condemned as stylistically unacceptable. Initial *but* is now acceptable in informal styles. As a stylistic device, however, it should be used sparingly.

See: **although, and,** co-ordination, **conjunction,** word order.

calque

A *calque* is a loan **translation** where the word or phrase is translated **morpheme** by morpheme from one language into the other. Calques from German include:

> *Battenberg > Mountbatten*

from French:

> *cordon bleu > blue ribbon*

and from Latin:

> *paganus* (person from heath) *> heathen*

Calquing is a marked feature of the English-related **pidgins and creoles** of West Africa and the New World where such calques as the following are found:

> *day clean*—dawn
> *dry eye*—brave (of a man), brazen (of a woman)
> *suck teeth*—disparage, insult

See: **creole, pidgins and creoles.**

Cameroon English

Cameroon has often been described as 'Africa in miniature'. Like Africa, it is multilingual (with over 200 indigenous languages for a population of under 9 million); it has known three colonial masters (Germany, France and England) as well as trading links with Portugal, Spain and the Netherlands; it has two official languages (French and English); and it has learnt the value of **lingua francas** (pidgin English, Ewondo Populaire, vehicular Hausa).

The following types of English are found in Cameroon:

1 Standard Cameroon English (SCE)
2 SCE with francophone influences
3 pidgin English (a much-used lingua franca, spoken by perhaps 50% of the population and becoming a mother tongue in some urban communities)
4 broken English

Since SCE is the variety favoured by radio announcers, it will be described here. Cameroon Pidgin will also be discussed because it is the most widely used language in the country and a language of considerable literary potential.

Phonology

1 SCE is non-**rhotic.**

2 There are fewer vowel contrasts in SCE than in **Received Pronunciation** (RP). Additional **homophones** are created by the merging of:

/i/ and /ɪ/ to /i/, *seat* and *sit* are both /sit/

/ɛ/ and /eɪ/ to /e/, *get* and *gate* are both /get/
/æ/ and /ɑ/ to /a/, *cats* and *carts* are both /kats/
/ɔ/ and /ɒ/ to /ɔ/, *nought* and *not* are both /nɔt/
/u/ and /ʊ/ to /u/, *fool* and *full* are both /ful/

3 There are no central vowels or centring diphthongs:

/ə/ > /a/, *better* > /beta/
/ɜ/ > /e/, *bird* > /bed/
/ʌ/ > /e/, *but* > /bet/
/iə/ > /ia/, *here* > /hia/
/ɛə/ > /ea/, *dare* > /dea/
/aiə/ > /aia/, *fire* > /faia/
/auə/ > /aua/, *power* > /paua/

4 /θ,ð/ are frequently replaced by /t,d/:

that thing > dat ting

5 There is a strong tendency to devoice /z/ and /bz,dz,gz/ in word-final position, thus causing the following pairs to become homophones:

nips and *nibs* > /nips/
carts and *cards* > /kats/
lacks and *lags* > /laks/

6 **Consonant clusters** tend to be split up, especially in word-initial position:

stop > /sɔtɔp/
trouble > /tɔrɔbul/

7 There is a tendency to nasalise vowels in words which occur in both English and French and which are nasalised in French:

baton > /batɔ̃n/
mason > /mesɔ̃n/
patron > /patrɔ̃n/

8 Under the influence of the **vernacular** languages and French, English tends to be spoken as if it were a syllable-timed language. Thus, all four syllables in *decolonise* receive equal stress.

Vocabulary
The main influences on the vocabulary of SCE are:
  1 the vernacular languages, giving items such as:

achu (type of food)
fon (chief)
yaa (chief's wife, female with power)

2 French, giving loans such as:

bon de caisse (cash voucher)
polycopy (photocopy, handout)
vignette (road-tax disc)

3 Pidgin, contributing words such as:

ashia (empathy formula)
cry-die (a wake)
pikin (child)

4 **Calques** from the local languages and French:

corn-stick < *kichi mbwasong* = cob
red-man < *kim bang* = European
certificate of individuality < *certificat d'individualité* = affidavit
court of first instance < *cour de première instance* = magistrate's court

5 **US English** is becoming increasingly popular and has provided such items as:

elevator—lift
guy—man
kickback—bribe
movies—films

Grammar

The grammar of SCE is essentially the same as other international standards but the following local usages are common:

1 the substitution of *all* for *both*:

Dynamo and Union, **all** *Littoral teams, are to meet in the semi-finals.*

2 the tendency to use certain adjectives as verbs:

She has been **pregnanted**.
They have **easied** *it.*

3 transforming mass into count nouns:

equipments (pieces of equipment)
woods (pieces of wood, blocks)

4 the hypercorrect use of *-ed* in the past tense of words such as:

broadcasted
shedded

5 names are usually written as surname + given name:

Mr Ngowah William

Cameroon Pidgin English has been widely used as a lingua franca throughout the country at least as far back as the German annexation (1884), and is the lingua franca of the police force, of prisons, and of urban schoolchildren at play. Although widely used and greatly loved, it has not been officially sanctioned by the government or given any status in the education system. The following extract from a story illustrates some of the features of the language:

Sɔm dei bin de nau, trɔki	Once upon a time, Tortoise
disaid sei i go bigin mek	decided that he would play
kɔni fɔ sɔm bif. I wan go	a trick on an animal. As he went
i mitɔp sɔm hamahama elefan	about he met a huge elephant
di chɔp fɔ bush.	eating in the forest.

See: **African English, pidgins and creoles, West African English**.

Canadian English

Canada has a population of 24.4 million, mostly of European origin, but with sizeable communities of Amerindians (250,000) and Inuit (17,000). Officially, the country is bilingual in English and French, but there is little functional bilingualism in Canada, largely because with the exception of the Province of Quebec the country is overwhelmingly anglophone. (In 1976, 81.5% of the population of Quebec claimed French as their mother tongue whereas the percentages for the other provinces were: British Columbia 1.6%, Alberta 2.5%, Saskatchewan 2.5%, Manitoba 5.5%, Ontario 5.7%, New Brunswick 33.6%, Prince Edward Island 5.6%, Nova Scotia 4.5% and Newfoundland 0.5%.)

Canadian English is becoming increasingly assimilated to US **norms**. There is free access along the 4,700 miles of shared border; many US radio and television programmes can be received in Canada; and over 75% of Canadians live within one hundred miles of the border.

As in most communities where English is spoken, we find regional, class and ethnic differences. The folk speech of Herring Neck, Newfoundland, is very different from that of Moose Jaw, Saskatchewan; the English of Quebec shows markedly more influence from French than does the English of British Columbia; immigrants from the Caribbean continue to use **creole** features; and working-class speakers are usually distinguishable from their middle-class contemporaries. The Canadian English of the media is, however, both influential and relatively homogeneous and it is this variety which is described.

Phonology
1 The entire country is **rhotic**; post-vocalic 'r' as in *war* and *ward* is prestigious.

2 When the diphthongs /aɪ/ and /aʊ/ occur before voiceless consonants, there is a strong tendency to replace them with /əɪ/ and /əʊ/, producing such contrastive pairs as:

/aɪ/	/əɪ/	/aʊ/	/əʊ/
pie	pipe	house(v)	house(n)
prize	price	loud	lout
side	site	mouth(v)	mouth(n)

3 Canadian English follows the US model in:
(a) the use of /u/ rather than /ju/ after /t,d,n/ as in:

/studənt/—student
/du/—due
/nuz/—news

(b) the voicing of /t/ between vowels and between /r/ and /t/:

/pɪdɪ/—pity
/fɔrdɪ/—forty

(c) the deletion of medial /t/ after /n/:

/tərɒnoʊ/—Toronto
/twɛnɪ/—twenty

(d) the use of syllablic /l̩/ or /əl/ where UK speakers use /aɪl/:

/fərtəl/—fertile
/mɪsəl/—missile

(e) the use of /e/ rather than /ɑ/ in the stressed vowel of tomato.
4 Canadian English follows the UK model in preferring:
(a) /i/ rather than /ɛ/ in the first vowel of:

/livər/—lever

(b) /ɪ/ rather than /aɪ/ in the second vowel of the prefixes:

/æntɪ/—anti
/sɛmɪ/—semi

(c) /u/ rather than /aʊ/ in:

/rut/—route

Vocabulary
1 Among the words borrowed from Amerindian and Inuit languages through Canadian English into world English are:

caribou pemmican toboggan (Amerindian)
igloo kayak parka (Inuit)

Most Canadians now use Inuit rather than Eskimo. (The word Eskimo is believed to derive from an Amerindian form meaning 'eaters of raw flesh'.)

2 Canadians use *riding* to mean **'parliamentary constituency'**.

3 Canadians tend to follow US English usage in vocabulary, preferring:

US	to	UK
bathroom		*lavatory*
clerk		*shop assistant*
gas		*petrol*
kerosene		*paraffin*
pantyhose		*tights*
pavement		*road*
sidewalk		*pavement*
truck		*lorry*

4 In a few instances, Canadian English follows UK usage, preferring:

UK	to	US
railway		*railroad*
tap		*faucet*
tin (of beans)		*can* (of beans)

5 In spelling, Canadian English tends to follow UK **norms**, preferring:

UK	to	US
labour		*labor*
programme		*program*
theatre		*theater*

Grammar

Speakers of Canadian English increasingly use the grammar of the standard language. The following features are apparent:

1 the use of what has been called 'narrative *eh*' as a tag in speech:

*Are you listening, **eh**? Well those shoes I bought, **eh**, are the most uncomfortable I've ever worn, **eh**. They hurt everywhere, **eh**, at my toes, **eh**, and my heels.*

Among younger Canadians, *eh* is often replaced by *right*:

*He came in, **right**, walked straight up to me, **right**, and stuck out his tongue.*

2 the nominative form of pronouns (especially *I*) is often used in structures involving *you* + *and* + *pronoun*:

*Between **you and I**/he...*
*He came in to see **you and I**.*
*The cost has to be borne by **you and I**.*

3 *Have you got* is preferred to *Do you have*:

Have you got *any fresh fruit?*

4 French **word order** of noun + adjective is seen in the names of the Great Lakes:

Lake Ontario
Lake Superior

and in a number of government agencies:

Agriculture Canada
External Affairs Canada

See: **UK and US English**.

cant

Like **argot**, *cant* is often used as a **synonym** for **jargon**. However, *cant* has a more specific meaning in that it is the term applied to speech or writing associated with a doctrine that is suspect. It may thus imply hypocritical piety, unacceptable political dogma, the secret language of the underworld or the stereotyped language of religious, political or scientific writers with whom we do not agree. When *cant* is used, it implies not only disagreement with what has been said or written but disapproval of the author.

See: **argot, etymology, patois**.

Caribbean English

In this account, the *Caribbean* comprehends a number of countries stretching from Bermuda, the Bahamas, through the Cayman Islands, Turks and Caicos, Jamaica, Puerto Rico, the Leeward Islands (including Antigua, St Kitts, Nevis, Anguilla, Monserrat, the Virgin Islands), the Windward Islands (including Barbados, Dominica, Grenada, St Lucia, St Vincent), Trinidad and Tobago, the ABC islands (Aruba, Bonaire, Curaçao) and the mainland coastal areas of Belize, Nicaragua, Costa Rica, Guyana and parts of Suriname. English is the official language of Bermuda, the Bahamas, the Caymans, Jamaica, the Leewards, the Windwards, Trinidad and Tobago, Belize and Guyana and in these countries it is spoken in a range of forms from standard to **creole** by approximately 5 million people. In coastal areas of Nicaragua, Costa Rica and Suriname English-related creoles are spoken, and in the other countries English is acquired by many as a second language. Throughout the region, therefore, we find a continuum of interlocking variants, ranging from creoles (which are the mother tongues of the majority of the population) to Standard English. (Such a spectrum of Englishes is often called 'a post-creole continuum'.) In the Virgin Islands, **US English** is the model. In all the territories historically linked to Britain, UK **norms** prevail but, because of the physical proximity of the USA and its penetration of the media, US English is becoming increasingly influential. This description concentrates on the standard end of the spectrum.

Phonology

1 The **accents** of Barbados and the Virgin Islands are **rhotic**; Jamaican and Guyanese speakers occasionally pronounce post-vocalic 'r'; the remaining speech communities are non-rhotic.

2 All syllables are more equally stressed in the Caribbean than in the UK or the US and there is more variation in the intonation of sentences.

3 The diphthongs /eɪ/ and /oʊ/ as in *gate* and *goat* are monophthongised to /e/ and /o/.

4 Schwa rarely occurs in relaxed speech. In words ending in -er, the vowel is often /a/, thus:

batter is often /bata/
fitter is often /fɪta/

In other unstressed syllables, either the full, unstressed vowel occurs:

instrument is /ɪnstrumɛnt/
panted is /pantɛd/

or /ɪ/ is used:

flannel is /flanɪl/

5 The centring diphthongs /ɪə/ and /ɛə/ (or their rhotic equivalents /ɪr/ and /ɛr/) are often merged so that *beer* and *bare* are homophones and realised as /bea/ or /bɛr/.

6 /θ,ð/ are frequently replaced by /t,d/, producing extra homophones in *tin* and *thin*, *with* and *wit*, *den* and *then*, *breed* and *breathe*.

7 The -ing form of the verb is frequently realised as /ɪn/ with:

/rʌnɪŋ/ becoming /rʌnɪn/.

8 **Consonant clusters** in word-final position which end in /t,d/ are often simplified. Thus:

act occurs as /ak/
best as /bɛs/
build as /bɪl/
sand as /san/
talked as /tɔk/

9 There is a tendency to substitute /kj,gj/ for /k,g/ when they are followed by back vowels:

cash > /kjaʃ/
gas > /gjas/

Vocabulary

1 Speakers from the Caribbean use the full range of the standard vocabulary. The region has, however, been settled or visited by many different people, all of whom have left linguistic traces on English. From African languages come *calalu* (vegetable), and *duppy* (ghost), from Arawakan comes *matapee* (basket), from Carib *cayman* (alligator), from Dutch *koker* (sluice), from French *bateau* (boat), from Hindi *dhal/dhol* (yellow pulse), from Portuguese *brigah* (cocksure, disdainful of others) and from Spanish *mantilla* (head covering for a woman).

2 Many English words have been extended in meaning:

mash up can mean 'destroy, ruin'
passage can mean 'money to pay the fare with'

3 Occasionally, tone is used to distinguish meanings, thus *station* pronounced with a mid tone followed by a high means 'the railway station', whereas when pronounced with a high tone followed by a mid tone it means 'police station'.

4 Rastafarian terminology changes regularly but items such as *Babylon* (oppression), *deaders* (meat) and *dreadlocks* (type of ringlets) are found throughout the Caribbean, as well as in the UK and the USA.

Grammar

1 Structures involving **active voice** predominate. Where passives occur, they usually involve GET:

*He **got** killed.*
*The car **got** mash up.*

2 *Will* is often replaced by *would*, especially when there is doubt about the proposition:

***Would** you buy me some new clothes?*

3 **Serial verb** constructions are common:

*Child, **run come go bring** those hats.*

4 Because of the reduction of consonant clusters and because of the influence from the creoles, the past tense, past participle and plural markers are occasionally deleted:

*The march has been **ban**. They **ban** it yesterday.*
*He went round all the place but there were no **job**.*

5 *Up* is added to a verb to indicate intensity or frequency:

*He **beat up** the boy.*
*He **ate up** his food every day.*

6 Questions are often in the form of statements but with rising intonation:

That is your ball?

Often *right* is used as a question tag:

You lost it, **right***?*

7 Collective nouns such as *government* and *jury* always function as singulars:

The **government** *is tackling the problem of unemployment.*

8 *My own* and *your own* are often preferred to *mine* and *yours.*

See: **Bahamian English, Barbadian English, Jamaican English, pidgins and creoles, Trinidadian English, West Indian English.**

case

The grammatical term *case* derives from Latin **grammar**, where **nouns** were described as having six cases: nominative, vocative, accusative, **genitive**, dative and ablative. A number of grammars of English even used the Latin-style **paradigm**:

	English	Latin
Nom.	lord	*dominus*
Voc.	O lord	*domine*
Acc.	lord	*dominum*
Gen.	lord's	*domini*
Dat.	to/for a lord	*domino*
Abl.	by/with/from a lord	*domino*

Latin nouns showed their relationship to other words in the sentence by their case endings. English nouns can play the same roles in sentences as their Latin counterparts but relationships are signalled mainly by **word order** and by prepositions rather than by case endings. For example, in the sentences:

The dog bit the child.
The child bit the dog.

the forms of *dog* and *child* do not change. It is word order that indicates which noun is the **subject** (in the nominative case) and which is the **object** (in the accusative case). Similarly, the meanings carried by the *-o* endings in the Latin word *domino* are indicated in English by the use of the prepositions *to/for/by/with/from* plus an article.

Case is not as relevant to the description of English as it was to Latin. Only one case occurs in English nouns, the genitive or possessive case indicated by *'s* or *s'*:

the boy's money
the boys' money

Even here, **possession** can also be indicated by the use of *of*:

the money of the boys

Indeed, the *of* construction is more likely with inanimate nouns:

the branches of the tree
the eye of the needle

In English, case is also found in the following **pronouns**:

Nominative	Accusative	Genitive
I	me	my/mine
he	him	his
she	her	her/hers
we	us	our/ours
they	them	their/theirs
who	whom	whose

(In some grammars, the forms *my, your, his, her, our, their, whose* are called 'possessive adjectives').

The pronouns *you* and *it* do not show differences between the nominative and the accusative but are marked for the genitive:

Nominative/Accusative	Genitive
you	your/yours
it	its

A number of difficulties occur with the use of pronouns in that speakers are not always certain whether to use the nominative or the accusative forms. The following rules should help:

1 The nominative is always used in subject position, including compound subjects:

John and I *hardly ever go fishing any more.*
She and John *are twins.*

(A useful rule to remember is that when the compound can be replaced by *we*, then the form *X and I* is obligatory.)

2 In formal speech and writing, the BE verb requires the nominative form both before and after:

It **was he** *who discovered the solution.*
Who is the Scarlet Pimpernel? **I am he.**

3 In formal speech and writing, the nominative is required in comparisons involving *than*:

He is taller than I.
She is taller than he.

4 The accusative case of pronouns is used when they are the objects in a sentence:

She loves him and us.
He visited John and me.

(When the compound can be replaced by *us* then *X and me* is obligatory.)

5 The accusative case of pronouns must be used after prepositions:

between you and me
before them
The money was left to him and me/us.

6 *Who* is the subject pronoun and *whom* the form used as an object:

Whom did you see?
He is the man whom we met in France.

and after a preposition:

To whom did you give it?
He is the scholar for whom the collection was made.

In colloquial speech, *whom* can sound pedantic and the sentences:

Who did you see?
He is the man we met in France.
Who did you give it to?

are more likely to be spoken than their more formal (and more correct) counterparts. Even in speech, however, if the pronoun comes immediately after a preposition, then *whom* must be used.

7 There are two points to be remembered concerning the use of the genitive case of pronouns. First, **apostrophes** should not be used with any of the pronouns above:

I prefer hers to his.
What is its name?
Why is theirs so much better?
Whose is it? Whose coat is it?

It is, however, essential to use an apostrophe with *one*:

One must do one's best for one's children.

Secondly, the possessive adjective should be used before **gerunds** (**-ing forms** used as nouns):

*His **arriving** so unexpectedly caused a number of problems.*
*I have encouraged **their taking part** in the marathon.*

See: **genitive, possession, pronoun.**

case grammar

Case grammar is a descriptive model devised by C.J. Fillmore in the late 1960s. Fillmore concentrated attention on the fact that many verbs involving movement or change (e.g. BREAK, CLOSE, TEAR) could occur in sets of sentences where a group of nouns could fill different slots in the sentence:

John broke the glass.
John broke the glass with the hammer.
The hammer broke the glass.
The glass broke.

It seems clear that, despite the surface difference in the sentences above, *John*, *glass* and *hammer* have consistent roles: John is invariably the **agent**, the hammer is always the instrument and the glass is the noun which receives the action. Fillmore suggested that, in **deep structure**, nouns are involved in **case** relationships with verbs. In some languages, such as Latin or Greek, the relationships show up as case endings; in other languages, however, the relationships may be signalled by **word order** and the use of prepositions or postpositions.

Fillmore's model is attractive in that it underlines the universality of certain relationships in language. Every speaker expresses views concerning agents and experiencers such as:

John hit Peter.

every society is aware that certain actions can only be performed with an instrument of some type; and we all understand sources and goals, time and place. In Fillmore's view the relationships are universal but the surface manifestations of case differ from one language to another.

See: **ergative, transformational grammar.**

catch phrase

A *catch phrase* is a fixed phrase or slogan popularised by an entertainer, a politician, an advertisement or the media. The popularity of a catch phrase is often temporary and many readers may have already forgotten Fritz Mondale's borrowed advertising slogan:

Where's the beef?

in the 1984 US Democratic Primaries. Other well-known catch phrases include:

Come up and see me sometime (Mae West).
If the Tories get up your nose, picket (Labour/TUC slogan).

See: **cliché, fad words, idioms.**

catch-22

The phrase *catch-22* derives from the name of a novel published by J. Heller in 1961. This phenomenon, also referred to as 'a no-win situation' and 'Hobson's choice', involves a person in circumstances where no move can lead to a satisfactory outcome. An early example of a catch-22 situation was a technique used in the reign of Henry VII (1485-1509) called 'Morton's Fork'. This was meant to curb the power of the barons by taxing them severely. Archbishop Morton reasoned that if a baron spent a lot of money, then he must have a lot which he could contribute to the king; alternatively, if a baron was not spending a lot of money, he must be saving a lot which he could contribute to the king.

catholic, Catholic

The word *catholic* with a lower case *c* is an adjective meaning 'universal':

*His interests as a scholar were **catholic**: he was not only fascinated by Creoles but found pleasure and stimulation in literature, philosophy and psychology.*

Catholic with a capital *C* can be both a noun and an adjective:

*He became **a Catholic** on his deathbed.*
*She was not very interested in **Catholic** dogma.*

In most parts of the world *Catholic* is equivalent to *Roman Catholic*.

causative

Many sentences in English can be shown to include a causal element in the verb:

Macbeth killed Duncan.

is the equivalent of:

> *Macbeth caused Duncan to die.*

and:

> *Mary improved the design.*

can be interpreted as:

> *Mary caused the design to be/become better.*

The same verb can occur in both *causative* and non-causative sentences:

> *Mary **cooled** the milk* (i.e. she caused it to cool).
> *Mary **cooled** down.*

and many adjectives and verbs are related causatively. Often **synthetic** causative verbs are formed by adding *-ate*, *-ify* and *-ise* to adjectives or nouns:

> *activate* (cause to become active)
> *beautify* (cause to become beautiful)
> *terrorise* (cause to become terrified)

See: **analytic, ergative, prime verbs, synthetic.**

Celtic influences

Celtic influence on English has probably been continuous over the last fifteen hundred years but may have been greatest:
1 when the Angles, Saxons and Jutes first arrived in Britain during the fifth century and
2 during the sixteenth to nineteenth centuries when large numbers of Celts moved into the cities and into London in particular

Because the Celts have been in an inferior position to the Germanic peoples who settled in Britain, much of the influence from Cornish, Irish and Scots Gaelic and from Welsh has either been denied or underestimated by scholars. Wrenn is fairly typical of English scholars in his claim (1958):

> Celtic influences have been sporadic and almost negligible...

and the following extract from the *Oxford English Dictionary* vol. 2, p.592 illustrates the too-easy dismissal of Celtic influences:

> Cog sb.2 [ME *cogge*, found from 13th c.: the Sw.*kugge*, Norw.*kug*, pl.*kugger*, in same sense, are evidently cognate; but the relations between them are not determined. The Celtic words, Ir., Gael.*cog*, Welsh *cocas*, uncritically cited as the prob. source, are (as usual in such cases) from English.]

In the case of *cog* sb. 2, the *OED* editors may be correct in dismissing the Celtic **etymology**, but the bracketed parenthesis is indicative of an attitude that tends to see all influence from the English–Celtic contact as one-way traffic.

During the invasion of Britain, many Celts fled to the fringes of the British Isles—Cornwall, Ireland, the Isle of Man, Scotland and Wales—but many of the women must have intermarried with the invaders, a fact that helps account for the preservation of topographical terms such as:

avon (river)
down (low hill)
tor (hill)

It is a truism that history is always the history of the conqueror and so it is not possible to say when or how other Celtic words entered English, but some did. From Irish: *bànshee, bog, brock* (badger), *colleen, leprechaun, trousers*; from Scots Gaelic: *cairn, loch, pibroch* (pipe music), *plaid, sporran, whisky*; and from Welsh: *bard, cromlech, eisteddfod, penguin*. In addition to the above, now widely recognised as deriving from Celtic languages, we find items of low prestige listed in English dictionaries as 'etymology unknown' but having Celtic **cognates** going back before the item was first recorded in English. Among these are: *cadge, cog* (cheat), *slob, spree* and *twig* (understand).

But the influence from Celtic was not limited to vocabulary. Contemporary English makes the following distinction:

I go/I am going

where French, for example, covers both with:

je vais

The Celtic languages have a tripartite distinction represented in Gaelic by:

téighim (GO + I)
táim ag dul (BE + I going)
bím ag dul (BE + habitual + I going)

The Celts thus make aspectual distinctions not regularly found in other West European languages. Indeed, according to Otto Jespersen, **progressive aspect** was not commonly found in English until early in the seventeenth century. It thus seems likely that Celtic influences contributed to the occurrence or at least reinforcement of the aspectual distinctions now made in English.

See: **Anglo-Irish, aspect, Hiberno-English, Scottish English, Welsh English.**

Central African English

None of the three countries which together form 'Central Africa' had English as a colonial language. The 34 million people of the Central African Republic, Zaire and the Congo still employ French as their official language but English is taught as the second foreign language in all schools. The English of this region resembles that of West Africa, especially countries such as Cameroon, where French is an official language.

See: **African English, Cameroon English, West African English.**

cheap, cheaply

In theory, the distinction between these two forms is clear: *cheap* is an **adjective** and *cheaply* an **adverb**:

> *He wanted to buy a cheap car.*
> *He sold it cheaply to get rid of it.*

Increasingly, however, *cheap* is used colloquially as an adverb:

> *He got it cheap.*

and a number of young speakers refuse to accept:

> *He got it cheaply.*

as an alternative. It is possible that *cheaply* will gradually disappear from the language and that the same form will function as both adjective and adverb just as forms like **better** do at present.

> *You couldn't find a better young man.*
> *He is getting better all the time.*

See: **adjective, adverb.**

'chestnuts'

The term *'chestnut'* is sometimes applied to areas of the language that people have very strong views on, such as: Should we ever split an infinitive? Why do people use *due to* when they mean *owing to*? Why have standards of pronunciation fallen? Why do people insist on using the word **aggravate** to mean 'infuriate'? In most discussion of **usage** we can predict that difficulties will be raised in three major areas:

   1 grammar (Which is correct: *none of them is coming/none of them are coming?*)

   2 pronunciation (Should it be 'controversy or con'troversy?)

   3 words (Why do people insist on misusing **unique** to mean 'rare'?)

See: **purist, split infinitive.**

Chinese English

It is impossible to trace exactly when English was first heard in *China*, but it is likely that some forms of English have been used on the Chinese coast since the middle of the seventeenth century, the English having established a trading post at Canton in 1640. It is also true that China Coast Pidgin English was an important **lingua franca** in the Pacific region, especially during the nineteenth century, and was influential in helping to form the Pidgin Englishes of Papua New Guinea, Samoa, the Solomon Islands and Vanuatu, as well as Plantation Pidgin in Northern Queensland. China Coast Pidgin English died out during the late nineteenth and early twentieth centuries, leaving small, localised traces in Hong Kong.

Today, the People's Republic of China is a country of over one thousand million inhabitants, a large number of whom (perhaps as high as 10%) have some knowledge of Standard English. English is recognised as a useful international lingua franca; the language is widely taught in schools, colleges and universities; and radio and television programmes on the English language allow workers (in the widest sense) to study the language in their spare time.

English is not a mother tongue in any part of China, nor is it necessary as an internal lingua franca, and so people acquire the standard language mainly through education. One's knowledge depends largely on linguistic ability and on the extent of one's exposure to the language, but it would probably be true to generalise that, in China, passive grammatical knowledge is greater than active fluency.

Phonology

No set of points can fully comprehend the variation that occurs in English in China, due mainly to mother-tongue dialect influences and to the country of origin of the teachers, but the following generalisations apply to many speakers.

1 Chinese English is essentially non-**rhotic**.

2 Since the voiced consonants /b,d,g/ do not occur in Mandarin Chinese, many speakers replace /b,d,g/ in English words by unaspirated /p,t,k/, the sounds used by native speakers of English in *spin*, *stick* and *skin*.

3 There is a tendency to impose a CVCV structure on English. This often involves introducing an epenthetic vowel into **consonant clusters** and adding a vowel to a word that ends in a consonant. Thus *act* is realised as /ækətə/, *six* as /sɪkəsə/ and *stand* as /sətændə/.

4 For some speakers of Chinese /n/ and /l/ are in free variation and so *linger* may be realised as /nɪŋgə/ or *announce* as /əlaʊns/. Others may use /n/ and /ŋ/ interchangeably, thus failing to distinguish between *ban* and *bang*.

5 The sounds /θ,ð,ʃ/ are all likely to be replaced by /s/:

thin /sɪn/
then /sɛn/
ship /sɪp/

and /tʃ/ is frequently replaced by /ts/ thus producing /tsaɪnə/ for *China*.

6 Vowels cause fewer problems but /ɛ/ tends to be realised as /aɪ/ so that the letter *x* is pronounced /aɪks/.

7 Because Chinese is a **tone language** with four contrastive tones, speakers of Chinese find English **intonation** difficult. They either carry over tonal distinctions to English or, in an effort not to do this, they frequently speak English within a very narrow intonation band.

Vocabulary
Apart from *silk* and *tea*, Chinese has given world English many words for prepared food:

chop suey
chow mein

for the martial arts:

kung fu
tai chi (shadow boxing)

for philosophy:

yin and *yang* (two elemental forces—mutually exclusive yet complementary)

and words derived from China's dynastic past:

kowtow (show deference)
yamen (office or residence of a public official)

A number of other words and phrases have entered English. Among them are *kaolin* (a fine, white clay), *pekinese* (dog), *shantung* (heavy silk), *shanghai* (kidnap, force someone to go somewhere or do something), *chop sticks* (quick + sticks, reinforced by *chop suey* meaning 'odds and ends of food') and:

Long time no see < *Hen jiu bu jian* (Very long no see)

Grammar
Chinese students aim to acquire standard International English but mother-tongue influences are seen in:

1 The marked preference for **active voice** where the passive might be more appropriate:

Some people told me.

in preference to:

> *I was told.*

2 The meaning carried by the **perfect aspect** in English is not realised in the verb phrase in Chinese but is carried by an adverbial or particle. Many speakers often confuse the simple past with past perfect, producing such sentences as:

> *I have spoken to him yesterday.*
> *I'm not hungry. I had already my dinner.*

See: **Hong Kong English, pidgins and creoles.**

circumlocution

Circumlocution is the use of an excessive number of words to state something that could be expressed more economically. Like **elegant variation** and **tautology**, it is a tendency to increase the length of an utterance, often in an attempt to impress listeners or readers. A number of terms are used for *circumlocution*, the most widely known of which are: **periphrasis, pleonasm, redundancy**, *roundabout expressions*, **tautology**, *verbiage*, **verbosity** and *wordiness*. There are three ways of eliminating the problem.

1 Unnecessary words should be removed. For example, all the words in parentheses can be dropped from the following phrases:

> *five (years of age)*
> *four (in number)*
> *it is true (to say) that*
> *pink (in colour)*
> *six foot (in height)*
> *triangular (in shape)*
> *until (such time as)*

2 Expressions involving circumlocutions should be rephrased:

> *at this moment/point in time* (now)
> *during the time that* (while)
> *five percentage points* (five percent)
> *in the event that* (if)
> *in the order of* (about)
> *in this day and age* (now/today)
> *shower activity* (showers)

3 Whole sentences and paragraphs should be assessed to see if they can be organised more simply and concisely. For example, the following sentence:

> *In the event that the robber, named Smythe, was unknown to the*

shopkeeper, and the shopkeeper to him, the curious feature of the situation is that he must have obtained his information about the shopkeeper's property as such from a third party. (42 words)

can be rewritten as:

Curiously, someone must have told the robber Smythe about the shop-keeper's property, because the two men did not know each other. (21 words)

Circumlocution is usually a symptom of a lack of discrimination or control. Most users could improve their **style** by checking sentence structure carefully and paying more attention to clarity and precision.

See: **fillers, periphrasis, pleonasm, redundancy, tautology, verbosity.**

class

This term is often applied to a set of items in a language which share certain formal properties, such as the ability to occur in certain positions in a sentence. Structuralists designed test frames to divide English words into *classes*. A frame such as:

$$(\text{the}) \ \dots \left\{ \begin{array}{l} \text{man} \\ \text{meaning seemed very} \\ \text{meat} \end{array} \right\} \dots$$

reveals some **adjectives** and a frame like:

The ... + s are here.

reveals some **nouns**. Different grammatical analyses subdivide English word classes in different ways but the following classes are recognised by most:

adjectives (*good, obvious*)
adverbs (*happily, truthfully*)
conjunctions (*and, if*)
determiners (*a, the*)
exclamations (*Oh! Wow!*)
nouns (*child, tree*)
prepositions (*at, in*)
pronouns (*I, which*)
verbs (*come, sing*)

Many individual words can occur in several word classes:

*Arthur's **round** table* (adjective)
*We walked **round** and **round**.* (adverb)
*They went for a **round** of golf.* (noun)

*He went **round** the bend.* (preposition)
*He **rounded** the corner at 90 miles an hour.* (verb)

Words are usually subdivided into those which belong to closed
sets and those which are found in open classes. By *closed set* we mean
that there are a finite number of items in the set. Conjunctions,
determiners, exclamations, prepositions and pronouns belong to
closed sets. Adjectives, adverbs, nouns and verbs belong to open
classes, which means there are many items in these classes and we
can add more. If we invented a new soft drink called 'shing' for
example, we would have a new noun, and if drinking shing became
popular, we might have a 'shing party' at which we would all
'shing', thus adding a new adjective and verb to the language.

clause

Not all models of English deal with *clauses* but for those that do a
clause is a unit of language smaller than a **sentence** and larger than
a **phrase**. A clause resembles a sentence in having a **subject** and a
predicate. Clauses can be subdivided into:

1 *main clauses* and *dependent/subordinate clauses* as illustrated by
the following sentences:

Main Clause	Subordinate Clause
He heard	*what you said.*
I know	*that you are tired.*

A subordinate clause can precede the main clause as in:

Subordinate Clause	Main Clause
If you do that	*you'll get into trouble.*

and a sentence may have several subordinate clauses:

(*If you take the road*) (*that turns left at the traffic lights*) [*you'll see a
signpost*] (*that will direct you.*)

The sentence above has a main clause (*you'll see a signpost*) and three
subordinate clauses.

2 **finite** and **non-finite** clauses. All the subordinate clauses above
are finite, that is, they have a verb which can take a subject from
the following set of pronouns: *I, he, she, it*. A non-finite clause
contains a non-finite verb form, that is, the infinitive (*to hide*), the
present participle (*hiding*) and the past participle (*hidden*):

Main Cl +	Finite Sub Cl	Main Cl +	Non-Finite Sub Cl
He thought	*I should hide.*	*He advised*	*me to hide.*
He insisted	*I was hiding it.*	*I was blamed*	*for hiding it.*
He knew	*we had hidden it.*	*We left it*	*hidden from view.*

Clauses can function in three different ways in a sentence:
1 as noun clauses:

*I heard **what he said**.*
*He wanted **to smoke**.*

2 as adjective/relative clauses:

*The man **who was leading** fell.*
*The man **leading the rest** fell.*

3 as adverbial clauses:

*He retired **after he lost**.*
*He retired **after losing**.*

Transformational grammar does not use the concept of *clauses* but deals with sentences which are embedded in other sentences. TG would describe such a sentence as:

The man who was leading fell.

as being composed of two simple sentences:

The man was leading.
The man fell.

with the first embedded in the second as follows:

The man (the man was leading) fell.

See: **finite, grammar, sentence, subordination, transformational grammar.**

cleft sentence

A *cleft sentence* is one in which a word or phrase has been highlighted by being given its own verb, thus producing a two-part or divided sentence. Clefting usually involves the formulas:

It is/was X who/that...
What (sentence) is/was...

and it permits us to highlight any part of the sentence except the verb. If we examine a sentence like:

Sally slipped on the ice last Sunday.

we can use clefting to produce:

*It was **Sally** who slipped on the ice last Sunday.*
*It was **on the ice** that Sally slipped last Sunday.*
*It was **last Sunday** that Sally slipped on the ice.*

Pronouns can also be emphasised this way so that:

She started it.

can become:

*It was **she** who started it.*

although such clefting is less common than:

She was the one who started it.

Cleft sentences using the second formula usually focus on non-human subjects or objects so that sentences such as:

I fancy a long, cool drink.
That legacy will be really useful.

can become:

***What I fancy** is a long, cool drink.*
***What will be really useful** is that legacy.*

See: **foregrounding**.

cliché

The term *cliché* is from the French word for a stereotype printing plate composed of movable type. A *cliché* is a trite, hackneyed word or phrase, once perhaps expressing insight, novelty or wisdom but now stale from overuse. Clichés take a number of forms:

1 single words or morphemes:

nice
situation
-wise (e.g. *pricewise*)

2 phrases:

at this moment/point in time
cool, calm and collected
foregone conclusion

3 metaphors:

at death's door
bamboo/iron curtain
make a mountain out of a molehill

4 formulas:

as far as I can see
mark my words
to be perfectly frank

5 nicknames:

John Bull (UK)
Rocky (heavyweight boxer)
Uncle Sam (USA)

6 quotations (often inaccurate):

a lean and hungry look (Shakespeare)
a little learning is a dangerous thing (Alexander Pope)
(often misquoted as 'a little knowledge')
tomorrow to fresh woods and pastures new (John Milton)
(often misquoted as 'fresh fields')

7 catch phrases:

a catch-22 situation
by and large
keep a low profile

8 foreign phrases:

par excellence (beyond comparison)
persona non grata (unacceptable person)
verb. sap. (a word is enough to the wise)

Clichés require little reflection on the part of the user or the recipient. They tend to express stock ideas and evoke stock responses. This automatic, unthinking response to clichés means that they can be useful in **propaganda** and it is because of this that many people have condemned them. George Orwell expressed his views on the use of clichés in this way:

> A speaker who uses that kind of phraseology has gone some
> distance towards turning himself into a machine. The
> appropriate noises are coming out of his larynx, but his
> brain is not involved as it would be if he were choosing
> his words for himself.
> 'Politics and the English Language' (1946)

There are no objective criteria by which we can say 'This is a cliché' any more than there are objective criteria for defining a work of art. If a word or phrase is frequently used, however, so that it has lost most of its original power, then it has one of the properties of a cliché. Many clichés involve aids to memory such as **alliteration** or **assonance**:

cold comfort
free and easy

suggesting that some, at least, are relics of an oral culture. Some of the original value of a cliché may be realised by a non-native user of English who may find phrases such as:

an iron hand in a velvet glove
gilding the lily

evocative and even poetic. Moreover, some languages require for-

mulaic references to indicate respect or solemnity, and an inexperi-
enced user of English may mistakenly substitute clichés for such
formulas, sometimes with surprising results, as in an Indian student's letter announcing his mother's death:

> *Sadly, I have to inform you, sir, that the hand that rocks the cradle*
> *has kicked the bucket.*

See: **address and reference, catch phrase, fad words, phatic communion,
propaganda.**

clipping

A *clipping* is a type of **word formation** in which a shorter word or
phrase is made from a longer one. Clipped words are normally colloquial and are more often spoken than written. Thus we find:

amp < ampere
Dip Ed < Diploma in Education

but not:

* univ < university
* trans < translated

which are unspoken **abbreviations**. Clipped forms may be based on
pronunciation:

nuke < nuclear weapon/power
pram < perambulator

and because they are used as full words, they take the same morphological endings as other English words:

phone phones phoning phoned

1 Clipped forms are often part of an in-group vocabulary:

exam lab prof vac (students)
goalie pro ref sub (football)
disco EP fan pop (music)

Because of their usefulness, some clippings have become part of our
everyday vocabulary:

bus < omnibus
cab/taxi < taxicab
gas < gasoline
sport < disport

Others coexist alongside their more formal sources:

auto automobile
photo photograph
plane aero/airplane
specs spectacles

2 Clipping of compounds and phrases also occurs, although this tendency is limited by the need to have within the expression a word that is unlikely to occur in many other contexts:

car < motor car
inter-city < inter-city train
transistor < transistor radio
typo < typographical error
video < video recorder

3 As with other subdivisions of language, clippings are not a totally discrete category. Some involve the clipping of more than one English word:

perm < permanent wave

or of a Latin phrase:

infra dig < *infra dignitatem* (beneath one's dignity)
mob < *mobile vulgus* (unstable crowd)

or the conjoining of two clippings:

hifi < high fidelity

and others may change as the items they describe become more familiar:

stereophonic record player > *stereo record player* > *stereo*
television set > *TV* > *telly*

4 Clipped forms may vary between the UK and the USA:

UK	USA
advert, ad	*ad* (advertisement)
chips	*French fries* (chipped/fried potatoes)
maths	*math* (mathematics)

See: **abbreviation, acronym, contraction, word formation.**

clothes

The terms for some items of clothing differ between the UK and the USA, even though many of the items are essentially the same. The reason for this is probably that dress has changed radically since the political separation between UK and US speakers, and both groups have introduced their own terms for the new garments. The commonest differences are:

UK	US
anorak	parka
braces	suspenders
dinner jacket	tuxedo
dressing gown	bathrobe
duffel coat	pea jacket
handbag	purse
press stud	snap
purse	change purse
pyjamas	pajamas
suspenders	garters
tights	pantyhose
trousers	pants, slacks
underpants	(under)shorts
vest	undershirt
waistcoat	vest

See: **Americanism, Anglicism, UK and US words, UK English, US English.**

codes

Codes are generally thought of as a means of restricting intelligibility to those who know how to interpret them. However, there are also codes, like the systems of semaphore, sign languages and morse, designed to promote intelligibility over obstacles such as deafness or distance. One such system is particularly useful in overcoming not only distance and interference but the potential ambiguity of the names of English letters. ('AC', for example, is barely distinguishable from 'SE'.) The spelling code is used by the police and armed forces, in international and civil aviation and marine communication:

A Alfa B Bravo C Charlie D Delta E Echo F Foxtrot
G Golf H Hotel I India J Juliett K Kilo L Lima M Mike
N November O Oscar P Papa Q Quebec R Romeo S Sierra
T Tango U Uniform V Victor W Whiskey X Xray Y Yankee
Z Zulu

and the numbers 5 and 9 are pronounced *fife* and *niner*.
The term *code* is used by sociolinguists to describe a variety of language and *code-switching* refers to a speaker's ability to move from one variety of language or even from one language to another in response to people or events.
Basil Bernstein used the terms 'restricted' and 'elaborated codes' in his discussion of the language used by children from different

social **backgrounds**. A restricted code was said to be marked by inexplicitness, simple vocabulary and syntax and by references to the here and now. Elaborated codes were thought to be explicit, well-organised, unrestricted with reference to time and place, and making use of precise vocabulary and the grammatical patterns of the standard language.

See: **semiotics**.

cognate

The term *cognate* refers to languages or units of languages which derive from the same source. Irish Gaelic, Welsh and Breton are cognate languages, all deriving in part at least from a Proto-Celtic language. Words like Latin *mater*, English *mother* and Gaelic *mathair* are cognate words deriving from a common **Indo-European** root.

When the subject, predicate or object in a sentence are lexically related as in:

> *A life has to be lived to the full.*
> *He now treats the treatment seriously.*

We can talk about a cognate subject, cognate predicate or cognate object.

See: **analogue, core vocabulary**.

cognitive

Cognitive meaning refers to those aspects of meaning which do not involve a subjective or emotional response. To say 'One plus one equals two' is obviously true and unlikely to evoke a strong positive or negative reaction. Other words are not so semantically neutral, however. The easiest way to illustrate the emotional content of some items is to contrast words which are almost synonymous:

> *artisan workman*
> *politician statesman*
> *resolute stubborn*

Each pair comprehends essentially the same *cognitive* meaning but our choice of one word rather than the other would imply an involvement. To describe someone as 'resolute', for example, is to suggest approval, whereas to describe the same person as 'stubborn' implies criticism.

See: **cliché, connotation, denotation, synonym**.

cohesion

Cohesion implies unity. When the term is applied to a word in English, it means that the word cannot take an infix:

unmanly

but not:

*munan or **malyn*

When the term is applied to a sentence, it means that no constituent in the sentence is obviously inappropriate or wrongly positioned:

She seemed to love everyone.

but not:

*She love to seemed everyone.

Cohesion is most frequently applied above the level of sentence to a text which is a unified whole and not just a collection of words or unrelated sentences. Cohesion often manifests itself in terms of **anaphora**:

*John Smith walked in. **He** was tall and handsome.*

as well as in consistency of vocabulary, tense and subject matter.

See: **anaphora, discourse analysis, linkage.**

coinage

A *coinage* is a new word formed according to the phonological possibilities of the language. Because of the many methods of word formation available to English users, coining is relatively rare, except in advertising and in the creation of trade names. Monosyllabic coinages tend to exploit hitherto unused slots in the language. For example, there are a number of monosyllabic words consisting of a consonant + -id:

bid did hid kid lid

but not all possibilities are used:

*cid fid gid jid

A coinage could thus be created by using one of these vacant slots. Such a word would be analogous in form with other -id words but it would also be novel.

Polysyllabic coinages tend to combine novel elements with conventional morphemes, so that the roots of *decombubelise* and *spifflicate* are novel but the affixes are regular.

A number of coinages such as:

fun pun quiz slang snob

have entered the language and, because they do not break any morphological rules, are indistinguishable from other words. Trade names such as *Kleenex* and *Sqezy* deliberately break the conventional rules of spelling but are in accord with the normal patterns of pronunciation.

See: **affix, derivation, word formation.**

collective nouns

The term *collective noun* refers to a singular noun that has a plural implication (e.g. *government*) and is used when the whole body (and not the constituent members) is being considered. The category *collective nouns* is not discrete, and it can be argued that some usages are midway between collective and **mass nouns**. For example, *team* is clearly a collective noun and *butter* is clearly a mass noun but it is not so easy to decide the status of such nouns as:

hair linen royalty

As a rule, we can classify nouns with animate members as *collective* (*committee, family, flock*) and those with inanimate or indistinguishable parts as *mass* nouns (*timber, straw, water*).

A collective noun takes a singular verb and is replaced by a singular pronoun in formal and written English:

*The jury **is** considering **its** verdict. **It has** been out for two hours.*

In informal styles, there is a tendency to use a plural verb form:

*The jury **are** considering the verdict.*

but, although this is acceptable in the spoken medium, there should be consistency of reference. To mix singular and plural usage as in:

*The jury reached **its** verdict although **they** disagreed on a number of points.*

would be regarded as an error of style and syntax.

There is a risk of a shift in number when a plural modifier comes between the collective noun and the verb:

*The team **was** cheerful.*
*The team of footballers **was/were** cheerful.*

In colloquial styles, words such as *family, government, team* are often used with plural verbs, but this usage should be avoided in writing.

Nouns of assembly may be regarded as a sub-category of collective nouns. Many of these, such as *a flock of sheep* or *a school of whales*, are well known but others are much rarer and are known only to collectors. Among these are:

an exaltation of larks
a kindle of kittens
a leap of leopards

Geese on the ground are *a gaggle* but in the air *a skein*. For practical purposes, the ordinary speaker needs relatively few nouns of assembly, several of which seem the result of lighthearted creativity rather than observation:

a charm of goldfinches
a watch of nightingales
a wisp of snipe

See: **countable and uncountable, every, mass nouns.**

collocation

Collocation, from Latin *collocare* meaning 'to place together', refers to the fact that words often occur together and that their meanings are in part conditioned by habitual co-occurrences. For example, the word *perch* can appear with such words as *fins, scales, swim, water*. In such contexts it is likely to mean *fish*. If, however, *perch* co-occurs with *alight, bird, branch* or *cage* it is likely to be either a verb related to 'sit' or a noun meaning 'a place on which to sit'.

Some collocations are more predictable than others. If we say *hale and ...*, the expected word is *hearty*. (Poets have often deliberately frustrated a reader's expectations by avoiding the normal collocations and producing such phrases as *once below a time*.) Others are less predictable, but a word such as *dog* is likely to occur with such items as *bark* or *bone*.

Function words such as *the* or *could* are relatively free of collocational restrictions. Semantically full words such as *knife* or *trot* are less free. Clichés (*at the eleventh hour*) and idioms (*bark up the wrong tree*) are fixed collocations, allowing little or no modification.

Occasionally, *collocation* is contrasted with *colligation*, from Latin *colligare* meaning 'tie together'. *Colligations* are sets of words which function in the same way. Thus, verbs such as APPEAR , CHOOSE and HAVE are said to colligate because they may all be followed by the to-infinitive:

He appears to have gone.
She chose to go on last.
We have to bear that in mind.

See: **cliché, context, idiom, idioms, vocabulary.**

colloquial English

Colloquial derives from Latin *colloquor* meaning 'to converse'. Its primary meaning thus relates to the spoken medium, so that a colloquialism is characteristic of or used in conversation. Martin Joos divided English styles into five main substyles:

Frozen
Formal
Consultative
Casual
Intimate

and *colloquial English* is most likely to be found in the two last categories. It implies 'informal', bears the additional feature of 'conversational' but is in no way inferior to 'formal'.

Colloquial is a more general term than **slang**. Whereas slang relates usually to nonstandard forms, a colloquialism may be standard or nonstandard. For example, the term *hobo* is a colloquial variant of the more formal *vagrant*, but both are standard. In contrast, the terms *deadbeat* and *shooler* (wanderer) are less widely known and the second, in particular, could be described as nonstandard.

Colloquial English is marked by spontaneity; simple vocabulary; reduced forms (*aren't* rather than *are not*); **fillers** (*you see*); and the use of words and phrases that are acceptable in speech but less so in writing (*a buck* [dollar], *between a rock and a hard place*).

Although *colloquial* is etymologically related to speech, colloquial English is often found in friendly **letters**, in certain sections of newspapers and in novels and plays where it is meant to create an impression of realistic speech.

See: **formal English, nonstandard English, slang, speech and writing, speech in literature.**

comparison and contrast

Comparison and *contrast* are procedures for determining the similarities and differences between two or more people, ideas, objects or things. Comparison focuses on likeness, as in Shakespeare's sonnet 18:

Shall I compare thee to a summer's day?

Many popular sayings are comparisons:

as bold as brass
as light on her foot as a cat at milking
too sweet to be wholesome

as are **similes**:

> O, my luve is like a red red rose
>   Robert Burns

and **metaphors**:

> And what is love? It is a doll dressed up
> For idleness to cosset, nurse and dandle.
>   John Keats

Contrast explores differences and is frequently employed in logical and/or persuasive writing in order to establish distinctions:

> No man can serve two masters for either he will love
> the one and hate the other, or he will serve the one
> and despise the other. You cannot serve God and Mammon.
>   Luke 17: 13

There is, however, some overlap between the words *compare* and *contrast* in that *compare to* stresses similarity and *compare with*, like *contrast*, stresses difference.

comparison of adjectives and adverbs

When **adjectives** and **adverbs** are used in a non-comparative way as in:

> That is a **big** car.
> He drives **carefully**.

they are referred to as *positive* or *in the positive* **degree**. Adjectives and adverbs can also occur in what is known as a *comparative form* or *in the comparative degree*:

> That is a **bigger** car than my last one.
> He drives **more/less carefully** than he used to.

The *superlative degree* involves a comparison of more than two:

> That is the **biggest** car I've ever had.
> He drives **most carefully** at night.

When only two items are involved in a comparison, the comparative form of the adjective must be selected:

> the taller of the two
> John is the older (of the two).

Monosyllabic and frequently-used disyllabic adjectives and adjectives used as adverbs form their comparative and superlative by adding *-er* and *-est* to the stem:

Positive	Comparative	Superlative
quick	quicker	quickest
lovely	lovelier	loveliest

Less common disyllabic and polysyllabic adjectives use *more/most* and *less/least*:

Positive	Comparative	Superlative
beautiful	more/less beautiful	most/least beautiful
ridiculous	more/less ridiculous	most/least ridiculous

Adverbs ending in -ly also take 'more/most' and 'less/least':

Positive	Comparative	Superlative
valiantly	more/less valiantly	most/least valiantly

Two adjectives, *far* and *old*, have two comparatives and superlatives:

Positive	Comparative	Superlative
far	farther/further	farthest/furthest
old	older/elder	oldest/eldest

For most purposes *further/furthest* and *older/oldest* should be selected.

A number of adjectives and adverbs are irregular, and these are among the most frequently used in the language:

Positive	Comparative	Superlative
bad/badly	worse	worst
good/well	better	best
ill	worse	worst
little	less	least
much	more	most

See: **adjective, adverb, degree.**

competence and performance

This distinction was introduced into **linguistics** by Noam Chomsky. *Competence* is defined as 'the ideal speaker-hearer's knowledge of his language' and *performance* as the 'actual use of language in concrete situations'. Competence is, as it were, the complete and perfect storehouse of linguistic knowledge that allows a speaker to:

1 produce and understand an infinite number of well-formed sentences

2 recognise errors and classify the degree of error involved, whether a slip, an understandable extension or a usage which breaks grammatical rules:

Sheats and Kelley (Keats and Shelley—slip)
I'll Bubu you. (an extension, a shift from noun to verb)
I knowed it. (breaking the rules)

3 recognise similarity of meaning under dissimilarity of form:

Jane followed Tarzan.
Tarzan was followed by Jane.

and differences of meaning under similarity of form:

I advised him what to say.
I asked him what to say.

4 recognise the possibility of one structure having several meanings:

Go to work on an egg. (three meanings at least)

Performance draws on competence, but whereas competence is perfect, performance can be faulty. It can involve hesitations, false starts, slips of the tongue, unnecessary repetitions, inattention and carelessness. Linguists try to describe competence by idealising performance, that is, by dredging away from actual language all performance accidents such as slips of the tongue.

The distinction between competence and performance is a useful one and one which all language users instinctively recognise. We have all, for example, corrected our own usage or been aware that our fluency was impaired because of illness or tiredness. We can only hypothesise about competence, however, by idealising performance.

The notion of *communicative competence* is a development of Chomsky's work. Research in this area derives from the fact that a native speaker not only has intuitions about language but about the variety of language most suitable at a particular time or place or in specific social contexts.

See: **langue and parole, speech and writing.**

complement

In its most general application, the term *complement* refers to anything that completes the **predicate**. It therefore comprehends everything which follows the verb and which is necessary to complete the state or action specified by the verb. According to this view, all the items in bold in the following sentences are *complements*:

*Maud rang **the doctor**.*
*Maud is **a doctor**.*
*Maud went **into the garden**.*

Most linguists give *complement* a more restricted meaning, applying it to words or phrases which follow a **copula**:

*John is **a doctor**.* (noun phrase complement)
*John appeared **foolish**.* (adjective complement)

*John was **out***. (adverb complement)
*John seemed **in a hurry***. (preposition phrase complement)

All these complements provide information on the subject and are called *subject complements*. In such sentences as:

*They elected John **President**.*
*She called John **an idiot**.*

the items in bold provide extra information on the object and are called *object complements*.

See: **BE, copula, predicate, verb phrase.**

compound

A *compound* is a lexical item formed by the process of:

base + base + (base):
bookcase (book + case)
notwithstanding (not + with + standing)

instead of the usual:

base + affix(es):
homely (home + -ly)

Compounding is a highly productive type of **word formation.**
1 The strongest stress normally falls on the first element of a two-word compound:

'blackbird (contrast: black 'bird)
'Whitehouse (contrast: white 'house)

but it may occur on a different syllable in polysyllabic words:

photo'phobia

2 Compounds may be single words:

clergyman

hyphenated words:

self-taught

pairs of words:

bee keeper

or hyphenated phrases:

a down-and-out
an up-and-coming star

These forms represent a continuum between the word and the phrase, many being in the process of change. Thus we find both:

book-maker and *bookmaker*
lion-tamer and *liontamer*

with UK users favouring more **hyphenation** than US speakers.

3 One group of compounds uses **morphemes** borrowed from Greek. Though usually full words in Greek, they may be bound morphemes in English. This type of compounding is a frequent source of new names for scientific and technological inventions and discoveries:

astronaut
biorhythm
thermonuclear

4 Several modern compounds are formed from a letter + a word:

T-square
S-bend
U-turn
X-ray

See: **affix, coinage, derivation, rankshifting, word formation.**

comprise, consist, constitute

These words are sometimes confused.
    Comprise means 'include' or 'contain' and is often found in descriptions of houses which are for sale:

*Desirable residence in sought-after neighbourhood **comprising** four downstairs reception rooms...*

Consist may be used in two ways, depending on the preposition which follows. *Consist in* means 'exist in' and it is often used of abstractions, especially religious abstractions:

*Charity **consists in** loving your neighbour.*

Consist of is the more usual collocation and means 'be made up of':

*The hip **consists of** a ball and socket joint.*

Constitute means 'form a whole, make up':

*What do you think **constitutes** their greatest threat?*

concord

Concord refers to a system in language where the choice of one element triggers off the use of a particular form of another element.

For example, in the following French sentences, the form of the adjectives and the verbs are determined by the noun:

Ma mère est petite. (My mother is small.)
Mon père est petit. (My father is small.)
Mes parents sont petits. (My parents are small.)

There is relatively little concord in English but we find it in the following circumstances:
1 In the non-past, the **subject** conditions the form of the verb:

I/you/we/they sing
he/she/it sing +s

The **base form** of the verb is used for all persons except the third person singular. There is no concord between subject and verb in the past:

I/you/he/we/they sang

Slightly different forms of concord affect BE, DO and HAVE.
2 Subject **complements** sometimes agree with the subject:

They are twins.
We were good students.

3 Certain pronouns trigger off the use of a particular form of the verb:

Neither (of them) has passed.
None (of them) has passed.

None is the equivalent of 'not one' and so it takes a singular verb. Increasingly, however, speakers use *none* as the negative equivalent of 'all' and so they use a plural verb:

None of them have passed (i.e. they have all failed).

4 **Everyone** causes problems. Most speakers say:

Everyone/every body has their problems.

but purists argue that since 'one/body' is singular, the correct form is:

Everyone has his/her problems.

5 In structures involving **continuous aspect,** BE triggers off the use of the -ing form of the following verb:

I am singing.
They were singing.

6 In structures involving perfect aspect, HAVE triggers off the use of the past participle of the following verb:

I have gone.
He has sung.

7 In **passive** structures, BE triggers off the use of the past participle of the following verb:

He was seen.
He has been seen.

See: **agreement, aspect, auxiliary, BE, DO, every, HAVE, nobody, passive voice.**

conditional

This term is applied to clauses which hypothesise:

If I were a blackbird, I'd whistle and sing.

or imply conditions:

Unless you change your routine, you can expect trouble.

The use of *if I were/was* is partly determined by the likelihood or unlikelihood of the hypothesis:

If I were a millionaire... (unlikely)
If I was there now... (likely)

When in doubt, *if I were* should be selected.
There is no conditional tense in English. Conditionality can be expressed by means of such subordinate conjunctions as:

as if
if
on condition that
providing that
unless

often in conjunction with modals:

*You **can** go **if** you promise to behave yourself.*
*I **won't** go **unless** you come too.*

Some grammarians insist that *should* must be used with the first person singular and plural:

I/we should go.

and *would* with the second and third persons:

You/he/she/they would go.

For many speakers, this distinction does not apply and *would* or its abbreviated version is used with all persons:

> I **would**/I'**d** *love to go if I had the time.*

See: **hypothetical, modality, verb phrase.**

conjunction

Conjunctions are joining words and in English we find two types: co-ordinating conjunctions (also called *co-ordinators*) and subordinating conjunctions (also called *subordinators*).

Co-ordinating conjunctions join units of equal status:

> *the man and the woman* (noun phrase + noun phrase)
> *He worked diligently and well.* (adverb + adverb)
> *It's either on my desk or in my bag.* (phrase + phrase)
> *I called but he didn't stop.* (sentence + sentence).

There is a finite set of co-ordinating conjunctions in English:

and	either...or	or	then
but	neither...nor	so	yet

Subordinating conjunctions introduce subordinate **clauses** (also called **dependent** clauses), often providing information on when, where, why or how an action or event occurred. The commonest subordinating conjunctions are:

after:	*He came after he made the announcement.*
(al)though:	*Although he was tired he went with them.*
as:	*The news finally sank in as he walked home.*
as...as:	*He left the house as soon as he could.*
as if:	*He behaved as if he owned the place.*
because:	*I went there because I wanted to.*
before:	*Sign this before you go.*
even if:	*I wouldn't have gone even if I'd been invited.*
if:	*If you play that tune again I'll scream.*
in case:	*Set another place in case she comes.*
more...than:	*She had more sense than I credited her with.*
since:	*We've been successful since she joined us.*
so that:	*They saved so that they could have a good time.*
till/until:	*Don't move till I come back.*
when:	*When you see her tell her I need help.*
whenever:	*Whenever I see her she's crying.*
where:	*You've put them where nobody can find them.*
wherever:	*Wherever you see Jack you're sure to see Jill.*
whether:	*He couldn't decide whether he should apply or not.*
while:	*Wait here while I do the shopping.*

Many subordinating conjunctions can also function as prepositions:

Subordinator	Preposition
*He arrived **after** I did.*	*He arrived **after** me.*
*He left **before** John did.*	*He left **before** John.*

See: **class, clause, co-ordination, sentence, subordination.**

connotation

Connotation refers to the extra association(s), usually emotional or social, that a word or phrase may have in addition to its denotative or referential meaning. For example, the words *boy, brat, child, kid, kiddy, lad, tot, wee'un* may all be used of a four-year-old boy, but their connotations vary from favourable or affectionate (*wee'un*) to hostile (*brat*). The emotional load of a word like *home* in contrast to *apartment* or *house* lies in its connotation. Social attitudes may affect the connotations of a word. Victorian prudery, for example, gave the words for trousers and underwear strong taboo connotations. And attitudes to race are often implied in the terms selected by a speaker or writer.

Certain words have stronger evaluative loading than others and this can vary from one **context** to another. For example, the terms *communist* or *fascist* may be used to whip up feeling at a political rally but appear relatively neutral in a book on modern history. Because connotations depend largely on context (or indeed on intonation), dictionaries cannot normally provide more than the denotative meaning, with perhaps a descriptive label such as 'derogatory' or 'vulgar'. Similarly, words that are denotatively equivalent, such as *girl* and *lass*, may have a variety of differing connotations (affection, class, region) that rule out synonymy.

The connotative force of words is often exploited in persuasive language such as advertising and **propaganda**. Most people have been attracted to a product or idea because of the pleasant, positive or prestigious associations conferred on it by loaded language. For different motives, poetry and descriptive prose depend on connotations to extend meanings and evoke particular sensations, but expository writing normally requires a more neutral vocabulary.

See: **cliché, denotation, euphemism, racist language, synonym.**

consonant cluster

A *consonant cluster* involves the co-occurrence of two or more consonants:

   state
   strip

English permits up to three consonants at the beginning of a syllable but there are strict rules as to the consonant sounds that can occur:

Position 1		Position 2		Position 3
		p		l/r/j
s	+	t	+	r/j
		k		l/r/w/j

The patterns above refer to sounds and not letters and can be illustrated by the words:

splash sprain spurious (pronounced 'sp + your + ious')
strain stew (UK English)
sclerosis screech squander skew

In word final position, English permits up to four consonants in a cluster:

exempts
glimpsed

Consonant clusters can cause pronunciation problems to both native and non-native speakers. The standard orthography illustrates how many clusters have been simplified in the past:

gnaw knight lamb

and the simplification continues:
1 clusters are reduced:

san(d)
vu(l)nerable

2 **intrusive vowels** are introduced:

ath(e)lete
chim(i)ney

See: **epenthesis, intrusive vowels, pronunciation.**

contemporary, contemporaneous

Contemporary refers to 'the same period of time, simultaneous' and may be used as a noun and an adjective:

*Wordsworth was a **contemporary** of Coleridge.*
Coleridge's poetry benefits from comparisons with the
*works of **contemporary** poets.*

Adjectival *contemporary* is increasingly used to mean 'modern, current' so that 'contemporary poets' in the example above could be ambiguous, meaning both 'poets of Coleridge's time' and 'poets of today'. Since both interpretations are possible, the need to use *contemporary* cautiously is clear.

Contemporaneous is an adjective meaning 'occurring at the same time'. It normally refers to events:

The Civil War and the Irish rebellion were **contemporaneous**.

but it is possible that it will take over the adjectival sense of *contemporary*, thus doing away with the present ambiguity.

context

The term *context* is used in three main ways.

1 It can refer to the words, structures and punctuation surrounding a particular word or usage. Out of context, words seldom have precise meanings, a fact that can be illustrated by the word *bear*. On its own it may evoke very different responses in the minds of different people, but in the following contexts we have no difficulty in giving it very specific meanings:

The brown **bear** *hibernates throughout the winter.*
He's in one of his moods—a regular **bear** *today.*
It is wrong to **bear** *false witness against a neighbour.*
She can't **bear** *the heat.*

In the first example, the use of *bear* as a noun and its **collocation** with *brown* and *hibernates* eliminate other possible interpretations. Similarly, in the fourth sentence, where *bear* is a verb and collocates with *can't*, the meaning 'tolerate/endure' is clearly indicated. The functions and relationships between words thus constitute a very specific meaning of *context*.

2 A more general use of the term is *literary context*. This normally includes the linguistic details mentioned above together with information about the genre (play, poem, novel), the type (lyric, ode, sonnet) and the time when it was written. **Alliteration** in an **Old English** epic, for example, can have a very different significance from alliteration in a short twentieth-century lyric.

3 A still more general use of *context* occurs in psycholinguistic and sociolinguistic studies, where it refers not simply to the linguistic environment but also to the extralinguistic details, often known as the *context of situation*. These details may include the ages of the participants, their sex or nationality, their gestures and movements, the time of day, the place or the occasion (a wedding, for example). Such information may shed light on entire utterances. The following forecast:

Outlook: warm and close.
Further outlook: a little sun.

takes on a different meaning when it is read out at a wedding celebration.

Because context plays an essential role in defining meaning, the quotation of something out of context can cause severe distortion and misrepresentation. The easiest example of this is the statement that 'There is no God' occurs in the Bible. It does, but in the context: 'The fool hath said in his heart: There is no God.'

See: collocation.

continuous aspect

The sentences:

> *It is boiling at 100 degrees centigrade.*
> *It boils at 100 degrees centigrade.*

have several differences. The first emphasises that the action is occurring now and is continuous whereas the second concentrates attention on the universality of the action. 'It' invariably boils at 100 degrees centigrade even if the action is not taking place now. The first sentence involves the use of the *continuous* or **progressive** aspect which is characterised by the use of BE plus the present participle of the following verb:

> *I am swimming.*
> *You were swimming.*

Continuous aspect can co-occur with perfective aspect as in:

> *He has been swimming.*
> *She had been swimming.*

See: aspect, auxiliary, Black English, progressive, verb phrase.

contraction

Contraction is a process whereby a word is phonologically reduced and attached to an adjacent form. It can be illustrated by:

> I + am > *I'm*
> they + have > *they've*
> dare + not > *daren't*

and is a feature of colloquial speech.

See: aphesis, apocope, clipping, elision, strong and weak forms, syncope.

controversy

The BBC receives many complaints about the pronunciation of *controversy*. Listeners object to announcers who stress the second syllable, insisting that the word should be pronounced with the strongest stress on the first syllable. The same listeners, however, would also criticise the stressing of the first syllable in *laboratory*, although both words had first-syllable stress in Britain until the 1930s. It would thus appear that the British speakers who say:

con'troversy

are following the same rule that shifted:

'laboratory

to:

la'boratory

in the UK.

See: **'chestnuts', purist.**

co-ordination

Co-ordination is the process of linking units of equal status, usually by means of a co-ordinating **conjunction**:

tall *and* handsome
time *and* tide
Come in *and* sit down.

but sometimes, especially when more than two units are involved, co-ordination is achieved by juxtaposition:

tall, dark *and* handsome
time, talk *and* tide
Come in, take off your coat *and* sit down.

In co-ordinated phrases and clauses, shared constituents can be elided:

my mother *and* (my) father
That very pretty girl came in and (...) sat down.

or replaced by **pronouns, auxiliaries** and **so**:

I saw the Swedish boy yesterday and recognised **him** at once.
You will be able to come, **won't** you?
I thought he was very handsome and said **so**.

See: **anaphora, conjunction.**

copula

This word, which derives from Latin *copula* meaning 'bond', refers to verbs such as BE which link a **subject** and a **complement**:

> *He is a doctor.*
> *He is in a hurry.*

The following verbs can also be used as copulas:

APPEAR:	*He appeared tired.*
BECOME:	*He became a nurse.*
GET:	*He is getting too big for his boots.*
GROW:	*He is growing taller all the time.*
LOOK:	*He looked suspicious.*
SEEM:	*He seems a very kind person.*

See: **BE, complement, verb phrase.**

core vocabulary

Our control of language determines the words we use (active vocabulary) and the words we understand but may rarely use (passive vocabulary). Most speakers have a unique inventory of words, acquired from the network of contacts (spoken and written) in which they are involved, but most speakers of a language also share a set of words for basic body parts and functions, common foods and activities. This shared vocabulary is known as the *core vocabulary*.

Morris Swadesh produced various lists of words (60, 100, 200, 400) which could be assumed to be known and used by all native speakers of a particular language. These lists included:

> animals commonly found in the area
> body parts and functions
> colours
> commonly-used clothes
> commonly-eaten foods
> kin relationships
> natural phenomena
> numbers
> pronouns
> question words
> references to location
> references to possession
> words relating to age (*young, old*) and size (*big, small*)

Since such words are frequently used in speech, they tend to be the least susceptible to change. (The core vocabulary of modern English is still almost exclusively Germanic in spite of centuries of contact with speakers of other languages.)

Linguists use core vocabularies to examine whether or not languages are related. The following lists in English, French and Gaelic, for example, suggest that the languages are related, albeit distantly:

English	French	Gaelic
cat	chat	cat
nose	nez	sron
father	père	athair
mother	mère	mathair
snow	neige	sneachta
one	un	aon
you	toi/vous	tu/sibh
old	vieux	sean
big	grand	mór

The closer the resemblance of the core vocabulary items and the more similarities there are, the closer the relationship between the languages.

Some linguists have evolved techniques for comparing core vocabularies and calculating the time since the languages or varieties of one language separated. The comparison of core vocabularies is known as *lexicostatistics* and the quantification techniques as *glottochronology.*

Although core vocabularies exist and are useful in assessing relationships, glottochronology is a controversial discipline. It assumes that languages change slowly and at a regular rate. In the words of Swadesh (1972):

One general rule applies to all forms of linguistic
change: It goes on slowly...

Our knowledge of **pidgins and creoles** over the past 400 years, however, shows us that fundamental phonological, lexical and grammatical changes can occur within a generation. In addition, glottochronology can in some cases give very wrong results. It is right when it tells us that UK and US English are closely related in time and space, but wrong when it indicates that English and Tok Pisin (the pidginised English of Papua New Guinea) diverged over two thousand years ago.

See: **cognate, pidgins and creoles.**

countable and uncountable

These terms are applied to certain types of **nouns.** *Countable* nouns are individual items that we can easily differentiate, number and pluralise. The singular can also be prefixed by *a*:

a/one chair   two chairs   ten chairs
a/one child   two children   ten children
a/one memory   two memories   ten memories

Uncountable or **mass** nouns denote amounts that can be divided but not separated into entities which can be numbered. We do not, for example, usually count sugar by the grain or water by the drop. Examples of uncountable nouns are:

cash   confidence
sand   soil

Uncountable nouns may be used with *some*:

some money not **a money*
some sand not **a sand*

with *the*:

the bread
the furniture

with a phrase equivalent to 'an amount of':

an ounce of tea
a ton of sand

or without an article:

I was filled with shame.

Such nouns are treated as singular and do not normally have a plural:

The news is not good.

The distinction between countable and uncountable nouns is neither wholly logical (some languages treat *hair*, *knowledge* and *luggage* as countable nouns, others as uncountable) nor wholly linguistic (*news* is uncountable but *news item* is countable). Moreover, a noun normally treated as uncountable may become countable when we refer to a variety:

Lactose and fructose are both **sugars**.

or to a specified amount:

One sugar or two?

The division between countable and uncountable nouns is language specific and arbitrary. In English, we make nouns countable when we concentrate on the fact that items are separable; when we focus on quantity, we make nouns uncountable. We may even use this distinction to differentiate meaning, so that the study of *people* (character observation) is not confused with the study of *peoples* (ethnology).

See: **collective nouns, determiner, fewer, noun.**

creole

A *creole* is a pidginised language adopted as the mother tongue of a speech community. In the process of becoming a mother tongue, the language is modified so as to fulfil all the linguistic needs of a community. We have historical evidence of the creolisation of many European-related pidgins over the last five hundred years: creole Englishes are found in the Caribbean, creole Dutch in South Africa, creole French in Mauritius and creole Portuguese in the Moluccas.

The processes by which a group of people learn the rudiments of a language not their own and are forced (by large-scale social disruption such as that caused by the Slave Trade) to pass this newly-acquired language on to their children as a mother tongue have been more in evidence since the fifteenth century than at any other period in the past. Nevertheless, the linguistic features associated with pidginisation and creolisation (such as the loss of **redundancies,** the dropping of **inflection** and concordial **agreement,** the exploitation of linguistic common denominators) have occurred many times in history, especially during times of conquest. The changes that became apparent in the English language in England after the Norman Conquest differ more in degree than in essence from the changes that occurred in the English of Jamaica during the period of the Slave Trade.

Pidgins and creoles have often been disparaged because they have been used by people of low social status. Linguistically, however, a creole is no different from any other mother tongue: it fulfils all the needs of its speakers and is modified to suit changing needs. Pidgins and creoles that are related to English (and there are at least sixty varieties along the trade routes of the world) have been stigmatised in the same way as dialectal Englishes have been stigmatised, because difference has been equated with deficiency and simplicity of structure with simplemindedness.

See: **mixed language, pidgins and creoles.**

curse and swear

In the idiolects of many speakers, these words are essentially synonymous, but for some speakers *curse* retains its meaning of 'malediction', 'wishing someone evil':

May the devil take you.

Swear originally meant 'take an oath, calling on God to witness that what is said is true', a meaning it still has in:

*I **swear** by Almighty God that the evidence I give will
be the truth, the whole truth and nothing but the truth.*

Casual swearing, when the names of heavenly beings were invoked in exclamations:

*God Almighty!
Lord God!*

was condemned by law in England in 1606. (Breaking the law could result in a fine of ten pounds, which was a great deal of money in the seventeenth century.) This law had three effects:

1 classical deities were invoked—a device used by Shakespeare and still found today:

*By Jove!
Jumping Jupiter!*

2 hidden swearing occurred:

Bloody < By our Lady
Drat < God rot you

3 substitutes (often alliterating substitutes) were found:

Crumbs < Christ
Jeepers < Jesus

More recently, *swearing* has taken on the meaning of exclamations involving 'four-letter words'.

See: **euphemism, exclamation, taboo words.**

dangling modifier/participle

A **phrase** or **clause** is described as *dangling, hanging* or *misrelated* when it is inappropriately attached to a word or when it is not related structurally to any part of the sentence. The following sentence taken from the *Daily Mirror* of 21 July, 1984, illustrates a dangling clause:

Laburnum seeds are best deadheaded when there are young children about because they are deadly poisonous.

The effects of such phrases and clauses may be confusing, misleading, comic or, in some instances, colloquially acceptable.

The commonest dangling modifiers involve **-ing forms, infinitives** or preposition phrases. In the following sentence, for example, 'driving' apparently modifies 'signposts':

There are no signposts driving through the Trough of Bowland.

In:

> *To get to the Trough of Bowland, signposts must be followed.*

the implied subject of the infinitive 'a motorist/a tourist' should be specified:

> *To get to the Trough of Bowland, a motorist must follow signposts.*
> *For a motorist to get to the Trough of Bowland, signposts must be followed.*

Similarly, more detail is required to make the next sentence acceptable:

> *At the age of three, his family left Burnley.*

'His family' cannot be 'at the age of three'. What is needed is a clause such as 'When he was three'. Only when the implied subject of both parts of the sentence is the same:

> *When **he** was three, **he** left Burnley.*

can the first clause be transformed into a preposition phrase:

> *At the age of three, he left Burnley.*

There are some **modifiers** that appear to contradict the rule:

> ***Assuming*** *that there are no interruptions, the job should take about two hours.*
> ***Knowing*** *him, the gift was no surprise.*
> *Roughly **speaking**, their house is five miles away.*
> ***Seeing*** *there is no alternative, this outfit will have to do.*
> ***To do*** *her justice, she tries very hard.*
> ***To give*** *her credit, she is always polite.*

Strictly, these modifiers are all misrelated: 'assuming' does not modify 'the job', 'knowing' 'the gift', 'speaking' 'their house', 'seeing' 'this outfit' nor 'to do/to give' 'she'. However, these constructions, and others like them, are distinguished from the earlier examples by the following facts:

they are colloquially acceptable
they behave more like **fillers** than modifiers
their verbs involve estimation, perception or mental processes
they all imply a first-person subject

The essential rule is to use modification carefully, ensuring that there is no chance of misinterpretation.

See: **fillers, infinitive, -ing forms, modifier, participle.**

data

The Latin singular *datum* meaning 'one piece of given information' is rarely used. Instead, the plural form *data* may be used with a plural verb:

> *The **data** collected so far make such a conclusion unlikely.*

Increasingly, the word *data* is used as a **collective** noun with a singular verb:

> *The **data** suggests that further research would be worthwhile.*

and, where necessary, with singular determiners:

> ***This data** is beautifully presented.*

See: **collective nouns, plurals of nouns.**

dates

UK and US conventions differ slightly in the writing of *dates*:

UK	US
9th October, 1984	October 9, 1984
9 October, 1984	9 October 1984
9 October 1984	

1 A form with commas is normally used when the full date is written within a sentence:

> *They planned to leave on 9 October, 1984.*

When the day of the week is added, another comma is used:

> *They planned to leave on Tuesday, 9 October, 1984.*

When only the month and year are used, the month is usually followed by a comma but this is not obligatory:

> *They planned to leave in October, 1984.*

2 Except in formal and legal documents, the day and year are usually expressed in Arabic numerals. In business **letters**, months with more than four letters are sometimes abbreviated:

> *9 Oct., 1984.*

When the whole date is written in numbers, the conventions are:

UK	US
9 - 10 - 1984 (day, month)	10- 9 - 1984 (month, day)
9 - x - 84	10 / 9 / 84
9 / 10 / 84	

3 When dates are spoken or read aloud, they should be:

the ninth of October nineteen eighty-four

or:

October (the) ninth nineteen eighty-four

4 Years and centuries should be written as follows:

200 BC
AD 323
the 1980s
the eighties
in 1983-84 (*in 1983-4)
nineteenth-century novels
the nineteenth century

5 In **footnotes,** dates may be abbreviated (*Oct.*, *19th century*).
It is clear that conventions are necessary in the writing of dates if we are to avoid ambiguity. The International Certificate of Vaccination specifically instructs:

Misunderstandings have arisen as to the date of issue, and therefore the period of validity, of International Certificates of Vaccination, due to differences in national or other practice of recording dates: for example, the 10th August, 1957, may be written as 10 Aug., 1957, or Aug. 10, 1957, or 10.8.57 or 8.10.57. These misunderstandings can be avoided if dates on International Certificates are always written thus:-

the *day* should be placed first in *Arabic* numerals;
the *month* should appear second in *letters*;
the *year* should come last in *Arabic* numerals.The above example would then appear as "10 August, 1957".

There is a growing tendency to get rid of all commas and there is a certain amount of choice in the writing of dates but whatever form a speaker or writer chooses should be used consistently.

See: **abbreviations, footnotes, punctuation.**

decimate

Decimate means 'reduce by one tenth'. Originally it applied to the practice of punishing troops for cowardice or mutiny by killing every tenth man. The word was generalised to mean the reduction by a tenth of anything countable, from fruit trees to profits.
Decimate is often used loosely as an emphatic and emotive word for the destruction of a large proportion of something:

*The drought has **decimated** their herds—fewer than half have survived.*

This usage should be avoided.

See: **problem words.**

declarative

The term *declarative* is identical in meaning to **indicative** and is applied to sentences of the form:

He is doing his best.
She doesn't sing well.

Both terms contrast with **imperative**:

Go away.

and **interrogative**:

Didn't you see anything?

See: **affirmative, imperative, indicative, interrogative.**

declarative question

A *declarative question* has the form of a statement:

You're leaving?

but has the intonation of a question when spoken and is marked by a question mark in writing.

A declarative question differs from a *rhetorical* question such as:

Do you think I was born yesterday?

in two ways:
1 A rhetorical question has the form of a question:

Was I tired?

2 A declarative question seeks an answer. A rhetorical question requires no answer since it is semantically equivalent to an emphatic declaration:

Do you think I'm stupid? (i.e. I'm certainly not stupid.)
Am I tired? (i.e. I'm extremely tired.)

See: **question.**

deep structure

The idea of a level of structure or **grammar** other than that revealed by actual samples of language was implied by traditional grammarians when they claimed that the subject of such a sentence as:

Go away.

was *you* (understood). Similarly, many structuralists expressed dissatisfaction with methods of analysis which did not make clear that superficial similarity could hide underlying differences.

Noam Chomsky specifically attempted to describe *deep structure* and to explain how the levels of language could be explicitly related. In his various writings since the publication of *Syntactic Structures* (1957) Chomsky and linguists influenced by him have shown how:

1 differing underlying patterns can have the same surface manifestation. This is particularly easy to show with regard to structures involving Ving + NP:

Visiting relatives (i.e. when they visit) *can be a nuisance.*
Visiting relatives (i.e. when we visit) *can be a nuisance.*

2 different surface structures can have the same underlying pattern:

We were terribly shocked and grieved when he died.
Our shock and grief at his death was terrible.
His death caused us terrible shock and grief.

Deep structures can be transformed into surface structures by a number of explicitly stated rules. Such rules allow us to account for:

1 **deletion**:

The card (I wrote the card) arrived late → The card I wrote arrived late.

2 **substitution**:

The man (I saw the man) was fat → The man that I saw was fat.

3 permutation:

He died last summer → Last summer he died.

4 insertion:

This is the cat → This is the cat that killed the rat.

See: **semantics, structuralism, transformational grammar, transformations.**

defining and non-defining relative clauses

Defining clauses (also called *restrictive clauses*) narrow the application of their **antecedents**:

the women who wore make-up... (i.e. only those wearing make-up) whereas *non-defining* or *non-restrictive clauses* extend our knowledge of the antecedent:

the women, who wore make-up... (i.e. and they wore make-up)

Defining relative clauses limit and reduce the application of the nouns they modify. In sentences such as:

The men escaped.
The ideas were impressive.

the subjects have almost general application. This application is reduced when we introduce defining clauses:

The men who carried torches escaped.
The ideas which Rachel put forward were impressive.

Defining clauses are not separated from their antecedents by commas and, in the spoken medium, the main and the defining clause constitute one tone group.

Non-defining relative clauses expand their antecedents by description or comment:

The men, who carried torches, escaped.
The ideas, which Rachel put forward, were impressive.

These relative clauses are marked off in the written medium by **punctuation**: commas, dashes or parentheses. In speech, such sentences would have two tone groups and pauses equivalent to the punctuation marks. A non-defining clause may be deleted without fundamentally altering the meaning and implication of the antecedent.

The distinction between defining and non-defining clauses is a significant one. If we contrast the difference in meaning between:

The women who had children left early (but only two left).
The women, who had children, left early (all left).

it becomes clear that punctuation and intonation can play crucial roles in determining the connection between a relative clause and its antecedent.

See: **antecedent, clause**.

definition

All *definitions* involving language are circular, a fact that is quickly revealed if we look up any word in a **dictionary**. If we want to know the meaning of *gibberish*, for example, and use *The Concise Oxford Dictionary* we are told that *gibberish* is:

Unintelligible speech, meaningless sounds, jargon, blundering or ungrammatical talk.

If we seek additional information we find that *jargon* is defined as:

> *Unintelligible words, gibberish ; barbarous or debased language ; mode of speech full of unfamiliar terms...*

And *The Concise Oxford Dictionary* is not alone in offering such circularity. It cannot be avoided. If for example there are N words in a language and we look up Word 1:

for Word 1 we get Word 2
for Word 2 we get Word 3
for Word 3 we get Word 4
for Word N we get Word N + 1

but there are only N words in the language and so circularity is unavoidable.

An alternative to a verbal definition is an *ostensive* definition, that is, we can point. If someone asks: 'What is a cow?' we can point to the animal or to a picture of the animal. Such definitions have two weaknesses:

1 few nouns are as easy to point at as *cow*. What could we do for *life* or *intelligence* or *God*?

2 unless the person already has a good idea of what a cow is, our pointing may be misunderstood. We might be pointing at horns or markings on the skin.

See: **dictionary**.

degree

Adjectives and adverbs can occur in three different forms, described as *positive*, *comparative* and *superlative degrees*:

Positive	Comparative	Superlative
amazing	*more amazing*	*most amazing*
fast	*faster*	*fastest*
huge	*huger*	*hugest*
foolishly	*more foolishly*	*most foolishly*

Occasionally, the constructions:

as amazing as/as foolishly as
less amazing/less foolishly
least amazing/least foolishly

are included in discussions of degree, the first described as *equative*, the second and third as *negative comparison*.

See: **adjective, adverb, comparison of adjectives and adverbs**.

degrees

Academic *degrees* are normally given after a person's name only in formal circumstances directly connected with the person's academic or professional activities. Thus a professor writing a reference may include degrees to indicate status and competence; and someone writing a formal letter to an academic, a clergyman or a professional person may give degrees and honours after the addressee's name. It is usually sufficient to give the highest degree received by the person, although catalogues, curriculum vitae and prospectuses often list all the degrees, as well as the institutions at which they were obtained. The practice of including degrees is distinct from that of using academic titles:

Dr Brown
Professor Brown

These are used in speech and are more likely than degrees to be given in informal correspondence.

The conventions for indicating degrees are:

John Brown, B.A. (*A.B.* if the degree is from Harvard)
Mary Brown, Ph.D.
John Brown, B.A. (*London*), *M.A.* (*Leeds*), *Ph.D.* (*Texas*)
Dr Mary Brown

The title 'doctor' and the degree are mutually exclusive and so the following should not be used:

*Dr Mary Brown, Ph.D.

There is a growing tendency to delete full stops in the marking of degrees, especially in the UK.

See: **abbreviations, address and reference.**

deixis

Deixis derives from *deiktos*, a Greek word meaning 'show, point out', and is related in form and meaning to *index* as in *index finger*. Deixis provides information on the **location** and temporal position of a speaker:

here (close in position to speaker)
there (far from speaker)
now (close in time to speaker)
then (removed in time from speaker)
I (speaker)

you (close to speaker)
they (distanced from speaker)

Deixis refers to all the units of language which provide information on the time and place of an occurrence:

adverbs: *here, now*
anaphoric reference: *the aforementioned, the latter*
demonstratives: *this, that, these, those*
pronouns: 1st, 2nd and 3rd persons
verbs: *bring/take, come/go*

and perhaps intonation. The unit which carries deixis is called a *deictic*.

See: **anaphora, bring, speaker orientation.**

deletion

Certain items can be deleted from sentences without interfering with the grammatical acceptability of the sentence:

That (big) dog can run (very) (quickly).

Such items tend to be adjectives, adverbs and co-ordinating conjunctions. In addition, shared constituents of compound phrases, clauses and sentences can be deleted:

my son and my daughter → my son and daughter
That's the stick which he picked up and which he shook at me → That's the stick he picked up and shook at me.

See: **deep structure, transformational grammar, transformations.**

demonstratives

There are two singular and two plural *demonstratives* in English (*this, that, these, those*) which can be used as **determiners**:

this/that chicken
these/those chickens

and as pronouns:

This/that is the answer.
These/those are the answers.

This/these imply proximity to the speaker and *that/those* imply distance from the speaker. None of the demonstratives is marked with regard to closeness or distance from the listener. English used to have a tripartite system with *yon* implying distance from both speaker and listener (and paralleling *yonder* in spatial orientation):

Speaker *this/these/here*

yon/yonder

Listener *that/those/there*

For most contemporary users of the language, however, *yon* and *yonder* are archaic or regional.

See: **deixis, speaker orientation.**

denotation

Denotation is the referential meaning of a word, as distinct from its emotional, social or regional associations. For example, the word *immigrant* may be defined referentially as a person who comes into a country of which he/she is not a native with the intention of permanent residence. This is the kind of denotative information given in most **dictionaries.** However, the word *immigrant* may also carry a range of emotional implications (such as colour, poverty) that vary according to personal experience, location and political or social attitudes. The additional associations are not the denotation but the **connotations** of the word.

Few words are exclusively denotative (even scientific or technical words may arouse strong feelings in some individuals, e.g. *ballistics, chromosome, ozone*) but the more neutral denotative references tend to predominate in expository prose.

See: **connotation, style, synonym.**

dependent

The term *dependent* is used in sentence analysis to refer to **clauses** other than the **main** clause. It is synonymous and in free variation with *subordinate*. In a sentence such as:

He said that you can come if you finish quickly.

we have a main clause:

He said

and two dependent clauses:

that you can come
if you finish quickly

Dependent clauses, as their name implies, cannot occur independently but rely structurally on another unit in a sentence.

The term *dependent clause* has been replaced by *embedded sentence* in transformational grammar.

See: **clause, embedding, subordination, transformational grammar.**

derivation

Derivation is a type of **word formation** involving the use of **prefixes** and/or **suffixes**. The addition of a prefix to the stem normally modifies the basic meaning with regard to negation (*un*happy), repetition (*re*affirm) and time (*ex*husband). The addition of a suffix to the stem normally causes the word to shift from one word class to another:

beauty (noun)
beautiful (adjective)
beautify (verb)

Suffixes should be distinguished from the inflectional endings *-s*, *-ed*, *-en*, *-ing*, *-'s*, *-er*, *-est*, which modify the function of a word, marking plurality, possession, a verb form or the comparative/ superlative forms of adjectives and adverbs. The basic difference between inflections and suffixes is that inflections do not change a word's class:

parent parents parents' —nouns
write writes writing written—verbs

whereas suffixes usually do.

Productive affixes are those where the meanings and implications are well known to native speakers, who can thus produce their own derivatives. Sometimes a new morpheme becomes productive in the language. This happened with *-nik*:

beatnik
kibbutznik
refusenik

and with *-gate* from *Watergate* which took on the meaning of government scandal, producing *Muldergate* in South Africa and *Kincoragate* in Ireland.

The word *derivation* is also used in the study of relationships between languages or between different stages of the same language. Thus we can say that many English terms associated with food and cooking *derive* from French and we can also say that modern *lord* derives from **Old English** *hlaf* + *weard* meaning the 'giver of bread'.

See: **affix, etymology, inflection, prefix, suffix, word formation.**

determiner

Structuralists coined the word *determiner* to designate a **class** of words that function like **attributive adjectives** and signal the appearance of a noun in English. The following are the most widely-used determiners in the language:

1 **articles** (*the, a/an*)
2 **demonstratives** (*this, that, these, those*)
3 **possessives** (*my, your, our...*)
4 **interrogatives** (*which, what, whose*)
5 **numbers** (*one, two..., first, second...*)
6 indefinite determiners: these are all the items that have a similar distribution to the above determiners but cannot be so easily classified. They include:

all, any, both, each, either, enough, every, few (fewer), less, more, most, much, neither, no, only, several, some.

A good test for a determiner is to check if the item has a similar distribution to *the*:

the good man	*the good men*
this good man	*these good men*
my good man	*their good men*
which good man?	*what good men?*
one good man	*all good men*
every good man	*other good men*

A number of determiners can precede articles:

all the trees
only the lonely

These are frequently referred to as 'limiters'.

See: **adjective, all, article, demonstratives.**

deviation

The terms *deviance* and *deviation* are applied to linguistic units which do not conform to the rules of the language. Thus, in English, a word such as:

*mna

a phrase such as:

*of out mind his

or a sentence such as:

*I am liking you muchly.

are deviant or 'ill-formed' because they break the phonological and syntactic rules of the language. (It is customary to mark a deviant form with an asterisk.)

As with so many aspects of language, there are no clear cut-off points between deviance and non-deviance. Deviation presupposes a **norm** but the norm can change. A question such as:

Is you is or is you ain't my baby?

is deviant, according to the rules of **Standard English,** but is acceptable in the song from which it is taken. Equally, a sentence such as:

I knowed she would come.

deviates from standard grammar but is acceptable in a number of regional **dialects.**

The notion of deviation is frequently invoked in stylistic analysis to account for a poet's exploitation of the language. Most poems use sentences containing words and phrases. Edwin Morgan, however, in 'Off Course' uses only noun phrases, two to a line, each beginning with 'the':

> the golden flood   the weightless seat
> the cabin song   the pitch black...

The effect of this pattern is of dislocation and, since the poem describes an astronaut adrift in space, the deviation from established syntactic forms reinforces the meaning.

Deviations may occur at any level of the language (**alliteration** and other phonic adornments can be seen in this light) but if the deviations are too many or too varied then comprehensibility may be lost.

See: **norms, style.**

dialect

No brief definition of this term will be totally satisfactory because the word *dialect* has been used in so many different ways. It derives ultimately from a Greek word meaning 'discourse, conversation, a way of speaking, a language of a country or district' and all these meanings, and several more, are implied by the term today. Indeed, *dialect* is so ambiguous that several linguists have tried to replace it with other terms such as:

cryptolect (a secret variety, e.g. Anglo-Romani)
ethnolect (an ethnic variety, e.g. Black English)
lect (any variety of language without social or regional implications)

register (a variety of language defined according to user)
sociolect (a variety used by a social class or occupation)

The word *dialect* has both scholarly and popular connotations.
Scholars have used the word to imply all of the following:

1 a language at different periods in its evolution
2 regionally-marked varieties of a language
3 socially-marked varieties of a language
4 the language of literature
5 the speech of the uneducated
6 the idiosyncratic language use of an individual
7 non-standard varieties of a standardised language
8 languages of the third world
9 languages of minority groups

The popular view of dialects overlaps the scholarly in that the
term is usually applied to:

1 regionally-marked speech
2 the speech of lower socio-economic groups
3 regional pronunciations

Popularly, *dialects* are also often associated with warmth, humour,
vitality, incorrectness, slovenliness, lack of intelligence. With so
many and such varied implications, the term *dialect* needs to be used
with care.

A dialect is not just a form of pronunciation. The word relates to
a variety of language and comprehends pronunciation, vocabulary
choice and syntax. A Yorkshire woman, seeing an old lady drop her
parcels, may say to her son:

Pick those [i.e. parcels] *up and carry them for her.*

or:

Sam 'er them up an' hug 'er them.

The first is standard English with a regional accent; the second is
an example of Yorkshire dialect.

Dialects are in no way linguistically inferior to any other mother-
tongue speech. They are perfectly adequate for the needs of their
speakers and can be easily modified to accommodate changes in
society. Usually, dialects do not have their own **orthography** and,
since most remain unwritten, they lack the prestige that accrues to
a standard language with a recognised system of writing. All dialects
can be given orthographies and any dialect could be moulded to suit
the needs of any society. **Standard English** was once a regional
dialect, considered by many to be incapable of expressing cultural
or literary aspirations.

It is not always easy to distinguish between a dialect and a language. Often the decision is made according to political rather than
linguistic criteria. As one cynic put it:

A dialect is a language without armies and navies.

Expressing essentially the same point another way, Swedish, Danish and Norwegian are classified as three languages although there is a high degree of interintelligibility among them. If the same degree of interintelligibility were found in African or South Pacific speech communities, the communities would be said to speak closely-related dialects. Attitudes to dialects are changing slowly but the claim made by Einar Haugen in 1972 is still widely applicable:

> As a social norm...a dialect is a language that is excluded from polite society.

As well as regional dialects, there are class dialects. Working-class people tend to have less formal education than their more affluent peers and often use a variety described as 'nonstandard' ('substandard' until the late 1960s). As far as English is concerned, working-class dialects show considerable similarities. First, they are all being influenced by the media and so are coming closer to **network norms**. Secondly, there is a 'standardness' about the nonstandard features that are found in working-class English from London to Adelaide or the Apalachians:

1 the tendency to use *them* as a demonstrative:

them boots

2 the tendency to simplify verb forms:

I see   I seen   I have seen

3 the tendency to use multiple negation:

I didn't say nothin'.

4 the tendency to use local pronunciation.

See: **Black English, creole, pidgins and creoles, style.**

dialectal, dialectic, dialectical

Dialectal is the adjective deriving from *dialect* and relates to varieties of a language:

> *There is considerable **dialectal** variation within Yorkshire.*
> *'Gotten' is considered **dialectal** in British speech.*

Dialectic is a noun referring to a type of logical procedure:

> *Plato's **dialectic** is characterised by dialogue.*

Dialectical is the adjective relating to *dialectic*:

> *Plato's **dialectical** methods have been imitated for centuries.*

diction

Diction, from Latin *dicere* (to say), has two commonly used meanings, one related to speech and the other to the choice of vocabulary. As a feature of speech or singing, diction refers to the enunciation of words. A speaker's diction may be clear and so good, or indistinct, and so poor. Good diction, the art of speaking clearly, was once considered an essential ingredient of good manners.

In relation to vocabulary, diction implies the selection of words. It is often referred to in the teaching of writing skills, where good diction involves the choice of clear, effective and appropriate words.

Poetic diction is a term, usually applied disparagingly to vocabulary items appearing in verse:

feathered friends = birds
finny tribe = fish
verdant meadows = green fields

See: **bon mot, poetic diction.**

dictionary

There are three main types of *dictionary*, each capable of providing a variety of information.

1 The *bilingual dictionary* aims primarily at the sort of **translations** that will help a person who is using two languages. This aim is usually fulfilled by dividing the book into two halves, each organised alphabetically. Thus an English–Spanish dictionary will devote the first half to English words for which Spanish equivalents are provided and the second half to Spanish words for which English equivalents are given. This method has been extremely successful in dealing with **Indo-European** languages where the stems of most **parts of speech** are isolatable and where the various forms of regular words begin with the same sound:

man men
hombre hombres

By its very nature, a bilingual dictionary is crude and oversimplified. It concentrates on **denotation** since it is impossible to take account of all **connotations** or language-specific viewpoints. To give an example: a speaker of English might look up *girl* in a French dictionary and find *fille*. This is denotatively accurate, but French people tend to use *jeune fille* for *girl* because *fille* can be used for *prostitute*. Bilingual dictionaries are perhaps more useful for jogging the memory or adding to something that one already knows than for providing entirely new information.

2 The *monolingual dictionary* provides information on meaning

and contextualisation. **Definitions** usually include **synonyms** and the most widely used **collocations** in which a word occurs. *Cat*, for example, may be defined as a *feline* and phrases such as *cat's cradle*, *cat o' nine tails* and *catspaw* explained. The monolingual dictionary may also provide information on:

(a) **etymology**. This provides information on how a word may have developed from an earlier word, or been taken over from another language. For example, *emu* is generally believed to come from a modification of Portuguese *ema* meaning 'rhea', another flightless bird.

(b) **pronunciation**. This can be useful but it also limits an English language dictionary because of the different pronunciations found in different parts of the English-speaking world.

(c) *forms of the word*. These may indicate irregular plurals, tenses, spellings, or provide other words that are etymologically related.

(d) *style markers*. Some dictionaries give more of these than others, indicating a range of descriptions from *formal* through *informal* to *colloquial*, **slang**, *vulgar* and *taboo*. Related to **style** markers are informative notes such as *archaic, ecclesiastical, obsolete, philosophy* or *scientific*. Such markers help a reader contextualise an unfamiliar word, but since they are not standardised one dictionary may label *vulgar* what another marks as *taboo*.

(e) **usage**. Some dictionaries, such as Webster's *Ninth New Collegiate Dictionary*, give a note on usage for problem words. This is a relatively new practice, incorporating some of the properties of usage guides and extending the usefulness of a dictionary as a reference work.

(f) *appendices*. Many dictionaries have appendices, each arranged alphabetically, giving information on such diverse subjects as **abbreviations**, weights and measures, universities and colleges, foreign words and **punctuation**. These extend the scope of the dictionary as a reference book, but are not really part of the lexicographical function.

3 A number of dictionaries have been compiled which focus specifically on some of the details listed under 2. These include 'etymological', 'pronouncing' and 'school' dictionaries. In addition, lexical relations such as synonymy and antonymy are provided in Roget's *Thesaurus* and its imitations; and specialised dictionaries dealing exclusively with **catch phrases** or **idioms** have been published.

All dictionaries are related in some way to vocabulary and usage and each is designed as a reference book. However, it is sometimes forgotten that a dictionary is the work of an individual or a team and is not, necessarily, guided by divine inspiration. It is useful to remember that all dictionaries, including the most revered, are best seen as helpful guides and not as absolute authorities.

See: **definition, denotation, etymology.**

differ from, differ with

Differ from is normally used in the sense of 'be different, show a difference':

> *Cultivated roses **differ from** wild ones in colour and shape.*
> *He certainly **differs from** the conventional salesman.*

Differ with normally means 'have a difference of opinion, disagree':

> *I **differed with** her over the colour scheme.*
> *We **differed with** the council over the rates.*

different from, than, to

There is some flexibility in the prepositions that follow *different*. Conventionally, UK usage has been *different from* in preference to *different to*:

> *The book was very **different from** what I expected.*

and US usage has been *different from* and *different than*:

> *The book was very **different from** what I expected.*
> *The book was very **different than** I expected.*

For some reason, the structures involving *different* can arouse strong feeling, many **purists** objecting to *different to* and *different than*. There seems to be little justification for such attitudes since all of these structures have been used since the seventeenth century, often in the writings of prestigious authors. Prejudice and purism are, however, strong forces and the *different from* structure is least likely to be stigmatised.

See: **'chestnuts', UK and US grammar.**

diglossia

Diglossia, from Greek *di* (twice) + *glossa* (tongue), is a term used in **sociolinguistics** to describe a community where two varieties of a language coexist, each with its own functions and with little admixture of varieties. Usually one variety has high status and the other low, the high variety being used for formal education, literature and religion, the low variety for intimate conversations and informal communications. Diglossia is found in some Greek communities (high variety: Katharevousa; low variety: Dhimotiki) and in Haiti (high variety: French; low variety: **creole**).

See: **pidgins and creoles.**

direct speech

The term *direct speech* is used to describe a set of conventions by which we express what someone is supposed to have said:

'Hello!' said Michael. 'Come in. We've all been waiting for you.'

Similar conventions are employed to indicate thought:

'What a beautiful girl!' he mused.

The assumption that there is such a category as direct speech is a convenient way of referring to the commonest means of representing speech in novels and stories, but it is more a description of the impression created by such speech representation than an isolatable category. Direct speech is seldom an actual record of what is said: we introduce conventions such as inverted commas and exclamation marks; we do not normally record such phenomena as hesitations, false starts, tempo, loudness or intonation; and what is given as 'thought' is an oversimplified stylisation of mental processes.

The relationship between direct and indirect (or **reported**) **speech** is often complex. The only direct speech samples that can be easily transformed into indirect speech (or vice versa) are those that are composed. Live speech is hard to transform into indirect speech as the following recorded utterance illustrates:

Well, you know like, I was never, er, never much of a
talker... But my brother now, well like take him...
By God, he could talk the hind leg off a donkey...

If we turn this into indirect speech we produce a version such as:

Paddy insisted that he had never been much of a talker but said that
we should consider his brother. He added with an oath that his brother
could talk the hind leg off a donkey...

but this version loses much of the quality of the original and the solution of replacing *By God* with *He added with an oath* is only partly successful.

The dichotomy *direct/indirect speech* is a simplification of the many representations of speech and thought that occur in literature. It is not always possible to say whether some samples such as:

'Will she never come?' he wondered.

are meant to represent speech or thought because many attributive verbs (*hypothesised, mused, pondered, theorised*) can represent both. Attributive verbs are a means of influencing the opinion of a reader. Almost all verbs of saying and thinking as well as many action verbs can be used in attribution:

ask, begin, cry, groan, hiss, hurry, imply, infer, insist, nod, preach,
rush, scream, screech, simper, squeak, squeal.

Our list is not meant to be comprehensive but it is sufficient to stress that the verb of attribution can imply the sex of a speaker (contrast *simper* with *thunder*), the state of mind (*groan, worry*), and whether or not the writer is in sympathy with the character (*hiss, wheedle*).

Direct speech is characterised by quotation marks. A **punctuation** mark at the end of the speech precedes the closing quotation mark. The first line of direct speech is indented from the left-hand margin. If a speech consists of more than one paragraph, each paragraph starts with an opening quotation mark, but a closing quotation mark is used only at the end of the speech or before a verb of attribution. In the conversion of direct into indirect speech, temporal, spatial and pronominal references and verbs like GO and **BRING**, which indicate **speaker orientation**, are moved one step further from the reporter:

'Come here at once,' shouted the teacher.
The teacher shouted that he should go there immediately.

The conventions involved in transposing from one mode to another suggest that speech can exist in more than one form without alteration of meaning. Reported speech is, however, less precise. Such a report as:

She said she would not go.

does not distinguish between:

'I will not go,' she said.

and:

'I would not go,' she said.

(Perhaps this is one reason why writers of detective stories often prefer reported speech.) Moreover, some conversions from direct to reported speech require changes such as the deletion of titles:

'Can I help you, madam?' he asked.
He asked (politely) if he could help her.

the substitution of more formal lexical items:

'Can I come too?' he asked.
He asked if he could also go.

the deletion of **exclamations**:

'O! You frightened me,' he exclaimed.
He exclaimed that she had frightened him.

and the expansion of **contractions**:

'We'll go tomorrow if it doesn't rain,' she promised.
She promised that they would go the following day if it did not rain.

Such changes inevitably affect meaning.

In reality, speech and its written representation are much more flexible, subtle and varied than the terms *direct* and *indirect/reported speech* suggest.

See: reported speech, speech and writing, speech in literature.

discourse analysis

Grammatical analysis tends to be limited to the **sentence**. Yet, it is clear to any sensitive user of language that there are many links between sentences in a continuous stretch of coherent speech or prose. *Discourse analysis* is the study of such links and of the patterns likely to occur in different types of discourse (narrative, conversation, religious ritual, political persuasion) and on certain occasions (marriages, funerals, christenings, bar mitzvahs).

Links between sentences add to the **cohesion** of a passage and these links are most apparent in:

1 consistency of tone (voice quality may contribute to cohesion in speech; stylistic appropriateness may achieve the same end in writing)

2 consistency of vocabulary (no item appears out of place in the context and lexical sets may occur, e.g. *game, set, match, fifteen, thirty, forty, love, deuce, advantage* would form a lexical set in a description of tennis)

3 consistency of **syntax** (we do not expect rapid and inexplicable changes in tense, aspect, location, narration)

4 **anaphora** (backward and forward references involving pronouns, auxiliary verbs, adverbials such as *finally, furthermore, later* and conjunctions, both co-ordinate (*and, but, either...or*) and subordinate (*because, if, when*).

See: anaphora, cohesion, discourse marker, linkage, parallelism.

discourse marker

Discourse markers are items of **linkage** which lend **cohesion** to a text. There are a number of types of discourse marker:

1 items which suggest addition: *as well as, furthermore, moreover*

2 items which suggest alternatives: *besides, either...or, however*

3 items which suggest cause and effect: *because, hence, so*

4 items which suggest conditions: *as long as, if, unless*

5 items which suggest sequences: *then, thirdly, to conclude*

6 items which suggest **time**: *afterwards, formerly, meanwhile*

7 noun substitutes: **pronouns**, *the former, the latter*

8 verb substitutes: **auxiliary** verbs, *DO (so)*.

See: anaphora, cohesion, discourse analysis.

disinterested, uninterested

Interested has a variety of related meanings, two of which are sometimes confused. One relates to personal advantage, profit and partiality:

> *He admitted that he was a director of the company under discussion and was thus an* **interested** *party.*

This use of *interested* is negated by *dis-*:

> *He is not a* **disinterested** *judge, because his brother is one of the contestants.*

The other meaning of *interested* relates to something that attracts attention or excites curiosity:

> *I was even more* **interested** *in sport when I was young.*

This use is negated by *un-*:

> *He was utterly* **uninterested** *in what was going on.*

Disinterested is often mistakenly used for the second meaning—so often, in fact, that it may in time become the acceptable form. For the present, however, it is advisable to distinguish between the uses.

See: **problem pairs.**

dissertation

The terms for written pieces of academic research or exposition differ slightly between the UK and the USA:

	UK	USA
c. 3,000 words	essay	report, essay
c. 10,000 words	long essay, paper	thesis
submission for doctorate	thesis	dissertation

although the terms *dissertation* and *thesis* are relatively interchangeable in both countries, implying a sustained piece of research.

Many of the conventions for academic writing are given under headings such as **argument** and **typescript**, but certain practices are peculiar to the essay, thesis or dissertation and certain procedures are thus advisable.

1 Find out about the regulations for binding (hard, soft, none) and colour, and follow the instructions of your institution concerning length, number of copies and acceptable methods of duplication. Also check the local conventions for the wording on the cover and title page.

2 The *Preface* follows the title page, and contains any essential

preliminary remarks about the dissertation and acknowledges any debts (e.g. to a supervisor). If there is more than one page to the preface, these pages should be numbered in small roman numerals (i, ii, iii) at the top right-hand corner. The preface should be as brief and simple as possible.

3 The *Contents* should follow the preface (on a separate page), numbered consecutively in roman numerals. Close to the left-hand margin, list the title of each section, chapter and major subsection within a chapter, as well as all appendices. Close to the right-hand margin, give the page number (arabic numerals) for each title in the list.

4 The *Abstract* should follow the table of contents, continuing the sequence of roman numerals.

5 The first page of text should begin the sequence of arabic numerals (1, 2, 3) that continues to the end of the **bibliography**. The text should be in double spacing, but within the text all indented **quotations** should be in single spacing. Acceptable conventions for endnotes and **footnotes** should be checked. (Footnotes are more difficult to type.) Footnotes should be in single spacing at the bottom of the page to which each note refers. Endnotes are typed at the end of each chapter or together at the end of the text, and should be in single spacing with a double space between each note.

6 An *Appendix* should be included only if its material does not fit logically or easily into the text itself and it should not be regarded as a 'rag-bag' for a badly organised dissertation. Appropriate material for an appendix would be a set of texts needed for the verification of claims made in the dissertation or the details of an experiment from which only some results have been drawn for the main argument of the dissertation.

7 The *Bibliography* should come at the end of all text including appendices or endnotes and should be in double spacing. A decision must be made on the author-title or author-date system, as this choice will have a direct bearing on the format of references and footnotes. A bibliography should normally consist of a single list organised alphabetically according to the last name of the authors.

8 **Abbreviations** should be kept to a minimum, so that the text and notes are readily interpretable. Among the appropriate scholarly abbreviations are:

cf.	confer = compare
ed., eds.	editor(s)
e.g.	*exempli gratia* = for example (e.g. is usually preceded by a comma)
et al.	*et alii* = and others (authors)
ff.	following, pp.22ff (Be more precise if possible.)
fig.	figure

ibid.	*ibidem* = in the same place (used for title already cited in note immediately above)
i.e.	*id est* = that is (preceded and followed by a comma; use 'that is' wherever possible.)
l., ll.	line(s), e.g. ll.22-3
MS., MSS.	manuscript(s)
n.d.	no date
n.p.	no place of publication
p., pp.	page(s), e.g. pp.23-4
pseud.	pseudonym
sc.	scene
sic	thus; used with brackets as an editorial comment
trans.	translator, translation, translated
viz.	*videlicet* = namely (use 'namely' wherever possible)
vol., vols.	volume(s)

9 The style of a dissertation should suit its audience. In relation to other styles, it is fairly formal. Some commentators have urged that first person pronouns should be avoided and **passive voice** preferred. However, whereas excessive use of 'I' may be egocentric or stylistically repetitive, it is unacceptable to be forced to refer to one's own contributions to knowledge (the main purpose of the thesis) in terms that imply either that the facts are well established or that the agent is unknown or insignificant. The best policy is to use first person references to highlight those parts of the research where the writer claims an innovation or a new interpretation.

10 It may be useful to organise the text into numbered subsections. For example, all sections of Chapter Two could begin with the number 2, followed by a full stop and the number of the section, and perhaps a further full stop and subsection. Thus 2.2.1 would indicate Chapter 2, second section, first subsection. Such numbering allows for easy cross-references that do not depend on knowing the page numbers of the final typescript. This system of numbering should be kept as simple and logical as possible, and the numbers should also precede the titles in the table of contents:

Chapter Two	The Poetry of Yeats	38
2.1	The Early Verse	41
2.1.1	The Early Lyrics	42

This numbering system has two additional advantages: it helps the writer to organise the material, deciding on the relative importance of ideas and arguments; and it allows the reader to locate sections in a dissertation that lacks the signposts we have in books (such as an index or the chapter title on each page).

See: **abbreviations, abstract, bibliography, footnotes, typescript.**

DO

DO can occur as a *dummy auxiliary* and as a full verb.

DO as a dummy auxiliary—DO has been called the *dummy auxiliary* when it has formal significance but little semantic value. It can be classified as follows:

1 DO occurs when no other **auxiliary** is present to allow:

(a) the formation of interrogative sentences:

You like it. Do you like it?

(b) the formation of negatives:

You like it. You don't like it.

(c) the formation of tag questions:

You like it, don't you?
You don't like it, do you?

(d) the occurrence of emphatic affirmation or denial:

You don't like it. I do.
You like it. I don't.

(e) comparisons in US English:

They have a bigger garden than we do.

2 DO triggers off the **base form** of the following verb:

Does she sing?

and, like the modals, it does not occur in non-finite constructions:

*to do sing *doing sing *done sing

3 DO exhibits past/non-past contrasts:

Does she sing?
Did she sing?

and agrees with its subject in non-past sentences:

I/you/we/they do know.
He/she/it does know.

DO as a head verb—DO can occur as a head verb:

I do my best.
They did their best work in the twenties.

When used as a head verb, DO needs the dummy auxiliary in the formation of interrogatives:

Did she do her best?

negatives:

They didn't do as much as they should have.

and emphatic assertion or denial:

> *They* did *do their best.*
> *They certainly* didn't *do their best.*

See: **auxiliary, dummy subject, modality, prime verbs.**

doublespeak

The word *doublespeak*, coined on **analogy** with George Orwell's 'New-speak', is the term used to describe language that is intended to conceal rather than reveal information. It is, for example, applied to the warnings on cigarette packets which say:

> *Smoking can seriously damage your health.*

(where the 'can' implies that it might not) instead of the more accurate:

> *Smoking has been shown to contribute to cancer and heart and lung disease.*

Doublespeak (occasionally also *doubletalk*) is a means of promoting a cause, whether political, commercial or ideological, by manipulating language. For example, a common answer by politicians to the question:

> *What are you going to do about unemployment?*

is:

> *This is a very serious problem and one that we are deeply concerned about.*

Such an answer avoids responsibility or blame, claims interest but does not commit anyone to doing anything.

One form of doublespeak relates to the use of unwarlike vocabulary in descriptions of war and weapons:

> *the theatre* (of war)
> *cruise* (a missile)
> *fat man* (a weapon)

See: **euphemism, gobbledygook, jargon, Newspeak.**

due to, owing to

There are some strong prejudices associated with the use of *due to* and *owing to*. According to **purists**, *due to* should be used only adjectivally, as a nominal **complement** which follows the noun it relates to:

*The delay was **due to** snow on the runway.*
*Her success will be **due to** her upbringing.*

Owing to should be restricted in function to phrases acting as adverbials:

***Owing to** the accident, train services will be disrupted.*
*There will be a delay, **owing to** the late arrival of BA623.*

There is no logical or linguistic reason for categorising *due to* and *owing to* in the way we have described. Nor is there any logical or culinary reason for preferring a fish fork to an ordinary fork when eating fish. Both are a matter of imposed convention.

See: **'chestnuts', purist.**

dummy subject

Occasionally, elements that are functionally significant but semantically negligible are introduced into sentences in English. These are known as *dummy* elements. The most frequently-used dummy is **DO** as in:

Do you want it?

There are two *dummy subjects*, *it* and *there*, in such sentences as:

It's a lovely day.
There are three twos in six.

Not all uses of **subject** *it* are dummy, as is clear if we **contrast**:

That lion is six years old. It (It = the lion) *was born in captivity.*

with:

It's going to rain. (It = ?)

When *there* is used as a subject, it is almost always a dummy element. It can, however, have locative implications in such sentences as:

There's the quotation we wanted.

See: **anaphora, auxiliary, DO, subject.**

dyad

The word *dyad* comes from Greek *dyo* (two). It is used in stylistic analysis to refer to pairs of words that habitually collocate:

by hook or by crook
might and main

Dyads (also known as *doubles*) occur frequently in bilingual communities where they are an easy way of ensuring understanding. Many developed in English after the Norman Conquest and some survive:

full and plenty (**Middle English** *full* + Norman French *plenté* = full)
goods and chattels (ME *god* + NF *chatel* = property)

A number of writers from the fifteenth century onwards have used dyads as a stylistic device and the technique was further ingrained in the language by the use of such phrases in the Bible as:

And Jesus spoke to the multitude saying...
And he waxed and grew strong.

It seems probable that such stylistic embellishment was a development of the use of dyads in post-Norman times.
Dyads may be adjectives:

hale and hearty

adverbs:

well and truly

nouns:

with a heart and a hand

and verbs:

aided and abetted

See: **cognate, euphuism.**

dynamic

Verbs in English are often subdivided into those which can, and usually do, occur in the **progressive**:

I am dancing and singing and enjoying myself.

and are frequently used in **imperative** structures:

Sing, dance and enjoy yourself.

These verbs are called *dynamic*.
A second type of verb, often referred to as *stative*, *essive* or *static*, rarely occurs in the progressive or the imperative:

I am tired.	not **I am being tired.*	**? Be tired.*
I have a cold.	not **I am having a cold.*	**? Have a cold.*

| *I like you.* | not | **I am liking you.* | **? Like me.* |
| *I see you.* | not | **I am seeing you.* | **? See me.* |

Among the commonest stative verbs are: BE, HAVE, RESEMBLE, and verbs of liking (LOVE), mental processes (REMEMBER, THINK) and perception (HEAR, SEE).

Most verbs in English can occur with and without progressive **aspect**. When dynamic verbs are used in a non-progressive way, they imply regular or habitual activity:

I go to work on the bus (i.e. usually).
I am going to work on the bus (i.e. on this occasion).

Stative verbs used without the progressive do not imply regular or habitual activity:

I like you (i.e. at the moment).
I remember you (i.e. now).

Verbs of perception co-occur with *can* when they imply that the activity is taking place at a particular moment:

I can hear you.
I can see you.

The term *dynamic* is used in **sociolinguistic** research to describe models of languages which attempt to illustrate the variation that exists and the changes that are taking place in a speech community at a particular time.

See: **aspect, fad words, stative and dynamic, verb.**

dyslexia

Dyslexia derives from Greek *dys* (bad) + *lexis* (word, speech) and is the technical term for a disability known also as 'word blindness'. It manifests itself early in a child's life: in his or her inability to differentiate between *p* and *9*, or *b* and *d* or any of the other letters which are similar in shape; or in an inability to remember the ordering of letters in a word, causing a child to write or spell *the* as *hte*, for example.

No one is certain how many children are affected by this problem, although the frequently-cited figure of ten percent is probably an underestimate. The danger is that children who confuse sets of letters and habitually misspell words will be considered unintelligent, whereas they seem to have visual problems associated with shapes, comparable to but not necessarily related to colour blindness.

See: **aphasia.**

each

Each can be used as a **determiner**:

> *Each man was supplied with a uniform.*

and as a **pronoun**:

> *Each had a map of the area.*

When *each* is used as a pronoun, it takes a singular verb:

> *Each chooses his own gift.*

In speech, pronominal *each* is almost invariably followed by *of them*:

> *Each of them has been given a month's salary.*

Some authorities insist on distinguishing between *each other* and *one another*, claiming that the first relates to only two:

> *John and Mary love **each other**.*

and the second to more than two:

> *John, Paul and Damian love **one another**.*

It would be extremely hard to support such a claim from contemporary usage.

See: **all, determiner.**

East African English

East Africa includes nine countries (Sudan, Ethiopia, Uganda, Somalia, Djibouti, Rwanda, Burundi, Kenya and Tanzania) and has a population of just under 120 million, although only a minority can speak English. Contact with English goes back to the late sixteenth century, but it was not until the nineteenth century that a large community of English-speaking expatriates settled in the area. Many of these settler families have remained in Kenya and this nucleus of mother-tongue English speakers has been reinforced in the present century by expatriates on short-term contracts.

Pidgin English did not develop in East Africa because Swahili (also called 'Kiswahili') already existed as a viable **lingua franca** throughout the area. Indeed, Swahili has replaced English as an official language and a medium of primary education in Tanzania.

Five main types of English can be distinguished in East Africa:

(a) mother-tongue English

(b) Standard East African English, the variety used by educated East Africans

(c) Standard East African English as spoken by Asians

(d) Arabic/Portuguese/Swahili-influenced English
(e) broken East African English.

Our description will focus on (b) since this is the prestigious norm for most East Africans.

Phonology

1 Standard East African English (SEAE) is non-**rhotic**.

2 There are fewer vowel contrasts in SEAE than in **Received Pro-nunciation**, with little distinction being made between the vowels in:

leave and *live* (usually /i/)
gnat and *net* (usually /e/)
far and *for* and *fore* (usually /a/)
pool and *pull* (usually /u/)

3 Diphthongs tend to be monophthongised. This is particularly true of /ei/ which is usually realised as /e/ so that *laid* and *led* are often indistinguishable.

4 The consonants /b/ and /v/ are often devoiced, especially in word-final position, so that *tab* sounds like *tap* and *have* like *half*.

5 The initial consonants in *thin* and *then* (that is /θ/ and /ð/) are realised as /s/ and /z/ or /t/ and /d/.

6 **Consonant clusters** such as str-, -nst and -ns tend to be split up:

straight > /setret/
against > /egenest/
dispence > /dɪspenɪs/

Vocabulary

Apart from the vocabulary found in all international varieties of English we find:

1 words from local languages, some limited to East Africa:

chitenge—cloth cover reaching from waist to ankle
panga—machete
pole—empathy formula
shamba—farm

and others well-known outside East Africa:

bwana—sir
safari—journey
uhuru—freedom

2 **calques** from local languages:

clean heart—pure
dry coffee—coffee without milk or sugar
hear—hear, feel, experience

3 English words with extended local meanings:

borrow—lend
duty—occupation
mono—first-year student
overlisten—eavesdrop
refuse—deny

Grammar
The syntax is derived from and very similar to Standard English in the UK. The main differences occur in:
1 the use of phrasal verbs. Sometimes the preposition is omitted as in:

leave for leave out
pick for pick up

or new phrasal verbs are coined:

come with (bring): *Come with that box.*
stay with (keep): *I'll stay with this one.*

2 There is a strong tendency to answer questions such as:

Isn't John in?

with 'Yes', if the implication is:

What you have said is correct. John is not in.

and with 'No', if the implication is:

What you have said is wrong. John is in.

3 'Is it/isn't it?' are the most frequently used question tags:

You didn't go, is it?
You said so, isn't it?

4 Many speakers use 'enjoy' without a reflexive pronoun:

It's a wonderful party. I'm really enjoying.

See: **African English, Kenyan English, Southern African English, Ugandan English.**

-ed forms

Often the term *-ed form* is used as a brief description of past tense forms in the English verb. This is because many regular verbs form their past tense by adding *-ed*:

arm armed
book booked
brand branded

It will be noticed that the term is derived from spelling and pays no attention to pronunciation in that the three endings above are pronounced /d/, /t/ and /ɪd/ respectively.

Like the verbs from which they derive, adjectives ending in -ed are normally pronounced /d/ after a vowel or a voiced consonant:

freed (*the freed hostages*)
heightened (*heightened tension*)

/t/ after a voiceless consonant:

dressed

and /ɪd/ after a d or a t:

raided rated

The /ɪd/ pronunciation can sometimes seem redundant. This may explain why verbs such as FIT and WET have lost their *-ed* endings in certain regions and why many verbs ending in *-t* or *-d* (BET, BURST, CAST, COST, CUT, HIT, HURT, LET, PUT, QUIT, SET, SHUT, SLIT, SPLIT, THRUST, UPSET, RID, SHED, SPREAD) either do not take *-ed* endings or are in the process of losing them.

A few other adjectives also have /ɪd/ forms:

aged (*an aged man*)   *blessed* (*that blessed day*)
crooked (*a crooked game*)   *dogged*   (*dogged determination*)
jagged (*a jagged outline*)   *learned* (*my learned friend*)
naked (*a naked infant*)   *ragged* (*a ragged beggar*)
rugged (*rugged country*)   *wicked* (*a wicked plot*)
wretched (*a wretched individual*)

A number of the forms above can be verbs:

He aged ten years in that one night.
He blessed the wine.
She crooked her little finger.
She learned easily.

and their *-ed* endings are not pronounced /ɪd/. Our **orthography** does not usually distinguish between the adjective *crooked* /krʊkɪd/ and the verb /krʊkt/ and this can sometimes lead to unintentional ambiguity as when a correspondent to the *Daily Mirror* (27 June, 1984) wrote on the subject of the Queen's appearance:

The Queen's hats don't upset me, either... It's the
large, old-fashioned handbag she always carries on
her crooked arm that irritates me.

The -ed ending is sometimes given a stress in poetry to complete a metrical pattern:

Thy bosom is endearéd with all hearts
Which I by lacking have supposéd dead...
        Shakespeare, Sonnet 31

It is possible that the pronunciation of the -ed endings of certain adjectives may have been reinforced by the set of adjectives which derive from Latin and end in -id. Among such adjectives are:

acrid horrid lucid lurid
morbid pallid rancid torrid

A number of adverbs also have the -ed pronounced as /ɪd/. The most widely used of these are:

allegedly assuredly supposedly resignedly resolvedly

See: **accent marks, -ed/-t forms, -en forms.**

-ed, -t forms

In **US English**, a number of verbs including BURN, DREAM, LEAN, LEAP, LEARN, SMELL, SPELL, SPILL and SPOIL are treated as regular, forming their past tense and past participle forms by adding *-ed*:

Don't burn yourself.
*He **burned** his finger.*
*He **has burned** his finger.*

In UK and UK-influenced English this usage is gaining in popularity but it is still correct to have:

*He **burnt** his finger.*
*He **has burnt** his finger.*

and a number of users distinguish between the forms, using *burned* for the past tense and *burnt* for the past participle. It is likely that the US usage which treats the verb as regular will gradually be accepted internationally.

In contemporary usage, the following system prevails:

UK and UK-influenced	US and US-influenced
dream/dreamt ~ dreamed/dreamt	dream/dreamed/dreamed
lean/leant ~ leaned/leant	lean/leaned/leaned
learn/learnt ~ learned/learnt	learn/learned/learned
smell/smelt/smelt	smell/smelled/smelled
spell/spelt ~ spelled/spelt	spell/spelled/spelled
spill/spilt ~ spilled/spilt	spill/spilled/spilled
spoil/spoiled ~ spoilt/spoilt	spoil/spoiled/spoiled

There is a tendency in UK-influenced usage to select the *-t* endings when the verb is to be taken literally:

*I **dreamt** all night.*
*I **leant** against the post.*

and the -*ed* endings when the verb is used metaphorically:

> He **dreamed** *of peace and brotherhood.*
> He **leaned** *on me to repay the money.*

See: -**ed forms, irregular verb, UK and US grammar.**

education

Many of the descriptive terms used in education in the UK and the USA differ, often in ways which can cause confusion to outsiders. The differences may be found at all levels so that a *pupil* at a *playschool* in the UK may be a *student* at a *nursery school* in the USA. The main differences are:

UK	USA
class, form	grade
primary school	grade school
public school	private school
secondary school	high school
state school	public school
technical college	junior college
university	college/university
1st year undergraduate	freshman
2nd year undergraduate	sophomore
3rd year undergraduate	junior
4th year undergraduate	senior
postgraduate	graduate
staff	faculty
lecturer	assistant professor
senior lecturer	associate professor
reader	associate professor
professor	senior/full professor
curriculum vitae/C.V.	résumé, C.V.
essay	paper, report, essay
homework	assignment
long essay, paper	thesis
maths	math
supervisor	adviser, mentor
thesis/dissertation	dissertation/thesis

See: **Americanism, Anglicism, graduate, UK and US words, UK English, US English.**

effective, effectual, efficacious, efficient

As with many words with related forms and overlapping meanings, there is sometimes confusion regarding the use of these four adjectives. All relate to *effect* or *result*.

Effective is applied to someone or something that can produce a satisfactory result or solve a problem:

*He's our most **effective** teacher. All his students do well.*
*Her technique for preventing rust is very **effective**.*

Effectual is applied to an action that fulfils its purpose or to a person capable of producing a desired effect:

*The talks were **effectual** in ending the strike.*
*He could hardly be described as **effectual**: he had wonderful ideas but never achieved anything.*

Efficacious is applied to something (usually a medicine) sure to produce a desired effect:

*It is not well known that pepper in warm milk is an **efficacious** remedy for hay fever.*

Efficient is applied to people and instruments that function well:

*She is highly **efficient**: she knows exactly where every file is and what is in it.*
*This particular engine does not make **efficient** use of oil.*

See: **problem pairs**.

Egyptian English

Throughout the nineteenth century, France and the UK vied for power in Egypt, especially after the building of the Suez Canal in 1869. UK influence increased in Egypt throughout the last quarter of the nineteenth century and Egypt was declared a British Protectorate in 1914. Egypt became a sovereign state again in 1922 but the English language continued to be used as an important medium in commerce, education, government and the media. The prestige of the English language diminished in 1956, when for a short time the UK and Egypt were at war, but the value of English as an international **lingua franca** has ensured that, after Arabic, English is the most widely taught language in the country, whose population is just under 45 million.

See: **North African English**.

either, neither

These words, which may function as **adverbs**, **determiners** and **pronouns**, tend to be pronounced differently in the UK /ˈaɪðə/ and the USA /ˈiðər/.

As an adverb in **negative** structures, *either* often occurs in sentence final position:

*We didn't see the play **either**.*
*They didn't go **either**.*

Adverbial *neither* and *nor*, in contrast, often occur in anaphoric reference and take the initial position:

Neither did we.
Nor did they.

(The construction using *nor* tends to be limited to formal or class-marked speech in the UK.)
Adverbial *either* and *neither* can be paired with *or* and *nor* respectively to imply two-part contrasts:

*It was **either** a yam **or** a sweet potato.*
*It was **neither** a yam **nor** a sweet potato.*

In practice, these 'two-part structures' often relate to more than two:

You can see him on either Monday, Wednesday or Friday.

If *either* occurs in initial position in this type of contrast, it can imply a threat:

***Either** you leave quietly or we'll call the police.*

Either...or/neither...nor take a singular form of the verb:

*It **was** either Pat or John.*
*Neither Pat nor John **has** said a word.*

Normally, the elements in such structures are equivalent (e.g. two phrases, two sentences, two adjectives, two verbs):

It was either the one with the bicycle or the one on skates.
Either he comes or he doesn't.
He was neither lame nor lazy.
She can neither work nor sleep.

Occasionally, for emphasis, the structures with *either...or* are not balanced, but in these circumstances *else* is often introduced:

He is either very stubborn or else he sees something that the rest of us can't.

Adverbial *either* and *neither* in balanced structures must be placed directly before the items they modify. Thus the sentences:

He'll either phone or leave a message.
He felt neither content nor comfortable.

are correct, whereas:

> *Either he'll phone or leave a message.*
> *He neither felt content nor comfortable.*

are incorrect, even though they are frequently heard in speech.

As determiners, *either* and *neither* cannot co-occur with other determiners and they are followed by a singular noun and verb:

> *Either answer is correct.*
> *Neither claim has any value.*

As pronouns, *either* and *neither* may occur on their own, triggering off a singular form of the verb:

> *Either is possible.*
> *Neither has any merit.*

They may also occur in the structure:

> (n)either + of + determiner + noun phrase (plural)

or:

> (n)either + of + pronoun (plural)

as in:

> *You can eat either of those peaches.*
> *Neither of them is ripe yet.*

See: **adverb, all, anaphora, concord, determiner, pronoun.**

elegant variation

There are three main types of *elegant variation*, each concerned with the substitution of learned or polysyllabic words or phrases for simple words:

> *It was subsumed under the rubric.*

rather than:

> *It was listed under the heading.*

1 People unused to the written medium are often tempted to use unnecessarily elaborate words and phrases. Long words are not automatically more appropriate than short ones: *ablutions, converse, epistle, imbibe* and *ratiocination* are rarely preferable to *wash, talk, letter, drink* and *reasoning* and there is no advantage in stylistic elaboration for its own sake. There are, it is true, established conventions for specific purposes (such as **letters**, essays, reports) but the language employed in all circumstances should be as simple, clear and precise as possible.

The preference for elegant variation resulted in the stylised **poetic diction** of some eighteenth-century verse against which Wordsworth reacted in his 'Lyrical Ballads'. Today, it is sometimes cultivated by writers whose mother tongue is not English:

The grim enthusiasm of her ardent lust was bubbling on her
romantic face, and her youthful glances of shyness. She
had got all the zests of the West and mettled her senses,
to bolster up alacrity, to crack love, romance and joke,
up to their highest mediocre of acme.
Miller O. Albert, *Rosemary and the Taxi-Driver*

2 The second type of elegant variation occurs in the work of professional writers who seek novelty or variety:

Keep in mind, however, a cautionary tale when planning a
continental motoring holiday. A British driver, thrown
temporarily off guard by a refuelling stop, pulled out of
a filling station forecourt onto the wrong side of the road.
In the acrimonious aftermath of the resulting collision,
the unfortunate miscreant lambasted the other motorist...
Observer Colour Supplement, 1 July, 1984

3 The aim of the third type is consciously humorous. It involves such substitutions as *obnoxious emanation* for *bad smell, a state of pecuniary disadvantage* for *broke* or:

You will always hear me chant this melody
Indicate the route to my abode.

for:

You will always hear me singing this song
Show me the way to go home.

Elegant variation is not just a matter of varying one's lexical choice. It may interfere with comprehension, give misleading information or evoke a humorous response when the writer may be aiming at sophisticated description.

See: **bombast, circumlocution, diction, poetic diction**.

elision

Elision involves the loss of sounds in speech or of letters in writing:

can + not > can't
there + is > there's
we + will > we'll

Vowels, consonants and entire syllables can be elided.

Literary samples of elision from Shakespeare's sonnets include such vowel elision as: *th'account, t'anticipate, y'have*. The function of elision in verse was mainly to regularise the **rhythm**. The type of Shakespearean elision illustrated is today found only in dialectal speech:

> *go + out > g'out*
> *the + other > t'other*

but the elision associated with auxiliary verbs:

> *I + would > I'd*

negation:

> *do + not > don't*

and the reduction of unstressed words like *and* and *of* occurs widely:

> *tea 'n' sympathy*
> *cuppa coffee*

The term *elision* comprehends **aphesis** (the loss of an initial vowel):

> *about > bout*

syncope (the loss of a sound or syllable medially):

> *February > Febuary, Febrary*

and **apocope** (the loss of a sound or syllable from the end of a word):

> *sand > san*
> *wetted > wet*

See: **aphesis, apocope, syncope.**

ellipsis

Ellipsis (plural *ellipses*) derives from Greek *elleipo* meaning 'come short/fall short' and it has two main applications.

1 It is the term for the omission from a **quotation** of words needed to complete it. The term is also applied to the full stops that signal the ellipsis. Ellipsis may occur at the beginning, the middle or the end of a quotation with three spaced dots indicating where the omissions have occurred:

> *. . .the clock that tells the time. . .*
> *Dialogue . . . consistently reflects the speech of the day.*

When ellipsis occurs after a complete sentence, the full stop should be followed by three stops:

> *The winter evening settles down*
> *With smells of steak in passageways. . . .*

The omission of one or more lines of poetry in a quotation may be signalled by a full line of spaced stops:

I've seen them come and seen them go
Like summer rain and winter snow.
. . . .
I've watched them, dumb.

and intrusions into a quotation must be enclosed in square brackets:

. . . [he] watched them, dumb.

The omission of a paragraph of prose from a quotation is indicated by three stops at the end of the preceding paragraph. In printed texts (as elsewhere in this book) a 3-dot leader, consisting of three unspaced dots, may be substituted for ellipsis. In a **typescript**, however, ellipses are preferable.

2 The term is used by linguists for the omission of a part of a sentence which is recoverable:

Where did Joanne go?
To Toronto.

We can reconstruct the full equivalent of the elliptical reply as:

Joanne went to Toronto.

See: **anaphora, punctuation, quotation.**

embedding

The term *embedding* is used in **transformational grammar** to refer to the process by which one **sentence** is included within another. For example, the sentence:

The man who came in is my father.

is a combination of two sentences:

The man is my father. + *The man came in.*

The second sentence is embedded in the first:

The man (the man came in) is my father.

and the repeated **phrase** 'the man' is replaced by a **pronoun,** in this example, 'who'.

Often, sentences involving non-finite verbs can be shown to involve embeddings:

His constant smoking of cigars irritates me.
(He smokes cigars constantly. + It irritates me.)
He asked me to help him.
(He asked me. + I helped him.)

Embedding differs from **co-ordination** in that the latter utilises co-ordinating conjunctions to join units of equal rank:

> He loves Mary **but** Mary doesn't love him.

See: **co-ordination, subordination, transformational grammar.**

emphasis

The term *emphasis* comprehends the many methods of putting extra **stress** on a sound, word, phrase or idea so as to give prominence to it. Emphasis may involve choices from all areas of the language and its effect may depend on a statistical change (e.g. regular increased volume, a ten percent increase in the number of negatives per paragraph) or on an unquantifiable impression created by a writer. In Dylan Thomas's phrase 'a grief ago', for example, there is no way of measuring mathematically the increased prominence given to 'grief' by its unexpected **collocation.**

The commonest types of emphasis are:

1 *Parallelism.* This device uses **repetition** of sounds as in Tennyson's:

> Over the rolling waters go
> Come from the dying moon, and blow
> Blow him again to me

of word:

> Sweet and low, sweet and low,
> Wind of the western sea,
> Low, low, breathe and blow
> Wind of the western sea!

or of **rhythm.** Many traditional ballads, for example, have four strong stresses in the first and third lines and three in the second and fourth:

> I wish the wind may never cease
> Nor fishes in the flood
> Till my three sons come home to me
> In earthly flesh and blood.

Often, as in all three examples above, several features (**alliteration, assonance,** rhythm, **rhyme**) co-occur and reinforce each other.

Such repetition need not be limited to poetry. It is a feature of oratory, excellently illustrated by Martin Luther King's 'I have a dream' sermon and can occur naturally in speech. The reduplicated adjectives in phrases like:

> a big, big mountain

for example, involve emphasis.

2 *Word Order*. The normal **word order** of:

Subject + Predicate + Object + Complement
I + called + him + a fool.

may be modified to:

A fool I called him.

emphasising 'a fool'. Such change of word order is common in **Yiddish-influenced English**:

So lucky I should be.

and in poetry:

Where dips the rocky highland
Of Sleuth Wood in the lake
  W.B. Yeats, 'The Stolen Child'.

3 *Figures of Speech*. Most of these are used for emphasis. For example in the following rhyming couplet from Alexander Pope, **antithesis** and anticlimax combine to highlight the trivial:

Here Thou, great Anna, whom three realms obey
Dost sometimes counsel take and sometimes tea.

4 *Deviation*. Deviations from the **norm** (like **inversion**) catch the reader's or listener's attention. The deviations may be in the imagery or unexpected adjectives as in Dylan Thomas's:

Her fist of a face died clenched on a round pain...

or in Charles Dickens's description of Mr Chadband in *Bleak House*:

Mr. Chadband is a large yellow man, with a fat smile,
and a general appearance of having a good deal of train
oil in his system.

5 *Proportion*. The amount of space devoted to each stage of an argument may indicate a writer's priorities. Similarly, the deliberate exclusion of something that is expected may represent a form of emphasis.

Emphasis is thus not simply, or even primarily, a matter of talking loudly or punctuating heavily. It permeates language at every level, reflecting and promoting certain attitudes and details. It may vary regionally and also socially, but most types of language involve emphasis of some kind.

See: **deviation, figurative language, foregrounding, parallelism, word order, Yiddish-influenced English.**

empiric, empirical, empiricism

These words all derive from a Greek word *empeirikos* meaning 'experience'.

Empiric is a derogatory term most frequently used by the medical profession with reference to a charlatan or a doctor who relies solely on experience. The word has been adopted by literary critics so that *empiric criticism* is untrained or unskilled criticism that does not take account of theoretical approaches to the study of literature.

Empirical and *empiricism* are philosophical terms applied to the practice of evolving rules to fit experience. *Empirical* has, however, been generalised to denote any procedure that relies on experience or observation alone, and it is sometimes used of an experimental method.

The term *empirical* is often used inaccurately by speakers and writers as an equivalent for *proven*.

-en forms

The term *-en form* is used as a synonym for *past participle*:

BE been *He has been...*
GO gone *He has gone...*
HAVE had *He has had...*
PUT put *He has put...*

As is clear from the list above, not all past **participles** end in -en but the term is used as a means of distinguishing between the past tense and the past participle of **verbs**. There is no difference in *form* between the past tense and the past participle of regular verbs:

I **walked** six miles yesterday.
I have **walked** six miles today.

but there is a difference in *function*.

See: **aspect, -ed forms, verb.**

English in the Indian Sub-Continent

Southeast Asia contains approximately one fifth of the world's population and the area is one of the most multilingual and multicultural on earth. Limiting this account to India (population c.714 million), Bangladesh (population c. 93 million), Pakistan (population c. 93 million), Sri Lanka (population c. 15 million) and Nepal (population c. 14.5 million), we are still dealing with an area where there are five language families and hundreds of mutually unintelligible languages (India alone has an estimated 850 languages in daily use). The need for **lingua francas** is thus obvious.

Because Britain was the colonial power in all these areas, English became the inter- and the intra-national language. Admittedly, English was associated with power, but it was not associated with a particular caste, region, religion, language family or group, and so even when it was phased out as an official language (as happened in India in 1965) it remained a language of education, culture, prestige and aspiration. As a link language it has often been preferred to a local lingua franca. This statement is particularly true of South Indian speakers, who often use English rather than Hindi in inter-state contacts.

As one would expect in such a large, highly populated area, we find a continuum of Englishes ranging from standard international English, indistinguishable in the written medium from the UK standard, through a spectrum of mother-tongue-influenced Englishes to pidginised varieties. Our description will concentrate on the standard end of the spectrum and, although it is difficult to offer firm generalisations for such a diverse area, we shall select those features which characterise the English of most people from the region.

Phonology

1 The **articulatory setting** tends to be retroflex, that is, the tip of the tongue curls slightly towards the roof of the mouth. The retroflexion affects all speech, but the consonants most particularly affected are /t,d,s,z,l,r,n/. (If the reader wishes to check the fundamental influence of retroflexion on pronunciation, he should curl the tongue slightly and then say aloud: 'What did you intend to do?')

2 The consonants /p,t,k/ are not aspirated in initial position, that is, they are not accompanied by the breath that characterises their articulation in most communities where English is spoken as a mother tongue. Since most native speakers of English use **aspiration** as a guide to distinguish between initial p, t, k, and b, d, g they tend to hear *bit* for *pit*, *den* for *ten*, *gum* for *come* and, since thousands of words are distinguished by initial p or b, t or d, k or g, the possibility for confusion is considerable.

3 Many do not distinguish between v and w or between n and ng, thus producing extra homophones in *vie* and *why*, *vine* and *wine*, *sin* and *sing*, and in *thin* and *thing*.

4 **Consonant clusters** involving s are often prefixed by /ɪ/, the vowel sound in *bit*, as in *ispeak*, *iscream*, *istatue*. Alternatively, the cluster is broken up by the insertion of a vowel as in *sicrew*.

5 Post-vocalic r is not pronounced in words such as *car* and *cart*. Nor is it used as a linking device in such phrases as *better or worse*.

6 There are fewer vowel contrasts than in **Received Pronunciation**, with such pairs as *par* and *paw* as well as *hot* and *hat* becoming homophones.

7 The diphthongs in words such as *gate* and *show* are monophthongised.

8 Fewer reduced vowels are used, thus the *a* in *about* is similar in quality to the *a* in *cat*.

9 The **stress** pattern is different from mother-tongue varieties. Often, all syllables are equally stressed or, when an attempt is made to reproduce the stress-timed pattern of English, the wrong syllable is stressed as in *de'finitely*.

Vocabulary

Many words in international English were adopted from the languages in the sub-continent, words like *bungalow, copra, chintz, curry, mango, pyjama/pajama* and *polo*. These are naturally also found in the English of the sub-continent, as are the majority of items current in Standard English. There are, however, four categories of words occurring in the English of this region which are sufficient, even in the written medium, to distinguish it from other varieties.

1 Items taken originally from Portuguese (*ayah, peon*); and from Arabic or Persian during the time of the Moghul Empire (*bakshish, chowkidar, sepoy*).

2 Items taken into English from the local **vernaculars**. Among these are the terms *ji* attached to a name as a means of expressing respect (*Guluji, Mamaji, Daddyji*); *Namaste* as a greeting (both hands are joined as in prayer while the word is said); items of clothing (*choli, dhoti, sari*); names of persons or trades (*dhobi walla(h), punka walla(h), saddarji*).

3 Items taken from English and modified in form: *co-sister* (brother-in-law's wife), *decoction* (concoction, usually an infusion), *delink* (abolish), *freeship* (scholarship), *inskirt* (undergarment, petticoat).

4 Words taken from English and modified in meaning: *batch* (group of people), *drumstick* (green vegetable), *jack* (authority), *stand first* (come first in an examination).

Grammar

Again, as with pronunciation, there is an enormous range of grammatical possibilities, often depending on the extent of one's education. The following patterns tend to characterise the English of the area:

1 Distinctions are not always made between **stative and dynamic** verbs. This means that most verbs are capable of occurring with the present **progressive**:

I am remembering you now.
He is seeing me often.

2 'BE + there' is used in existential constructions such as:

What will you eat? Vegetable is there; rice is there.

Mother-tongue speakers of English would prefer to use a construction involving HAVE:

We have vegetables and rice.

3 Inversion of subject and predicate is rare after the question words *what, when, where, which, who, how*:

What you've been doing?
How you've been able to buy this fine house?

4 There is a tendency to omit *the* when the reference is generic:

We all went to look at solar eclipse.
Let's go to pictures.

5 Many speakers from the region use a universal **tag**, often *isn't it?* but occasionally *not so?*:

You will come again, isn't it?
Your children are still schooling, not so?

6 Prepositions are often used differently:

*He backed out **in** the last moment.*
*That goonda fellow has just torn **off** my notes.*
*The streets are jamming **up** with traffic.*

7 Word compounding often follows a rule that reverses the order found in native English, thus:

board notice for notice board
glass pane for pane of glass
key bunch for bunch of keys

See: **Pakistani English, Sri Lankan English.**

enormity

Enormity strictly used refers to the great wickedness of a crime or action:

*We were shocked by the violence last night and after twenty-four hours we are only beginning to recognise the full **enormity**.*
    Margaret Thatcher (interviewed after inner city riots)

Frequently, however, especially in speech and in loose writing, *enormity* is used as a synonym for *size*:

*We were impressed by the **enormity** of the park.*

enquire, inquire

The spellings *enquire/inquire* and *enquiry/inquiry* are interchangeable. Both forms are correct throughout the English-speaking world. There is a slight tendency to prefer the *en-* form for the verb:

> *We **enquired** about the times of the services.*

and *in-* for the noun:

> *The **inquiry** opens tomorrow.*

but this is a tendency and not a fixed rule.

In the UK *enquiry/inquiry* is pronounced /ɪnˈkwaɪərɪ/ as if it were *in + choir + ee* whereas the US **pronunciation** is usually /ˈɪnkwərɪ/.

See: **pronunciation**.

epenthesis

This term refers to a process which is almost the reverse of **syncope**. *Epenthesis* involves the inclusion of a vowel or consonant medially in a word, often making the word easier to pronounce:

film > filum
chimney > chimminey/chimbley

It most frequently involves the insertion of a short neutral vowel into a **consonant cluster**:

strong > sᵊtrong

and is frequently found in the English of people whose mother tongues do not have the consonant clusters found in English or whose mother tongues have a CVCV structure (i.e. consonant vowel consonant vowel, e.g. *nama, pita*). English permits a maximum of three consonants in initial position and four in word final position:

CCCVCCCC *strengths* /strɛŋkθs/

and in non-mother-tongue English these clusters are often broken up by epenthetic vowels so that *screw driver*, for example, is realised as 'sukuru daraiva'.

A form of written epenthesis occurs in words like *debt* and *doubt*, which used to be written *dette* and *dout* but had the b inserted by scholars who felt that the English words should reflect their Latin origins in *debitum* and *dubitare*. Many other words had their spellings changed so that their classical origins might be more easily seen. These include:

adventure (previously aventure)
baptism (previously bapteme)

catholic (previously cat(t)olic)
language (previously langage)
perfect (previously parfit)

It seems probable that until the early seventeenth century these words continued to be pronounced in the old way but gradually, under the influence of the written medium, the pronunciation too changed.

See: **consonant cluster, intrusive vowels and consonants, spelling pronunciation, syncope.**

epigram, epigraph, epitaph, epithet

The **morpheme** *epi* derives from a Greek form meaning 'upon'. These four words are sometimes confused because of their similar appearance and because of a certain overlap of meaning.

An *epigram* originally meant an inscription (often on a tomb). The word is now used to describe a short, pithy saying, often in a balanced, antithetical structure:

> *If the hill will not go to Mahomet, Mahomet will go to the hill.*
>   Francis Bacon, 'Of Boldness'

As a literary term, an *epigram* refers to a short poem in two parts, the first setting the scene and the second making a concise and often unexpected point. An example of such verse is:

> *Go, smiling souls, your new-built cages break,*
> *In heaven you'll learn to sing, ere here to speak,*
> *Nor let the milky fonts that bathe your thirst*
> *Be your delay;*
> *The place that calls you hence is, at the worst,*
> *Milk all the way.*
>   Richard Crashaw, 'To the Infant Martyrs'

An *epigraph* is an inscription in stone, on a coin or on a statue:

> *E pluribus unum* (From many one)
> *Look on my work, ye Mighty, and despair.*
>   P.B. Shelley, 'Ozimandias'

The word *epigraph* is also applied to a motto or quotation at the beginning of a written work or at the beginning of a section of the work:

> *Guns don't kill people, people kill people.*
>   D. Bolinger, *Language the Loaded Weapon.*

An *epitaph* is an inscription on a tomb:

Here lieth the mortal remains of X
The Lord hath given
The Lord hath taken away.

Epitaph is used in a broader sense to refer to a commemorative verse such as the one written by Ben Jonson on the death of his daughter in 1616:

Here lies, to each her parents' ruth
Mary, the daughter of their youth...

The term *epithet* has three related meanings, only the first of which is fully acceptable:
1 an adjective or adjective phrase:

deceptive water
faithful and loving heart

2 the entire noun phrase in which the epithet occurs:

marked men

3 an insulting or obscene description of a person:

a politician invariably under the influence of alcohol or someone's pursestrings

ergative

Ergative comes from a Greek **verb** meaning 'cause, bring about, create' and the term is applied to the relationship that exists between such sentences as:

The plane landed at Lima.

and:

The pilot landed the plane at Lima.

where the **subject** of a verb becomes the **object** of the same verb and a new subject is introduced as the cause or agent of the action. The term *ergative* is new but the phenomenon it refers to is not. It was introduced to help explain the fact that many verbs in English could occur in both **transitive** and **intransitive** sentences:

The stick broke.
John broke the stick.

Among these are verbs of change, either in position or state, such as BREAK, CLOSE, CHANGE, COOK, GROW, MOVE, START, STOP, SPLIT, TEAR and their synonyms.

One of the main stylistic values of such verbs is that they allow the speaker to avoid naming the agent, in other words, they are very useful in making excuses:

The dinner burnt.
The car stalled.
My shirt tore.

There is one other phenomenon related to the subject of ergativity: the increased use in speech and writing of verbs with non-logical subjects:

The plane is now boarding at Gate 21.
Your windows need painting.
This book reads well.
The dress washed beautifully.

See: **active voice, case grammar, passive voice, verb.**

ersatz

This word was taken into the language from German in the late nineteenth century and applied to an artificial (often inferior) substitute or imitation:

*This is **ersatz** coffee. It's made from roasted acorns.*
*Don't you get the feeling that everything is **ersatz** these days? **Ersatz** milk that never knew a cow? **Ersatz** food—all monosodium glutamate and flavouring!*

especially, specially

These **adverbs** have essentially the same meaning but can have different functions and emphases.
  Especially tends to occur before a preposition + noun phrase:

*We love eating muffins, **especially** in the winter.*

or before a subordinate clause:

*You must eat well, **especially** if you are working late.*

Specially is more likely to occur before a verb or adjective:

*It was **specially** designed to suit their needs.*

and can be prefaced by *extra-*:

*It was **extra-specially** good of you.*

ethnolect

An *ethnolect*, from Greek *ethnos* meaning 'race, people', implies the linguistic behaviour characteristic of an ethnic group. The term has been applied to **Black English, Gypsy** English and **Yiddish-influenced English** but has wider applications. The speech patterns of a Scot which are habitually found in the language of other Scots may be regarded as an *ethnolect*.

Ethnolinguistics studies language in relation to race.

See: **Anglo-Romani, Black English, dialect, Gypsy, Yiddish-influenced English.**

etymology

Etymology derives ultimately from the Greek word *etumos* meaning 'true, actual'. The word now refers to the study of the origins and history of the forms and the meanings of words. For example, we know something of the etymology of *Saturday*, which derives from Old English *Saetern(es)daeg* from Latin *Saturni dies* (Saturn's day). *Saturday* is etymologically related to *saturnic* (affected by lead poisoning) and *saturnine* (of a gloomy disposition) but few speakers of English would relate Saturday semantically to either of these words.

However, not all etymologies are clear. Some words, such as *humbug* have been adapted from languages which are less well documented than Latin and others like *hype* (elaborate promotion of a record, book or film) may have more than one etymology. *Hype* may derive from Greek *hypo* meaning 'under', from *hypodermic* (under the skin), and from the Greek prefix *hyper* meaning 'over', as in *hyperbole* and *hypermarket*. Multiple etymologies are commonly invoked in the explanation of creole vocabularies. For example, the word *dɔti*, which is found in most Atlantic pidgins and creoles related to English, almost certainly derives from Twi *dɔti* meaning 'soil, earth, clay' reinforced by English *dirt/dirty*.

See: **barbarism, borrowing, dictionary.**

euphemism

A *euphemism* is a word or phrase that is substituted for one that is regarded as too explicit, offensive or unpleasant:

dirty *unhygienic*
dying *terminally ill*
poor *underprivileged*

Euphemisms may be ephemeral in that a new word may take on the connotations of the word that it replaced and thus no longer serve a euphemistic purpose:

water closet   toilet

They may be specific to a region (UK *toilet* can be impolite in parts of the USA where *bathroom* or *restroom* may be preferred) or to an occupation (politics, the military). They may also vary according to the speaker's viewpoint, so that a gunman who is regarded favourably by the speaker may be referred to as *a freedom fighter* whereas if he is regarded unfavourably he may be described as *a terrorist*.

Euphemisms can be useful. There are, for example, a great many related to death and dying, suggesting our reluctance in the English-speaking world to face the fact of non-existence. Some of these are serious and others humorously dismissive, but all serve the purpose of distancing us from the reality:

Serious	Humorous
be interred	*push up daisies*
go to heaven	*kick the bucket*
pass away	*cash in your chips*

Some of the humorous equivalents for *die* are quite callous, but it is often appropriate to use euphemisms in expressing sympathy, when gentler expressions are preferred to the starkness of *die* and *death*.

Euphemisms may be described as a means of directing our thoughts away from unpleasant realities: old age, death, obesity or poverty; or from bodily excretions.

Euphemisms are part of the language of advertising and can be useful in persuading groups not to be pressurised into thinking less of themselves:

Big is beautiful.
Black is beautiful.

If used as part of military indoctrination, they can make killing more acceptable by providing dehumanising terms for the enemy:

gooks
jungle-bunnies
terrs

and by describing war as *a military campaign* to *pacify* enemies or *liberate* friends. Weapons are made less frightening by being *named* rather than described:

Big Boy
Minuteman

or they are referred to as *hardware* or *systems*.

Euphemisms exploit the language's capacity for metaphorical expansion. This capacity is in itself neither good nor bad, but we should always be aware of the power euphemisms can have to reveal our thoughts and our attitudes to other people.

See: **cliché, connotation, curse and swear, doublespeak, propaganda, taboo words**.

euphuism

Euphuism (from a character called *Euphues*, created by John Lyly in 1579) is a style of writing popularised in England in the late sixteenth century but having roots that go back to the fourteenth. The word is applied to a highly contrived, intricate **prose style** characterised by **alliteration**, elaborately balanced constructions, carefully selected words, phrases, clauses, rhetorical questions, patterned comparisons and **similes**, classical and scriptural allusions, and by a desire that the prose should be seen to be 'crafted'. The following extract is an example of euphuism:

> *But his minde was so blemished with detestable qualities,*
> *and so spotted with the staine of voluptuousnesses, that he*
> *was not so much to be commended for the proportion of his*
> *bodie, as to be condempned for the imperfection of his minde.*
>   Robert Greene, 'The Carde of Fancie'.

See: **alliteration, assonance, discourse analysis, elegant variation, parallelism, style**.

every

Every functions as a **determiner**:

> *Every person in the village tried to vote.*

The word *every* and compounds involving *every-* (*everybody, everyone, everything*) take singular nouns and verbs:

> *Every detail is perfect.*
> *Everybody was delighted.*

The only exception to this rule is when *every* precedes a cardinal number:

> *We visit her every three days.*

in contrast to ordinals:

> *We visit her every third day.*

Every causes problems of **agreement** in such structures as:

> *Everyone should do ——— best.*

In the spoken medium, the usual solution is:

*Everyone should do **their** best.*

but, since every + body/one/thing is singular, grammarians insist the construction should be:

*Everyone should do **his** best.*

where *his* comprehends *her*. Many speakers object to the sexism implicit in the choice of personal adjective and advocate the use of:

*Everyone should do **his or her/her or his** best.*

or reversion to the preferred spoken form:

*Everyone should do **their** best.*

Many others feel uncomfortable with all the solutions and are uncertain what to use here and in **question tags** involving *any-, every-, some-*:

Anyone can do it, can't he/she/they?
Everybody has rights, haven't they?/hasn't he/she?
Somebody locked the door, didn't they/he/she?

There are no easy answers to this problem. It seems only reasonable, however, that language should not be used to offend people or to reinforce stereotypes. If it is true that 'the Sabbath was made for man [and woman] and not man [or woman] for the Sabbath' it seems equally true that language must serve its users. The simplest solution and the one that will most easily be accepted (because it is already the preferred form in speech) is the use of *they/their* as the pronominal and adjectival forms triggered off by *any-, every-* and *some-*.

See: **agreement, concord, determiner, sexist language**.

everyone, every one

Everyone can usually be replaced by *everybody*. It is singular and refers to people:

Everyone here is always in a hurry.
Everybody here is always in a hurry.

Every one can usually be replaced by *every single one*. It refers to animate beings (excluding human beings) and to inanimate nouns:

*I counted **every one** myself and not a single sheep was missing.*
*He must really love garden gnomes! He bought **every one** in the shop.*

except, excepted, excepting

Except as a preposition implies exclusion:

> *He'll talk about anything **except** religion and politics.*

It is followed by the accusative forms of personal pronouns:

> *He likes everyone **except me/us/them**.*

and by the base form of the verb:

> *We'll do nothing **except eat, sleep, swim and relax**.*

In certain regions *except* can occur as a conjunction meaning 'unless':

> ***Except** you do what you're told, you'll not get far.*

but the use of *except* as a conjunction is archaic and recessive.

Excepting and *excepted* are used to imply exclusion in relatively formal structures involving *not, without* and *always* as in:

> *We'll all attend, **not excepting** the children.*
> *We'll all attend, the children **not excepted**.*

Excepting precedes the noun phrase and *excepted* follows it. The uses above are grammatical but unusual and would be avoided by many speakers.

exclamation

Exclamation derives from Latin *ex + clamare* meaning 'to cry out, utter loudly' and implies a type of **emphasis** that is signalled by certain conventions: **intonation** (in speech), the exclamation mark (in writing), by specific words (e.g. *how, what*) and by changes in **word order**.

1 A statement may be converted into an exclamation simply by a change of intonation or by the use of an exclamation mark:

> He was furious. > *He was furious!*

2 *How* is used in exclamations. We can have:
(a) how + adjective:

> *How lovely!*

(b) how + adjective + subject + predicate:

> *How tall they are!*

(c) how + adverb + subject + predicate:

> *How beautifully she sings!*

(d) how + subject + predicate:

How he ran!

3 *What* also occurs in exclamations, in such structures as:
(a) what + (a/an/the) + noun:

What a fool!
What luck!
What the heck/dickens!

(b) what + (a/an) + adjective + noun

What a rotten day!
What terrible luck!

(c) what + (a/an) + (adjective) + subject + predicate

What courage they have!
What a fantastic performance they gave!

4 Rhetorical questions are often used as the equivalents of emphatic statements:

Am I tired! = I'm extremely tired.
Can he run! = He can run exceptionally well.
Was she angry!= She was very angry indeed.

Negative rhetorical questions may function as emphatic positives:

Aren't they sweet! = They are very sweet.
Isn't he fast! = He's extremely fast.

5 Wishes expressed with *if only* are often exclamatory:

If only I'd known!
If only I could have my life over again!

Conventionally, a sentence that is syntactically incomplete is acceptable if it ends with an exclamation mark:

You told!
An ice cube!
Even worse!

In addition, the heavy use of exclamation marks in the language used to describe a character may suggest to a reader that the character is young, shallow, emotional or given to exaggeration.

See: **emphasis, punctuation, sentence, style.**

exposition

Exposition is a form of discourse. It is concerned with explaining or clarifying ideas and tends to be marked by detailed analysis, definition of terms, the use of comparisons and contrasts, all of which may be supplemented by diagrams, graphs, illustrations or maps.

See: **argument, definition, discourse analysis, narration, style.**

fact

The word *fact* is used in a variety of ways, some of them inaccurate or misleading. In the phrase *the true facts* as in:

> *She tried to unearth* **the true facts**.

the adjective is redundant, since something that is untrue cannot be a fact.

Often, *fact* is used as a **filler** or **discourse marker**, included more for **emphasis** or **linkage** than for its meaning:

> *As* **a matter of fact**, *I don't think so.*
> *In fact, you're probably right.*

The phrase *the fact* can be obligatory in sentences where a noun phrase is required between a preposition and the conjunction 'that':

> **He did not take account of that she was ill.*
> *He did not take account of **the fact** that she was ill.*

See: **discourse analysis, discourse marker, fillers.**

fad words

Various terms such as *fad words* or *vogue words* are applied to items that are popular for a relatively short time and are used more for their effect than for their precise meanings. Many are emotive adjectives which reveal more about the user's attitude than about the object described (*brilliant, fantastic, phenomenal, wonderful*) and others are words which are popularised by the media (*ambience, charisma, macho*).

There are fashions in *fad words*, the following being popular in the 70s and early 80s: *absolutely* (yes), *accomplish* (do), **affirmative** (yes), *burglarise* (burgle), *dialogue* (conversation), *image* (reputation), *proceed* (go), *simplistic* (simple), *terminate* (end), *transportation* (transport), *utilise* (use).

Such choices resemble **elegant variation**, but they are used not only to impress but to be fashionable. Because they are overused, they take on some of the characteristics of **clichés**. The following list includes a number of words, many of them excellent in the right contexts, which have been diminished by over-exposure: *charismatic, democratic, disadvantaged, importantly, interface, meaningful, ongoing,* *relevant, situation, state of the art, third world, traumatic, viable.* Such fashionable words can lose popularity almost as quickly as they gain it. They are tokens of a society where novelty often has more appeal than accuracy.

Just as there are fashions in *using* words, so are there fashions in *criticising* certain words. Many **purists** object to the use of *hopefully* as a sentence **modifier** or of *talk with* rather than *talk to.* The criterion for condemning a particular usage should be the desire to keep the language flexible and expressive, accurate and effective.

See: **'chestnuts', cliché, elegant variation, jargon.**

false etymology

A *false etymology* is an incorrect description and history of a word, phrase or morpheme. To claim, for example, that *ptarmigan* derives from Greek because a number of words such as *pterodactyl* and *ptomaine* (poisoning) are Greek is a false etymology. (Its actual **etymology** is the Gaelic word for the bird, *tarmachan*.)

Most false etymologies are the result of accident or circumstance. For example, many of the African words in the first edition of *The Dictionary of Jamaican English* were traced to Twi, suggesting a strong Ghanaian influence on **Jamaican English**. When the **dictionary** was first compiled (late 50s and early 60s) there were very few dictionaries of West African languages available, but there was an excellent dictionary of Twi. Subsequent research has shown that a high proportion of the words found in Jamaican English and Twi are also found in many other West African languages.

A common type of false etymology arises from a wrongly interpreted morpheme. The *bikini* swimming suit was named after the Pacific atoll Bikini but, since it referred to a two-piece suit, *bi-* was interpreted as 'two' and the term *monokini* applied to the bottom half of a bikini.

See: **etymology, folk etymology, flammable.**

family tree

The terms for describing family relationships in any language reflect the structure of the society. For example, mother-tongue speakers of English use only a limited number of terms, which are differentiated according to generation and also usually according to sex:

(*parent*) *father mother* (*uncle aunt*)
child son daughter (*nephew niece*)
sibling brother sister (*cousin*)

(The bracketed items derive from French.)Other generations are indicated by prefixing *grand* (originally from French) or *great*:

> *grandparent grandmother grandson*
> *great-aunt great-nephew great-grandparent*

and relationships created by marriage also derive from the same
terms:

> *?parent-in-law father-in-law mother-in-law*
> *stepchild stepson stepdaughter*

Such a simple system is very inadequate in many societies in
India, Africa and the South Pacific and so the English kinship terms
are extended by including items such as *co-sister* (brother-in-law's
wife) in India, *co-wife* (wives of the same husband) in West Africa
and *small papa* (maternal uncle) in Papua New Guinea.

The idea of the nuclear family is often an idealisation, taking little
account of changes (like divorce) or the relationships that can arise
from remarriage.

The metaphor of *family trees* is often applied to languages, so
that it is commonplace to refer to French and English as 'related
languages' or to Indo-European as the 'parent language' of both.
This metaphor is then often illustrated by means of such tables as:

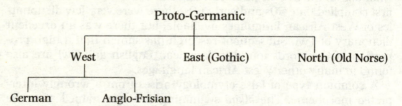

As a metaphor, the table above is useful, but it is utterly unrealistic
to pretend that all linguistic change is orderly and that all influences
are in one direction only. Recent experience shows us that even so-
called 'dead' languages like Hebrew can be resurrected and can
become the mother tongue of people whose ancestors had abandoned
its use. And if we consider the types of English spoken in Jamaica
and Sierra Leone we see considerable similarities which can be accounted for as follows:

1 Many West Africans from the Sierra Leone region went to
Jamaica in the early seventeenth century.

2 In the late eighteenth century, many Jamaicans went to Sierra
Leone and helped to found Freetown.

3 In the nineteenth century, some Sierra Leoneans went to
Jamaica to work.

4 In the late nineteenth and early twentieth centuries, mission-

aries from Jamaica went to various parts of West Africa, including Sierra Leone.

Such interaction between peoples cannot be limited to the last four centuries and graphically illustrates the dangers of assuming one-way traffic in linguistic influences.

See : **etymology**.

female, male ; feminine, masculine

A study of the way these terms are used reveals a lot about popular attitudes to the roles played by men and women.

The words *female* and *male* are often used descriptively and objectively to refer to the sex of people, animals, insects and plants :

*The people of Papua New Guinea often refer to a **female** child as 'pikinini meri'.*
*The **male** swan is called a cob.*
***Female** spiders have been known to eat the **male** after mating.*
*The stamen is the **male** reproductive organ of a flower.*

There is, however, a tendency to regard *male* as basic and *female* as derived or parasitic, so that if *female* (or one of its synonyms) does not precede a profession we are likely to assume that the person is male :

a female pilot
a lady judge
a woman doctor

In similar vein, a number of linguists working on feature analysis where, for example, a bull could be described as being :

+ noun
+ animate
+ male
+ adult...

have chosen to describe a cow as :

+ noun
+ animate
− male
+ adult...

The terms *feminine* and *masculine* are used objectively in descriptions of **gender**. In many languages, all words are either *feminine* or *masculine* and the pronoun used to refer to a word is the equivalent of either *he* or *she* :

La table est petite. Elle est... (The table is small. It is...)
Le jardin est petit. Il est... (The garden is small. It is...)

The fact that there is nothing intrinsically female about a table, for example, is illustrated by the fact that the word for 'table' is masculine in Irish. Similarly, *salt* is masculine in French, Italian and Portuguese but feminine in Spanish and neuter in German.

See: **gender, sexist language**.

fewer, less, lesser

Fewer and *less* are both comparatives but they are used differently. *Fewer* modifies **countable** nouns and *less* modifies uncountable quantities:

> There are **fewer people** here because we've had **less sun** this year.
> We are eating **less sugar** and **fewer potatoes** than before.
> They have learned even **less** than we imagined.

The distinction between *fewer* and *less* is easily taught and remembered but is a distinction that is probably being lost, with *less* being increasingly used to modify both countable and uncountable nouns. Even the BBC in a news broadcast reported:

> There were **less policemen** on duty today.

using a form which would have been stigmatised a few years earlier; and *The Times* used the headline:

> Connors to play in **less events**.

Lesser occurs only as an attributive adjective in relatively formal styles:

> He is the **lesser** man.
> Choose the **lesser** of the two evils.

See: **problem pairs**.

figurative language

The term *figurative language* has two related meanings.

1 The first involves **metaphor** and focuses on what happens when X is expressed in terms normally associated with Y. For example, a *soft* cushion is an ordinary literal description with the adjective deriving from sensory perception. However, when *soft* is used to describe something that is not literally soft (*a soft job, a soft option, a soft smile*) then we are using figurative language. Such non-literal use of language may be observed in all social activities and at all levels of formality. If we limit ourselves simply to body parts, we can

see how widely they have been extended from their literal bodily applications:

> *to nose out the truth*
> *the mouth of a river*
> *to shoulder responsibility*
> *to foot the bill*

It is virtually impossible to speak *without* using metaphor because metaphor is, in the words of I.A. Richards, 'the omnipresent principle of language'.

2 Figurative language can also refer to language embodying figures of speech. The commonest figures of speech (apart from *metaphor*) are:

analogy (*birds of a feather*)
antithesis (*Hair today, bald tomorrow*)
apostrophe (*Romeo, Romeo, wherefore art thou?*)
bathos (*A man, a master, a marvel...a mouse*)
climax (the high point of the action)
hyperbole (*an Olympus to a molehill*)
irony (*Marie Antoinette: Now don't lose your head over these revolutions!*)
metonymy (*He was called to the bar.*)
oxymoron (*a noiseless noise*)
personification (*the laughing brook*)
simile (*as fat in the forehead as a hen*)
synecdoche (*Two heads are better than one.*)

See: **litotes, meiosis, metaphor, paradox, syllepsis.**

Fijian English

The Republic of *Fiji* is made up of a conglomeration of 300 + small islands, just over 100 of which are inhabited. The islands were explored by Captain Bligh (after the mutiny on the *Bounty*), annexed by Britain in 1874 and granted independence in 1970. Today's population of under one million is multiracial (46% indigenous Fijians, 50% immigrant Indians and 4% made up of Chinese, Europeans, South Sea Islanders) and multilingual, with English, Fijian, Hindi, Urdu, Tamil, Telugu, Gujerati and Chinese being spoken, with radio programmes in English, Fijian and Hindi, and with two daily and one monthly newspaper in English and weeklies in both Fijian and Hindi.

English is the official language of the Republic. It is the main language of commerce, education and government, the one language capable of bridging racial, cultural and linguistic barriers, and Fijians often claim with pride that the new day dawns first in Fiji, making the local English daily (founded in 1869) 'the first newspaper published in the world today'. The standard norm in Fiji approximates to Standard **New Zealand English** largely because of three facts: many teachers in Fiji are from New Zealand; the two most important school examinations are the New Zealand School Certificate and the New Zealand University Entrance Examination; and many Fijian students go to New Zealand for tertiary education. There are a number of differences, however, most of them attributable to the influence of the mother tongues.

Phonology

1 All accents are non-**rhotic** and all speakers tend to speak English as if it were a syllable-timed language.

2 Speakers of Fijian tend to have a smaller vowel inventory than New Zealanders, often eliminating centring diphthongs (as in *dear*, *hair*, *liar*, *shore* and *sure*), using /a/ rather than schwa in words such as *ago* and *father*, and monophthongising the vowels in *goat* and *gate*.

3 Speakers of Indian origin tend to preserve the retroflexion of their mother tongues and to carry over some of the speech habits found in Indian English.

Vocabulary

Local **borrowings** into English are limited. Fijians tend to use Fijian among themselves and the same is true of other linguistic groups, with the result that the vocabulary is very similar to New Zealand English. Among the commonly-used local words are:

roti—type of bread
taro—edible plant

Grammar

1 **Yes/no questions** are often distinguished from statements by intonation and/or the use of a **tag**:

He's coming today?
He's coming, yes?
He's coming, isn't it?

Wh-questions, too, frequently have the **word order** of statements:

When she is coming?
Why she said that?

2 Mass nouns such as *information* are often treated as count nouns:

I have received these informations.

See: **English in the Indian Sub-Continent, New Zealand English.**

fillers

Unrehearsed speech is often marked by *fillers*, that is, words and phrases which are unnecessary semantically but useful in preserving a **rhythm**, avoiding uncomfortable silences and associating the listener with the conversation. Among the most frequently used fillers are:

> *as everybody knows/says*
> *as it were*
> *at this moment in time*
> *by and large*
> *from where I stand*
> *in (actual) fact*
> *in my opinion/view*
> *just let me say/add*
> *kind of/ sort of*
> *right and proper*
> *you know/you see*

Many stylists condemn fillers as being unnecessary, clumsy or imprecise but there is good reason to believe that fillers contribute to the fluency of speech. Originally, the *Français Fondamental* course had no fillers but teachers found that conversations were stilted and unnatural until they introduced such fillers as *alors*, *eh bien*, and *mais vous voyez*.

See: **catch phrase, phatic communion.**

finite

The term *finite* is applied to a **verb** (phrase) which takes a **subject** ([*you*] *sang*), can show contrasts in **tense** ([*you*] *sing/ sang*) and in **agreement** ([*you*] *sing/ [he] sings*) and which can occur alone in an independent sentence or main **clause**:

> [*they*] *sing*
> [*they*] *have sung*
> [*they*] *are singing*
> [*they*] *are sung*
> [*they*] *have been singing*
> [*they*] *have been sung*

The non-finite parts of the verb are the infinitive (*to sing*), the present participle (*singing*) and the past participle (*sung*).

Clauses containing finite verbs are called 'finite clauses':

> *when he arrived*

whereas clauses containing non-finite verbs are called 'non-finite clauses':

on arriving
having arrived

See: **verb**.

first, firstly

Many stylists and publishing houses insist that *firstly* should not be used. This attitude is illustrated by Eric Partridge's claim:

firstly is inferior to *first*, even when *secondly*, *thirdly* follow it. (*Usage and Abusage* 1982: 120)

The advocated system is thus: 'First... secondly... thirdly... finally/last.' Since *first* means 'preceding all others in time, order or significance' it is unnecessary to use the -ly form. Nevertheless, *firstly* has been used since the sixteenth century, is increasingly widely used today and is acceptable in all but the most formal of styles.

See: **'chestnuts'**.

flammable

Many users of English have trouble distinguishing *flammable*, *inflammable* and *non-flammable*. *Flammable* and *inflammable* both mean 'easily set on fire' with *inflammable* being more likely to be used of emotions and *flammable* of volatile substances. Difficulties arose because the *in-* **prefix** in English is often used to negate words:

edible inedible
hospitable inhospitable

and so *inflammable* became ambiguous.

The normal warning now used to mark chemicals and substances which can be easily ignited is *flammable* with *non-flammable* being the negative.

flaunt

Flaunt has several meanings in contemporary English:
1 display oneself in public
2 wave something ostentatiously
3 display something or someone ostentatiously or impudently
4 treat rules contemptuously
The fourth usage probably arose from confusion with *flout*:

He flouted the rules.

and consequently some stylists argue that *flaunt the rules* is incorrect. Many contemporary writers use *flaunt* to mean 'treat contemptuously' and *flout* is rapidly becoming archaic.

See: **'chestnuts'**.

folk etymology

Folk etymology is the alteration of a learned or unfamiliar word by ordinary users of a language. The alteration involves reinterpretation towards a similar sounding, more familiar word or **morpheme** so that the term makes more apparent sense to the user. *Sill* is an unfamiliar word in Northern Ireland and so *window sill* has been transformed into *windy stool*; and in Cameroon, *blindfool* replaces the less meaningful *blindfold* in both literal and metaphorical uses:

> *We used smoke to **blindfool** (i.e. mesmerise) the bees.*

Folk etymology has always been involved in vocabulary change and development. *Forlorn hope*, for example, has been reinterpreted from Dutch *verloren hoop* meaning 'a lost group', and *bridegroom* has two morphemes which are meaningful to contemporary users of English (bride + groom) but the second involves folk etymology. *Bridegroom* comes from **Old English** *bryd* (bride) + *guma* (man) but *guma* was replaced because it ceased to be meaningful. And the exclamation *Great Scott!* is probably an anglicisation of *Gruss Gott!* reinforced by the prestige of Scott of the Antarctic.

Contacts between speakers of different **dialects** or different languages increase the likelihood of folk etymologising. In the Isle of Man, we find *lemoncholy* (melancholy), in South Africa *coronations* (carnations), British soldiers referred to Ypres as *Wipers, damsel jam* and *Welsh rabbit* are widely used by dialect speakers in England for *damson jam* and *Welsh rarebit*, and in Ireland and parts of the USA we find such examples as:

> *cowcumber* for *cucumber*
> *piano rose* for *peony rose*
> *sparrow grass* for *asparagus*

Folk etymology can provide productive morphemes. The compound *Hamburger steak*, for example, was clipped (see **clipping**) to *hamburger*. Coincidentally, *ham* looked and sounded like a description of the meat, and *burger* began to be treated like a free morpheme, giving such forms as:

> *baconburger*
> *beefburger*

steakburger
turkeyburger

or indeed a *burger* for any kind of heated meat sandwich.

Although some folk etymologies, like *bridegroom*, enter the standard language, the pressure of written norms usually limits folk etymologies to speech and oral cultural traditions.

See: **etymology, false etymology.**

food and drink

With *food and drink* as with so many areas of culture there are considerable differences in UK and US terminology. The commonest differences are listed below:

UK	USA
angel cake	plain cake, angel food cake
aubergine	eggplant
bap	hamburger bun
biscuit (sweet)	cookie
chips	French fries
courgettes	zucchini
crisps	chips
grill	broil
jam	jelly
jelly	jello
kipper	smoked herring
marrow	squash
milk	cream
mince	chopped/ground hamburger meat
neat (i.e. without water)	straight
porridge	oatmeal
scone	biscuit
single cream	table cream
soft drink	soda, pop
spirits	liquor
sultanas	raisins
sweets	candy
swiss roll	jelly roll
swede	rutabaga
takeaway	fast food
whiskey cocktail	highball
with ice	on the rocks

Some foods are characteristically British:

bubble and squeak (fried mashed potato and cabbage)
Cornish pasty (meat and vegetables in pastry)

Lancashire hotpot (type of stew with layers of meat, onions and potatoes)
stout (type of beer)
Yorkshire pudding (baked batter eaten with meat and gravy)

(An interesting phenomenon is the proliferation of words for types of bread: *bap*, *barm bread*, *bridge roll*, *bun*, *cob*, *granary*, *oven bread*, *shuttle*, *soda bread*... many of which are regionally marked.)

There are also some characteristically American foods:

blueberry pie
corn bread
hominy grits (cooked corn kernels)
pumpkin pie
root beer (carbonated soft drink)

See: **Americanism, Anglicism, meals, UK and US words**.

footnotes

A *footnote* is a reference or explanation usually occurring at the bottom of a page. The style of a footnote should follow established conventions so that the reader may use the information easily and profitably. This style should also be consistent with that used for references and bibliographical details.

It is essential to acknowledge your sources not only when you quote directly from another writer but also when you rephrase or paraphrase what someone else has written. Cite the original source of a **quotation**, naming a secondary source only when the primary source is unobtainable. If you do not acknowledge your debt to another writer you may be accused of **plagiarism**. It is not, however, necessary to give references to familiar sayings, line references for very short poems, or detailed information about something that is widely accepted as common knowledge.

Footnotes must be numbered consecutively throughout an article or chapter. Never number notes by pages. Type each number in arabic numerals, slightly above the line, after any punctuation. Do not use full stops or parentheses with the footnote numbers. The footnotes themselves may be typed at the end of each chapter or article. If they are printed in this position they are often known as *endnotes*. If footnotes are typed at the foot of the page (in a **dissertation**, for example), they should be in single spacing with a triple space between the text and the first footnote and with a double space between footnotes. The first line of the footnote should be indented five spaces, and the footnote number should be slightly raised and separated from the note by one space.

See: **abbreviations, bibliography, dissertation, quotation, typescript**.

foregrounding

Foregrounding is a stylistic term with two main implications.

1 Its broader implication refers to ways in which linguistic details may be emphasised. This type of foregrounding involves **deviation** from an established **norm** and may be illustrated by the disruption of the rhythmic pattern in a poem, by heavily punctuated passages in a novel, by the occurrence of patterned **alliteration,** by the use of incongruous **collocations** or by violating the set conventions for the representation of speech and narrative. It is a means of establishing a hierarchy of significance whereby the reader is consciously or unconsciously made aware of the structural and/or semantic priorities of the writer. In 'The Outing: A Story', for example, Dylan Thomas uses unconventional narrative techniques to foreground his ideas:

> *If you can call it a story. There's no real beginning or*
> *end and there's very little in the middle. It's all about*
> *a day's outing, by charabanc, to Porthcawl, which, of course,*
> *the charabanc never reached, and it happened when I was so*
> *high and much nicer.*

2 The narrower meaning of *foregrounding* (or *fronting*) refers to changes in **word order** whereby an object, complement or other sentence component is shifted to the beginning of a sentence or poetic line for **emphasis**:

> *A fool he called me.*
> *A gold medal was what he won.*
> *It was the butler he saw.*

A good example of foregrounding is attributed to St Philip Neri who, on seeing a criminal taken to the scaffold, said:

> *There but for the grace of God go I.*

Foregrounding is frequently used for emphasis in poetry:

> *No longer mourn for me when I am dead,*
> *Than you shall hear the surly sullen bell*
> *Give warning to the world that I am fled*
> *From this vile world with vilest worms to dwell.*
>   Shakespeare, Sonnet 71

It often occurs in informal speech:

> *That I must see.*
> *Found her, did you?*

and in humorous prose (often combined with other devices such as functional shift and word play):

> *The spectacle that followed is already a legend of awfulness.*

*A man called Wolper, famous for such things, devised it, and
this was, one trusts, his masterpiece. Wolper than this
we do not get. This was the Wolpest. You thought 76
trombones was the conventional showbiz hyperbolic maximum?
Shame on you! Wolp had ordered 96. Hell, there were 48
sousaphones. And 144 trumpets. A gross, I believe
it's called.*
    Observer, 5 August, 1984, p.22

See: **cleft sentence, deviation, Irish English, Yiddish influences.**

foreign words in English

English speakers have always borrowed words from other languages
and indeed an examination of the *foreign words found in English*
provides interesting insights into the contacts made by speakers of
English and their attitudes to the people and items contacted.

The process of anglicising the pronunciation (and sometimes the
spelling) of a borrowed word is erratic. Words in popular use (*café,
parka/anorak*) are easily absorbed, whereas those limited in use may
retain their non-English spelling and pronunciation (*Angst, con-
sommé, sotto voce*). In the written medium, words that are still regarded as foreign are italicised. Pronunciation is a useful guide to
what is and what is not regarded as foreign although it is not
infallible. (Some speakers, for example, still rhyme *trait* with *day*
while others rhyme it with *date.*) Another guide is pluralisation and
agreement (*cactuses, this data is available..., lingua francas*).

Some speakers include foreign words in their English for reasons
of prestige. French and Latin, for example, are still associated with
culture, education and privilege and it is not uncommon in parliamentary debates in Britain to find an educated speaker attempting
to put an uneducated colleague at a disadvantage by using such
fixed phrases as:

a fortiori (with stronger reason)
a priori (from the former)
amour propre (self esteem)
bête noire (pet hate)

The inclusion of such phrases may be more a symptom of snobbery
than of education and may be more useful for communicating attitude than meaning. There is no intrinsic merit in peppering one's
English with foreign words or phrases. Many have become part of
the language and may be used freely but others that are intended to
put a listener at a disadvantage should be avoided.

See: **accent marks, borrowing, italics.**

foreword, preface

A *foreword* is an introductory essay or statement at the beginning of a book and is normally written by someone other than the main author of the work. In contrast, a *preface* is an introduction to a book, article or thesis written by the author. A preface usually includes the author's aims, refers to any points of difficulty or dispute, comments on any assistance received, and acknowledges permission to reprint anything in the copyright of another author.

formal English

In the spectrum of English **styles**, *formal English* is at the opposite end to **slang**. It is characterised by particular choices at all levels of the language: slower speech with less **assimilation** and vowel reduction; choice of words (*acquire/receive* instead of *get*, *enjoyable* instead of *nice*); **formulas** (*Dear Sir/Madam, Yours faithfully*); syntactic choices (infrequent use of first person singular pronoun, full negative form *not*, occurrence of passives); and longer, more complex sentences. Formal English is suitable for academic writing, business **letters**, job applications, speeches, and in contexts in which ceremony and impersonality predominate.

Formal English is in no way superior to informal English. Each is appropriate to a particular context and the use of formal English in a context where it is not required is as inappropriate as the wearing of a heavy coat on a hot day.

See: **colloquial English, register, style.**

formula

The plural is *formulae* in **scientific** or **formal English** and *formulas* in other contexts. Formulaic patterns occur in all languages and help individuals to deal with conventional encounters. Often, slight variations in a formula can indicate different levels of formality : *Dear Sir* is formal and impersonal, whereas *Dear Bob* is informal and friendly.

Many formulas are phatic, easing interpersonal transactions: *Hello!, Hi!, How are you?, How do you do?, You're welcome! I'm sorry for your trouble/I'd like to express my sympathy on your recent bereavement.* Some are not meant to be taken literally. *How do you do?*, for example, does not invite detailed information on one's health.

See: **phatic communion.**

functional shift

Functional shift describes the movement of a word from one **class** to another. For example, a noun such as *sandwich* is now frequently used as a verb:

*I was **sandwiched** between two of the biggest men I've ever seen.*

A similar shift is apparent with trade names as in:

*Will you **hoover** the floor for me?*

and:

*Did you **Maclean** your teeth today?*

The shifts can be from noun to verb (as above), verb to noun (*drive-in, take-away*), adverb to verb (*He has upped the prices.*), adjective to noun/verb (*This green has a lot of yellow in it./The Greening of America*), conjunction to noun (*You and your ifs and buts!*) and almost any word can be turned into a verb if slotted into the frame:

I'll ——— you!

A functional shift that is considered unacceptable is known as an *impropriety*. A word may be acceptable in one region and an impropriety in another. The verb *suicide* is generally considered an impropriety in the UK, but is fully accepted in the USA where, according to *Webster's Ninth Collegiate Dictionary*, it was first recorded in 1841. Some usages are borderline (e.g. *to author, to deadpan*) and others seem to have little chance of being adopted: we have *to bugle/drum/fiddle/pipe/trumpet/whistle* but not **to cello/guitar/piano*. Usefulness often determines whether or not a functional shift is accepted but there is an arbitrary element here as in other types of **word formation**.

With many English words we cannot be absolutely sure which class the word first appeared in, but in contemporary English the tendency is usually to shift from noun to verb. This movement may reflect our need to name new objects, discoveries and inventions (*satellite, orbit, shuttle*) and then, as these become familiar, our need to refer to their functions. Thus we have first a *tape-recorder* and then *to tape-record/tape*. Many such changes are quickly accepted because of their wide applicability.

If used to excess, the practice of functional shifting may lead to confusion. It can also, however, be a source of succinctness in the language.

See: **multifunctionality, word formation.**

fused sentence

The terms *fused* and *run-on* sentence are applied to a sentence such
as the following from a major newspaper:

> *Yorkshire were always up with the required scoring*
> *rate, their biggest enemy was the weather.*

which consists of two sentences and should have a conjunction, a
semi-colon or a full stop/period after 'rate'.

Fused sentences should be avoided.

See: **sentence**.

future

In some languages, *future* **time** is signalled by a change in the form
of the verb:

English	French	Latin	Spanish
I see	*je vois*	*video*	*veo*
I shall see	*je verrai*	*videbo*	*vere*

In English, futurity does not involve a modification of the headverb
as it does in French, Latin and Spanish. It is most frequently signalled
by five patterns, all of which tend to collocate with such temporal
adverbials as *soon, tomorrow, next week*.

1 will/shall + the **base form** of the headverb:

> *She will do her best.*
> *We shall succeed.*

Traditionally, *will* was said to mark futurity with second and third
person subjects:

> *you/he/she/it/they will go*

whereas 'shall' occurred with first person subjects:

> *I/we shall go.*

but there is considerable regional variation regarding the use of
will/shall, with 'will' being the preferred form, irrespective of subject,
in Ireland, Scotland and parts of the USA. In formal writing, it is still
advisable to follow the rule, but in speech the problem disappears
because '*ll* is used irrespective of person:

> *I'll go and he'll go and she'll go. In fact, we'll all go.*

2 BE going + to infinitive:

> *I'm going to work harder next year.*

There are a number of variants of this pattern including:

BE about to: *He's about to retire.*
BE on the point of: *He's on the point of retiring.*
BE to: *He's to retire.*

3 BE + the present participle of the headverb:

I'm resigning next month.
He's arriving this afternoon.

4 will/shall/'ll + be + present participle of the headverb:

He'll be arriving on the noon train.
I shall be wearing black.
They'll be leaving soon.

5 the non-past **tense**:

He leaves for Paris at dawn.
She arrives tomorrow.

See: **auxiliary, head, tense, verb.**

Gambian English

The population of the Gambia (West Africa) is approximately 600,000 and the official language is English. The Gambia came under British jurisdiction as early as 1588 and was governed for parts of the eighteenth and nineteenth centuries as part of the Crown Colony of Senegambia. It gained its independence in 1965.

Apart from *Gambian English*, which forms part of the spectrum of **West African Englishes**, there are two useful **lingua francas**, namely Wolof (an African language which is frequently used between anglophone Gambians and francophone Senegalese) and Aku, an English-related **creole**, derived from Sierra Leone Krio.

See: **creole, pidgins and creoles, Sierra Leone English, West African English.**

gender

The word *gender* is used in linguistics as a means of classifying nouns into such categories as masculine, feminine or neuter. There are essentially two types of gender:

1 natural gender, where the sex of the item in the real world determines its classification in a language. Thus, in English, a woman is a **female** and is classified as being *feminine* and a man is a male and is classified as being *masculine*.

2 grammatical gender, which has little or nothing to do with sex

in the real world but where the term *feminine*, for example, is applied because a word has a particular ending (Latin *insula* meaning 'island') or because it may be modified by the feminine form of an article or adjective as in Spanish:

Esta naranja es muy cara. (This orange is very dear.)

Unlike languages such as Latin or French, English makes little use of grammatical gender. Nouns are either masculine, feminine or neuter and they take the appropriate pronoun:

The man was tired. **He** *had been awake all night.*
The woman was tired. **She** *had been awake all night.*
The dog was tired. **It** *had been awake all night.*

There are, however, some exceptions to this pattern.

Some nouns refer to animate beings of indeterminate sex (*baby, cat, child, member, parent, pet, student*). Ignorance or options concerning the sex of the referent can lead to awkwardness about *he or she* since there is no singular pronoun serving both. Increasingly, *they* is being used as a singular for this purpose:

Will each individual please check that **they** *have completed the necessary forms.*

Many guides to usage repeat that *he* has traditonally served for references to both sexes, a practice that was introduced into English in the seventeenth century.

Feminine endings and masculine and feminine forms of nouns do occur, but they are unsystematic and are declining in popular use (*waitress, actress, comedienne, lady doctor*). Most poetesses and actresses would prefer to be called poets and actors, and so, incidentally, be taken more seriously. Where the gender distinction persists, it is usually socially significant as in such sets as:

lord lady
duke duchess
king queen

Certain machines or vehicles over which man has traditionally had control are referred to as *she*, namely ships, motorbikes and, to a lesser extent, cars. In a similar way, the sun (powerful) and day (light, pleasant) have been depicted in English literature as masculine, whereas the moon (weaker) and night (dark, less pleasant) have been portrayed as feminine. West African Pidgin English takes this a step further, calling the right hand *manhan* and the left *wumanhan*. The perception of a country as masculine or feminine probably reveals something about national parental or sex roles: Germany, for example, is a fatherland, whereas Ireland is Mother Ireland or 'Dark Rosaleen'.

See: **female, sexist language.**

genitive

The term *genitive* is normally applied to a case ending which is attached to **nouns** to indicate **possession**:

John's book
It is John's.

In English, there are two methods of indicating possession:

the dog's tail
the tail of the dog

and it is the first method, signalled by the case ending *'s* which is referred to as the genitive **case**. The *'s* method of indicating possession is more likely to be used with animate nouns:

John's foot
the cat's foot/paw
the foot of the hill

The genitive marker can be attached to phrases:

the King of England's six wives
the man at the bottom of the street's wife

although this phenomenon is more likely to occur in speech than in writing. The *'s* marker is also frequently attached to temporal nouns to indicate relationships such as duration:

a day's time (i.e. within a period of twenty-four hours)

and appropriateness:

a winter's tale (i.e. a tale suitable for winter).

See: **apostrophe, case, of, possession.**

gerund

The name *gerund* is given to **-ing forms** which are derived from **verbs** and which can function as nouns:

Being and doing are more important than having.

Although gerunds function as nouns, they retain some of the attributes of verbs in that they can often take an object:

Smoking cigarettes can seriously affect your health.

and be modified by an adverb:

Smoking regularly can seriously affect your health.

When gerunds occur in such structures as:

He does not approve of my smoking.

the possessive adjective is frequently replaced in colloquial speech by an object pronoun:

> *He does not approve of me smoking.*

The possessive form of the adjective is more acceptable in formal contexts but the object pronoun is widely used in what Henry Sweet describes as 'the speech of slippered ease'.

See: **-ing forms, noun, verb.**

GET

GET is perhaps the most frequently used **verb** in English. It has such a wide range of literal and metaphorical meanings that it is possible to construct a lengthy utterance without using any other verb:

> *When it got light, he got up and got dressed quickly. He*
> *got himself some breakfast, got his papers together and*
> *got ready for work. He got a newspaper at the corner, got*
> *the 7.20 bus to town and got to his office by 7.50. After*
> *getting the lift to the sixth floor he got to his desk by*
> *his usual time and got down to the job at once.*

Because GET is so frequently used in speech, it has often been criticised in writing and teachers have warned generations of children to avoid *get* and **nice**. It is stylistically inappropriate to overuse any word but it is equally inappropriate to avoid GET altogether.

GET can occur in five main structures:

1 with a direct object where it can mean 'acquire, catch, gain possession of, obtain, receive':

> *He **got** a prize for his poem.*
> *They all **got** a cold.*

2 with a direct object + a to-infinitive it is equivalent to 'cause, persuade':

> *She **got** him to stop smoking.*

3 with a direct object + adjective/adverb/preposition phrase it means 'cause to become, come or go':

> *I **got** my shoe wet.*
> ***Get** the children out.*
> ***Get** it out of the house.*

4 with an auxiliary + a direct object/to-infinitive/past participle it is the equivalent of 'have':

> *I've **got** $20.*
> *He's **got** to go.*
> *You should **get** those repairs done now.*

5 with a direct object + a past participle it can function like a passive:

*She has **got** herself elected.*
*He **got** his son suspended.*

In **UK English**, the past tense and past participle of *get* are identical:

*I **got** a letter from him this morning.*
*I've **got** a new computer.*

In **US English**, *gotten* is used as the past participle:

*I've **gotten** a new computer.*
*He's **gotten** a big raise in pay.*

It is not used, however, when *have got* means 'must':

*I've **got** to go.*

See: **prime verbs, UK and US words, US English.**

Ghanaian English

Ghana in West Africa has a population of approximately 12 million, many of whom speak the official language of the country, English. Britain established six coastal settlements in Ghana in the seventeenth century and English was acquired by many Ghanaians as a second language. The quality of *Ghanaian English* has always been closely modelled on British **norms** and Ghanaians tend to pride themselves on the excellence of their English. The country attained independence in 1957 and English has continued to be the most widely-used language in education, politics, commerce and literature.

See: **African English, West African English.**

gobbledygook

The word *gobbledygook* was coined by a Texan congressman, Maury Maverick, to describe the verbose, pompous language of official communications. Such language is often meaningless to the average user of English but continues to be used in official documents, possibly as a way of impressing the lay person.

In many countries the Plain English Campaign has tried to counter the worst effects of gobbledygook by writing 'translations' of the more confusing official forms and documents and by offering advice on how such forms should be written.

Gobbledygook can be wasteful of both time and money. *The Guardian* (24 July, 1979), for example, describes how the Department of the Environment produced a form for a loft insulation scheme which was so confusing that thousands of forms were incorrectly completed. Salford Council printed a special guide to accompany the form but no one could understand that either!

Obviously, it would be simpler and more economical if official, legal and business documents could be written in clear, intelligible English in the first place. We would then be spared the verbal inflation which can transform seven words from the Lord's Prayer:

> *Give us this day our daily bread*

into the following seventy-six:

> *We respectfully petition, request and entreat that due and*
> *adequate provision be made, this day and the date hereinafter*
> *subscribed, for the satisfying of these petitioners'*
> *nutritional requirements and for the organising of such*
> *methods of allocation and distribution as may be deemed*
> *necessary and proper to assure the reception by and for said*
> *petitioners of such quantities of baked cereal products as*
> *shall, in the judgment of the aforesaid petitioners,*
> *constitute a sufficient supply thereof.*
> The Observer, 27 February, 1977

See: **circumlocution, jargon.**

gofer

Gofer (also *gopher*) derives from *go for* and refers to someone who runs errands:

> *As well as two people at the desk, we're going to need a gofer.*

The word probably became popular not only because it filled a gap, but also because it sounds the same as *gopher* (a small burrowing animal). Less common analogous forms are *dufer* (do for) and *godufer* (go do for).

good

Good is normally used as an **adjective** or **noun**:

> *They did a good job.*
> *Your work is not good.*
> *It's for your own good.*

Both *good* and *well* can be used to express physical states:

> *I feel good.*
> *I feel well.*

with *good* in such contexts being equivalent to a more emphatic *well*.

Occasionally and mostly in speech, *good* occurs as an **adverb**:

I do it good.
He was fixed good and proper.

Such usage is to be avoided in formal contexts.
Good can be used as an adjectival intensifier in such sentences as:

We walked a good six miles.
You stayed a good three hours.

See: **adjective, adverb, better.**

gradable

Gradable has three main uses:

1 It can be applied to **adjectives** and **adverbs** to describe the fact that they can occur in positive, comparative and superlative forms:

Positive	Comparative	Superlative
big	bigger/less big	biggest/least big
likely	more/less likely	most/least likely

2 The term is used in semantics to refer to adjectives like *good/bad*, *high/low*, *soft/hard* which have no absolute values. A *big fly* is smaller than a *small bird* because *big* is understood to imply 'big in the context of flies'. These adjectives are often described as 'implicitly graded adjectives' and they are different from adjectives such as *male/female* which are absolute. To state, for example:

X is not male.

implies:

X is female.

but to state:

X is not bad.

does not imply:

X is good.

3 It is occasionally applied to **parts of speech** which can substitute for each other but which differ in degree:

a	chip	of	very	nice marble
a	piece	of	terribly	nice marble
a	block	of	extraordinarily	nice marble

See: **adjective, adverb, antonym, comparison of adjectives and adverbs, degree, semantics.**

graduate

Although the essential meaning of *graduate* is shared by speakers in the UK and the USA, there are a number of differences in usage.

The noun *graduate* (pronounced /ˈgrædʒʊət/) normally refers to the holder of an academic degree:

*She is a **graduate** of Delhi University.*

In the UK a person who is studying for a higher degree is normally referred to as a *postgraduate* whereas *graduate* suffices in the USA.

The commonest use of the verb *graduate* (pronounced /ˈgrædʒʊeɪt/) in both the UK and the USA is as an intransitive verb with the meaning of 'receive an academic degree':

*They **graduated** from Harvard in 1976.*

In the USA, the verb can also be used transitively to mean 'grant an academic degree':

*They **graduated** 600 students.*

See: **degrees, education.**

grammar

The word *grammar* is not an easy one to define because it has been used to comprehend many different facets of, and approaches to, language. Yet all definitions of *grammar* have one thing in common: they all deal with the ways in which larger units of language such as **sentences** are constructed from smaller units.

1 *Normative (Prescriptive) Grammar* implies the body of rules necessary to use the language 'correctly'. Such grammars tend to *prescribe* not *describe* socially-acceptable usage. They tell us, for example, that:

To whom did you refer?

and:

He is taller than I.

are correct, whereas:

Who did you refer to?
He is taller than me.

are incorrect. Normative grammars are unpopular in academic circles today but, although they were aimed at the middle classes and at people who were attempting to better themselves, the core of what they taught was accurate.

2 *A Descriptive Grammar* tends to be based on a corpus (speech or

writing or both). It does not prescribe any particular usage but may generalise from the particular corpus studied to the language as a whole.

3 *A Comparative/Contrastive Grammar* compares/contrasts two languages, A and B, usually to help speakers of A acquire B or vice versa. Such grammars tend to point out the areas of potential difficulty likely to be met by speakers of A (or B) as they learn language B (or A).

4 *A Pedagogic Grammar* is designed specifically for teaching purposes and so may grade the language in terms of what is easy to learn. A grammar that concentrates on teaching a particular section of English, for example, to a special group of people such as scientists or economists is often described as ESP (English for Special/Specific Purposes).

5 *Intuitive Grammar* is the innate knowledge of a language possessed by a native speaker, a knowledge which enables a speaker to make 'infinite use of finite means' by producing and understanding acceptable utterances and to evaluate degrees of acceptabilty by recognising, for example, that:

   a flaming fist

is more acceptable than:

   **a foot fist*
   **flaming fist a*

6 *A Theoretical Grammar* attempts to theorise about the nature of Language as well as about individual languages. Such grammars often deal with the common denominators that are found in all human languages.

7 *Transformational* (*Generative*) *Grammars* postulate two levels of language (surface structure and **deep structure**) and attempt to relate the levels systematically.

In many UK grammars, the term *grammar* tends to refer to one level of language only, namely **syntax** (i.e. all that is not **phonology** and all that is not **semantics**). Increasingly, however, and especially in US grammars the term comprehends all levels of language:

   Phonology—the study of sounds and sound patterns
   Morphology—the study of words and affixes
   Syntax—the study of groups of words
   Semantics—the study of meaning

and models of grammar try to reproduce the native speaker's ability to associate sound with meaning and meaning with sound.

See: **linguistics, transformational grammar.**

guess

The expression *I guess* is a colloquial discourse marker popularised by speakers of US English. It is similar in function to:

> *I believe/feel/imagine/reckon/suppose*
> *in my opinion/view*
> *it seems to me*

and serves to make an assertion less dogmatic:

> *I guess you're right.*
> *You're right, I guess.*

See: **shibboleth, UK and US words.**

Guyanese English

The *Co-operative Republic of Guyana*, formerly *British Guiana*, was a British colony from 1814 until 1966 when it gained its independence. It became a republic within the Commonwealth in 1977. The population of under 1 million has English as an official language but many Guyanese speak an English-related **creole**, called Creolese.

See: **Caribbean English, pidgins and creoles, West Indian English.**

Gypsy/gypsy

The word *Gypsy* derives from *Egyptian* because it was believed that the Romani people came from Egypt. In fact, they came from India and the Romani language has still a great deal in common with other Indic languages such as Hindi and Sanskrit.

When the word is used to refer to a Romani, then an upper case 'G' should be used, just as it is when we refer to an *American*, a *Canadian*, a *Catholic* or a *Jew*, because the word *Gypsy* covers both race and culture.

Because Gypsies have often been treated as social outcasts, the term *gypsy* has been extended to include 'wanderer, wanton, untrustworthy' and the derived verb:

> *I was **gypped**.*

is as racist and offensive as the equivalent:

> *I was **jewed** out of it.*

See: **Anglo-Romani, racist language.**

h silent and dropped

The initial *h* is often silent in words originally borrowed from French:

heir(loom)
honest
hour

and this usage, together with the regional (and nonstandard) tendency to drop initial *h* from words like:

ham
house
husband

has caused some confusion in the pronunciation of words beginning with the letter *h*. The confusion is not limited to individuals: Webster's dictionary recommends *an historic occasion* but not *an hotel* while Collins's dictionary prefers *a historic decision*.

The rule formerly applied was that *an* should be used before a word beginning with *h* when the initial syllable was unstressed:

an habitual offender
an hereditary title
an historian
an hotel
an hysterical outburst

This rule is gradually disappearing and *h* is being treated like other consonants.

The social stigma attached to dropping initial *h* has resulted in **hypercorrections** where an *h* is prefixed to words (*heggs* for *eggs*) which should not have them. The pronunciation of *h* as *haitch* and not *aitch* is also a hypercorrection.

See: **accent, hypercorrection, shibboleth.**

hardly, scarcely

Hardly and the more formal *scarcely* are somewhat unusual **adverbs** in that they can cause inversion when used as temporal adverbs:

...Hardly are those words out
When a vast image out of Spiritus Mundi
Troubles my sight...
    W.B. Yeats, 'The Second Coming'

and they overlap with negatives and resemble some modals in their ability to introduce shades of doubt into a sentence:

He was not a fiend.

He may not have been a fiend.
He was hardly a fiend.

They may function as adverbs of degree:

*We could **hardly** bear to wait.*
*I can **scarcely** hear you.*

in which role they tend to occur after the subject and auxiliary (if there is one) but before the headverb (cf. *almost, nearly, quite*). In this role, they carry a **negative** implication (cf. *barely, rarely, seldom*) but denote not an absolute negative (such as *not, never*) but a degree of negativity ('almost not'):

*We **scarcely** knew him.*
*That's **hardly** fair.*

and are approximately equivalent to:

We almost didn't know him.
That's almost unfair.

They may also function as temporal adverbs, usually co-occurring with the past perfect and a *when* clause:

*I had **hardly** opened the letter when I realised my mistake.*
*They had **scarcely** spoken when their differences became apparent.*

These usages are similar to constructions involving *no sooner*, which however takes a *than* clause:

I had no sooner opened the letter than I realised my mistake.

The essential function of words like *hardly* and *scarcely* is to provide a degree of subtlety or uncertainty that the absolute contrasts of positive and negative do not allow.

See: **adverb, head, modality, negation.**

HAVE

HAVE is a **prime verb,** is irregular in its **morphology:**

Non-past: (I/you/we/they) *have,* (he/she/it) *has*
Past/Past Participle: *had*
Present Participle: *having*

and can function as both as an **auxiliary:**

*She **has** been all round the world.*

and as a full verb:

*He **has** a lovely home.*

As an auxiliary, HAVE

1 occurs in Position 2 of the **Verb Phrase** if there is a modal:

*We may **have** seen an intruder.*

2 triggers off the past participle of the verb that follows:

*You could **have** hidden.*

3 can occur in non-finite constructions:

***having** seen the problem*
***to have** played for the Barbarians*

4 can be followed directly by *not/n't*:

*I **have** not (haven't) heard the results yet.*

5 can exhibit past/non-past contrasts when it occurs initially in the verb phrase:

*He **has** sung.*
*He **had** sung.*

6 can exhibit morphological changes in the non-past, depending on the number and person of the subject:

*I/you/we/they **have** seen the film.*
*John/Mary/it **has** seen the mouse.*

There are some differences between UK and US uses of HAVE as a full verb. Generally, speakers of **UK English** do not use the dummy auxiliary with HAVE:

UK	USA
Have you any wool?	*Do you have any wool?*
Has she a computer?	*Does she have a computer?*

In colloquial speech in the UK *HAVE got* is the preferred form:

Have you got any wool?
Has she got a computer?

See: **auxiliary, GET, UK and US grammar**.

head

If we look at the sentence:

That young man in blue may have seen the Boston burglar.

we can isolate two **noun phrases**:

that young man in blue
the Boston burglar

and one **verb phrase**:

may have seen

Each phrase has a *head* or *headword*, the element of central importance around which other elements may cluster in a fixed order. In
our example, the heads are *man*, *burglar* and *seen*.

A noun head or headnoun can be a proper noun:

ancient Egypt

a pronoun:

it

a deverbal noun (or **nominalisation**):

our arrival

or a common noun:

the tree on my left

The order of items in a noun phrase is:

Determiner + Modifier(s) + Head + Modifier(s)

where only the head is absolutely obligatory:

D	M	H	M
the	mythical	man	in the moon
a	short, fat	man	on my left
		man	

The headword or headverb in a verb phrase is the unit which occurs
finally:

Modal + Auxiliary HAVE + Auxiliary BE_1 + Auxiliary BE_2 + Head

and where the head alone is obligatory:

Modal	HAVE	BE_1	BE_2	H
may	have	been	being	watched
	has	been	being	watched
may		be		watched
		is	being	watched
				watched

See: **auxiliary, noun phrase, verb phrase.**

headlines

The language of *headlines* shares many features with **journalese**
and with advertising: use of **abbreviations, acronyms, alliteration,**

ambiguity, rhyming, **puns**, unusual **word order** and simple (often predictable) vocabulary. It has, however, a number of features which allow us to discuss headlines as a sub-genre of journalism.

1 Not only are the words in headlines often short, but they are frequently used as shorthand sensationalism:

*Blazing busman **horror***
Blood** flows in Brixton's **orgy** of **violence
*Five burned to death in **sex ban fury***

Words commonly occurring in such contexts are: *curb, cuts, horror, freeze, mole* (i.e. 'spy'), *orgy, probe, snag, switch, vow.*

2 The grammar of headlines results from a desire to create a strong impact in a short space. Subjects and auxiliaries may be omitted:

[Miners have been] *Starved back to work*

as may copulas:

Shaun [is] *on right line*

articles:

[A] *Tight rein for Robert*

and genitives:

Maggie['s] *praise for pit war police*

3 A headline may consist of a series of nouns, sometimes as many as four:

Leeds Bus Crash Drama
Motorway Madness Fog Pileup

These are often difficult to unravel.

4 If a finite verb occurs, the non-past tense is preferred:

*Martina **wins** again*

but non-finite verbs are common:

*No-go areas **ruled** out*

and futurity is frequently signalled by an infinitive:

*Government **to be asked** for help*

See: **journalese, telegraphese.**

hear, listen (to)

The verb *HEAR* implies perceiving sounds whereas *LISTEN* implies making a conscious effort to hear:

*We **heard** the sound of the boys talking.*
*We **listened** to what they were saying.*

When the emphasis is on the receiver's effort, LISTEN is used. Thus, we may *hear* a talk, recital, performance or broadcast but *listen* to records when we play them ourselves. This distinction is similar to that between SEE and LOOK (at).

HEAR is used with the meaning of 'perceive with the senses' in some varieties of English such as the pidgins used in Cameroon and Vanuatu. This meaning is apparent in the Cameroonian proverb:

Man wei i bɔn i biabia na i go fɔs hia di smɛl.
(One who burns his beard will first notice the smell.)

Similarly, in Standard English, HEAR can have a wider application than aural perception when it is used as a loose synonym for BE-LIEVE:

*I **hear** John has been injured.*

Verbs of perception (HEAR, SEE) rarely occur with progressive aspect whereas LISTEN and LOOK frequently do:

*How can you **hear** when you **aren't listening**?*
*He didn't see me although he **was looking** in my direction.*

See: **aspect, see.**

hendiadys

Hendiadys derives from Greek *hen dia dyoin* meaning 'one through two' and refers to a combination of words such as:

nice and tired

where 'nice and' functions as a modifier of 'tired', the expression meaning 'nicely tired'. Other frequently used examples are:

fine and dandy
good and ready
nice and warm
well and truly

See: **figurative language.**

hiatus

This term is applied to a phonological phenomenon. When two vowels are juxtaposed and both are clearly enunciated, a break occurs between them which is known as *hiatus*. There is, for example, a hiatus after *pre-* in *preempt* and after *re-* in *reassess*. The word *hiatus*, deriving from Latin *hiare* meaning 'to yawn', can be somewhat misleading in that it suggests a gap or silence between two vowels, whereas in normal speech we usually introduce a glide from one to the other.

Different regions deal with hiatus in individual ways. Occasionally the hiatus is reinforced by a glottal stop:

my own > /maɪʔoʊn/

or, in certain contexts, such as:

awe-inspiring
law and order

people from the south of England introduce an intrusive 'r':

awe-rinspiring /ɔrɪnspaɪərɪŋ/
lawrand order /lɔrənɔdə/

In formal speech, it is advisable to employ hiatus between juxta-posed vowels.

See: **elision, intrusive vowels and consonants**.

Hiberno-English

Hiberno-English refers to the English used in Ireland by people whose ancestral mother tongue was Gaelic. It has two main sub-varieties: Southern Hiberno-English, where the strongest non-Gaelic influence is Southern British, and Northern Hiberno-English, where Scottish influence has been strong.

Both sub-varieties are **rhotic** and are marked by:
1 strong **aspiration** of syllable-initial /p,t,k/:

pin /pʰɪn/, *tin* /tʰɪn/, *kin* /kʰɪn/

2 a tendency to use clear l (i.e. the l sound in *light* and not the l sound in *gull*) in all contexts.

3 a tendency to use Gaelic words, albeit with English endings:

banshee (fairy woman) *banshees*
keeny (cry, lament) *keenying*

4 a tendency to use Gaelic-inspired verbal constructions:

She came in and her singing.
I'm after seeing the child.

5 a tendency to use Gaelic-inspired idioms:

There's good buying on the potatoes today.
She hasn't her sorrows to seek.

6 a tendency to use Gaelic-derived metaphors, similes and pro-verbs:

The year is wearing thin.

as mean as get out
There's a truth in the last drop in the bottle.

The easiest way to distinguish between Southern and Northern Hiberno-English is to examine the pronunciation of *three trees*. Speakers of Southern Hiberno-English say:

tree trees

while speakers of Northern Hiberno-English say:

three threes

See: **Anglo-Irish, Irish English.**

hire, lease, let, rent

There is some overlap and a certain amount of confusion on the part of UK and US speakers with regard to the precise usage of these verbs.

Hire is most commonly used to mean 'pay for the temporary use of something':

*We **hired** a marquee for the garden party.*

A second meaning of 'allow the temporary use of something for payment' is less widely used but is perhaps growing in popularity, especially when *hire* co-occurs with *out*:

*We **hired out** the marquee that was badly damaged.*

In the UK *hire* usually refers to a short-term agreement and does not include people or accommodation:

*He **hired** a car/bus/bicycle for a week.*
*The car was **hired (out)** to John Smith.*

In the USA, *hire* is most frequently used to mean 'give a job to someone':

*We should be able to **hire** 400 new workers next year.*
*You're **hired**.*

Lease means 'pay for the use of something for a specified time' or 'allow the paid use of something for a specified time':

*The British **leased** Hong Kong until 1997.*
*The Chinese **leased** Hong Kong to the British until 1997.*

Let meaning 'provide accommodation for an agreed payment' is more common in UK than in US English:

*She **lets** the cottage to the same family every summer.*

Rent like *hire* can mean 'pay for the temporary use of something':

*Mary **rented** the house from her father.*

In UK usage, *rent* usually implies a longer period of time than *hire*:

> We **hired** *a car for a week.*
> We **rented** *the same cottage for twenty years.*

and can be used for accommodation as well as property. In US usage *rent* is common for both short and long-term contracts:

> We **rented** *an automobile for a week.*

See: **antonym, household and accommodation.**

homonym, homograph, homophone

Homonym comes from Greek *homo* (same) + *onyma* (name) and refers to words which have the same spelling and pronunciation but different meanings:

> *post* 1 piece of timber 2 affix to a wall (*post a placard*) 3 send a letter 4 place where soldier is stationed 5 after (*post-war*)

Words which have the same spelling but which differ in meaning, origin and possibly also in pronunciation are called *homographs* (i.e. written the same way):

> *bear* 1 animal 2 endure

Words that are pronounced the same way but which have different meanings, spellings or origins are called *homophones* (i.e. same sounds):

> *pail pale*
> *pair pare*

Words may be homophones in some regions but not in others. In Southern British English, for example, the following are homophones:

> *paw poor pour*

as are:

> *Mary marry merry*

in some speech communities in the USA.

See: **antonym, synonym.**

Hong Kong English

Hong Kong has two official languages, namely Cantonese and English, although Cantonese is much more widely spoken since it is the mother tongue of 98% of the 4+ million people in the colony.

English has considerable prestige in Hong Kong because it is the language of most international trading and a good command of the language is essential in business.

Phonology

The accents of most speakers are influenced by their Cantonese mother tongue and so have much in common with those described for **Chinese English**. In addition, the following tendencies are apparent:

1 the use of fewer vowel contrasts, with /i/ being used for /i/ and /ɪ/, as in *seat* and *sit*, /u/ being used for /u/ and /ʊ/ as in *cooed* and *could* and /a/ being used for both /æ/ and /ɒ/ as in *hat* and *hot*.

2 the use of /o/ and /e/ instead of /oʊ/ and /eɪ/ in words such as *boat* and *bait*.

3 the occasional substitution of /s/ for /ʃ/ so that *ship* sounds like *sip*.

4 the lack of aspiration with initial /p,t,k/ so that mother-tongue speakers of English often hear Hong Kong *pet* as *bet*, *tin* as *din*, *cut* as *gut*. Some speakers use a glottal stop rather than /p,t,k/ when these sounds appear finally in a word:

map > /maʔ/
at > /aʔ/
pick > /piʔ/

5 the occasional substitution of /r/ for /l/:

English > /iŋgriʃ/
willing > /wiriŋ/

6 the simplification of **consonant clusters** either by omitting a consonant at the end of a word (especially when the word ends in /t,d/):

band > /ban/
last > /las/

or introducing a vowel into an initial cluster:

grass > /gᵃras/
state > /sᵉtet/

Vocabulary

1 Vocabulary items have been adopted from Chinese but the popular ones are those which relate to clothing or food and they are widely known throughout the English-speaking world:

cheongsam (dress with high collar and slits in skirt)
chop suey (dish with vegetables and meat)
chow mein (dish with meat, vegetables and noodles)

2 A few examples of China Coast Pidgin English have been recorded in Hong Kong in the 1970s. Among these are the use of *piecee* in counting:

One piecee, two piecee...

and *number one* to mean 'best, excellent'.

3 *Gwailo* meaning 'devil' is occasionally used as a disparaging term for an expatriate.

Grammar
Most users of English approximate to the standard norms in writing but the following features are found in spoken English:

1 a tendency to treat all nouns including *fruit* and *work* as count nouns:

three fruits   four works

2 the recapitulation of the subject:

*My English **it** is not good.*

3 frequent deletion of *a/an*:

I work in office.

4 the occasional use of the wrong third person singular pronoun, with *he* being used for *she*:

*This is my mother. **He** is on holiday here.*

See: **Chinese English.**

hopefully

Hopefully as an **adverb** modifying a verb in such sentences as:

*They waited **hopefully** for their results.*
*It is better to travel **hopefully** than to arrive.*

has always been acceptable. As a sentence **modifier**, equivalent to 'it is to be hoped', *hopefully* has been considered unacceptable by many writers and clumsy by others.

Kenneth Hudson (1977) includes *hopefully* in *The Dictionary of Diseased English*, referring to it as 'German/American' and mentioning 'certain dangers in its use'. *Hopefully* has been criticised in the USA as well as the UK, and *Webster's Ninth New Collegiate Dictionary* (1983) notes 'the irrationally large amount of critical fire' drawn by the usage, critical fire that is not aimed at other similar sentence modifiers such as *fortunately/unfortunately*, *interestingly* and *presumably*.

In spite of all the adverse criticism levelled at *hopefully* it is now firmly established as a sentence modifier throughout the English-speaking world.

See: **adverb, 'chestnuts', dangling modifier, modifier, purist.**

household and accommodation

Many of the terms relating to the structure, functioning and occupation of the home are different in the UK and the USA. The commonest differences are:

UK	USA
aluminium	aluminum
blind (on window)	shade
block of flats	apartment building
camp bed	cot
chest (of drawers)	bureau, dresser
clothes peg	clothes pin
cooker	stove
cot	crib
cupboard	closet
curtains (heavy)	drapes
dummy (for a baby)	pacifier
dustbin	garbage/ash/trash can
eiderdown	comforter/quilt
elastic band	rubber band
estate agent	realtor
first floor	second floor
flat (rented)	apartment
flat (owner occupied)	condominium/condo
garden	yard
ground floor	first floor
hotel rate (+ meals)	European plan
hotel rate (room only)	American plan
kettle	tea kettle
larder	pantry
let	lease/rent
lift	elevator
lodger	roomer
maisonette	flat
methylated spirits/meths	denatured alcohol
net curtains	sheers
paraffin	kerosene
power point/socket	outlet/socket
semi-detached	duplex
sideboard	buffet
single storey open-plan	ranch house

skirting board	baseboard
tap	faucet, tap
(thermos) flask	thermos bottle
washbasin/sink	sink
wash	wash up
wash up	do the dishes
Welsh dresser	hutch

Many of the US terms are widely understood in Britain and other parts of the world and some (e.g. *socket* and *sink*) are replacing their UK equivalents.

See: **Americanism, Anglicism, hire, UK and US words.**

hybrid

A *hybrid* is a word composed of elements from more than one language:

Cumberland—Celtic (Cumbri) + Old English (land)
feminism—Latin (femina) + Greek (-ismos)
Grimstone—Norse (Grim) + Old English (stan)
refill—Latin (re-) + Old English (fyllan)
television—Greek (tele-) + Latin (videre)
womanise—English (woman) + Greek (-izein)

The term is also occasionally applied to a pidgin or **creole** which incorporates elements from two or more languages. A sentence such as:

Wuna bin giv mi palava boku.—You gave me a lot of trouble.

from a West African Pidgin English derives *wuna* from Igbo, *bin*, *giv* and *mi* from English, *palava* from Portuguese and *boku* from French.

See: **pidgins and creoles, word formation.**

hypallage

Hypallage, deriving from Greek *hypo-* (under) + *allassein* (exchange), is a figure of speech in which the attributes of one element of a statement are transferred to another element. Thus a descriptive adjective may be shifted from the noun to which it applies to another noun. A well-known example of such a transferred epithet comes from Gray's *Elegy in a Country Churchyard*:

*The ploughman homeward plods his **weary way**.*

The natural headnoun of 'weary' is 'ploughman' and not 'way' but the adjective is transferred for emphasis.

Other more commonplace examples of hypallage are:

*He bade her a **sad farewell**.*

(presumably it was 'he' and not the 'farewell' that was 'sad')

*There was an **awkward silence**.*

See: **figurative language**.

hyperbole

Hyperbole derives from Greek *hyperbole* meaning 'excess'. It is a figure of speech employing extravagant exaggeration in order to emphasise a detail or a succession of details. We find such colloquial uses of hyperbole as:

There were millions of people in the stadium.
We had a pizza the size of today and tomorrow.
The news spread like a bushfire in a drought.

It is occasionally used in poetry, as when Richard Crashaw in 'The Weeper' describes Mary Magdalen's eyes as:

Two walking baths, two weeping motions,
Portable and compendious oceans.

See: **figurative language**.

hypercorrection

In all speech communities where nonstandard variants exist, certain forms are stigmatised. The stigmatised forms may relate to pronunciation (*girl* rhyming with *oil*, *'ouse* for *house* or *walkin'* for *walking*), to choice of words (*a brave day* for *a fine/good day*, *lonesome* for *lonely*), to prepositional use (*for to go* instead of *to go*, *take for* instead of *take after*), to verb forms (*I seen* for *I saw*, *he shoulda went* for *he should have gone*).

Often, in the process of modifying towards the standard, a speaker will overcompensate and produce hypercorrect forms such as *garding* for *garden*, *heggs* for *eggs* or *I have did/saw*, and speakers who worry about using adjectives as adverbs have produced *more importantly* for *more important*, *thusly* for *thus*, *singlehandedly* for *singlehanded* and *badly* for *bad* as in:

*How are you? Not too **badly**.*

Hypercorrection is common in speakers who are or who would like to be socially mobile upwards.

See: **h silent and dropped, (more) importantly, Standard English**.

hyphenation

Hyphenation refers to the process of joining words or morphemes by means of a hyphen. The word *hyphen* comes from Greek *hypo* (under) + *hen* (one) and it is a **punctuation** mark used to indicate:
 1 **compound** words:

father-in-law
life-form

 2 compound attributive adjectives:

foot-and-mouth disease
mother-tongue speakers

 3 the breaking of a word at the end of a line
 4 the **syllables** in a word:

hy-per-son-ic

Hyphenation is much commoner in compound words in the UK than in the USA.

See: **compound, punctuation, syllable.**

hypothetical

A *hypothetical* situation is one that may or may not occur or have a parallel in the real world. Hypothetical questions/statements often involve the use of an *if* clause and the modal *should/would/'d* in the main clause:

*If you had such power, what **would** you do?*
If I had your talent, I'd be a lot more confident.

When BE occurs in the *if* clause there is a tendency to use *were*, irrespective of the number of the subject, if the hypothesis is far-fetched or improbable:

*If **I** were a blackbird I'd whistle and sing.*
*If **they** were us they'd feel the same.*

In colloquial English, there is a growing tendency to use *was* with first and third person singular subjects, especially when the suggestion is possible:

*If **I** was a teacher I'd have firm ideas on discipline.*

See: **modality, subjunctive.**

-ic, -ical words

Many **adjectives** have two forms, one ending in *-ic* and another in *-ical* (*classic/al, economic/al, historic/al*) and there is no comprehensive rule which allows us to predict which ending is likely to be correct in any specific context. It seems, however, that -ical adjectives are more widely used than -ic adjectives and are also more likely to be used metaphorically:

*Keats has often been praised for his **lyric** gifts.*
*John was **lyrical** in his praise of the meal.*

Some adjectives are only found with an -ic ending: *academic, alcoholic, allergic, analgesic, artistic, Byronic, catholic, dramatic, emphatic, fantastic, ferric, linguistic, phonetic, phonic, tragic, semantic, specific, syntactic, traumatic.* Some of these adjectives used to have -ical endings (*fantastical, tragical*) and some are used in popular speech with -ical endings (*academical, dramatical*) but such forms are regarded as nonstandard. Many recent adjectives are coined with -ic endings only (*bionic, electronic, morphophonemic, synthetic, systemic*).

A number of adjectives occur only with the -ical ending: *clerical, clinical, critical, heretical, geological, grammatical, lexical, musical, physical, radical, technical, topical, tropical.*

A few adjectives can occur with both -ic and -ical endings and with the forms being in free variation: *arithmetic(al), egotistic(al), fanatic(al), geometric(al).* It is probably true that the -ic ending is more likely to occur in the written medium and the -ical variant in the spoken.

A number of frequently occurring adjectives exist in both forms but with a difference in their meanings: *classic(al), comic(al), economic(al), historic(al), lyric(al), politic(al).* The differences may be illustrated by such sentences as:

*His plans make good **economic** sense.*
*He's **economical** to a fault—perhaps 'mean' would be a more accurate label.*
*Tomorrow will be an **historic** occasion—the tenth anniversary of independence.*
*There are quite good **historical** documents from the period.*

Many nouns also end in *-ic*, including *arithmetic, clinic, fanatic, music.*

See: **adjective**.

identifying relative clause

This term is an alternative to **defining clause** and refers to a clause which limits or reduces the scope of the nouns or noun phrases it modifies:

*The women **who wore seat belts** escaped.*

The clause in bold tells us that only those women who wore seat belts escaped.

See: **defining and non-defining clauses.**

idiom

Idiom comprehends the specific characteristics of a language, **dialect** or speech community. Idiom is not based on logic, nor is it the same in two languages or indeed in the same language at different times in its history. It may comprehend the syntactic, lexical and semantic idiosyncrasies of a language and seems to be learnt as we absorb the customs and conventions of our society.

Idiom may change with time. Shakespeare, for example, could form interrogatives and negatives without the use of the dummy **auxiliary DO**:

Like you this?
I like it not.

Today, these structures are unidiomatic, although they are still intelligible.

Idiomatic units may be words, phrases, syntactic structures (as above) or rhetorical devices. For example, we normally say:

*She cares for **sick** children.*

and not:

She cares for **ill children.*

Idiomatically *sick* tends to be used attributively and *ill* predicatively:

*She's a **sick** child.*
*She's very **ill** indeed.*

Similarly, we can say:

*I **bumped into** my friends in town.*

but not (without a marked change of meaning):

I **bumped off/onto/over my friends in town.*

The patterns for **figurative language** and rhetorical devices are also conventionalised. We can transfer epithets, for example, in only very limited ways, so that it is acceptable to say:

*It was a **sad** journey.*

implying that the one who made the journey was sad, but it is not usual to say:

It was an **ebullient journey.*

although the person who made the journey may well have been ebullient.

Because there are no general rules by which we can analogise about idiomatic usages, this area can present particular difficulties for learners of a language. For example, a fluent user of English as a second language may still not be aware that the expression:

*There's **no question** of your doing the book.*

implies a negative and the opposite of what was intended:

*There's **no doubt/debate** that you will do the book.*

Problems of idiom arise in even the most apparently straightforward of statements. Where English has:

I am thirsty.

French has:

J'ai soif (I have thirst).

and Gaelic:

Tá tart orm (BE thirst on me).

and an examination of different translations of the Bible will reveal many differences not only of nuance but of fundamental meaning.

Much of this book is concerned with the idiom of English, the conventions, habits and idiosyncrasies that allow speakers of English to express their aspirations, fears, ideals, prejudices and preoccupations in a unique manner.

See: **hypallage, idioms, synonym.**

idioms

Idioms can be defined as phrases whose meanings cannot be deduced from an understanding of the individual words in the phrase. Thus the following expressions mean 'die':

bite the dust
go to the happy hunting ground

although a knowledge of the meanings of 'bite', 'dust', 'go', 'happy', 'hunting', 'ground' would not help us to interpret the phrases.

Idioms can be totally opaque (i.e. there is no resemblance whatsoever between the meaning of the idiom and the meaning of the individual words):

a hat trick (taking three wickets with successive balls)

semi-opaque (where part of the phrase is used literally):

eat humble pie (forced to behave humbly)

or fairly transparent in terms of **metaphor**:

> *burn the candle at both ends*

Some idioms are totally fixed. We rarely find:
1 word substitution. We can have:

> *kick the bucket*

but not:

> **kick the pail*
> **kick a pail*
> **hit the bucket with the foot*

2 nominalisation. We have:

> *bite the dust*

but not:

> **the biting of the dust*

3 comparatives or superlatives:

> *once in a blue moon*

but not:

> **once in a bluer moon*

4 change of number:

> *raining cats and dogs*

but not:

> **raining a cat and a dog*

Others allow some variation:

> *cut a handsome/fine/sorry figure*
> *blind alley(s)*

The commonest types of idiom are:
1 noun phrases:

> *a wild goose chase*

2 preposition phrases:

> *by the skin of his teeth*

3 rhyming or alliteratively linked phrases:

> *odds and sods*
> *hale and hearty*

4 frequently used **similes**:

> *as fit as a fiddle*

5 verb + adverb:

give in (yield)

6 verb + preposition phrase:

be in the black/pink/red

7 metaphorical use of body parts:

finger a criminal
head for the hills

Colours are sometimes used quasi-idomatically:

white coffee
white wine

are not 'white' and:

red tape

is neither 'red' nor 'tape'.

See: **dyad, metaphor, simile.**

-ie, -o endings

-ie(-y) endings can:
1 indicate affectionate diminutives:

Billie
doggie

2 imply an informal approach to a person's place of origin:

Aussie < from Australia
townie < from a town

3 be used as a mild form of abuse or as a means of reducing fear or tension:

commie < communist
leftie < left of centre politically

-o is less widely used as a **suffix** than *-ie* but it occurs in:

boyo
bucko
cobbo < cobber (friend)

words implying that the person described has all the attributes normally associated with a young man.

Other examples of *-o* as a suffix suggest addiction and disapproval:

dipso < a dipsomaniac
metho < a drinker of meths/denatured alcohol
wino < a drinker of wine

although in Australia the *-o* ending is often used as a simple colloquial ending:

arvo—afternoon
salvo—member of the Salvation Army
smoke-o—tea break

See: **Australian English.**

ill, sick

There is some overlap between these words. They both relate to bad health, with *ill* being the preferred formal variant in the UK.

Ill can refer to a temporary state of discomfort or nausea:

*She felt quite **ill** when she saw their injuries.*

In the UK it can also refer to longer term or serious illnesses:

*He is seriously **ill** and his condition is being monitored every fifteen minutes.*

Ill is normally used predicatively (i.e. after the subject and predicate). In UK usage *sick* has two main implications.
1 When used predicatively, it usually implies vomiting:

*I feel **sick**. I'm going to be **sick**.*
*He's just been **sick**.*

2 When used attributively (i.e. before a noun) it usually refers to chronic or long-term illness:

*She nursed her **sick** husband for eighteen months.*

Ill is the preferred usage and can cover both transitory and chronic bad health. *Sick* is still used, however, in such fixed phrases as:

off sick
on sick leave
a sick joke

In US English *sick* can cover a wider range of illness than in the UK:

*Our teacher is **sick**.*
*I'm **sick** to my stomach.*
*He's a very **sick** man.*

It has also been extended metaphorically to mean 'tired of':

*I'm **sick** of baseball.*

See: **idiom, UK and US words.**

imagery

The term *imagery* occurs frequently in discussions of literature. It is often used vaguely to cover:

1 the descriptive words and phrases in a literary text, especially those relating to the senses:

The sensuous **imagery** *in Keats's 'Eve of St Agnes' in part accounts for the popularity of the poem.*

2 the use of **figurative language,** especially similes and metaphors:

Discuss the thematic **imagery** *in* King Lear.

See: **figurative language, metaphor, simile.**

imperative

Imperative structures are used in giving commands:

Go away.
Don't put it on my chair.

The verb form used in affirmative imperatives is the **base form** of the verb (identical to the **infinitive** without 'to'). In negative imperatives, the base form of the verb is usually preceded by *Don't* but very occasionally negative commands involve *Let* and *May*:

Let *me never hear you say such a thing again.*
May *you never lack company.*

The second person pronoun *you* is not normally used in imperative sentences, although it can occasionally be used for emphasis:

You *come here at once.*

Occasionally, imperative structures do not involve verbs:

Home!
Out!

Such imperatives are indicated by intonation in speech and by an exclamation mark in writing.

The imperative does not show person contrasts because it always implies a second person subject. Nor does it show tense changes, referring always to the future, immediate, proximate or remote:

Do it at once.
Do it as soon as you can.
Do it before you die.

See: **auxiliary, curse and swear, Hiberno-English, indicative, subjunctive.**

imply, infer, insinuate

These three verbs are often confused. They are related in meaning in that they are all associated with the processes by which meaning is conveyed. *Imply* and *insinuate* are concerned with production and *infer* with reception.

Imply derives from Latin *implicare* (to involve) and means 'hint' or 'suggest something indirectly':

> He **implied** that he would not tolerate any opposition.

Infer derives from Latin *in* + *ferre* (to bring in) and means 'deduce' or 'come to a conclusion based on what is implied by someone or something else':

> I can't **infer** anything from such conflicting pieces of data.

Infer has been used so frequently for *imply* that it is possible its specific meaning will be lost.

Insinuate derives from Latin *in* + *sinuare* (to curve) and is closely related to *imply* in that they both specify production. However, *insinuate* normally carries unpleasant, derogatory connotations:

> He **insinuated** that we were little better than liars.

See: **problem pairs.**

(more) importantly

The use of *importantly* instead of *important* as a sentence **modifier** has attracted hostility from **purists**, who object to such sentences as:

> More **importantly**, our exports are being affected.

It is not, however, surprising that people have analogised with pairs of similar words such as:

> *impressive/impressively*
> *notable/notably*
> *serious/seriously*

and created a distinction between *important* used as an adjective and *importantly* used as an adverb.

See: **hopefully, hypercorrection, modifier.**

indicative

The terms *indicative* and *declarative* are interchangeable and refer to verb phrases, clauses and sentences which make statements. They contrast with **imperative, interrogative** and **subjunctive**:

Be a good boy.	Imperative
He is (not) a good boy.	Indicative
Is he (not) a good boy?	Interrogative
If only he were a good boy.	Subjunctive

See: **imperative, interrogative, mood, subjunctive.**

individual

Use of the noun *individual* to mean 'person' has been severely criticised. H.W. Fowler in *A Dictionary of Modern English Usage* (Oxford, Oxford University Press, 2nd ed. revised Ernest Gowers, 1983: 279) quotes a description of *individual* as 'one of the modern editor's shibboleths for detecting the unfit' and the *Oxford English Dictionary* declares its use to be a 'colloquial vulgarism'.

There is little objective evidence to explain why *individual* should have been given such unfavourable attention but as a synonym for *person* as in:

He's a strange individual.

it has been regarded as inferior. The 'proper' use of the noun *individual* is when it contrasts with a group:

In the long term, the new agricultural policy will benefit all farmers, but in the short term individuals may suffer.

It is acceptable, in all but the most formal situations, to use *individual* as a synonym for *person*.

See: **'chestnuts', shibboleth.**

Indo-European

Indo-European is a classification label for a family of related languages, all of which are thought to be descended from Proto-Indo-European as in the following **family tree:**

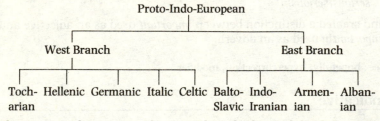

The West and East Branches are then further subdivided so that Celtic comprehends Breton, Irish and Scottish Gaelic and Welsh; Germanic can be subdivided into Danish, Dutch, English, Flemish,

German, Icelandic, Norwegian and Swedish; and Balto-Slavic can be subdivided into Bulgarian, Czech, Latvian, Lithuanian, Polish, Russian and Serbo-Croatian.

Among the languages in Europe which are not classified as Indo-European are Basque and Finnish.

See: **family tree.**

infinitive

This term usually applies to the non-finite part of the verb prefixed by *to*:

to go (simple infinitive)
to have been swimming (complex infinitive)

although some linguists prefer to call such forms *to-infinitives*.
Infinitives are negated by being preceded by *not*:

*I asked him **not to go**.*
*I couldn't persuade her **not to swim**.*

In many languages, the infinitive is a single form:

French	Latin	English
aimer	*amare*	*to love*
porter	*portare*	*to carry*

and such forms could not be split. Because Latin could not have a **split infinitive**, there developed the belief that split infinitives such as:

to boldly go

should be avoided in English. Such usage is common in colloquial English as is the anaphoric use of *to* in such exchanges as:

Why didn't you go?
*I didn't want **to**.*

The to-infinitive can also function as a noun:

***To err** is human.*

See: **split infinitive, verb phrase.**

inflection/inflexion

Inflection (formerly called 'accidence') refers to **suffixes** which do not change word classes but which indicate such relationships as:
    1 plurality:

boy boys

2 possession:

the boy's books
the boys' books

3 tense or aspect:

look looks looked looking

4 grading of adjectives and adverbs:

big bigger biggest
slowly more slowly most slowly

See: **affix, derivation, suffix.**

-ing forms

Traditional grammars divided *-ing forms* such as *dancing* and *walking* into three categories:
 1 present **participles,** where they were part of the **verb phrase**:

*They have been **dancing** together all night.*
*He was **walking** home because he had missed the bus.*

2 **adjectives**:

*I can't find my **dancing**/**walking** shoes.*

3 **gerunds,** -ing forms which functioned as nouns:

***Dancing** is good for you.*
*I enjoy **walking**.*

The term *-ing form* is neutral as to the function of a verb-derived -ing form.
 In Standard English WANT is usually followed by the past participle:

*Do you **want** your windows **cleaned**?*

Increasingly, however, in colloquial UK English, the -ing form is replacing the past participle:

*Do you **want** your windows **cleaning**?*

Many stylists object to this usage but since it is in many instances the preferred form of the young, it is likely to become acceptable.
 Spelling problems can arise when *-ing* is added to certain verbs. The general rules are:
 1 When a verb ends with a silent *e*, the *e* is deleted before *-ing*:

bridge	*bridging*	*live*	*living*
fatigue	*fatiguing*	*sue*	*suing*

The main exceptions to this rule are verbs which end in *ee, inge, oe* and *ye*:

agree	*agreeing*	*see*	*seeing*
singe	*singeing*	*swinge*	*swingeing*
canoe	*canoeing*	*shoe*	*shoeing*
eye	*eyeing*	*dye*	*dyeing*

Where the loss of an *e* would result in ambiguity so that *dying* (ceasing to live) and *dyeing* (colouring) would become identical, the tendency is for the *e* to be retained. Where the loss of the *e* would not cause confusion, as in *eying*, the form without *e* is permitted.

2 When a verb ends in *ie*, the *ie* is replaced by *y* before *-ing*:

die	*dying*	*tie*	*tying*
lie	*lying*	*vie*	*vying*

See: **aspect, gerund, participle, verb phrase.**

innuendo

Innuendo (pl. -oes/-os) is a type of **irony** consisting of an oblique or indirect allusion, often reflecting maliciously or injuriously on a person's character, reputation or ability:

The tenor sang in tune several times during the evening.
He works hard, does everything himself, doesn't like delegating.

Innuendo works by implication rather than by overt comment.

See: **irony.**

instrumental

Many languages can express the relationship 'by means of a noun/with a noun' by using a **case** ending traditionally referred to as *instrumental*. The term is applied in **case grammar** to nouns such as 'hammer' in the following sentences:

*He broke the window with a **hammer**.*
*The **hammer** broke the window.*

The *instrumental* is the case of the inanimate object causally involved in the action of the verb. The term *instrumental* can thus be applied to 'knife' in:

*He opened the moneybox with a **knife**.*

because the **agent** 'he' caused the moneybox to open by using a knife.

See: **case grammar.**

intensifier

The term *intensifier* is normally applied to a set of **adverbs** (e.g. *very*, *terribly*, *too*) which intensify the meaning of an adjective or adverb:

He is $\left\{ \begin{array}{l} \text{very} \\ \text{really} \end{array} \right\}$ funny even though he talks $\left\{ \begin{array}{l} \text{so} \\ \text{very} \end{array} \right\}$ slowly.

The simplest test for an intensifier is to see if it can replace *very*.

In UK usage, a number of intensifiers (e.g. *awfully*, *frightfully*) are class marked. They tend to be used by upper-class speakers and by people who are keen to improve their social standing.

A number of adjectives (e.g. *absolute*, *mere*, *sheer*) which tend to be used attributively have also been described as intensifiers:

*It's **absolute** lunacy!*

See: **adjective, adverb.**

interrogative

The word *interrogative* is applied to **sentences** which ask questions:

Are you tired?

There are two types of interrogative sentence: those like the above which expect a *yes* or *no* answer, and sentences which begin with a **question** word (e.g. *How?*, *When?*, *Who?*, *Why?*) and cannot receive a *yes/no* answer:

Why are you going?

Yes/no questions involve the **inversion** of the subject and predicate when the predicate is BE, HAVE or the modals:

He is handsome. Is he handsome?
He has arrived. Has he arrived?
He can't swim. Can't he swim?/Can he not swim?

DO is required with other verbs:

He likes milk. Does he like milk?

Non-*yes/no* questions involve the use of interrogative adjectives:

*I saw a man. **Which** man did you see?*

interrogative adverbs:

*I saw a man. **When** did you see him?*

and interrogative pronouns:

*He said this. **What** did he say?*

Occasionally, the intonation of questions is used with a declarative structure to form an interrogative sentence:

You're tired?

See: **declarative question, inversion, question, question tag, sentence.**

intonation

Intonation can be most simply described as the melody of speech utterances: a falling melody usually signals statements or questions using question words:

He's coming.   —   ⁻   —

When is he coming?   —   —   _   _   _

and a rising melody tends to indicate a yes/no question:

Is he going?   _   _   —   ⁻

Intonation can also indicate a speaker's attitude to a listener or to the subject matter, since it is involved in implying respect, admiration, insolence, sarcasm, disbelief and enthusiasm.

It seems very likely that intonation may vary between regions, so that one person's request may have the melody of another person's command.

See: **paralinguistic features, tone languages.**

intransitive

This term is applied to **verbs** which do not take an object:

She arrived.
It suddenly emerged

Many verbs in English, especially those involving change or movement, can occur in both **transitive** and intransitive constructions:

*The prior **rang** the bell.*
*The bell **rang**.*

and many others can occur in pseudo-intransitive structures.

*We **eat** at 8.*

is clearly related to:

*We **eat dinner** at 8.*

and:

*The potatoes **are selling** at 20c a pound.*

can be derived from:

> X *is selling potatoes* at 20c a pound.

The difference between a pseudo-intransitive and an intransitive sentence is that a transformed sentence can elicit an object for pseudo-intransitive verbs:

> *What do we eat at 8? Dinner.*
> *What is selling at 20c a pound? Potatoes.*

whereas no object can be elicited for an intransitive verb:

> **What did she arrive?*
> **Whom did it emerge?*

See: **active voice, ergative, transformations, transitive, verb.**

inversion

Inversion involves reversing the order of a series or part of a series:

> *He is clever.* → *Is he clever?* (ABC → BAC)

The commonest form of inversion in English involves changing a statement into a **question** by inverting the subject and BE/DO/HAVE/modals:

He is a fool.	→ Is he a fool?
He doesn't like X.	→ Doesn't he like X?
He has been singing.	→ Has he been singing?
He won't come.	→ Won't he come?/Will he not come?

See: **interrogative, transformations.**

Irish English

English is an official language in Eire (population 3.5 million) and the official language of Northern Ireland (population 1.5 million). *Irish English* is the general term for the various types of English used in the island. These varieties can be simplistically represented as follows:

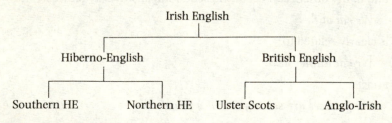

The diagram is oversimplified in that it suggests that the subvarieties are discrete, whereas they influence each other and are all influenced by media norms.

See: **Anglo-Irish, Hiberno-English, Ulster Scots.**

irony

Irony derives ultimately from Greek *eiron* meaning 'dissemble'. The term is applied to a figure of speech which is characterised by being interpretable on at least two levels. For irony to function, both meanings must be understood.

The simplest form of irony is the use of words to imply the opposite of what is actually said. This is also known as sarcasm, and its implication is usually derogatory. For example, to say:

You're a real friend.

to someone who has just let you down is an ironic way of stressing your disapproval of the behaviour. Intonation plays a significant role in sarcasm. Related to this form of irony are excessively polite forms of address (as a put-down):

Well, Mr Brian Jones, I believe you have a complaint.

and mock heroic types of verse, where a trivial subject is discussed in inflated language. Alexander Pope's *Dunciad*, for example, parodies the title of the *Iliad* and the technique of Milton's *Paradise Lost* in such lines as:

High on a gorgeous seat, that far outshone
Henley's gilt tub, or Flecknoe's Irish throne.

Dramatic irony occurs when a character in literature says something which is meaningful at one level to the character and at another level to the reader/audience. In Kenjo Jumbam's novel *The White Man of God*, for example, the events are narrated by a boy who does not fully understand the implications of the adult conversations that he recounts to the reader.

Related to dramatic irony is *tragic irony* or *irony of fate*. This literary convention was popular in Greek tragedy and involves a cruel reversal of fortunes at the very moment when the hero's expectations seem likely to be fulfilled. Such a tragic reversal occurs in *Oedipus Rex* when Oedipus, at the moment of his greatest achievement, discovers that he has unknowingly murdered his father and married his mother.

Socratic irony is often involved in philosophical discussions. It is a method of argument which pretends ignorance in order to question an opponent closely and so reveal his inconsistencies and false assumptions.

Irony need not always be serious or shocking. Nevertheless, because of the power of irony to present an idea from an unusual viewpoint, its most memorable examples tend to make ethical or moral comments.

See: **figurative language, innuendo, parody, problem words, satire.**

irregular verb

Most **verbs** in English are regular in that they form their past tense by adding *-ed* in the written medium, /ɪd, d, t/ in the spoken:

> *pelt* + *ed* /pɛlt + ɪd/
> *stay* + *ed* /steɪ + d/
> *look* + *ed* /lʊk + t/

and their marked non-past by adding *-s* in the written medium, /ɪz, z, s/ in the spoken:

> *bridge* + *s* /brɪdʒ + ɪz/
> *spray* + *s* /spreɪ + z/
> *trick* + *s* /trɪk + s/.

All verbs which do not follow these rules are *irregular*. Some like BE and HAVE are very irregular; others like SAY only slightly irregular.

All new verbs coined since the seventeenth century have been regular and many, such as CLIMB, MELT, SWELL, WREAK, and, more recently, STRIVE have been regularised. Only three verbs have become irregular since the seventeenth century: DIG, SPIT and STICK.

A number of verbs are treated differently (in terms of form) in the UK and the USA, the most widely used of which are:

UK and UK-influenced	US and US-influenced
dive/dived/dived	dive/dove and dived/dived
fit/fitted/fitted	fit/fit/fit
get/got/got	get/got/gotten and got
quit/quitted/quitted	quit/quit/quit
wake/woke/woken	wake/waked/waked

and two have markedly different pronunciations:

UK and UK-influenced	US and US-influenced
ate rhymes with *get*	*ate* rhymes with *gate*
shone with *gone*	*shone* with *bone*

See: **-ed, -t forms, -en forms, GET, verb.**

-ise, -ize

The practice of adding *-ise/-ize* to a noun or adjective to form a verb is well established:

brutalise hospitalise legalise transistorise

The -ise/-ize ending is Greek in origin but it is not restricted to words of Greek origin:

computerise < Latin *computare* (count)
idolise < Greek *eidolon* (phantom)
mesmerise < Dr F.A. Mesmer

A number of **purists** have objected to some -ise/-ize verbs because they duplicate the meanings of other verbs:

finalise = conclude, end, settle

or because they are associated with **jargon**:

politicise

The form -ise is widely used in the UK whereas -ize is preferred in the USA, but there is a growing tendency to prefer the -ize ending even in the UK, except for such verbs as:

advertise	advise	arise
chastise	circumcise	compromise
despise	devise	disguise
excise	exercise	improvise
merchandise	promise	revise
supervise	surmise	surprise

See: **spelling**.

italics

Italics are indicated in manuscripts and **typescripts** by single underlining. Italics should be used sparingly, but convention suggests that the following should be italicised:

1 Titles of published books (but not the Bible, books of the Bible or the Koran), journals, magazines, plays, motion pictures, long poems, operas, ballets and long musical compositions. Quotation marks and not italics are used for the titles of radio and television programmes, articles, chapters and short stories:

Jane Austen's *Emma*
the journal *Abbia*
Tennyson's *In Memoriam*
Handel's *Messiah*
Chapter 4, 'Whatever happened to Mesopotamia?'

2 The names of ships, aircraft and some spacecraft:

HMS *Endurance*
SS *Nimitz*

When an apostrophe s occurs with such a name it is not in italics:

Columbia's home base

3 Foreign words and phrases that have not been assimilated into English. These are not always easy to identify although a non-English pronunciation is a good guide and most dictionaries indicate whether or not italics are needed. Examples are:

billet doux
sine die

Roman script should, however, be used for proper names and for quotations from other languages:

He insisted that the discussions were terminated *sine die*
and added that the striking workers would soon learn the
force of the French proverb 'Tout s'avise a qui pain faut'.

4 In course papers, academic articles, **dissertations** and theses, italics should be used sparingly. In botanical and zoological studies italics are conventionally used for the names of genera, species and varieties, but roman script for higher ranks (phyla, classes, orders).

See: **punctuation.**

Jamaican English

English is the official language of Jamaica, which has a population of approximately 2.3 million and which was under British rule for just over 300 years when it achieved independence in 1962. The term *Jamaican English* comprehends a continuum of Englishes from Standard English to Creole English. Most varieties of Jamaican English show some influence from West African languages in terms of borrowed words:

ackee okro (food)

loan translations:

corn stick (corn cob)
suck teeth (disparage)

and proverbial wisdom:

When the chicken is merry, the hawk is near.

See: **Caribbean English, pidgins and creoles, West Indian English.**

Japanese English

Japan is composed of several islands in the North Pacific. The population of over 118 million is homogeneous in culture and language and Japanese is spoken without significant differences throughout the country. English is not an important means of communication within Japan but it is used when dealing with foreigners, irrespective of their place of origin.

English is regarded as the most useful foreign language, and most children from the age of twelve attend English classes for at least six years. The classes are oriented towards written examinations and so oral skills tend to be neglected. Similar statements can be made about universities. English literature is well taught and frequently studied but most university students would find it easier to discuss Hamlet's soliloquies than to direct one to the nearest post office.

The business world is somewhat different. Nearly all Japan's considerable overseas trade is conducted through English. Most firms of any consequence need personnel able to communicate efficiently in English and many send future executives to anglophone countries to acquire the necessary skills.

English is occasionally used in written advertisements, especially for imported goods such as whiskey, and pop music in English is played and sung. It is the music and the rhythms, however, rather than the meanings that are enjoyed.

As English is not widely used in Japan, it would be misleading to describe a specifically Japanese phonology, vocabulary and grammar. The influences from the mother tongue are considerable, however. Most Japanese students find it hard to differentiate between /l/ and /r/ or /f/ and /v/; /t/ and /d/ or /s/ and /z/ often replace /θ/ and /ð/; intrusive vowels are introduced into **consonant clusters** at both the beginning and the end of words; and the vowel contrasts in English are considerably reduced.

English words associated with technology (e.g. *computer*) and imports (e.g. *jeans*) are occasionally adopted into Japanese and some Japanese words have found their way into international English. Among such words are:

rickshaw < *riki* (power) + *sha* (vehicle)
saki < *sake* (fermented rice)
satsuma < *Satsuma* (province famous for mandarin trees)
sushi < *sushi* (rice garnished with raw fish)
tycoon < *taikun* (great prince)

The greatest problems experienced by Japanese students acquiring English grammar are article usage and the distinction between singulars and plurals (neither of which exist in Japanese). They also tend to omit *if* from conditional clauses, again due to the influence of Japanese, where condition is indicated not by a conjunction but by an inflection in the verb.

jargon

The term *jargon* has been used so loosely and with so many meanings, nearly all of which have been pejorative, that it may be useful to indicate the five overlapping senses currently covered by the word:

1 a confused, confusing, unintelligible form of language
2 a strange, outlandish language or **dialect**
3 a simplified, hybrid language
4 the specialised, technical language of a particular group
5 pretentious language involving **circumlocutions**, polysyllabic words and vague expressions

Common to all of these applications is the assumption that jargon is unintelligible to an outsider, but the fact that we cannot understand a variety does not mean that it is either gibberish or debased. Technical vocabularies, whether used by linguists, plasterers, seafarers or cricket enthusiasts, may permit very precise communication exchanges and in so far as they perform such a role they are of value. Technical terminology such as *archiphonemes* (linguists), *hawks* (plasterers), *fathoms* (seafarers), *silly mid-on* (cricketers) are, however, out of place in everyday English.

See: **argot, cant, circumlocution, cliché, gobbledygook, slang.**

jejune

Jejune, pronounced /dʒɪˈdʒun/, derives from Latin *jejunus* (fasting) and it usually implies 'scanty', 'lacking in substance', 'devoid of interest'. Recently, possibly because users have been influenced by French *jeune* meaning 'young', it has also been used as a synonym for 'naive', 'unsophisticated'. Many **purists** object to the 'slide' of meaning but such mobility is natural in language and not necessarily a sign of 'decay'.

See: **'chestnuts', problem words, purist, semantic change.**

journalese

Journalese was originally a term applied to the language of newspapers but it has been extended to cover the journalistic traits which can be found in some radio and television programmes. The word has strongly derogatory connotations and cannot be accurately applied to all newspaper language. It refers to characteristics of style which arise from the necessity to attract and retain readers and by limitations of time and space. The commonest features of journalese are:

1 use of **abbreviations,** initials and **acronyms**:

Aussies KO Poms [Australians beat English at cricket]
SAM-busters [surface-to-air missiles] *shield Royal jet*

2 **alliteration.** This device is used mainly in headlines as a means of attracting attention:

Sad Sister's Story
Pitt and the Pendulum

3 **ambiguity.** This may be intentional:

Martina, shaken not stirred

or accidental:

The Cockney millionaire, the bionic racer with legs pinned together with screws and plates, was a magnificent third on the treacherously flooded Kyalami circuit.

4 language intended to play on a reader's emotions:

The Pittsburg team has given new life and new hope to one two-year-old child but what about the thousands of other children for whom there will be no life-saving transplants?

5 first names, nicknames and titles:

Fritz fights back as Gary loses heart
Newlywed rock superstar Elton John...

6 compression of ideas often found in pre-nominal modification:

Runaway mother-of-five Marion Leadbetter hugged her 11-year-old son Jason yesterday and vowed: 'I'll never leave you again.'

7 omission of articles and auxiliary verbs:

Police appalled by savagery of attack

8 **puns.** Punning is perhaps the most popular word game in journalese. It occurs in headlines:

Bitter suite

and also within stories:

Mystic [an eagle owl], *owned by rare-bird keepers Liz and Eddie Hare, from Chilham, Kent, was invited to show off his educational talons by local headmaster Brian Robinson.*

9 rhyming is most likely to occur in **headlines**, especially those relating to sport:

Ray lets his play have the final say

10 stock words and phrases: Police tend to *hunt/quiz/track* criminals who are *hardened rapists/mass murderers/sex fiends* whose victims are often *runaway boys/girls/teenagers*. The story may be a *drama/mystery/riddle/shock/tragedy*. Favourite words are: *ace, axe, bid, clash, cut, fury, glory, grass roots, hit, jinx, live-in lover, outrage, quit, rap, slam, stampede, storm, threat, walk free/tall, wed* and frequently-used phrases include:

marathon bargaining session
narrowly averted walkout
ruggedly handsome

See: **headlines, telegraphese**.

just

In the spoken medium, the **adverb** *just* has relatively little constant semantic content but is used with different **intonation** patterns to indicate different attitudes. For example:

*She was **just** beautiful.*

can, depending on intonation, mean:

She was extremely beautiful.
She was beautiful (but not talented).
She could be described as beautiful but only just.

Just can occur in several positions in a sentence with the position affecting its meaning, as is clear from the words that can substitute for *just* in the different examples:

***Just** wait till your father comes home!* (only)
*Hey! **Just** a minute!* (wait)
*They **just** don't know any better.* (simply)
*She knows **just** what to say.* (exactly)
*It's **just** enough.* (barely)
*They've **just** arrived.* (very recently)
*He passed his exams—**just**!* (with nothing to spare)

The use of a **modifier** with an absolute such as *perfect, sublime* or *unique* is unacceptable, since there cannot be degrees of absolutes. However, the colloquial use of *just* with an absolute implies emphasis rather than modification:

*It's **just** perfect!*

In the UK *just* occurs with inversion in class-marked rejoinders:

She jumped magnificently.
Didn't she just!

and seems to be an upper-middle-class equivalent of the equally unorthodox working-class emphatic:

Would you like some tea?
I wouldn't half! (i.e. Yes indeed.)

In UK usage when *just* means 'a moment ago' it tends to co-occur with the present perfect:

I have just seen him.
John has just left.

whereas in US English it frequently co-occurs with the simple past:

We just heard the news.
Mary just called by.

See: **adverb, intonation, presently.**

KEEP

KEEP is a **prime verb,** which means that it is one of the most frequently used verbs in the language. It can function as a semantic equivalent of 'be faithful to':

He always keeps his word.

'control':

I could hardly keep my temper.

'manage':

You kept a boarding-house, didn't you?

'preserve':

The cream kept her skin soft.

'restrain':

Don't keep him from doing what he wants.

and 'retain':

They kept all the money they collected.

Keep also collocates with the preposition *at* to indicate persistence:

He'll keep at it until he drops.

with *on* + a present participle to mark repetition:

She kept on practising until she got it right.

and with *up* to suggest competition:

It will be hard to **keep up** *with the Joneses now.*

See: collocation, prime verbs.

Kenyan English

English is a significant language in *Kenya* (population about 18 million). It is spoken natively by African-born Whites, but for the majority of Kenyans it is acquired as a second language and reflects the influence of various mother tongues. In spite of certain pressures on the government to introduce African languages such as Kikuyu as **lingua francas**, English is still used in advertising, the Civil Service, commerce, the law courts, local literature, the media and at all levels of education.

See: **East African English**.

King's/Queen's English

The terms *King's/Queen's English* are determined by the sex of the ruling British monarch and do not imply different varieties. The King's English of 5 February, 1952, when George VI was king, is indistinguishable from the Queen's English of 6 February, 1952, when Elizabeth II succeeded her father.

Both terms are a relic of the influence of the English court in establishing the prestigious variety of English which subsequently developed into the standard language. The power of the monarchy in affecting attitudes to language is still strong. In 1984 Prince Charles used Tok Pisin, the Pidgin English of Papua New Guinea, when opening the newly-built house of parliament in Port Moresby, and the pidgin which had often been disparaged attracted widespread positive interest and publicity in Britain.

By *King's/Queen's English* most users imply correct speech and **usage** and, in particular, the standard **norms** of Southern Britain. The terms are most frequently invoked when a puristic user of English laments the 'slovenliness' or 'inaccuracy' of a modern usage.

See: **accent, network norms, purist, Standard English**.

langue and parole

These terms were introduced into **linguistics** by the Swiss linguist, Ferdinand de Saussure. *Langue* represents the pooled language knowledge of a speech community. *Parole* refers to actual instances of speech uttered by an individual on a specific occasion. *Parole* is very similar to the Chomskyan term *performance* but *langue* differs from *competence* in that *langue* is the language knowledge possessed by a speech community, whereas *competence* is the knowledge of a language possessed by an ideal speaker-hearer.

See: **competence and performance, transformational grammar.**

latinate models of grammar

Many **grammars** of English were based on descriptions of Latin. Nouns were declined as if they had six **cases** and two numbers (singular and plural):

	Singular	Plural
Nominative	*sailor*	*sailors*
Vocative	*O sailor*	*O sailors*
Accusative	*sailor*	*sailors*
Genitive	*sailor's/of a sailor*	*sailors'/of sailors*
Dative	*to/for a sailor*	*to/for sailors*
Ablative	*by/with/from/in a sailor*	*by/with/from/in sailors*

In English, however, only two case differences, *sailor* and *sailor's*, are marked in the singular, and two in the plural, *sailors* and *sailors'*. (It will be noticed that the difference between the genitive singular *sailor's* and the nominative and genitive plurals exists only in the written medium.)

Verbs were uneconomically conjugated:

	Present	Past	Future
1st person singular	*I go*	*I went*	*I shall go*
2nd person singular	*you go*	*you went*	*you will go*
3rd person singular(masc)	*he goes*	*he went*	*he will go*
3rd person singular(fem)	*she goes*	*she went*	*she will go*
3rd person singular(neut)	*it goes*	*it went*	*it will go*
1st person plural	*we go*	*we went*	*we shall go*
2nd person plural	*you go*	*you went*	*you will go*
3rd person plural	*they go*	*they went*	*they will go*

and described as being in the **indicative** mood (declarative):

you go/went
you don't go/ didn't go

the **imperative** mood (order):

go
don't go
let us go

or **subjunctive** mood (verb used in expressing a wish or in a subordinate clause):

> *Far may he go.*
> *...if he go astray*

Latin could not end a sentence with a preposition, take an accusative pronoun after BE or split an infinitive and so such structures were condemned in latinate models of English grammar.

The values of such models were:

1 their clarity. It was easy for a user to know what was right and what was wrong

2 their ability to suggest underlying similarities in all languages.

Their main weaknesses derived from the facts that:

1 they did not recognise that each language is unique and must be described in its own terms

2 they were prescriptive and did not fully allow for the changes that occur in all living languages.

See: **grammar.**

latinism

A *latinism* may be:

1 a word, phrase or **idiom** borrowed from Latin:

> *This is known as a* codex.
> *The case was held* in camera.
> *That's another reminder of 'Sic transit gloria mundi'.*

2 the preference for a style involving Latin-derived words:

> *He **proceeded** to **affix** the **insignia**.*

rather than:

> *He went on to pin on the badges.*

3 the use of constructions based on Latin models:

> *Having acquired the title, he felt fulfilled.*
> *Of arms and the man I sing.*

Much of our vocabulary derives from Latin and few English speakers are conscious of the Latin roots of such words as *difficult, grace, ludo* or *innocent*. Latinisms involve the conscious use of learned language. They are a feature of formal prose and can be pretentious in speech or expository writing.

See: **elegant variation, foreign words in English.**

lay, lie

The verbs *lay* and *lie* are sometimes confused because their meanings and some of their forms overlap.

Lay meaning 'put someone or something down' is phonologically regular: lay, laying, laid, laid. It is usually transitive:

Lay the baby on her side.
*They **laid** down the rules at their first meeting.*

Lie meaning 'be down, recumbent' is an **irregular verb,** its forms being: lie, lying, lay, lain. It is intransitive:

*I have been **lying** in the sun.*
*The baby **lay** there, sleeping peacefully.*

The most frequent confusion of these verbs involves the use of *laying* for *lying*:

* He was just **laying** there, doing nothing.

See: **ergative, problem pairs.**

learn, teach

These are reciprocal verbs:

*Mary is **teaching** John German.*
*John is **learning** German from Mary.*

and like other reciprocal verbs such as **BORROW** and LEND one verb is often over-applied. In many nonstandard varieties of English, LEARN is used for both the productive and the receptive activities:

*He learned me to whistle.

Standard usage has TEACH when the meaning intended is 'instruct, cause someone to learn' and LEARN when the meaning intended is 'study, receive instruction'.

See: **antonym, borrow.**

letters

For most *letters*, the appropriate style is signalled by the subject matter (congratulations, gossip, job application, sympathy) and by the addressee(s) (contemporary, parent, manager of a firm, bereaved friend). The two main types of letter are personal and official and the conventions differ slightly in the UK and the USA.

The writer's address is given at the top right-hand corner of the first page. The lines of the address start either directly below each other or each line starts two letter spaces to the right of the line above. The date comes immediately below this address. A small margin is left at the right-hand side of the page.

In a business or official letter, the addressee's name and address are given close to the left-hand margin and two spaces lower than the date. The margin on the left-hand side is conventionally wider than that on the right. Men's names may be given as *Mr Jones, Mr J. Jones, Mr James Jones* or, increasingly rarely, as *James Jones, Esq.* Forms of women's names include *Ms Jones, Mrs Jones, Miss/Mrs/Ms A. Jones, Miss/Mrs/Ms Anne Jones* with *Ms* being the preferred form for younger women. It has been a convention for a married woman (but not a widow) to be addressed by the first name or initial of her husband (*Mrs J. Jones, Mrs James Jones*) but this practice is declining. Professional titles take the place of Miss, Mr, Mrs and Ms (*Dr A. Jones, Professor J. Jones*) and first names are used with *Dame* and *Sir* (*Dame Rebecca West, Sir Clive Sinclair*).

A one-line space is left between the recipient's address and the salutation *Dear X* which occurs close to the left-hand margin. Formal business letters begin *Dear Sir* or *Dear Madam*; less formal letters imply varying degrees of intimacy by such uses as *Dear Ms Jones, My dear James*. The main differences between salutation conventions in the UK and the USA are:

UK	USA
Dear Mr Jones	*Dear James Jones*
Dear Sirs	*Gentlemen*
Dear X,	*Dear X:*

The first sentence of the letter begins with a capital letter and starts underneath the end of the salutation but one line down. Subsequent paragraphs are indicated by indenting five spaces. If indentation is not used, double spaces are left between paragraphs.

Letters opening with the formal greetings *Dear Sir(s), Dear Madam* or *Gentlemen* close in the UK with *Yours faithfully* and in the USA with *Yours sincerely, Sincerely* or *Yours truly*. Letters with less formal greetings may use a range of endings, *Sincerely, Yours, Best wishes, Love* or an individual conclusion such as *Aloha, Peace, Stay well*. Each of these endings conforms to the spacing for paragraphs and is followed by a comma.

The writer's name is typed or printed below the signature in formal letters and, if the writer has a special function, this is given either after or directly under the name:

Anne Jones, Head of Department
James Jones
Club Secretary

See: **address and reference, addresses, dates.**

lexical verb

In **verb phrases** one to five verbs may co-occur as a unit:

(he) *watched*
(he) *may have been being watched*

The final verb in the sequence is known as the *headverb* or *lexical verb*; the others are known as **auxiliaries**. Auxiliary verbs tend to signal grammatical relationships such as **modality**:

(he) *may watch*

or the **passive**:

(he) *was watched*

whereas lexical verbs convey meaning:

(he) *may watch*
(he) *may follow*

See: **auxiliary, head, verb phrase**.

lexicography, lexicology

Lexicography refers to the compiling of dictionaries and the principles involved in such compilation. Traditionally, **dictionary** makers have studied **vocabulary** in alphabetical order. *Lexicology*, on the other hand, refers to the study of vocabulary and includes the history, development and organisation of words. Lexicology is the wider discipline and may study words from the points of view of antonymy, collocations, hyponymy, idiom, synonymy, toponymy and polysemy.

See: **dictionary, lexicon, vocabulary**.

lexicon, lexis

Lexicon derives from Greek *lexikon* (pertaining to words) and is used to mean:

1 an alphabetically-arranged inventory of the words of a language together with their definitions
2 the **vocabulary** of a language (spoken or written)
3 the vocabulary of a speaker or group of speakers
4 the vocabulary employed in a text
5 the inventory of **morphemes** in a language

The word *lexis*, which derives from the Greek *lexis* meaning 'speech, word', is often used as a synonym for *vocabulary*, especially a subset of the entire vocabulary of a language:

> The **lexis** employed by this writer is largely Anglo-Saxon in origin.

See: **dictionary, vocabulary.**

like, as

Like is a **preposition** used in comparisons:

> It looks **like** a fossil.

It is frequently used as a **conjunction** in US English:

> He spent money **like** it was going out of style.

and this usage is gradually replacing *as* and *as if* in casual English:

> She doesn't love you **like** I do.
> She sings **like** she has no ear for music.

In formal contexts, *as* is preferred to *like* as a conjunction. It may be followed by a prepositional noun phrase:

> **As in his other stories**, the truth was not rigidly adhered to.

by a clause:

> Do **as you would be done by**.

or by a clause with inverted word order:

> He is intelligent, **as are his sisters**.

See: **as, simile.**

like, love

Many languages have only one verb covering the semantic areas of both *like* and *love* (for example, French *aimer*) and in English there is a considerable overlap in their usage. They both imply affection, with *love* usually being stronger:

> I **like** John but I **love** James.

enjoyment:

> I **like** baseball and Mary **loves** cricket.

and desire:

> I'd **like** a pizza and I'd really **love** some ice cream.

Like rather than *love* is used to indicate approval:

> I **like** *his character and his taste in cars.*

and choice:

> *You can do what you* **like**.

Love rather than *like* is used to indicate strong family ties:

> *She* **loves** *her family.*

patriotism:

> *We all* **love** *our country.*

sexual attraction and (as a noun) gratification:

> *John and Mary really* **love** *each other.*
> *At that stage, they had not made* **love**.

The noun *like* is limited in meaning to 'equal':

> *We shall never see his* **like** *again.*

It can be pluralised, however, and occur in such sentences as:

> *We've got to know all his little* **likes** *and dislikes.*

Occasionally, in regionally-marked English, *like* is used as a **filler**:

> *He came in,* **like**, *but he didn't stay.*
> *I haven't seen him,* **like**.

See: **fillers**.

lingo

The word *lingo* probably comes from Portuguese *lingoa* (language, tongue) and it tends to be used contemptuously for:

1 non-native varieties of languages, such as pidgins, which have often been referred to as 'bastard lingos'

2 foreign languages, especially non-prestigious ones:

> *I don't understand the* **lingo**.

3 the vocabulary of a specialised subject:

> *Some doctors have developed a* **lingo** *to cover their own ignorance. A temperature they can't explain, for example, is labelled PUO—pyrexia of unknown origin.*

4 the language of a particular group of people:

> *The* **lingo** *of the crew of the SS Mary Jane was a type of English.*

See: **cant, jargon, pidgins and creoles**.

Lingua Franca

Lingua Franca derives from Italian and means 'Frankish Tongue'. When written with capital letters it refers to a simplified language used in the Mediterranean as a means of communication between trading partners who did not share a mother tongue. It probably predates the Crusades but the crusaders helped to spread Lingua Franca because it facilitated communication between Christian and Muslim and among the multilingual crusaders.

The vocabulary of Lingua Franca was Romance, **inflections** were dropped and the **syntax** was simple, regular and fixed, thus making Lingua Franca one of the earliest known pidgins. Its value continued throughout the period of European expansion, mainly because its structure remained stable even when the vocabulary differed from place to place. Travellers were recommended to learn it as recently as 1746:

> In the first place it is requisite for the person that designs to travel into those parts [i.e. Guinea and the Americas] to learn languages, as English, French, Low Dutch, Portuguese and Lingua Franca.
>
> John Barbot, 'A description of the coasts of north and south Guinea'

Molière used a form of it in *Le Bourgeois Gentilhomme*:

Se ti sabir,	If you know
Ti respondir ;	You reply
Se non sabir	If you don't know
Tazir, tazir.	Be quiet, be quiet.

The Portuguese variety of Lingua Franca was known as Sabir and its use can be attested along most of the trade routes of the world, probably giving world English the words *palaver*, *pickaninny* and *savvy*.

The term *lingua franca* with lower case letters was gradually extended to mean any language employed to facilitate communication between people with different mother tongues:

*Pidgin English is a **lingua franca** in West Africa.*
*French was once the **lingua franca** of the diplomatic service.*

Since the phrase is Italian, its etymologically correct plural is *lingue franche* as in:

*English and French are **lingue franche** in the Common Market.*

but increasingly its plural is being anglicised to *lingua francas*:

*There were three main **lingua francas** in the country.*

See: **pidgins and creoles.**

linguistics

Linguistics is the scientific study of language. Language has been studied as far back as our records go but the attempt to study language with objectivity and precision is essentially a twentieth-century phenomenon.

Linguistics studies all aspects of language including:

Phonology — the study of sounds and sound patterns
Morphology — the study of morphemes or meaningful combinations of sounds
Lexicology — the study of words
Syntax   — the study of meaningful combinations of words
Semantics   — the study of meaning

and each of these areas has its own subdivisions and areas of overlap.

Modern linguistics has drawn attention to the differences between speech and writing and between diachronic studies (where a language is examined over a period of time) and synchronic studies (where a language is examined at a particular time and/or place). Distinct subdisciplines have also developed: *descriptive* linguistics sets out to establish the rules governing a particular language; *contrastive* linguistics compares and contrasts languages, usually to improve language teaching; and *transformational* linguistics attempts to show the relationships between surface structure and the underlying patterns of language.

Among the hybrid disciplines which are studied by linguists are:

psycholinguistics — which studies the relationships between language and the mind
sociolinguistics — which concentrates on the uses of language in society
stylistics   — which uses linguistic insights to examine style, particularly literary style

See: **grammar**.

linkage

Linkage may be defined as the patterning that gives **cohesion** to a text. It may involve intonation, rhythm, alliteration, assonance and rhyme in the spoken medium and any devices, such as repetition, which link one part of a text with another.

See: **anaphora, cohesion, discourse analysis, discourse marker, parallelism.**

literary genre

The word *genre*, from French *genre* meaning 'kind, type', is used in describing categories of artistic compositions in literature, music and painting. A *literary genre* is a subdivision of literature according to purpose (a lyric poem versus a prose drama), structure (a short story versus a novel) or technique (prose versus verse). The three basic genres are poetry, drama and the novel, but finer distinctions are introduced into literary discussions to facilitate the particular analyses being made.

See: **literature, style, stylistics.**

literature

Literature, deriving from Latin *litteratura* (writing), is a term that has expanded in meaning. It can refer to any type of written material:

Have you seen that literature they sent me on gardening?

but it is most frequently applied to:
1 imaginative works (written and spoken) that show elements of permanence
2 works noted for their form or expression
3 works exhibiting a particular physical form (e.g. a sonnet)
4 works long or short, ancient or modern, written or spoken, which evoke a profound response on the part of the listener or reader
5 the distilled wisdom, customs, beliefs and culture of a people
6 'What oft was thought but ne'er so well expressed' (Alexander Pope)
The 'definitions' of literature given above are all partial, but most critics would agree that a creator of literature uses language with power and flexibility, producing a linguistic arrangement that perfectly unites form and meaning.

See: **literary genre, speech in literature, stylistics.**

litotes

Litotes derives from Greek *litos* (simple). It is a figure of speech involving **understatement**:

I have some feeling for him. (i.e. I love him very much.)

and frequently occurs when an affirmative is stressed by negating its opposite:

He wasn't what you might call poor. (i.e. He was very rich.)

Litotes often depends on intonation for its full effect and so is frequently found in speech.

See: **figurative language, meiosis, understatement.**

little

The word *little* can function as an **adjective**:

*a **little** house*

as an **adverb**:

*He **little** knows the troubles that await him.*

as a noun:

*She gave away the **little** that she had.*

and can have different implications, depending on its context. With **countable** nouns it refers to size:

*There was a **little** horse in the stable.*

and with uncountable nouns to quantity:

*There was **little** news from Beirut.*

1 As an adjective, *little* is usually attributive:

*What a lovely **little** garden!*

and often implies an attitude such as affection or contempt:

*It's such a pretty **little** village.*
*You horrible **little** man!*

In the UK, *little* is occasionally used to indicate dislike (and social condescension) rather than size:

*She has gone out with that dreadful **little** man.*

The predicative use of *little* is regional:

She's only little.

2 *Little* is not normally gradable as a **modifier** of countable nouns (*small* being preferred when comparatives and superlatives are required):

the little/small horse
the smaller horse
the smallest horse

Occasionally, however, children use the forms *littler* and *littlest* and a number of television programmes such as 'The Littlest Hobo' have adopted their usage.

The comparative and superlative forms of *little* as a modifier of uncountable nouns and as an adverb are *less* and *least*:

little news   less news   least news
*He cared **little** about me.*

*He cared **less** about me than about the others.*
*He cared **least** about me.*

3 The formula 'little + uncountable noun/clause' has negative implications:

*There was **little reason** to smile.*
*There is **little joy** in this world.*
*There is **little we can do about it**.*

Similar implications apply when *little* is used as an adverb:

*Tonight we shall talk about a **little-known** hero.*

4 The formula 'article + little + singular uncountable noun' has positive or neutral implications:

*There was **a little sunshine**.*

And there is a similar implication when *a little* is used as a **complement**:

*There is **a little** we can do to help.*

See: **adjective, adverb, complement, countable, gradable, noun.**

location

Some languages can express the *location* of an action by means of case endings. Thus in liturgical Latin:

Urbi et orbi (To the city and to the world)

indicates location by means of the *-i* endings. English does not have *case* endings to indicate location but uses such devices as prepositions:

at/in/near/under the desk

locative adverbs:

here/there

preposition phrases:

on a hill

adverbial clauses:

*He hid it **where he used to hide his money**.*

and the choice of verb:

***Bring** it to me and then **take** it to your father.*
***Come** here at once and don't **go** out again.*

See: **bring, case, GET, speaker orientation.**

main

The adjective *main* is used in contrasts to identify the most important unit in a group. A *main clause* is the **clause** that is most like a sentence in being able to occur in isolation, whereas a **dependent** or *subordinate* clause cannot stand alone:

Main clauses	Subordinate clauses
You must come	*when you are free.*
We have succeeded	*in annoying you.*

Main verb is a synonym for *headverb* and distinguishes the semantically full verb from **auxiliaries**:

(*I*) *may have been* **sleeping**.

See: **auxiliary, clause, head**.

MAKE

MAKE is a **prime verb** with two main functions:
1 as a semantic equivalent of 'create', 'construct':

God **made** *the world.*
She **made** *all her own furniture.*

2 as a **causative**:

You **made** *me love you* (you caused me to love you).
They always **make** *us laugh* (cause us to laugh).

Ambiguity can occur when both the 'construct' and the 'causative' meanings are possible:

She made that reel.
    (a) She constructed that spool/bobbin
    (b) She caused that to spin.

MAKE can be used in the following patterns:
1 MAKE + object + base form of verb:

We made her go.

2 MAKE + to + verb + object/preposition phrase:

I was made to take another test.
We were made to wait for hours.

3 MAKE + object + object complement:

He made the garden beautiful.
They made him president for another term.

4 as an **analytic** equivalent of **synthetic** sentences:

He made the point clear(er).—He clarified the point.
He made a complaint.—He complained.

MAKE also occurs in innumerable **idioms** including:

make a mountain out of a molehill (exaggerate)
make believe (pretend)
make (both) ends meet (manage on little)
make fun of (mock)
make faces (grimace)
make good (succeed)
make love (have sexual intercourse)
make out (pretend)
make time (progress)
make waves (create a stir)
make with the (produce)

Non-native speakers of English occasionally have difficulty in distinguishing between MAKE and DO, largely because many languages either only have one verb to fulfil the functions of both DO and MAKE:

English	French
I *did* my homework.	*J'ai fait mes devoirs.*
I *made* a cake.	*J'ai fait un gâteau.*

or because the equivalent verbs are differently distributed:

English	Afrikaans
What are you doing?	*Wat maak jy?*
It doesn't matter.	*Dit maak nie saak nie.*

The usual, although by no means absolute, rule for distinguishing DO and MAKE is to use DO for actions and work:

I'll do the cleaning if you'll do the cooking.

and to use MAKE for the creation of some specific result, whether abstract or concrete:

We'll make new plans.
I'll make an apple pie.

See: **idioms, prime verbs**.

malapropism

The term which denotes the incorrect use of a word, usually a learned word, derives from the name of a character *Mrs Malaprop*, in R.B. Sheridan's play *The Rivals* (1775). Mrs Malaprop's name is an anglicisation of *mal à propos* (in an inappropriate manner). She confuses such words as:

allegory and *alligator*
allusion and *illusion*

and yet is appalled when her command of English is criticised:

> *An aspersion upon my parts of speech! Was ever such a brute! Sure, if*
> *I reprehend anything in this world, it is the use of my oracular tongue*
> *and a nice derangement of epitaphs.*
>   Act 3 Scene 3

In spite of giving her name to the phenomenon of incorrectly-used words, Mrs Malaprop was not the first literary character to use *malapropisms*. Shakespeare's common characters often delight in polysyllabic words which *sound* impressive but are inappropriate. The gravediggers in Act 5 Scene 1 of *Hamlet*, for example, use:

> *crowner's quest* for *coroner's inquest*
> *so offended* for *se defendendo* (justifiable homicide)
> *argal* for *ergo*
> *modesty* for *moderation*
> *imperious* for *imperial*

Malapropisms occur frequently in the spoken medium:

> *He was shot **ajaxing*** (highjacking) *the lorry.*
> *She was beginning to feel better after her accident but now **compen-***
> ***sations*** (complications) *have set in.*

and in written work where the writer has not learned to distinguish between 'eloquence' and supposed 'elegance'.

See: **elegant variation, folk etymology**.

Malawian English

Malawi was formerly Nyasaland. It became a British protectorate in 1891, joined Northern and Southern Rhodesia (now Zambia and Zimbabwe) in a federation from 1953 to 1963, gained its independence in 1964 and became a republic in 1966.

English is the official language of the 6.6 million inhabitants of Malawi although it is the mother tongue of only a very small percentage. It shares many characteristics with the English heard in East and South Africa and is gradually establishing its own literature in English.

See: **East African English, South African English, Southern African English**.

Malaysian English

The Federation of *Malaysia* came into being in 1963. It was composed of West Malaysia (the former Federation of Malaya), East Malaysia (formerly the British colonies of Sabah and Sarawak) and Singapore.

Singapore seceded in 1965 to become an independent republic. Malaysia's estimated population of almost 15 million is multicultural and multi-ethnic, with Malays making up approximately 44% of the population, Chinese 40%, and with considerable numbers of Tamils and other Indians.

English was the main medium of instruction until 1970 when Bahasa Malaysia (a modified version of Malay) was introduced. Since then, English has gradually changed from being a second language for most young Malaysians to being a foreign language. The recent deterioration in the quality of English in Malaysia has been observed by educationists and employers and, because of the value of English in international trade, steps are being taken to reverse the slide in standards.

English is still regularly used in commerce, the law and the media in Malaysia and is similar in form and function to the English used in Singapore.

See: **Chinese English, English in the Indian Sub-Continent, Singapore English**.

maxim

A *maxim* is a pithy statement intended to improve moral conduct:

> *People who live in glass houses shouldn't throw stones.*

They are still popular in speech but are rarely found in modern literature, although their popularity in the past is suggested by their frequent appearance in Shakespeare's plays:

> *Give every man thy ear, but few thy voice...*
> *Neither a borrower nor a lender be...*
>   Hamlet Act 1 Scene 3

The term *maxim* is often used more loosely to describe also **aphorisms** and **proverbs**.

See: **aphorism, proverb**.

maybe, perhaps

These two words are virtually synonymous, but *maybe* tends to be more widely used in informal, colloquial speech:

> **Maybe** *he's sleeping.*

whereas *perhaps* tends to occur in more formal contexts:

> **Perhaps** *he's asleep.*
> *This is* **perhaps** *his finest work.*

May and *be* are written as two words when they occur in the relatively formal pattern: 'It + may + be + (complement) + that':

*It **may be true** that he is ill.*

and when the modal *may* occurs with auxiliary BE:

*He **may be** arriving tomorrow.*

See: **modality**.

meals

The terms for *meals* often provide information on one's social and regional origins. In middle- and upper-class society in Britain the terms used are:

breakfast (first meal of the day)
lunch (usually light meal in the middle of the day)
(tea) (optional light snack around 4 pm)
dinner (larger meal in the evening)

whereas in working-class communities the meals are:

breakfast
dinner (largest meal of the day)
tea (lighter meal eaten around 6)
(supper) (optional snack meal around 9 - 10 pm)

In other parts of the world, different customs prevail. In Guyana, for example, *tea* is often the first meal of the day; in Southern Africa it is often the equivalent of *morning coffee*; and in West Africa *tea* may refer to any snack involving a hot drink (tea, coffee, cocoa, hot chocolate).

Nowadays, most people eat the sort of meals they prefer at the times that are most convenient to them, but some ambiguities can occur since times are often indicated by reference to meals:

I'll be back before lunch.
I saw her around tea time.
They returned just after dinner.

See: **food and drink**.

measurements

Although most English-speaking countries now use metric units of *measurement*, old imperial measurements have been retained, especially in popular speech, for distances:

It's about six miles from here.

for length:

> *twelve yards of linen and a nine-inch zip*

and for a person's height:

> *He's six foot three and she's five foot five.*

With regard to people's weight, many countries use pounds:

> *She's 114 pounds.*

whereas the UK still commonly uses stones (fourteen pounds) and pounds:

> *She's eight stone two.*

and liquids are measured in gallons, quarts and pints as well as in litres. The equivalences are:

Imperial	Metric
inch	2.54 centimetres/25.4 millimetres
foot (12 in)	.305 metres/30.5 centimetres
yard (3 ft)	.914 metres/91.4 centimetres
mile (1760 yds)	1.626 kilometres
pint	.568 litres
quart (2 pints)	1.136 litres
gallon (8 pints)	4.546 litres
ounce	28.35 grams
pound (16 oz)	.454 kilos/454 grams

See: **money, numbers.**

meiosis

Meiosis comes from the Greek word *meiosis* (diminution). It is a figure of speech closely related to **litotes** in that it involves **understatement**. Most stylisticians today only use the term litotes but a few preserve meiosis for understatement which has the specific intention of raising our esteem for the item apparently disparaged:

> *How can we help this poor little mite?*
> *He's not much but he's all I've got.*

See: **litotes, understatement.**

Mentalism

Mentalism is a branch of psychology which contrasts sharply with **Behaviourism**. Whereas the latter insists that the only objective evidence for psychological research is behaviour, that is, actions and responses to stimuli, the former values such subjective data as can be established through introspection. Behaviourism and Mentalism have both influenced linguistics. Behaviourists have argued that when a child is born its mind is blank and all language knowledge is the result of conditioning, experience and stimulation; Mentalists claim that children are born with a predisposition to acquire language and that the speed of a child's **acquisition of language** can in part be accounted for by the child's inherited linguistic abilities.

See: **acquisition of language, Behaviourism**.

metalanguage

Each subject tends to have a vocabulary of its own. In a discussion of geography, for example, we would expect to find words like *continents*, *contours*, *oceans* and *plate tectonics*. *Metalanguage* is the specific variety of language used to describe language. Many of the descriptions in this book involve metalanguage. The study of metalanguage is metalinguistics.

metaphor

The word *metaphor* derives ultimately from Greek *metapherein* (transfer). It is a figure of speech in which A is covertly identified with B. In:

John bellowed.

for example, John (A) is described as behaving like a bull (B) in that *bellowing* specifically refers to the noise made by bulls. The figurative extension of meaning that characterises metaphor may occur with nouns:

*We lost **touch** with that **branch** of the family.*

verbs:

*She **broke** his heart.*

adjectives:

*He gave me a **dirty** look.*

adverbs:

*They applauded **warmly**.*

and phrases:

*They **took account** of our views.*
*He **tore up** the road.*

Metaphor is, in the words of I.A. Richards, 'the omnipresent principle of language', a claim that is easy to accept when we try to find
a passage or sentence without metaphor. It occurs in the figurative
use of body parts, including:

> the arm of a chair
> the back of a house
> the foot of the hill/foothills
> the last leg of a journey
> the nose of a plane
> the spine of a book
> in the teeth of a storm

Many such metaphors are 'dead', that is, we are no longer conscious
of their figurative nature when we use them, although certain regional metaphors, using identical techniques, strike us as non-literal:

> the **eye** of a bottle—Papua New Guinea
> the **heel** of the hand—Ireland

Metaphors may be subdivided into a number of categories:
1 *animistic* metaphors, giving animate qualities to inanimate
nouns:

> Darkness **brooded** over the land.
> This river **runs** through the city.

2 *concretive* metaphors, giving physical substance to abstractions:

> a **fully-developed** idea
> a **pincer** movement

3 *dehumanising* metaphors, applying non-human attributes to
people:

> She's **pot-bellied**.
> The children **crowed** with delight.

4 *deifying* metaphors, attributing divine qualities to people:

> an **omnipotent** ruler
> Mona Lisa's **eternal** smile

5 *humanising* metaphors, which give human qualities to non-
human nouns:

> the **inconstant** moon
> a **brave** attempt

6 *synaesthetic* metaphors, in which the qualities associated with
one sense are applied to another:

> a **loud** colour
> She sang **sweetly**.

In all successful metaphors, the objects compared must have certain similarities and yet be sufficiently different for their juxtaposition to arouse a sense of novelty.

See: **figurative language, idioms, imagery, simile, synaesthesia.**

metathesis

Metathesis, which comes from Greek *metatithenai* (transpose), involves the transposition of sounds in a word, usually to break up a **consonant cluster** and on **analogy** with other words. Many contemporary commentators use:

  nucular for *nuclear*

to avoid the unusual combination of 'nucl-' but also, no doubt, under the influence of such words as *circular*, *insular*, *particular* and *singular*.

Metathesis may be historical and now fully accepted:

  crud > *curd*
  gars > *grass*

or contemporary and stigmatised:

  dirndl > *drindle (skirt)*
  pretty > *purty*

See: **consonant cluster.**

metonymy

Metonymy comes from Greek *meta* + *onyma* (change + name) and is a figure of speech in which someone or something is referred to by an associated item:

  The pen [a writer] *is mightier than the sword* [a soldier].

Many such usages are conventionalised:

  the crown represents the monarchy
  the press represents the newspaper industry
  the turf represents horse-racing

and:

  address the bench means 'speak to the judge(s)'
  a silk means 'a Queen's Counsel' (in the UK a higher-level barrister)

See: **figurative language, synecdoche.**

metre

Metre is regulated **rhythm**. All utterances are to some extent rhythmic, involving an indeterminate number of stressed and unstressed **syllables**:

> / x x /
> *What did you say?*
> x /   x x / x   /   x   / x
> *I can't hear a single word you're saying.*

In English poetry, we regulate the number of stressed syllables:

Till a' the seas gang dry, my dear x / x / x /, x /
And the rocks melt wi' the sun x x / / x x /
And I will luve thee still, my dear, x / x / x /, x /
While the sand o' life shall run. x x / x / x /

Often, as in the ballad stanza from Burns, we find a pattern of four strong stresses in lines one and three and three strong stresses in lines two and four. The metre of a poem is the rhythmic melody, divorced from the words. Often, when we forget the words of a verse, we remember the metre and by repeating the metre we can gradually recall the words.

Just as English grammar was forced into a latinate mould, so too was English verse. Latin verse could be subdivided into feet and so four types of poetic foot were used in a description of English verse:

anapest x x /—two unstressed + one stressed syllable
dactyl / x x—one stressed + two unstressed
iamb x /—one unstressed + one stressed
trochee / x—one stressed + one unstressed

With some verse, especially children's rhymes, the foot works reasonably well:

Mary had a little lamb / x / x / x /
Its fleece as white as snow x / x / x /

Little Miss Muffet / x x / x
Sat on a tuffet / x x / x

but irregularities are often found in less trivial verse. In Milton's sonnet 'On the Late Massacre in Piedmont':

Avenge, O Lord, thy slaughtered saints, whose bones
Lie scattered on the Alpine mountains cold;
Ev'n them who kept thy truth so pure of old,
When all our fathers worshipped stocks and stones

we find the pattern:

x / x /, x / x /, x /
/ / x x x / x / x /;
x x / x / x / x / x /,
x / x / x / x / x /.

The number of stressed syllables per line is regularly five, whereas the unstressed syllables vary from five to six and the positioning of the unstressed syllables is regular only in lines one and four.

English verse does not fit easily into Romance patterns because English is a stress-timed language whereas the Romance languages are syllable-timed. In stress-timed languages, stressed syllables are produced at regular intervals of time and the number of unstressed syllables may vary; in syllable-timed languages, however, the syllables are produced at equal intervals of time with the number of stresses being random. It is the occurrence of a regular pattern of stressed syllables, often with an irregular pattern of unstressed syllables, which gives English poetry its characteristic rhythm.

See: **parallelism, rhythm, stress, syllable**.

Middle English

Middle English refers to the variety of English spoken and written mainly in England from the twelfth to the fifteenth century. During this period, English changed from an inflected Germanic language, virtually inaccessible to any modern speaker, to a relatively uninflected language with extensive Romance **borrowings**. The differences between **Old English** and Middle English are perhaps clearest when we contrast passages which deal with the coming of Spring:

> Holm storme weol,
> won wið winde: wynter yþe beleac
> is-gebinde, oþðæt oþer com
> gear in geardas, swa nu gyt doð,
> þa ðe syngales sele bewitiað,
> wuldor-torhtan weder.
>   *Beowulf*, 1131-36

> Whan that Aprill with his shoures sote,
> The droghte of Marche hath perced to the rote,
> And bathed every veyne in swich licour
> Of which vertu engendred is the flour;
>   Chaucer, *Prologue to the Canterbury Tales*, 1-4

The *Beowulf* passage contains words that we recognise: *storm, wind, winter, come, now, was* and *weather*, but the meaning of the passage is lost to most speakers of contemporary English. Chaucer's passage, on the other hand, is relatively easy to understand when we master the spelling conventions and relate *shoures* to *showers*, *droghte* to *drought*, *rote* to *root*, *veyne* to *vein* and *swich* to *such*.

A comparison of the two passages will also show the increase in Romance vocabulary (from 0% in *Beowulf* to 23% in Chaucer), a swing from alliterative patterning to rhymed verse and a movement away from **inflections** to fixed **word order** and prepositions.

See: **Old English.**

mixed language

The term *mixed language* has frequently been applied to **pidgins and creoles,** which are *mixed* in the sense that they often show influences from more than one language. Thus, in the Cameroon Pidgin sentences:

Dat pikin sabi chɔp gari. (That child loves eating gari.)
Ma haus big pas ɔl. (My house is biggest.)
Baiam giv mi. (Buy it for me.)

English has provided ten of the thirteen words; Portuguese has provided two (*pikin* 'child' and *sabi* 'know, be able to'), Igbo has provided one (*gari* 'grated cassava') and African languages have provided the structure of the comparison and the imperative. (In Lamnso, for example, the sentence would be rendered:

Lav yem kuh shaah sidzem.
House my big pass all.

and the Yoruba equivalent of the third sentence is:

Ra a fun mi. (literally 'Buy it give me.')

Mixing is not, however, limited to pidgins and creoles. It is found in all communities where two or more languages are in use. The following example of English cum French cum Latin was recorded in Guernsey in 1631:

The prisoner ject un brickbat a le dit Justice que
narrowly mist, et pur ceo immediately fuit Indictment
drawn pur Noy envers le prisoner, and son dexter manus
ampute and fix al Gibbet sur que luy mesme immediatement
hange in presence de Court.

Puerto Rican teachers often condemn 'Spanglish', the blending of Spanish and English by bilinguals:

Yo quiero improve mi vocabulary. (I want to...)
Mi papa es muy protective. (My father is very...)

and children growing up in bilingual homes often produce mixed utterances:

> *C'est a me! My pomme!* (It's mine! My apple!)

and advertisers often blend languages:

> *Les meilleurs blue-jeans du monde!* (The best jeans in the world!)
> *Haar-do à la mode.* (Fashionable hair-do.)

English itself is a mixed language, a fact that becomes clear if we examine almost any sentence. Of the seventeen words in the previous sentence, six (*mixed, language, fact, clear, examine, sentence*) are from French. Many fixed phrases such as *attorney general* or *mission impossible* show the influence of Latin and French in having the adjective after the noun; others such as *alter ego, infra dig, qui vive, savoir faire* have been adopted without change; and the possessive structure 'the daughter of my first wife' as opposed to 'my first wife's daughter' reflects the influence of the French equivalent 'la fille de ma première femme'.

See: **borrowing, foreign words in English, pidgins and creoles.**

modality

Modality refers to the attitudes expressed by a speaker towards the statement or proposition being made:

> Utterance → Modality + Sentence

Such attitudes (both conscious and unconscious) may express ability, compulsion, desire, insistence, intention, obligation, permission, possibility, willingness and uncertainty.

In English, modality can be signalled by:

1 *Modals*, nine verbs: *can, could, may, might, must, shall, should, will, would*, which form a subclass because of the way they pattern and because of their meanings.

(a) Modals occur in the first position in the VP:

> He **might** be coming.

(b) They are mutually exclusive:

> *He **might can** go.

(c) They trigger off the base form of the following verb:

> I **must** go.

(d) They take the negative not/n't directly:

> She **may not** come.
> I **can't** go through with it.

(e) They do not occur in non-finite constructions:

*musting
*to might
*shall + ed

(f) They do not exhibit past/non-past contrasts in the same way as other verbs. *May* and *might* can appear in structures where past/non-past contrasts are not involved:

*I **may** go to London tomorrow.*
*I **might** go to London tomorrow.*

and *must* has two different 'pasts' depending on its meaning:

Non-past	Past
He **must** come here often.	He **must have** come here often.
	He **had to** come here often.

(g) They can all refer to the **future**, but with varying degrees of certainty:

*He **will** come.*
*He **may** come.*
*He **should** come.*

2 *Quasi-modals* of two kinds:

(a) verbs like *dare, need, ought to* and *used to* which share some of the syntactic characteristics of modals:

*I **daren't** move.*
*You **needn't** bother.*
*He **ought** to have been practising.*
*She **used to** be bothered by such things.*

(b) verbs which share much of the meaning of modals. These include:

BE to	— *She **is to** try tomorrow.*
BE able to	— *He **isn't able to** work so hard now.*
BE about to	— *I'm not **about to** throw it all away.*
BE going to	— *They're **going to** regret this.*
HAVE to	— *We **have to** change these reports.*
HAVE got to	— *You've **got to** help.*
HAD better	— *It'd **better** be good.*

3 *Intonation.* By varying our **intonation**, we can modify meaning as in:

You'll go all right! = { *I'll see to it!*
{ *Over my dead body!*

In the written medium, modality is often signalled by verbs of attribution and their modifiers:

She hoped/insisted/pleaded/urged wistfully.

4 *Word order.* The clearest examples here are the differences between statements, questions, orders and blessings/curses:

You are going away.
Are you going away?
Go away.
May you never know want!/May you never know rest!

5 *Modifiers* such as:

Maybe *he'll come.*
Perhaps *he'll come.*

Modals are among the most frequently-used verbs in the language and yet they are among the most difficult to define. This may be because a certain amount of 'bleaching' (i.e. loss of meaning) is going on. We might, for example, ask if there are any clear differences between the modals in:

May/can/might *I have the salt, please?*
Will/would/can/could *you pass the potatoes, please?*

In addition, there is a tendency now to use some of the modals to describe facts rather than possibilities:

You **may** *be big* (i.e. you are big) *but that won't save you.*
You **will** *remember* (i.e. you are sure to remember) *that September 8 is an important anniversary for us.*

See: **auxiliary, mood, quasi-modal, verb phrase.**

modifier

A *modifier* is a unit which is structurally dependent and which qualifies the meaning of other units, usually nouns, verbs, **adjectives**, **adverbs** and sentences. The usual modifiers are adjectives, which qualify nouns:

big *winnings*

adverbs, which qualify verbs, adjectives, other adverbs and sentences:

He ran **quickly.**
very *big winnings*
He ran **very** *fast.*
It is not, **however,** *clear why he behaved in this way.*

and preposition phrases:

the man **in the moon**
He was sitting **on my left.**

Occasionally, however, other sentence units such as determiners:

the army

auxiliaries:

It may not work.

and dependent clauses:

The man who introduced the subject is my uncle.
They left when the row started.

are also described as *modifiers*.

Frequently, especially in journalism, several modifiers co-occur as in this extract from *The Times* (18 September, 1984):

The Paris-based, German-born, fan-collecting, fast-talking, computer-brained designer makes a state appearance in London tomorrow...

In traditional **grammars**, adjectives were said to *qualify* nouns and adverbs to *modify* verbs, adjectives, sentences and other adverbs. Today, the nouns *modifier* and **qualifier** and the verbs *modify* and *qualify* are used interchangeably, with *modifier/modify* being the preferred terms.

See: **adjective, adjunct, adverb, parts of speech**.

money

A precise sum of *money* is given in figures and symbols:

25c—twenty-five cents
50p—fifty pence
£5.75—five pounds seventy-five pence
$10.95—ten dollars ninety-five cents
£2,500—two thousand five hundred pounds
$50,000—fifty thousand dollars

Less commonly, round figures are spelt out.

For sums involving larger amounts, the usual conventions are:

$2bn—two billion (i.e. two thousand million) dollars
£25m—twenty-five million pounds
£65K—sixty-five thousand pounds

The UK originally used *billion* to mean 'one million million' but the term is now used with its US meaning.

In contexts, sums of money are treated as singular:

$2m is being spent on repairs.

Often, when a sum is used as a modifier, it is spelt out:

a two million dollar repair bill

although there is a growing tendency to use figures here too:

a $2m repair bill

See: **billion, numbers.**

monologue

A *monologue* (derived from *mono* + *logue* on analogy with *dialogue*) or soliloquy is a speech made by one person. The dramatic monologue is a literary convention which allows a character to communicate his thoughts directly to an audience. Shakespeare's plays contain a large number of monologues, delivered mainly by the hero. A dramatic monologue differs from a speech in that a speech has an overt addressee (as well as the audience) whereas a monologue is the equivalent of a character speaking his thoughts aloud.

As well as dramatic soliloquies, the term *monologue* covers poems which are addressed to, but never involve replies from, another person. Robert Browning uses this poetic technique in such poems as 'Andrea del Sarto'.

Colloquially, the word *monologue* is often applied to the speech of a person who talks *at* rather than *with* a listener.

mood

Mood is closely related to **modality** in linguistic discussions. Traditionally, mood was applied to verbs to distinguish between the forms used in making statements (i.e. **Indicative** Mood):

I am (not) tired.

in giving orders (i.e. **Imperative** Mood):

Be quiet.

and in marking verbs in subordinate clauses or in making wishes (i.e. **Subjunctive** Mood):

I insist that you be in at ten.
Things would be different if I were in charge.
Long live the Queen!

See: **imperative, indicative, modality, subjunctive.**

morpheme

The word *morpheme* derives ultimately from Greek *morphe* meaning 'form'. A morpheme is composed of one or more **phonemes** (the smallest units of sound in a language) and is the smallest unit of **syntax**.

There are two types of morphemes:
1 free morphemes, which can occur as separate words:

help

2 bound morphemes, which cannot occur independently. The -s
which can mark plurality is a bound morpheme (or 'bound form'):

tree trees

Affixes, too, are bound morphemes:

un- + *help* + *-ful*

but occasionally, a bound morpheme may be used as a free form:

*Are you **pro** or **anti**?*
*He's my **ex**.*

See: **affix, morphology, word formation.**

morphology

Morphology is the study of the structure of **words**, which are regarded
as free **morphemes** or combinations of morphemes. Morphology comprehends two main areas of study:
1 **inflection**, which is concerned with the various forms in which
a word may exist:

cat cats
do does did doing done
early earlier earliest

2 **word formation**:

amazingly < amaze + ing + ly
bookcase < book + case
brunch < breakfast + lunch
globetrot < globetrotter
kleenex < clean + X

See: **affix, derivation, word formation.**

morphophonemics

Morphophonemics comprehends two main areas of study:
1 the phonological factors that may affect the form of **morphemes**.
For example, the negative morpheme *in-* varies according to context:

illegal
immoral
irreparable

2 the factors that may affect the form of **phonemes**. For example, the 'p' sound is slightly different in each of the following words:

pit
spit
sip

multifunctionality

Many words in English are *multifunctional* in the sense that they can function in a variety of roles:

*I bought a **square** table.* (adjective)
*They used to meet in the **square**.* (noun)
*I can't **square** that with my conscience.* (verb)

Multifunctionality is a feature of uninflected languages and of **pidgins and creoles**:

Smɔl *no bi sik.* — 'Smallness' is not an illness.
Wi bin pulam **smɔl**. — We pulled it gently.

See: **functional shift, pidgins and creoles.**

mutation

The word *mutation*, which derives from Latin *mutare* meaning 'change', is applied to the vocalic sound changes which mark:
1 certain plurals:

foot feet
man men
mouse mice

2 certain verbal distinctions:

do did done
sing sang sung
write wrote written

mutual

Mutual has long been a **shibboleth**, its correct use implying education and prestige, its incorrect use being associated with carelessness and poor education. The puristic attitude towards *mutual* is summed up by the Fowlers in *The King's English* (1958: 65) where they link the misuse of **individual** and *mutual*, adding that *mutual* is 'a very telltale word, readily convicting the unwary'.

The word *mutual* denotes a response, attitude or action that is equal, contemporaneous and shared by two. Thus we find:

mutual affection/assistance/attraction/respect/trust
mutual dislike/distrust/distaste

Mutual modifies a singular noun:

John and Fred grew up together and their **mutual affection** *is as marked today as it ever was.*

The well-known **solecism** *our mutual friend*, which was perpetuated by Dickens in his novel of the same name, is unacceptable because it refers not to a relationship between two but to the feelings of two towards a third. One of the reasons for this usage is the ambiguity of the correct form:

our common friend

Mutual needs to be distinguished from *reciprocal*, which refers to actions and feelings which are a response to others. Thus if A treats B kindly, it is likely that B will reciprocate A's kindness. The kindness would thus be *reciprocal* rather than *mutual*.

It is semantically useful to maintain the distinction between *mutual* and *reciprocal* but it seems likely that *mutual* will gradually become acceptable as applying to more than two in the same way that *between* is being extended to contexts in which **among** would be more appropriate.

See: **among, 'chestnuts', individual, shibboleth.**

naivete, naivety

The word *naïve* was borrowed from French *naïf/naïve*, meaning 'natural', over three hundred years ago, and many users continue to use the dieresis to indicate that the word is disyllabic. There is considerable vacillation on the part of native speakers with regard to the derived noun with the forms *naïveté, naiveté, naivete* and *naivety* all being acceptable. Since the words have become firmly established in English, it seems reasonable to use *naive, naively* and *naivety*, but, whatever forms are chosen, they should be used consistently.

See: **accent marks, foreign words in English.**

name

In most traditions, naming is highly significant. The choice of *Beverley* for a daughter or *Todd* for a son may suggest upward social mobility, just as the naming of a daughter after her maternal grandmother is common in matriarchal societies.

In the past, a name was endowed with the spirit of its owner. To know a person's or a god's name was to have power over him. We have relics of such beliefs in the commandment:

Thou shalt not take the name of thy God in vain.

and in fairytales such as 'Rumpelstiltskin', where the discovery of the captor's name weakens his power. In the more recent past, Christians named their children after a saint such as Mary or Peter, who was meant to be the child's patron and model, or after a Christian virtue such as Faith or Makepeace.

Throughout the world where English is used as a first or second language, most users have at least two names, one or more given names and a family name:

Joanne Brown
Ahmed Mubarak

In parts of Africa and the Indian sub-continent, the family name is often put first:

(Ms) Pushpa P.T.
(Mr) Nfon Donatus

even when signing one's name. In the USA it is not uncommon to find such male hierarchies as:

John Brown
John Brown Jr
John Brown III

The titles *Senior/Sen* and *Junior/Jr* are occasionally found in the UK and Australia but they tend to suggest US influence, as does the use of an initial before a given name as in:

J. David Brown

Double-barrelled names tend to arise in three main ways:
1 a woman may add her husband's surname to her own. Thus on marrying John Smith, Mary Brown may become:

Mary Brown-Smith

2 a man (*John Brown*) may take on his mother's maiden name:

John Hamilton-Brown

3 where surnames are common (as with Jones, Rees, Vaughan in Wales), double-barrelled names can be a way of distinguishing families. Again, the wife's name precedes the husband's. Thus Mary Vaughan and Evan Rees may become Mary and Evan Vaughan-Rees.

See: **address and reference.**

narration, narrative

The terms *narration* and *narrative*, both from Latin *narrare* (tell a story), cover a number of meanings, all associated with giving an account of a sequence of events.

Narration usually applies to:

1 the act or process of giving an account

2 a traditional form of discourse, the others being **argument**, *description* and **exposition**.

Narrative has three main meanings:

1 a continuous account in speech or writing, usually in chronological order. It may include dialogue, present a particular viewpoint, tell a story or give an account of an event or series of events. Spoken narrative conventionally uses non-past verbs (often referred to as the 'present historic') to describe past events, and uses demonstrative adjectives and locative adverbs to create an impression of the here and now:

> *This fellow comes up to me here. He looks at me and says:*
> *'Could I tap you for a tenner?'*
> *'For a tenner,' says I, 'you could hit me with a hammer.'*

2 A distinction can be made between simple narrative, in which events are recounted in chronological order, and more complex narrative, in which events are recounted in an order that suits a preconceived plot. For example, if we label the events in a story A, B and C, then simple narrative uses the sequence A B C, whereas a detective story might use the technique B C A, where the full nature of A is not revealed until the end, and a psychological thriller may have A C B, where the precise motivation is not revealed in its chronological context.

3 More narrowly, *narrative* can be applied to the portions of a novel or story that are not conversation. It is not always easy to draw a line between fictional speech/thought and narrative, but essentially narrative provides background information, is expected to be reliable, has a first- or third-person narrator, and conforms more closely than speech to the written norms.

See: **argument, direct speech, exposition**.

negation, negative

Negation involves the contradiction or denial of an **affirmative** statement. In English, negation is normally carried by the *negative* marker *not/n't* either alone or in combination with the negative response *no*:

> *Did he say anything? No, he didn't*
> *Will he do it? No, he won't.*

Negation can also be marked by:
1 negative **morphemes**:

happy unhappy
legal illegal
loyal disloyal

2 negative words beginning with *n*:

neither...nor
never
none
nothing
nowhere

3 negative verbs such as:

deny
doubt
negate

4 **adverbs** such as *hardly, seldom, rarely*:

I **hardly** *ever see him.*
He **seldom** *says anything.*
She **rarely** *goes anywhere.*

5 intonation:

You'll go all right! (i.e. over my dead body)

Until the seventeenth century, double or multiple negation was widely used as a form of emphasis, as in:

Nor go neither; but you'll lie like dogs, and yet say
nothing neither.
     Shakespeare, *The Tempest*, Act 3, Scene 2

Then, grammarians introduced the rule that 'two negatives make an affirmative' and so Shakespearean-type emphasis became nonstandard. In spite of the rule, however, such examples as:

He didn't say nothing.
They wouldn't give nothing to nobody.

occur in mother-tongue dialects of English throughout the world.
   In colloquial speech, we often use what has been called 'transferred' negation with verbs of thinking:

He doesn't think they'll come. (He thinks they won't come.)
I don't believe he said it. (I believe he didn't say it.)
I don't suppose she'll come. (I suppose she won't come.)

In balanced structures, such as:

*He **neither** spoke **nor** listened.*
***Neither** John **nor** his brother can sing.*

nor and not *or* should be used.

See: **affirmative, either, parallelism.**

neologism

A *neologism* is a newly-created word or phrase, or the use of an established word with a new meaning:

*Have a **wazzy** weekend!* (wazzy = exciting, fun-filled)
*What do you think of his **punk** hair style?*
do-nothingism

Purists often express disapproval of neologisms, regarding them as unnecessary **barbarisms**. Gradually, however, neologisms, like **slang**, either disappear or are accepted into the language. Many neologisms associated with drugs are quickly discarded but others (e.g. *psychedelic*) are absorbed. The terminology associated with computers (e.g. *formatting, menu, muffin, parallel interface, ram*) contains many neologisms, which are rapidly being accepted into the language.

See: **coinage, jargon, slang.**

network norms

Although there is a standard written English which is essentially the same throughout the English-speaking world, there are numerous regional pronunciations. A form may be associated with educated speakers in one area and be of low status in another: postvocalic *r* in words like *port*, for example, has very different connotations in the USA and in southern UK. In each area of the world where English is a mother tongue or frequently-used second language there is a prestigious spoken variety which is used and spread by radio and television. These *network norms* are based on educated speech, but because they are based on *speech* and not *writing* they tend to be less formal, less complex and more open to the changes that are taking place in the language (the use of *less* where *fewer* would occur in the written medium, for example, and the extension of *between* to references involving more than two). In addition, since world-wide reporting is commonplace and since television programmes are widely circulated, regional network norms are becoming increasingly alike, with US norms, in particular, influencing the style of media journalists throughout the world.

See: **accent, Received Pronunciation, rhotic, Standard English.**

New Zealand English

New Zealand became a British colony in 1840 and was granted dominion status within the Commonwealth in 1907. Its population of 3.1 million is made up of approximately 10% Maoris and 90% settlers mainly from the British Isles. *New Zealand English* is very similar in pronunciation and syntax to **Australian English** and, in view of their shared history (New Zealand, for example, was administered in the 1840s as part of New South Wales) and the place of origin of their settler communities, these similarities are to be expected. It is in the area of vocabulary and especially in those items derived from Maori that New Zealand English is most clearly distinguishable from its neighbour.

Phonology

1 With the exception of a small community of Scottish settlers in the south of New Zealand's South Island, New Zealand English is non-**rhotic**.

2 The vowel sound in words such as *bit, is, ship* tends to be schwa:

/ðəs əz ðə bət aɪ laɪk/—This is the bit I like.

3 The front vowels in words such as *peck* and *pack* are close so that *peck* is often heard as /pɪk/ and *pack* as /pɛk/. *Pick* is realised as /pək/.

4 The long vowels in *beat* and *boot* are centralised and occasionally diphthongised so that *beat* is realised as /bɪit/ and *boot* as /bɪʉt/.

5 There is a tendency to merge the centring diphthongs in *hear* and *hare* so that, for many speakers, such pairs are **homophones**.

6 The vowel sound in *nut* is often identical with the sound in *not*, both being realised as /nɒt/.

7 The *l* sound tends to be dark in all contexts, so that the *l* in *light* sounds like the *l* in UK *full*. In words where the *l* is syllabic, as in *bottle*, it is often realised as a vowel /bɒtu/.

8 The velar nasal /ŋ/ can occur initially in Maori names such as *Ngaio* but most speakers other than Maoris realise such words as if they began with *n*.

Vocabulary

Much of New Zealand's vocabulary is shared with Australia, the UK and the USA, but a number of words have been adopted from Maori including place names:

Moana (Lake)
Rotorua (Two lake)

names for birds, animals and plants:

hapuku (fish)
huhu (beetle)
kiwi (bird)
kumara (sweet potato)
rata (tree)

and for indigenous culture:

haka (war dance)
hui (celebration)
kia ora (good health)

and settler:

pakeha (white person)

Grammar

Standard New Zealand English is indistinguishable from the standard written language in Australia and the UK. Many **dialect** features such as the use of *I done* and *them things* occur in the speech of the less well educated members of the community but, on the whole, New Zealand English is homogeneous and, in grammar, close to media **norms**.

See: **Australian English.**

news

The noun *news* is uncountable:

We've just had some very good news.
an item/piece of news

and although it looks plural *news* functions as a singular:

*The **news is** good.*
*Such good **news travels** fast.*

Other words that are formally plural but can function as singular are:

1 the names of familiar maladies:

collywobbles (**folk etymology** of *cholera morbus*)
measles
mumps

2 the names of certain games:

billiards
checkers
draughts

3 some words ending in -ics:

aerobics
athletics
mathematics
politics

See: **countable, -ic, -ical words.**

Newspeak

The term *Newspeak* was invented by George Orwell in *Nineteen Eighty-Four* (1948) to describe a variety of language designed as a means of controlling thought. The word has subsequently been expanded and used with a lower case *n* to refer to the ambiguities and contradictions often found in the language of **propaganda**. In this latter usage *newspeak* is similar in meaning to **Doublespeak** or *double talk*.

Many of the features of Newspeak are evident in other varieties of English:

1 **multifunctionality**. In Newspeak all words (including *if* and *when*) can be used as nouns, verbs, adjectives and adverbs.

2 linguistic irregularities are reduced. Orwell, for example, eliminates *thought*, making *think* work as both noun and verb and regularising the past tense to *thinked*. Many pidgins use similar techniques. In Cameroon Pidgin English, we have:

Tink nau. Ma nem bi wɛti? (Think now. What is my name?)
Wi bin tink sɔm fain tink. (We thought some fine thoughts.)

In addition, in Newspeak the **morpheme** *-ful* is used to mark adjectives and *-wise* to mark adverbs. The pidgin of Papua New Guinea uses very similar devices in that the morpheme *-pela* indicates an adjective:

arapela bikpela haus (another big house)

and *-im* marks a transitive verb:

Em i bagarap pinis. (It's ruined.)
Em i bagarapim haus bilong mi. (He ruined my house.)

3 vocabulary is reduced. Negatives are signalled by *un-* so that *warm* is replaced by *uncold*; emphasis is carried by *plus* and *doubleplus* (*pluscold, doublepluscold*) and other meanings are carried by *ante-, down-, post-* and *up-*.

All of the devices described by Orwell occur naturally in varieties of English and are not inherently good or bad. What Orwell was stressing was that language is our means of coming to terms with our individual universes, that our individuality is in part a consequence of our idiosyncratic command of our language, and that our minds can be controlled, in part at least, by language.

See: **affix, circumlocution, Doublespeak, euphemism, pidgins and creoles, propaganda, word formation.**

nice

The adjective *nice* provides a clear example of the semantic changes many words in English undergo. *Nice*, deriving from Latin *nescius* (ignorant), came into English in the fourteenth century with the meanings of 'foolish' and 'silly' as well as 'ignorant'. One hundred years later *nice* could also mean 'wanton' and 'lascivious'. From *wanton* its meaning extended to 'shy' and then 'precise' as in:

> *a nice distinction*

By the eighteenth century it had developed its contemporary meaning of approval:

> *a nice meal* (I enjoyed it.)
> *a nice person* (I approve of this person.)

and can now be applied to anything from activities to zebras. Because of its wide applicability and vagueness, *nice* is often criticised by teachers.

Recent uses of *nice* suggest that its semantic shifting is not at an end. It is now frequently used to mean the opposite of 'pleasant'. Tone of voice can make:

> *O that's nice! That's really nice!*

mean:

> 'That is not at all pleasant or acceptable.'

See: **aggravate, cliché, phatic communion, semantic change.**

Nigerian English

Nigeria, with an estimated population of 80 million, is one of the wealthiest countries in Black Africa. Its links with Britain go back to the fifteenth century, when Portuguese traders first complained that English adventurers were travelling to the West Coast of Africa. Independence was granted in 1960 and in 1961 Nigeria became a Republic within the Commonwealth.

As well as being the most populous country in Africa, Nigeria is one of the most multilingual. An estimated 400 languages are spoken within its borders. The three largest of these are Hausa (spoken by 26.7% of the population), Igbo (10.7%) and Yoruba (17.8%). These, together with Pidgin English, are widely used throughout the country.

English is the official language and also the educated **lingua franca** of Nigeria. It is the medium of education in all but the first three years of primary school, the language of official and formal functions, and the language of international and elite intertribal communications. It is also the dominant language of the press, with 13 daily and 15 weekly newspapers in English, and more air-time on radio and television is devoted to English than to any other language.

English began to be taught formally in Nigeria in the nineteenth century and in the course of over a hundred and fifty years a distinctive variety has emerged. As in other anglophone communities, the English in Nigeria is not a single, homogeneous language but a cluster of subvarieties which include:

(a) Pidgin English
(b) mother-tongue-influenced English
(c) the Indian-influenced English of many teachers and traders
(d) standard Nigerian English
(e) expatriate mother-tongue English

And such a subdivision hides the fact that standard Nigerian English is spoken with different accents, owing to the influence of the mother tongues and of distinct regional policies in education. For example, *pan* and *fan* may be **homophones** for some Hausa speakers, *bus* and *buzz* or *cheer* and *sheer* for Yoruba speakers, and *light* and *right* for speakers of Tiv or Idoma.

Phonology

1 All varieties of Nigerian English are non-**rhotic**. Received Pronunciation (RP) is still a prestigious accent and educated speakers show varying degrees of sophistication in their approximation to it.

2 There are fewer vowel contrasts than in RP, with many speakers conflating /i/ and /ɪ/ to /i/, /ɔ/ and /ɒ/ to /ɔ/ and /u/ and /ʊ/ to /u/, thus making homophones of *sheep* and *ship*, *nought* and *not*, *fool* and *full*.

3 The central vowels /ə/, /ʌ/ and /ɜ/ are replaced by front or back vowels, usually under the influence of spelling. Thus:

/əgoʊ/ > /ago/ (ago)
/bʌt/ > /bɔt/ (but)
/bɜd/ > /bɛd/ (bird)
/tʃɜtʃ/ > /tʃɔtʃ/ (church)

4 The diphthongs in *bay* and *go* are monophthongised; those in *bear* and *beer* are sometimes monophthongised and sometimes realised as /ea/ and /ia/.

5 The consonants /θ,ð/ as in *thin* and *then* are realised as /t,d/ in the south and as /s,z/ in Northern Nigerian English.

6 The /ʒ/ sound that occurs finally in *orange* /ɒrɪnʒ/ is realised as /dʒ/ in the north and as /ʃ/ in the south.

7 **Consonant clusters** are often modified either by vowel **epenthesis** as in /arɛndʒimɛnt/ for *arrangement* or by **apocope** as with /lɪs/ for *list*.

8 The rhythm and stress patterns of the mother tongues affect Nigerian English. The syllables in polysyllabic words are often more equally stressed than in RP and emphasis is sometimes suggested by a change of intonation. Thus, a Nigerian speaker who wishes to stress his intention to go may not give emphatic stress to *will* in:

I will go.

but change the falling tone on *go* to a fall-rise *gŏ*.

Vocabulary
Nigerian English differs from other varieties of English in four main ways:

1 Words are borrowed from Nigerian languages:

akara (bean cake) (Hausa)
chĩchĩ (fritter) (Igbo)
bolekaja danfo molue (public transport) (Yoruba)

2 There are **calques** from the mother tongues:

smell pepper (suffer)
spray money (attach money to musicians, dancers as a mark of appreciation)
wash an event (celebrate an event by 'washing' it down with drinks)

3 Many words and phrases have been given additional meanings:

battery charger (person who repairs batteries)
essential commodities (scarce consumer goods)
Well done! (greeting to someone at work)

4 A number of words have been created in Nigeria, some on analogy with English words. The *-ee* morpheme, for example, is more productive:

arrangee (someone who arranges illegal money exchanges)
decampee (one who switches to a different political party)

Others derive from **acronyms**. The Joint Admission and Matriculation Board, for example, has led to *jambite* meaning a first-year undergraduate student and the War Against Indiscipline has produced *wai*, meaning 'a type of crusade'.

Grammar
Most educated Nigerians use standard grammar, especially in writing, but the following features are widespread:

1 the use of *could* and *would* for *can* and *will*:

I could remember that you came this morning.
This is to inform you that there would be a meeting tomorrow.

2 the use of uncountable nouns as countable:

*Thank you for your **advices**.*
*We have ordered **these equipments**.*

3 the definite article is sometimes omitted:

***Aircraft** is fully booked.*

or inserted where it is not required:

***The** life after death is a reality.*

4 the use of *no + any* by Hausa speakers:

*I have **no any** friend.*

5 the use of verbs in a reciprocal sense without *each other*:

We have known for ten years.
We saw this morning.

and the tendency to use *themselves* where *each other* is required:

They really love themselves.

6 the different use of prepositions:

*The victim died **by** twelve o'clock.*
*Mr Olu is the principal **for** our school.*
***On** the long run, this won't work.*

Nigerian Pidgin is widely used as a lingua franca, especially in coastal and large urban communities. Like Nigerian English, it differs from region to region, reflecting the speaker's mother tongue and degree of exposure to Standard English. It has been used in literature by novelists, poets and playwrights and it can be found, mainly for humorous purposes, in some newspapers and on radio and television. The following extract from Chinua Achebe's story *Civil Peace* gives an idea of the flexibility of Nigerian Pidgin English:

'My frien, why you no de talk again. I de ask you say you
wan make we call soja?'
'No.'
'Awrighto. Now make we talk business. We no be bad tief.
We no like for make trouble. Trouble done finish. War done
finish and all the katakata wey de for inside. No Civil War
again. This time na Civil Peace. No be so?'
'Na so!'

See: **African English, pidgins and creoles, West African English**.

nobody, none, no one

Nobody, meaning 'no person', is singular and like *no one* takes a singular verb:

> **Nobody has** to know.
> **No one knows** anything.

No one occurs in two forms, *no one* and *no-one*, with the first form gaining in popularity.
    There are difficulties in agreement when **question tags** occur:

> *Nobody knows, does he/she/do they?*
> *No one had the answer, had he/she/they?*

Grammarians insist that since *nobody* and *no one* are singular and since *he* comprehends *she* the correct **tags** should be:

> *Nobody knows,* **does he?**
> *No one had the answer,* **had he?**

but many feminists suggest that the colloquial usage with *they*:

> *Nobody knows,* **do they?**

should be adopted.
    Etymologically, *none*, from Old English *nan* meaning 'not one', is also singular and should be followed by a singular verb:

> *None* **was** *wasted.*

None is, however, often followed by the construction 'of + plural NP' and in these circumstances the plural form of the verb occurs in colloquial speech and increasingly in the written medium:

> *None of their efforts* **were** *wasted.*

> *Nobody, no one* and *none* can occur as objects as well as subjects:

> *I saw* **nobody.**
> *I met* **no one.**
> *I like* **none** *(of them).*

but, colloquially, we are more likely to use:

> *I didn't see anybody.*
> *I didn't meet anyone.*
> *I don't like any (of them).*

See: **all, concord, every, number.**

nominalisation/nominalization

The term *nominal* is often used as a synonym for a **noun**, a **pronoun**, a **noun phrase** or a structure which can function as a subject, object or noun complement:

*The professor lost **her** mortarboard.*
***She** lost **it**.*
*The order was founded to look after **the poor**.*
***To err** is human.*

Nominalisation is the process of forming nominals from other word classes:

good (adj) → *goodness*
see (verb) → *seeing* (*Seeing is believing.*)
arrive (verb) → *arrival*

See: **noun, noun phrase.**

nonce words

Nonce words are created, consciously or unconsciously, 'for the nonce', that is, on or for a particular occasion. They look and sound like English words in that they do not break the phonological constraints of the language, but they are ephemeral.

Nonce words can result from conscious humour:

*He's wonderful, maybe even **twoderful.***

a slip of the tongue:

tinty moothpaste

a false analogy:

*He's becoming **Englified.*** (cf. verified)

or blends:

finicky + *pernickity* → *firnickity*

Often, advertisers use nonce-type words as product names:

Nescafé < Nestlé's coffee/café

although if these or any other nonce creations cease to be ephemeral, then they cease to be nonce words.

See: **coinage, word formation.**

nonstandard English

As well as a written standard language which is accepted (with minor differences) throughout the English-speaking world, there are several types of *nonstandard English* in existence:

1 regional dialects. In Yorkshire, for example, one may hear:

He were stood at pit gate, were he.

2 working-class dialects:

I shoulda went out and bought them boots.

3 mother-tongue-influenced English. This category includes a wide spectrum of Englishes which are influenced phonologically, lexically and syntactically by the speaker's mother tongue:

You should pick the child (pick up the child) *at two.*

(This type of English is often referred to as 'L$_2$ English'. L$_1$ = a mother tongue, L$_2$ = one's first foreign language, L$_3$ = one's second foreign language. A Nigerian, for example, might have Hausa as an L$_1$, English as an L$_2$, Yoruba as an L$_3$ and Pidgin English as an L$_4$.)

4 inadequately acquired English, where false analogies or false learning strategies can produce:

I have breaked it.
I have not the people seen.

See: **dialect, pidgins and creoles, Standard English.**

norms

A *norm* may be regarded as the habitual language use of a group. The group may be as small as a village community or as large as all the speakers of **US English**. The norm is useful in providing a fixed point from which a series of comparisons may be made. For example, the norm of **Received Pronunciation** (RP) in the UK provides a basis for pronunciation comparisons between speech in Lancashire and in Cornwall as well as between either of these and RP. There is, however, a tendency for a norm to become a prestigious standard and for variations to be regarded not simply as 'different' but as 'inferior'.

The study of norms has proved useful in many branches of linguistics. The selection of norms of pronunciation, for example, has helped in the **sociolinguistic** studies of ethnic groups and urban communities. **Stylistics,** too, often utilises the notion of norms. A poetic sentence such as:

Me he condemns!

which has the structure Object + Subject + Predicate may be seen to deviate from the pattern of the usual English sentence Subject + Predicate + Object.

Scientific English can be shown to have a marked preference for passive constructions, pre-nominal modification and polysyllabic vocabulary:

A specified quantity of pulverised, pre-tested ammonia crystals was added to the solution.

See: **deviation, network norms.**

North African English

The countries described under this heading are Morocco, Tunisia, Algeria, Libya, Egypt, Mauritania, Mali, Niger and Chad and the disputed territory of Western Sahara. The population of the area is just over 113 million and the ten countries have known four colonial powers: Britain, France, Italy and Spain. With such diversity, it would normally be hard to offer generalisations, but for all these countries the Islamic religion and Arabic are unifying forces. English is most widely used in Egypt but it is widely taught as a second European language in all francophone territories and as the first foreign language of Libya.

Phonology
Although the phonology of individuals differs according to their exposure to and competence in English, the following features are widespread:

1 The prestige English of the region is non-**rhotic**, but US influence combined with **spelling pronunciation** is causing a change, so that post-vocalic *r* is becoming common in words such as *far* and *farm*. In other positions, the *r* is often rolled.

2 Length differences in vowels are rarely preserved so that:

weep and *whip* are realised as /wip/
not and *nought* are realised as /nɔt/
fool and *full* are realised as /ful/

3 /ɛ/ as in *ten* is often raised to /ɪ/, causing *ten* to be realised as *tin*.

4 The diphthongs /eɪ,aɪ,ɔɪ/ are often replaced by /e,a,ɔ/.

5 Initial /p/ is often not aspirated and so /p/ and /b/ are not fully contrasted, resulting occasionally in the confusion of sets such as *pump* and *bump*.

6 /tʃ/ and /dʒ/ as in *chop* and *judge* are often replaced by /ʃ/ and /ʒ/, causing words such as *chop* and *shop* to be confused.

7 /θ,ð/ are often replaced by /t,d/ or, especially in word-final position, by /s,z/.

8 The *l* sound tends to be clear in all positions and to sound identical in *light, fill* and *kettle*.

9 Intrusive vowels are often introduced into **consonant clusters**:

string > /sɪtrɪŋ/
months > /mʌntɪz/

10 The velar nasal /ŋ/ is variously realised as /ŋk/, /ŋ/, /ŋg/ and /n/.

Vocabulary
Apart from the many **borrowings** from Arabic for words associated with religion and culture:

Koran
muezzin
mullah

influence from French in the francophone countries encourages the use of items such as:

auto /oto/ for car
fifteen days for fortnight
mandate for money order

In addition, there is a tendency to confuse near synonyms in such lexical sets as:

hear/listen
know/learn/discover
see/look
strange/foreign

Grammar

1 The **copula** is often omitted:

She teacher.
We happy.

2 Adjectives are sometimes used as nouns:

*He didn't tell me the **important** (thing).*
*I work at the **British** (Council).*

and the comparative is sometimes used where a superlative is required:

*She is the **older** (i.e. oldest) child in the family.*

3 The noun phrase is often recapitulated within a relative clause:

*That's **the man** I saw **him** yesterday.*
*She followed **the girl** that I met **her** on the bus.*

4 Intonation is often used to distinguish statements from *yes/no* questions:

He has come?

and the word order in wh-questions tends to be untransformed:

What he is doing?
When you are coming?

5 Articles cause many problems: *a* is sometimes omitted:

This is shop./This shop.

sometimes relaced by *one*:

You want one orange juice?

and, especially with abstract nouns, replaced by *the*:

We all need the love.

Some and *any* tend to be avoided:

I bought lovely oranges in the market.
We haven't money.

6 The preposition *to* is often used after *bring, buy, give, send, tell* and *owe*:

*He **brought to me** the message.*
*She **gave to me** a beautiful present.*

and *from* often replaces *than* in comparatives:

*He is older **from** me.*

7 *Very* is frequently replaced by *too*:

*This mountain is **too** high.*

See: **African English.**

noun

Traditionally, a *noun* was defined as a 'naming word' or 'the name of a person, animal, place or thing' and such definitions, although vague, are still useful. Recent definitions of nouns tend to concentrate on their *form* and *function* rather than on any semantic criteria. As far as form goes, it can be shown that most nouns change to indicate plurality and **possession**:

Singular	Plural	Possesssion Singular and Plural	
the cat	the cats	the cat's tail	the cats' tails
the dog	the dogs	the dog's tail	the dogs' tails
the horse	the horses	the horse's tail	the horses' tails

In speech, plurality and possession in regular nouns are both signalled by the addition of /s/, /z/ or /ɪz/ to the base form of the word. In the written medium, *s* or *es* indicate plurality, an apostrophe + *s* indicates singular possession and *s* + an apostrophe indicates plural possession.

Nouns in English can be subdivided in different ways:

1 They can be either *masculine, feminine* or *neuter*:

bull	cow	book
man	woman	flower
stallion	mare	tree

2 Nouns can be either *proper* or *common*:

Ahmed	*boy*
Egypt	*country*
Arabic	*language*

Proper nouns (and the names of languages are proper nouns) always start with a capital letter, whereas common nouns begin with a small letter:

French fruit
Spanish spider

3 Nouns can be either *concrete* (i.e. they can refer to objects that have a material existence) or *abstract* (i.e. they can refer to ideas, concepts or qualities):

coin	*intuition*
dinner	*duty*
elevator	*jealousy*

4 Nouns may be either **countable** or **uncountable** (or *mass*). A countable noun can be preceded by *a*:

a tree

can have both a singular and a plural form:

a house   houses

and can, as its name suggests, be counted:

one banana   two bananas   ten bananas

Whereas singular countable nouns can be preceded by *a*, uncountable nouns tend to be preceded by *some*:

some butter   some sand

An uncountable noun cannot normally be pluralised and cannot be counted:

beef *two beefs/beeves
fun *ten funs
rain *five rains

5 In English, there are a number of **collective nouns** such as:

collection committee flock

which are singular in form but which refer to a number of people, animals or things. Such nouns tend to occur with singular forms of the verb and are replaced by singular pronouns:

*The collection is priceless. **It** took years to assemble.*

Nouns can function as subjects:

Trees should not be cut down.

objects:

*He always gave **money** to the poor.*

and as complements:

*That was **John**.*
*They elected him **President**.*

They can follow prepositions:

in the trees

and be replaced by pronouns:

John was President.
He was this.

See: **collective nouns, countable, gender, noun phrase, plurals of nouns, proper nouns.**

noun phrase

A *noun phrase* is a nominal group with a **noun** as headword:

a happy child
a girl in blue

A headword is the unit of central significance around which other units cluster in a set order. We can have several noun phrases in a sentence:

The old house *was sold to* **the highest bidder** *for* **an undisclosed figure**.

There are four types of noun phrases in English which have essentially the same distribution and which can often substitute for each other. These are:

1 *Substantive phrases* which have the basic pattern:

(Determiner) (Modifiers) Headword (Modifiers)

where only the headword is obligatory:

D	Modifier(s)	Headword	Modifier(s)
		people	
some		people	
some	ordinary	people	in glasshouses
some	nice, ordinary	people	who don't throw stones
	nice, ordinary	people	leading decent lives

2 *Proper names*, both unmodified:

J.B. Ackroyd

and modified:

the beautiful Ms Green
our Fido
47-year-old father of two, Brian Matthews

3 *Pronouns*, which can be subdivided into:
(a) personal:

I you we

(b) possessive:

yours ours theirs

(c) reflexive:

herself himself ourselves

(d) demonstrative:

this that these those

(e) interrogative:

who? which?

(f) relative:

that which whose

(g) distributive:

all (of you)   both (of us)

(h) indefinite:

any some

Pronouns are used to replace other noun phrases:

The people we met *were called Smith.*
They *were called Smith.*

4 *Nominalisations*, that is, nouns derived from other parts of speech:

*descend   Their **descent** was rapid.*
*poor   The **poor** seem to be getting poorer.*

Noun phrases can function as **subjects**:

The people *wanted to leave.*

objects:

*Have you read **much poetry**?*

and **complements**:

  *What is **the problem**?*

They also occur after **prepositions** in preposition phrases:

  with all my heart

See: **complement, head, nominalisation, noun, object, pronoun, subject.**

number

Number is used in the classification of words which can display a contrast between singular and plural:

  The cat likes me.
  The cats like us.

Number is thus apparent in nouns, non-past verbs and, to a lesser extent, in pronouns.

  Number often corresponds to life:

Tabby/he	likes John.
Ginger/she	likes Mary.
The cats/they	like them.

but the correlation is not perfect. There are, in English, nouns which are singular in form but plural in reference:

  congregation jury

or plural in form but singular in reference. These include certain games:

  checkers draughts

illnesses:

  measles mumps

and studies:

  physics psycholinguistics

In addition, certain uncountable nouns like *sugar* refer to quantities rather than specific entities.

  With regard to verbs, number is only apparent in the non-past:

Non-past	*Past*
He likes cheese.	He liked cheese.
We like cheese.	We liked cheese.

although, again, there is not a one-to-one correlation between grammar and life. The third person singular only affixes an *s* or *es* to the

base form of the verb, whereas the first and second persons singular and the first, second and third persons plural take the base form:

I/you/we/they/Tom and Jerry like apples.
he/she/it/Tom likes apples.

Personal pronouns have been subdivided into first, second and third persons singular and plural:

Person	Singular	Plural
1	I/me/my/mine	we/us/our/ours
2	you/your/yours	you/your/yours
3 fem.	she/her/hers	they/them/their/theirs
masc.	he/him/his	they/them/their/theirs
neut.	it/its	they/them/their/theirs

Although *we* is plural, it is not equivalent to *I* + *I* + ... but rather to *I* + *you* + *he/she/they*.

See: **collective nouns, concord, countable, news, plurals of nouns.**

numbers

The conventions which apply to *numbers* can be summarised as follows:

1 Use words for:

(a) numbers *one* to *twelve*. When numbers above twenty are spelt out, they should be hyphenated (*twenty-two*). Figures can be used to avoid too many hyphens:

a 22-year-old cyclist

(b) round figures *a thousand, two million*

(c) numbers which occur with *per cent*, especially at the beginning of a sentence, but figures plus the % symbol are preferable in the middle of a sentence and in notes and tables.

2 Use figures for:

(a) numbers from 13 upwards

(b) before **abbreviations**:

2 kg
3 km
5 cc
6 pm (but *six o'clock*)

(c) percentages, except at the beginning of a sentence

(d) for **dates**, except in very formal writing

(e) in addresses:

7 Becket Avenue
1234 Becket Drive

(f) for exact sums of **money**:

£3.95
$2.63

3 The following conventions should also be adhered to:
(a) Use a comma after thousands and millions:

16,124
1,346,925

Full stops/periods are more common in continental Europe:

16.124
1.346.925

(b) Place the decimal point half-way up the number:

0·5

In continental Europe a comma is used:

0,5

(c) With consecutive numbers, keep the last two digits:

12-14
234-48
1254-59

(d) Indicate the plural of a figure with *s*:

all the 3s
twelve 5s
1990s

(e) The figure '0' is normally called *nought* in the UK and *zero* in the USA. It is also referred to as *0* (pronounced *oh*) in a series of numbers:

My car registration number is six nine oh. (UK)

as *zero* in temperature measurements:

*The temperature will fall below **zero** tonight.* (UK and US)

as *nil* is sports matches:

*Coventry lost two-**nil**.* (UK)

and as *love* in tennis matches:

*She's leading forty-**love**.* (UK and US)

In **US English**, there is a tendency to leave out *and* in such numbers as 105 and 250:

UK	US
one hundred and five	one hundred five
two hundred and fifty people	two hundred fifty people

The symbol ♯ is frequently used to indicate *number*:

number thirty-five (UK) ♯ *35* (US)

and throughout the English-speaking world *megaton* can be used for *one million tons*:

a twenty megaton bomb

See: **age, billion, measurements, money, UK and US words.**

object

Many verbs can co-occur with two or three noun phrases:

John loved his cat.
Mary wrote John a letter.

Such verbs are **transitive**, that is, they can take an *object*. Verbs like BRING, BUILD, GIVE, MAKE, WRITE can take both a direct and an indirect object:

Subject	Predicate	Indirect Object	Direct Object
John	built	Mary	a house.
Mary	gave	him	the money.

An indirect object can be moved and preceded by the prepositions *for* or *to*:

John built a house for Mary.
Mary gave the money to him.

A direct object can be identified as follows:
1 It normally follows the **predicate** in finite sentences:

I saw Penelope.

If, for stylistic purposes, the object is foregrounded, then it precedes the **subject** as well as the predicate:

Penelope I saw.

2 There is no concordial **agreement** between the predicate and the object:

He loves his cat.
He loves his cats.

3 It can only occur with a non-passive predicate:

Subject	Predicate	Object
The detective	overheard	the thief.
The thief	was overheard.	

4 The most frequently occurring objects are nouns:

*I enjoy **baseball**.*

noun phrases:

*I have enjoyed **every single game**.*

and object pronouns:

*The dog followed **me** home.*

The object pronouns are: *me, him, her, us, them* and *whom*. Other pronouns such as: *you, it, this* can occur as both subjects and objects. Occasionally, the object can be a finite **clause**:

*She described **what she had seen**.*
*I denied **that I had said it**.*

or a non-finite clause:

*He wanted **to go home**.*
*They denied **being involved**.*

5 The object does not occur in **question tags**:

*She saw him, **didn't she**?*

6 The object relative pronoun may be omitted:

*the letter **that** I wrote*
*the letter **which** I wrote*
the letter I wrote

7 The object may be omitted with pseudo-intransitive verbs:

He shaved (his beard) this morning.
She wrote (a letter) to her son.
We usually eat (lunch) at noon.

See: **transitive, verb phrase.**

of, off

The words *of* and *off* derive from the same **Old English** root and they are sometimes confused or compounded in regional **dialects**:

*The wind took the roof from **off of** the house.*

They are, however, clearly distinguished in the standard language.
Of is a **preposition** which can be used to indicate position:

the bottom of the road

attributes:

the wisdom of Solomon

origin or status:

> *the barber of Seville*
> *a man of means*

material used:

> *a sword of gold studded with precious stones*

contents:

> *a cup of coffee*

cause:

> *She died of pneumonia.*

possession:

> *the wealth of Croesus*

relationships:

> *a cousin of my father's sister-in-law*

part of a whole:

> *most of the money*

weights and measurements:

> *a pound of tomatoes*
> *a metre of this material*

and time in the USA:

> *a quarter of two (1:45)*

When *of* occurs as an indicator of possession, it can often be replaced by a structure involving an **apostrophe** + s:

> *a daughter of a king = a king's daughter*
> *daughters of kings = kings' daughters*

Such replacement is unlikely:
1 when the nouns involved are inanimate:

> *the leg of a table → the tableleg* (*the table's leg)

2 when the phrase is idiomatic:

> *a hair of the dog* (a drink)
> *the dog's hair* (literal)

Of occurs in the structures:
1 NP + of + NP:

> *the time of your life*

2 Adjective + of + NP:

hard of hearing

3 **Adverb** + of + NP:

out of sight

4 VP + of + NP:

die of grief

Off can occur as an adverb:

The plane took off on time.

as a preposition:

They ran him off the road.

and as an adjective:

an off day

Unlike *of*, *off* normally has locative force, implying distance or movement away from something:

The house was still ten miles off.
They moved off quickly and were soon out of sight.

Thus, the *off side* of a car is the driver's side (away from the kerb) while the *near side* is the passenger's side (close to the kerb).

See: **location**.

okay

Okay (also written *O.K.*, *OK*) is widely used in informal language as an expression of agreement:

*Will you take it? **Okay**.*

as an adjective:

*He's **okay** now.*

as a noun:

*We got his **okay** yesterday.*

and as a verb:

*I don't think he'll **okay** the party.*

There is no satisfactory **etymology** for *okay*. Some linguists claim that it derives from an **abbreviation** of *oll korrect*, a variant form of 'all correct'; others that it was borrowed from the *O.K. Club* which was founded in 1840 by supporters of a presidential candidate who came from Old Kinderhook in New York; a few suggest that it is a variant of the Scottish expression *Och aye*; and Africanists have pointed out that many West African languages have expressions of agreement such as *oki*, *oka* and *okai*. Whatever the etymology, the word, which was first recorded in the early nineteenth century, is one of the most frequently used in the English language.

See: **etymology**.

Old English

Old English (also referred to as *Anglo-Saxon*) is the name given to the varieties of English spoken in parts of England from about AD 450 to 1100 and with written documents from the seventh century. Old English was composed of Germanic dialects, derived from the dialects brought to Britain by the Angles, Saxons and Jutes in the middle of the fifth century and mutually intelligible with many Germanic dialects in Scandinavia and northwestern Europe. The Old English dialects were highly inflected: all nouns, both animate and inanimate, had grammatical **gender**, adjectives agreed with the nouns they modified, **predicates** agreed with subjects, and an elaborate system of **case** endings permitted considerable freedom of **word order**.

Many of the most frequently-used words in the language (*child, man, woman, BE, COME, GO, bad, good, full*) derive from Old English, but the language changed dramatically between 1100 and 1400: inflections and grammatical gender were largely lost and much vocabulary was adopted from French. An indication of the fundamental differences between Old English and contemporary varieties can be given by juxtaposing a brief passage from the Gospel of St Mark in Old English with the same passage from the New English Bible:

Old English	Contemporary English
Her ys godspellys angyn Hælyndes Cristes, Godes Suna. Swa awriten is on ðaes witegan bec Isaiam, 'Nu ic asende minne engel beforan ðinre ansyne, se gegearwað ðinne weg beforan ðe...'	Here begins the Gospel of Jesus Christ the Son of God. In the prophet Isaiah it stands written: 'Here is my herald whom I send on ahead of you, and he will prepare your way...'

See: **inflection, Middle English**.

only

In popular usage, *only* is often placed in front of the verb:

I only bought a coat.

or between the auxiliary and the headverb:

*I've **only** bought a coat.*

In speech, we avoid potential **ambiguity** by emphasising the word that *only* relates to:

I've only bought a coat. (and not a Rolls Royce)
I've only bought *a coat.* (though I also fancied a skirt)

In the written medium, however, it may not always be clear whether *only* modifies the subject, the predicate, the object or the **adjunct**. For precision, therefore, *only* should be placed immediately before the sentence unit it modifies:

Only Jane got a rise last week.
Jane only got a rise last week.
Jane got only a rise last week.
Jane got a rise only last week.

Other limiters that need to be treated similarly include *even, exactly, just, merely, nearly* and *simply.*

See: **adjunct, ambiguity**.

onomatopoeia

Onomatopoeia is the use or creation of words which denote an action or object by suggesting a sound associated with the action or object. Thus, for example, *buzz, crunch, fizzle, hiss* and *hum* convey meaning largely through sound effects.

The link between sounds and meaning is usually completely arbitrary. The chemical compound of hydrogen and oxygen is known variously as:

agua eau wasser water uisce

and none of these words bears more than a conventionalised connection with H_2O. Other words like *cuckoo* and *peewit* derive their form from the sounds reputedly made by these birds. However, even onomatopoeic sounds can differ from place to place: a dog barks *bow wow* in some parts of the English-speaking world and *wuff wuff* in others; and an anglophone rooster begins the day with *cock-a-doodle-doo* whereas his West African counterpart uses *kukaruku*.

A number of scholars have pointed out that certain sounds in English regularly occur with a particular meaning. Thus *sl-* has unpleasant connotations in:

slime slink slither slush

(although not in *sleep* and *slim*). *Fl-* and *gl-* are respectively associated with movement and light:

flee flow flutter
gleam glisten glow

and the vowel sound in 'hunt' /ʌ/ is usually associated with physical effort, as in:

grunt munch thump

When sounds or combinations of sounds frequently occur with a specific meaning, the phenomenon is referred to as **sound symbolism**. Poets frequently use sound symbolism to reinforce their meanings. Thus fricatives like /s, z, f, v/ occur when friction, effort or continuity of movement is stressed, just as plosives like /p, b, t, d, k, g/ are often found in war poetry.

Sound symbolism is most frequently used in English to appeal to the ear, but it is occasionally used in connection with the other senses. Expressions like *yum yum* can imply that food tastes good, wolf whistles suggest appreciation of the female form and *yuch!* is occasionally a response to something that is unpleasant to the touch.

See: **sound symbolism, synaesthesia**.

oral tradition

Every community in the world has a language and a **literature**, that is, a spoken or written compendium of significant beliefs, laws, stories and traditions. All such literatures were originally oral in that they existed only in the spoken medium and were passed down by word of mouth from one generation to another. (There is a growing tendency to use the word *orature*, from *oral* + *literature*, for traditional wisdom found only in the spoken medium.)

Since *oral traditions* could easily be lost or forgotten, people have made extensive use of mnemonic devices (memory aids) such as:

1 **alliteration**:

Look before you leap.

2 **antithesis**:

The old dog for the hard road, and the pup for the path.
Easy killed and easy cured.

3 **assonance**:

A bird in the hand is worth two in the bush.

4 repetition, of word or structure:

They hadn't sailed a league, a league,
A league but barely three,
When the sky grew dark, the wind grew strong
And gurly grew the sea.

5 rhyme:

An apple a day
Keeps the doctor away.

6 formulaic openings and conclusions:

Once upon a time...
And they lived happily ever after.

See: **literature.**

orchestrate, organise

Orchestrate and *organise* have ostensibly similar meanings when they relate to arranging events in an effective way. However, in media reports *orchestrate* is often used unfavourably and *organise* favourably. This tendency results in covert influence:

*It was an **orchestrated** demonstration against the government.*
*It was an **organised** event and passed off peacefully.*

See: **connotation, propaganda.**

orthography

Orthography derives from Greek *orthos* (straight, upright) + *graphos* (writing) and it can refer to:
 1 the study of a writing system or writing systems
 2 the principles of **spelling** in a particular language or group of languages.

See: **morpheme, punctuation, spelling.**

oxymoron

Oxymoron from Greek *oxus* (sharp) + *moros* (stupid) is a figure of speech involving two semantically exclusive or contradictory terms:

devoted enemies
false truth
peaceful war

Oxymoron, like **paradox**, often features in poetry where literal truth may be sacrificed to emotional impact.

See: **figurative language, paradox.**

Pakistani English

Pakistan, which gained its independence from the UK in 1947, has a population of approximately 93 million. Originally, Pakistan (which is in part an **acronym** for Punjabi + Afghan + Kurd + Sind) consisted of the modern state of Pakistan (West Pakistan) and the state of Bangladesh (East Pakistan) but after the war of 1971 Bangladesh (population about 90 million) became an independent state. The official languages of Pakistan and Bangladesh are Urdu and Bengali respectively, but English is the most important non-indigenous language in both countries, being used extensively in commerce, education, literature and international dealings. The varieties of English used range from standard international English with a local accent through mother-tongue-influenced forms to a limited type of English used by taxi-drivers, waiters and people involved in the tourist industry.

Islam is a more significant force in Pakistan and Bangladesh than in India and so there are more lexical items derived from Arabic and Urdu in the English of Pakistan and Bangladesh than in India.

See: **English in the Indian Sub-Continent.**

palindrome

Palindrome derives from Greek *palindromos* meaning 'running back again'. It involves an arrangement of letters and words giving the same message backwards and forwards:

> *bib*
> *Malayalam*
> *radar*
> *Able was I ere I saw Elba.*
> *Eros saw Bob was sore.*
> *Madam, I'm Adam.*
> *Todd eyed Dot.*

Papua New Guinean English

Papua New Guinea, which was a United Nations Protectorate known as 'The Territories of Papua and New Guinea', gained independence from Australia in 1974. The country has a population of just over 3 million with some 700+ languages in daily use. English is one of the official languages of the country, as is Tok Pisin (Talk Pidgin), an English-related Pidgin, and it is the Pidgin rather than Standard English that is most frequently used in Parliament, commerce and in much internal interaction.

Educated speakers from Papua New Guinea approximate to standard **Australian English**, although their pronunciation usually reflects the patterns of their mother tongues. In general, Papua New Guineans can be distinguished from Australians of similar education in that they tend:

1 to use fewer vowel contrasts, so that *bit* and *beat* are often **homophones**

2 to use fewer diphthongs, so that *gate* and *take* have /e/, rather than /eɪ/

3 to devoice voiced consonants at the end of a word, so that *bead* can sound like *bit* and *bag* like *back*

4 to simplify **consonant clusters**

5 not to distinguish between *he* and *she*

6 to use stative verbs with the **progressive**:

I am knowing him well.

7 to use prepositions differently:

We must voice out our opinion.
I will discuss about this tomorrow.
Are you aftering (i.e. following) *him?*

8 to use an invariable **tag**, *isn't it?* or *not so?*

He has arrived, isn't it?

9 to use vocabulary items from their own culture:

bilum (type of woven bag)
kunai (type of grass)
taro (type of food)

10 to show some influence from Tok Pisin.

Tok Pisin is lexically related to English but is not easily understood by a mother-tongue speaker of English. It has an official **orthography**, is highly regarded by the government and is used for many purposes in the country and in dealings with neighbouring countries like the Solomon Islands, where a closely-related Pidgin exists. The simplest way of highlighting the differences between Tok Pisin and English is to juxtapose a verse from the Gospel of St Mark 1:6:

Tok Pisin	Standard English
Na Jon i save putim klos ol i bin	And John was clothed
wokim long gras bilong kamel, na	with camel's hair, and
em i pasim let long namel bilong en.	with a girdle of skin about him.

See: **Australian English, pidgins and creoles.**

PARADIGM   330

paradigm

Paradigm comes from Greek *paradeiknynai* meaning 'show side by side'. In language studies, the word refers to a table which sets out all the inflected forms of a **part of speech**. Paradigms relating to nouns are called *conjugations*; those relating to verbs are called *declensions*.

Latin-based grammars of English used to provide such paradigms for nouns as:

	Singular	Plural
Nominative	lord	lords
Vocative	o lord	o lords
Accusative	lord	lords
Genitive	lord's	lords'
	of the lord	of the lords
Dative	to/for the lord	to/for the lords
Ablative	by/with/from/in the lord	by/with/from/in the lords

and for verbs:

	Tense	Singular	Plural
First Person	Present	I sing	we sing
Second Person		you sing	you sing
Third Person		he/she/it sings	they sing
First Person	Past	I sang	we sang
Second Person		you sang	you sang
Third Person		he/she/it sang	they sang
First Person	Future	I shall sing	we shall sing
Second Person		you will sing	you will sing
Third Person		he/she/it will sing	they will sing

Paradigms work well for inflected languages such as Latin but are not particularly useful in illustrating contemporary English.

See: **case, case grammar, grammar, inflection.**

paradox

Paradox, from Greek *para* (beyond) + *doxos* (opinion), is a figure of speech involving an apparent contradiction, as in Donne's 'Batter my heart' sonnet:

> ... *for I*
> *Except you enthrall me, never shall be free,*
> *Nor ever chaste, except you ravish me.*

Paradox is often used in religious language, perhaps because it stresses the impossibility of expressing attributes of the divine in human terms:

A man who saves his life will lose it.
I am the beginning and the end, the alpha and omega.

More recently, the term *paradox* has been applied to a person whose behaviour seems contradictory.

See: **figurative language, oxymoron**.

paragraph

Paragraph derives from Greek *paragraphein* (write beside) and was a system devised to draw attention to a section of text. Paragraphs developed in prose in much the same way as stanzas developed in verse: to indicate a sequence.

Externally, a paragraph is a visual aid, signalling a step in an argument or discussion. Internally, it should contain one central point supported by homogeneous subject matter. Successive paragraphs should offer a sequence of steps leading towards a conclusion.

There are no fixed rules as to the length or complexity of a paragraph. Long paragraphs may be necessary in making coherent points in a philosophical or formal essay. Short paragraphs may, on the other hand, be more suitable in **letters** and types of journalism where a detailed examination of ideas and views is not required.

A paragraph may be signalled by indenting the first word five letter spaces or by leaving a double space between paragraphs, but not both.

See: **argument**.

paralinguistic features

Paralinguistic features are defined in two main ways:
1 features of speech such as breathiness, giggling, lisping, loudness, which are meaningful in terms of conveying attitudes and responses, but are not as integrally involved in linguistic messages (nor as fully studied) as **intonation**
2 the gestures that acompany speech and include eye contact, posture and body movements. Often these bodily accompaniments to speech are referred to as *kinesics*.

Paralinguisic features tend to be acquired as we learn language (children, for example, usually have to be taught to keep quiet in church) and they differ from country to country, often even from region to region. Some, like laughing to express amusement and scratching the head to indicate uncertainty, tend to be widespread, but others such as a victory 'V' sign are more limited. Occasionally, the same gesture can mean different things. It is rude in western society to stick out one's tongue at visitors, although this same gesture is reported to have been a mark of courtesy in ancient Tibet.

See: **speech and writing.**

parallelism

Parallelism is the arrangement and repetition of linguistic elements for stylistic effect. Parallelism can apply to sounds, vocabulary, syntax and semantics or to a combination of some or all of these. It is regularly employed in poetry, oratory and persuasive language and can be discussed in terms of:

1 *assonance*, the repetition of the same vowel sounds. We can, for example, compare the words *Bunyan, swung, strummed, one, sprung* and *up* in:

> *When Bunyan swung his whopping axe*
> *And forests strummed as one loud lute,*
> *And timber crashed beside his foot*
> *And sprung up stretching in his tracks.*
>   Richard Wilbur, 'Folk-tune'

2 *alliteration*, the repetition of the same consonant:

> *Round and round the rugged rock the ragged rascal ran.*

3 *metre*, where the pattern of stressed and unstressed syllables is regular, as in traditional ballad stanzas like:

> *I saw the old moon late last night*
> *With the new one in its arm*
> *And if we go to sea, my lord*
> *I fear we'll come to harm.*

4 *rhyme*:

> *You'll wonder where the yellow went*
> *If you clean your teeth with Pepsodent.*

5 *morphology*, where the same **morpheme** is repeated often with expansion, as in the following extract from Shakespeare's Sonnet 116:

> *...Love is not love*
> *Which **alters** when it **alteration** finds,*
> *Or bends with the **remover** to **remove**.*

6 *lexis*, where words are repeated for emphasis, as in the following line from Milton's *Samson Agonistes*:

Dark, dark, dark, amid the light of day.

7 *syntax*, where similar sentence patterns may be used:

...if you prick us do we not bleed? if you
tickle us do we not laugh? if you poison us
do we not die?
    Shakespeare, *The Merchant of Venice*, III.i.58-60

8 *semantics*, where the same idea is repeated using different lexical items. An example of this occurs when Macbeth (II.ii.60-61) suggests that no amount of water can wash the crime of murder from his hands, but rather the blood will:

The multitudinous seas incarnadine,
Making the green one red.

In ordinary expository prose, parallelism can be regarded as a type of **co-ordination**, linking elements that are already logically connected. Thus an adjective is parallel to another adjective, a noun to a noun or a verb to a verb:

*I felt **foolish, self-conscious and clumsy**.*
*We all have **homes and families** to consider.*
*He **huffed** and he **puffed** and he **blew** the house down.*

a phrase to a phrase:

*She had **an Italian accent and an angelic expression**.*

and a clause to a clause:

*He is totally consistent in **what he says and how he does it**.*

Parallelism is a feature of **similes**:

dead as a dodo/doornail

proverbs:

When trouble comes in through the windows love goes out through the doors.

and underlies the mnemonic devices in oral literature.

See: **alliteration, assonance, metre, oral tradition.**

paraphrase

Paraphrase from Greek *paraphrazein* (to recount) is an alternative version of a text, a version that changes the *form* but not the content of an utterance. The paraphrase may involve:

1 **transformations** such as:

Jack killed Jill.
Jill was killed (by Jack).
the killing of Jill by Jack
Jack's killing of Jill

2 producing a humorous version as with:

The Lord and I are in a shepherd/sheep situation, and I am in a position
of negative need.

for:

The Lord is my shepherd, there is nothing I shall want.

3 producing an amplification of original material:

In the couplet:
If this be error, and upon me proved,
I never writ, nor no man ever loved.
Shakespeare claims that if the views which he has expressed
in the previous twelve lines are wrong and can be shown to be
wrong, then it follows that neither he nor anyone else has
ever truly loved.

See: **parody, précis.**

parody

Parody derives ultimately from Greek *para* (near) + *oide* (song) and
refers to a composition which imitates the style of a serious work for
comic effect.

A parody may work by reproducing the *form* of a passage while
changing the *content* as in the following passage which imitates the
form of the wedding service:

Dearly beloved, we are come together here today to auction
this vase and this cup to the highest bidder. If they have
once passed from their present owners into a new home, it
will be folly to revoke the bond. Therefore, let anyone
who knows of an impediment to the sale come forward. Let
such a person speak now or forever hold his peace.

Many poets have been parodied, among them A.E. Housman.
Housman's structures are closely followed in version A, whereas
version B parodies the pessimism, the subject matter and the use of
'lad':

Wake ; the silver dust returning
Up the beach of darkness brims

And the ship of sunrise burning
Strands upon the Eastern rims.

Wake; the vaulted shadow shatters,
Trampled to the floor it spanned,
And the tent of night it tatters
Straws the sky-pavillioned land.
    A.E. Housman, 'Reveille'

(A) *Rest; the golden ball declining*
Over mountains gleaming red,
And the galleon-moon reclining
Longs to raise her silken head.

Rest; the vaunted daylight trembles
Parted from the earth it held,
And the force of night assembles,
Darks the sun-tormented veld.
    L.J. Todd

(B) *What! still alive at twenty two,*
A clean upstanding chap like you?
Sure, if your throat's hard to slit,
Slit your girl's and swing for it.

Like enough you won't be glad
When they come to hang you, lad;
But bacon's not the only thing
That's cured by hanging from a string.
    Hugh Kingsmill

Some works parody both the *form* and *content*. Fielding's novel *Shamela*, for example, aimed to ridicule Richardson's *Pamela* in the title, in the epistolary style and in the content. Whereas Pamela was meant to be a poor but virtuous maiden whose virtue was eventually rewarded by an offer of marriage from the Squire, Shamela achieved the same end by carefully exploiting her attractions.

Usually, a parody focuses on one specific piece, but types can also be ridiculed. Jane Austen satirises Gothic novels in *Northanger Abbey*, and modern love songs are occasionally parodied by the selection of over-used rhymes such as 'moon/June/spoon/tune', 'kiss/bliss' and 'tender/surrender'.

For maximum effect, parody depends on the addressee having some knowledge of the work being ridiculed.

See: **irony, paraphrase, satire.**

participle

Traditional grammarians referred to the verb forms ending in *-ing* which followed the **progressive auxiliary BE** as *present participles*, for example, 'singing' in:

*They are **singing**.*

The verb forms that followed the auxiliary HAVE and the passive auxiliary BE were called *past participles*:

*She has **arrived**.*
*We weren't **seen**.*

Many modern linguists prefer the terms **-ing forms** and **-en forms** because so-called *present participles* can be used adjectivally:

*the **swaying** trees*

and do not have to refer to the present:

*He **was travelling** all day yesterday.*

Similarly, so-called *past participles* can be used adjectivally:

*the **forsaken** merman*

and need not refer to the past:

*She **will be employed** from the first day of next month.*

See: **auxiliary, gerund, -ing forms.**

parts of speech

Traditional grammars were based on Greek and Latin models and the following parts of speech were taken over and applied to English:

Adjective	(e.g. *pretty*)
Adverb	(e.g. *quickly*)
Article	(e.g. *the*)
Conjunction	(e.g. *and*)
Interjection	(e.g. *wow*)
Noun	(e.g. *house*)
Preposition	(e.g. *in*)
Pronoun	(e.g. *we*)
Verb	(e.g. *arrive*)

and defined in such ways as:

An adjective qualifies or describes a noun.
An adverb modifies a verb.

An article is an adjective-like word. There are three
articles in English, the definite article *the* and
the indefinite articles *a* and *an*.
A conjunction is a joining word.
An interjection is an exclamatory word that expresses
emotion.
A noun is the name of a person, animal, place or thing.
A preposition is a word placed in front of a noun or
pronoun to show the relationship of that noun (or pronoun)
to other elements in the sentence.
A pronoun is a word that can replace a noun.
A verb is a doing word. It may express an action, a
state or condition.

Modern linguists have criticised traditional definitions. *Redundancy*
is a noun in:

Most workers worry about redundancy.

but it is hardly the name of a person, animal, place or thing. Equally,
the pronoun *he* does not replace just the noun in:

The tired old man in the threadbare clothes walked home.
He *walked home.*

It replaces the entire noun phrase, 'the tired old man in the threadbare clothes'. Contemporary linguists prefer to look at the *form* and
functions of units in speech and offer definitions based on such criteria. Nouns, for example, tend to form their written plurals by
adding *-s* (occasionally *-es*):

window windows
potato potatoes

and they tend to fit into such test frames as:

$$\text{The} \underline{\quad\quad} \text{were} \left\{ \begin{array}{l} \text{old} \\ \text{tired} \\ \text{bad} \end{array} \right.$$

Using the criteria of form and function we can distinguish two
main types of words in English: *open* sets which contain a large,
potentially infinite number of units and *closed* sets which contain a
finite set of units. The open set contains four **classes**: nouns, verbs,
adjectives, adverbs; the closed set contains six: determiners, pronouns, auxiliaries, prepositions, conjunctions, interjections/
exclamations. This list is not dissimilar to the one provided by
traditional grammarians. Perhaps the greatest difference between
traditional and modern grammarians is the insistence of the latter
group that a word can only be fully classified by examining the ways

in which it can function. For example, although *the* is usually an article (determiner), it can function as a noun in such a sentence as:

> *I can't find a single the in that entire passage.*

See: **class, multifunctionality.**

pass, passed, past

The word *pass* when used as a verb is regular in form:

> *pass   passes   passing   passed   have passed*

Past is not a verb but can function as an adjective:

> *I've been very busy this past year.*

an adverb:

> *They walked past without saying a word.*

a noun:

> *He lives in the past.*

and as a preposition:

> *She ran past the entrance.*

The use of *past* as a verb in such sentences as:

> **We past the time playing cards.*

is incorrect and unacceptable.

passive voice

Transitive verbs (i.e. verbs which can take objects) can occur in two types of sentences:

> A *The cat chased the mouse.*
> B *The mouse was chased (by the cat).*

A-type sentences are called *active* and it will be noticed that the subject is typically the agent or instigator of the action or event. B-type sentences are called *passive* and they are usually characterised as follows:

  1 The subject is typically the recipient of the action.
  2 The predicate involves BE + the past **participle** of the headverb.
  3 The agent need not be mentioned:

> *The mouse was chased.*

When the agent is not specified, we have what is called a *truncated* or *non-agentive* passive.

4 The agent, when present, is introduced by *by*.

5 The rule for transforming an active into a passive sentence is:

$NP_1 + V_{trans} + NP_2 \Rightarrow NP_2 + BE + \text{past participle } V \, (+ \text{ by } NP_1).$

In colloquial speech, GET rather than BE can occur in passives:

*He **got** beaten up.*
*We'll **get** massacred.*

See: **active voice, ergative, participle, transformations, voice.**

patois

This term, pronounced /'patwa/, originally referred to non-metro-politan French. Gradually, it was expanded to mean:

1 a nonstandard **dialect** of French

2 a French **creole** such as the variety spoken in Martinique

3 a creole, irrespective of its lexical source language. Many speak-ers of Jamaican creole refer to their mother tongue as 'patois'.

4 a regional dialect

5 a special language of an occupation or group

A *patois* like a *dialect* differs from the standard language in pho-nology (sounds and sound patterns), morphology (the forms words can take), vocabulary and syntax. All of these differences can be seen if we juxtapose a Jamaican creole sentence with its English equivalent:

Di nyam a fi mii. (The food is mine.)

See: **dialect, pidgins and creoles, West Indian English.**

perfect

Traditional grammarians referred to structures involving HAVE + V_{en} as *perfect tenses* thus:

I have gone—present perfect
he had gone—past perfect (also 'pluperfect')
we shall have gone—future perfect
to have gone—perfect infinitive

Modern linguists refer to the structure involving HAVE + V_{en} as *perfect aspect* rather than *perfect tense* because **tense** relates strictly to **time** whereas **aspect** refers to the continuity of an action or to its completion.

See: **aspect, tense.**

period

The *period* (USA) or *full stop* (UK) is appropriate in the following positions:

1 at the end of sentences: sentences that are not exclamations or questions are closed with a period.

2 to end **footnotes**. Footnotes, even when they do not contain a verb, are conventionally treated like full sentences.

3 for **ellipsis**: three spaced periods.

4 for **abbreviations** that end with a lower case letter, e.g. *Lat.* for *Latin*. (There is a growing tendency to reduce periods in abbreviations.)

5 with parentheses. The position of the period should suit the sense.

6 in quotations: US practice includes commas and periods within quotation marks:

He is puzzled by 'The Waste Land.'

UK practice prefers the period outside the quotation marks but this practice varies according to publishers' house styles.

7 after verbless proverbs or well-known expressions:

Always a bridesmaid, never a bride.
One man, one vote.

8 between dollars and cents, pounds and pence:

$5.95
£4.21

The period should not be used:

1 after a title, such as that of an essay or book, unless the title ends the sentence:

*Far from the Madding Crowd. is a great book.
I really enjoyed Far from the Madding Crowd.

2 after footnote numbers

3 at the end of items in a table

4 after an abbreviation which has a period or after a period, exclamation mark or question mark which appears in quotation marks or italicised at the end of a sentence:

The article was called 'John Brown Esq.'
She was a journalist employed by **Which?**

See: **abbreviations, ellipsis, numbers, punctuation.**

periodic sentence

A *periodic sentence* is a complex, formal structure that reserves an essential piece of information, usually contained in the main clause, for the end of the sentence. Early writers of English prose often imitated the Ciceronian period (or sentence) which compressed an entire argument into one sentence. The following sentence from Milton's *Of Reformation in England* (1642) illustrates the technique:

> *Then, amidst the hymns and hallelujahs of saints, some one may perhaps be heard offering at high strains in new and lofty measure to sing and celebrate thy divine mercies and marvellous judgments in this land throughout all ages, whereby this great and warlike nation, instructed and inured to the fervent and continual practice of truth and righteousness, and casting far from her the rags of her old vices, may press on hard to that high and happy emulation to be found the soberest, wisest and most Christian people at that day, when thou, the eternal and shortly expected King, shalt open the clouds to judge the several kingdoms of the world, and distribute national honours and rewards to religious and just commonwealths, shalt put an end to all earthly tyrannies, proclaiming thy universal and mild monarchy throughout heaven and earth; where they undoubtedly, that by their labours, counsels and prayers, have been earnest for the common good of religion and their country, shall receive above the inferior orders of the blessed, the regal addition of principalities, legions and thrones into their glorious titles, and in supereminence of beatific vision, progressing the dateless and irrevoluble circle of eternity, shall clasp hands with joy and bliss in overmeasure for ever.*

Although long periodic sentences have remained prestigious in serious prose writings, they are rare in contemporary prose. When used skilfully as a rhetorical device, a periodic sentence produces a climax, as in the following advice offered to readers by Francis Bacon:

> *Read not to contradict and confute; nor to believe and take for granted; nor to find talk and discourse; but to weigh and consider.*

Parallelism is often used to support the periodic technique.

See: **foregrounding, parallelism, rhetoric**

periphrasis

Periphrasis, from Greek *peri* (around) + *phrazein* (to declare), is, like **circumlocution**, a method of expressing something in a roundabout way:

He gave a positive response.

for:

He said yes.

Periphrasis is often found in **pidgins and creoles**:

gras bilong hed (hair = grass belong head)
pikinini bilong diwai (fruit = children belong tree)

See: **circumlocution, gobbledygook, pidgins and creoles.**

person

When *person* is used in a linguistic context it refers to the marking of the relationships between participants in discourse. In English, distinctions of person are made in the set of **pronouns**:

First person singular 'speaker'	= I
First person plural 'speaker + others'	= we
Second person singular 'addressee'	= you
Second person plural 'addressees'	= you
Third person singular 'person referred to'	= he/she
Third person singular 'thing refered to'	= it
Third person plural 'people/things referred to'	= they

English indicates person in the verb in the non-past tense, where the first and second persons singular and the first, second and third persons plural take the base form of the verb:

I/you/we/they love.

and a third person singular subject takes -*s*/-*es*:

He/She/It/The friend loves.
He/She/It/The friend watches.

See: **pronoun, speaker orientation, speech and writing, verb.**

phatic communion

Bronislaw Malinowski created the term *phatic communion* to describe the language used by people to establish bonds rather than to exchange information. In phatic communion, it is not so much *what* one says as *that* one speaks which is significant. In English, phatic communion often involves comments on the weather, on one's general health or one's family:

> *Nice day!*
> *How are you? And the family?*

A great deal of our conversation with people we do not know well is of the phatic variety. Silence may be golden when we are in the company of intimate friends but it can be threatening or offensive when we are with strangers or acquaintances.

Most societies have stylised *phatic courtesies* for greetings:

> *Hello! Hi! Good morning!*

introductions:

> *This is my brother, John.*
> *How are you?/How do you do?*

requests:

> *Could you let us have the order immediately?*

polite orders:

> *Would you mind shutting the door, please?*

excuses:

> *I'm sorry I'm late. There was more traffic than I expected.*

thanks:

> *Thank you very much.*
> *You're welcome./Don't mention it.*

and for farewells:

> *See you soon.*
> *Have a nice day.*

The form of the courtesy may vary in different regions but the need for such formulaic utterances is felt by all communities.

See: **fillers, paralinguistic features.**

phenomenon

The word *phenomenon* derives from the Greek verb *phainein* (to show). Its plural is *phenomena*, a form which is sometimes incorrectly used as a singular. (A similar misuse occurs with *criterion/criteria*.)

In early uses, *phenomenon* was a philosophical term meaning 'something that is perceived by the senses' but its meaning has been extended to include:

1 an occurrence or fact that is of scientific value and worthy of study

2 an unusual event, fact or occurrence

3 any notable fact, person or occurrence

See: **plurals of nouns.**

Philippine English

The Philippines, made up of a group of approximately 7,000 islands, has a population of just over 48 million, 52% of whom claimed in the 1980 census that they could speak English. This would make the Philippines the third largest English-speaking country in the world after the USA and the UK. The country was a Spanish colony from 1565 to 1898 when, as a result of the Spanish-American War of 1898, it was occupied and governed by the USA until independence was granted on 4 July, 1946.

It is not clear how many indigenous languages are spoken in the Philippines but the number is unlikely to be lower than 85 and may well approach 300. A local vernacular, Tagalog, was selected as a national language in 1937, taught as a subject in all primary and secondary schools from 1946 and renamed *Pilipino* in 1959. In 1973, parliament decided to form a common national language, to be called *Filipino*. This was a standardised, common-core variety of Tagalog and this language is gradually replacing English in certain domains, including early education and local business transactions.

Philippine English is based on Standard US **norms**. The extent of the influence of the mother tongues usually depends on the length and the quality of a speaker's education.

Phonology

1 The **articulatory setting** tends to be dental rather than alveolar (as in the USA) and all words involving the sounds /t, d, s, z, l, r, n, tʃ, dʒ/ are affected.

2 Word-initial /p, t, k/ are usually not aspirated and so native speakers of English often mistake words like *pet, tin* and *cull* for *bet, den* and *gull*.

3 Word final /b, d, g/ tend to be devoiced and heard as /p, t, k/.

4 The consonants /f, v/ are usually replaced by /p, b/:

five > paib

and /t, d/ are regularly substituted for /θ, ð/:

thing > ting
then > den

5 Only voiceless sibilants occur with the result that /s/ is substituted for /z/:

hens > /hɛns/

and /ʃ/ for /ʒ/:

rouge > /ruʃ/

6 Post-vocalic *r* is favoured but the /r/ is a flap rather than a continuant.

7 **Consonant clusters** tend to have intrusive vowels when they occur in initial position:

school > *eschool*
string > *sitring*

and to be reduced in word-final position:

banned > *ban*
friends > *frien(s)*

often leading to errors of tense or agreement.

8 There is no regular distinction between /i/ and /ɪ/ as in *beat* and *bit*, /u/ and /ʊ/ as in *pool* and *pull* and /ɒ/ and /oʊ/ as in *got* and *goat*.

9 Philippine English tends to be syllable-timed rather than stress-timed and so there is little vowel reduction and many disyllabic and polysyllabic words are accented on syllables which are usually unaccented in US English:

'*achieve*
'*deceive*
'*deco*'*rate*

10 *Wh*-questions, like yes/no questions, have a rising intonation.

Vocabulary

1 Many words associated with local culture have been absorbed into Philippine English:

buko (type of lollipop)
sarisari (food store)
tao (ordinary person)

Others have been taken over from Spanish:

career (college course)
carretela (horse-drawn vehicle)

2 English words are used with a local meaning:

jeepney (modified jeep used for public transport)
stepbrother (half-brother)
stepsister (half-sister)

3 Different phrasal verbs occur:

It's up for you. (i.e. up to you)
He was sounding off his ts and ds. (i.e. sounding)

4 Many mass nouns are treated as countable:

advices hairs furnitures informations

Grammar
1 The **articles** *the/a/an* have a different distribution. When the noun is non-specific, there is a tendency to avoid articles:

Everyone has car now.
Majority of the respondents answered no.

Where it is specific but unknown to the listener *one* is often preferred to *a/an*:

*He has bought **one** beautiful house.*

Often *this* is preferred to *the*:

*She spent all **this** money.*

2 The word order of **direct speech** is often used in indirect speech:

*I don't know **where is he**.*
*He is asking **where did you get your bag**.*

3 Often **aspect**, rather than **tense**, is emphasised:

*He **is going** every day.* (US He goes every day.)
*She **has visited** me yesterday.* (US She visited me yesterday.)

4 There is often lack of agreement between subject and predicate:

*He usually **come** here on Mondays.*

5 Often third person singular pronouns and possessive adjectives are used without regard to gender:

*My mother **he** buy me one fine dress.*
*She gave me **his** address.* (i.e. her address)

See: **US English.**

philology

Philology, coming from Greek *philos* (friend) + *logia* (learning) and meaning 'love of learning', was originally applied to the study of:
1 literature (often literature of an earlier period)
2 the language used in the literature.
Today, the term is most frequently applied to the scientific study

of language and particularly to the study of the changes undergone by a language over a period of time.

See: **etymology**.

phoneme

A *phoneme* is usually defined as the smallest significant unit in the sound system of a language. There are three phonemes in each of the following words:

pin /pɪn/
beef /bif/
shed /ʃɛd/

Each language has its own set of distinctive sounds which can be arrived at by studying minimal pairs such as:

pit and *bit* revealing /p/ and /b/
pin and *pen* revealing /ɪ/ and /ɛ/
pin and *pick* revealing /n/ and /k/

These words are only differentiated, in each case, by one distinct sound or phoneme.

See: **phonetics, phonology**.

phonetics

Phonetics is the scientific study of speech sounds. It provides a systematic method of describing and transcribing all the sounds of all languages.

The chief organs of speech are the lips, teeth, tongue, palate, uvula, pharynx, vocal cords and lungs, and the mobile organs are in constant movement when we speak.

There are two main types of speech sound: consonants and vowels. Consonants are formed when the airstream is restricted at some point. At each point of contact two consonants can be formed: a voiceless consonant, made when the vocal cords are open and not vibrating, and a voiced consonant, made when the vocal cords vibrate. Consonants are defined in terms of:

1 *their place of articulation*. In English, the main points of articulation are *bilabial* (involving the two lips as with /p/), *labio-dental* (involving lip and teeth as with /f/), *alveolar* (involving the alveolus or ridge behind the top teeth and the tongue as with /t/), *palatal* (involving the tongue and the hard palate as with /j/), *velar* (involving the tongue and the the soft palate as with /g/) and *glottal* (involving the glottis as with /h/).

2 *their manner of articulation*. The chief subdivisions for English are:

(a) *Plosives* or *stops*. These involve complete closure of the mouth. The air pressure builds up and is released with plosion. (US descriptions prefer the term *stop*.) There are three sets of plosives in English:

/p, b/—bilabial plosives (*pit, bit*)
/t, d/—alveolar plosives (*tin, din*)
/k, g/—velar plosives (*cull, gull*)

(b) *Fricatives*. These involve incomplete closure in the mouth. The sounds are made with audible friction. English has the following fricatives:

/f, v/—labio-dental (*fine, vine*)
/ʍ/—labio-alveolar (sound of 'wh' in *which*)
/θ, ð/—dental (*thin, then*)
/s, z/—alveolar (*sing, zing*)
/ʃ, ʒ/—palato-alveolar (*ship, azure*)
/h/—glottal (*hat*)

(c) *Approximants*. These involve a degree of narrowing but no audible friction. These consonants are sometimes referred to as 'frictionless continuants' or 'semi-vowels'. English has the following approximants:

/j/—voiced palatal (*yes*)
/w/—voiced labio-velar (*wet*)
/r/—voiced alveolar (*red*). (The r sound is pronounced differently in different regions. In the USA it tends to be retroflex, in Scotland trilled or rolled. In **Received Pronunciation** it initiates syllables only and does not occur after a vowel.)

(d) *Laterals*. These sounds are made when the air pressure is blocked by the tip of the tongue but allowed to escape around the sides of the tongue. Occasionally, *l* is classified as an approximant.

/l/—voiced alveolar lateral

(e) *Affricates*. These sounds involve complete closure as for plosives, followed by a slow release of air. The English affricates are:

/tʃ, dʒ/—post-alveolar (*chin, gin*)

(f) *Nasals*. These sounds are made by diverting the airstream through the nose. There are three voiced nasals in English:

/m/—bilabial nasal (*dim*)
/n/—alveolar nasal (*din*)
/ŋ/—velar nasal (*ding*)

Vowels cannot be defined by touch because they demand an open

passage in the mouth. The following vowels occur in Received Pronunciation and in General American English:

	RP	GAE	monophthongs
1	i	i	— long, front vowel (*bee, ease, keep*)
2	ɪ	ɪ	— short, front vowel (*in, kit*)
3	ɛ	ɛ	— short, front vowel (*epsilon, get*)
4	æ	æ	— short, front vowel (*apple, hat*)
5	ɑ	ɑ	— long, back vowel (*arm, palm*)
6	ɒ	ɒ	— short, back vowel (*operate, got*)
7	ɔ	ɔ	— long, back vowel (*awe, lawn, saw*)
8	ʊ	ʊ	— short, back vowel (*foot, put*)
9	u	u	— long, back vowel (*boom, true*)
10	ʌ	ʌ	— short, central vowel (*up, strut*)
11	ɜ	ɜr	— long, central vowel (*urge, church, fur*)
12	ə	ə	— short, central vowel, called 'schwa' (*the*)
	RP	GAE	diphthongs
13	eɪ	eɪ	— narrow diphthong (*age, cape, day*)
14	əʊ	oʊ	— narrow diphthong (*over, home, go*)
15	aɪ	aɪ	— wide diphthong (*I, file, sty*)
16	aʊ	aʊ	— wide diphthong (*owl, loud, allow*)
17	ɔɪ	ɔɪ	— wide diphthong (*oil, join, toy*)
			diphthongs in RP only
18	ɪə	ɪr	— narrow diphthong (*ear, hear*)
19	ɛə	ɛr	— narrow diphthong (*air, hair*)
20	ɔə	ɛr	— narrow diphthong (*short, war*)
21	ʊə	ʊr	— narrow diphthong (*sure, poor*)

Every language has its own distinct set of phonemes and each
variety of English has a distribution of sounds that differs to some
extent from the system described above.

See: **articulatory setting, phoneme, pronunciation.**

phonology

Phonology is the scientific study of sounds and sound patterns in
a particular language. The phonology of an individual language
describes the unique patterns into which the phonemes of that language can be arranged.

See: **phoneme, phonetics.**

phrasal verb

A *phrasal verb* is a sequence of words involving a verb and one or
more particles:

get away with (*He could get away with murder.*)
put down (*The whole herd had to be put down.*)

Phrasal verbs can be shown to be units by the way they function.
A one-word verb can often be substituted for a phrasal verb:

blow up—explode
drop off—sleep

and the elements may continue to co-occur when the sentence is
transformed:

*What could he **get away with**?*

Phrasal verbs are sometimes subdivided into *adverbial* and *prepositional* sub-types. The former involve sequences of verb + adverb
where the adverb may be separated from the verb:

*He **tore up** the paper.* ⇒ *He **tore** the paper **up**.*
*He **looked up** his friend.* ⇒ *He **looked** his friend **up**.*

and prepositional verbs involve verb + preposition:

*He **went into** the house.*
*They **were** all **in** the red.*

Many phrasal verbs are idiomatic in the sense that their meanings
cannot be deduced from the meanings of the individual parts:

*She **put off** (delayed) her departure.*

See: **idioms, prepositional verb, verb phrase.**

phrase

In traditional grammar, a *phrase* was defined as a sequence of words
which functioned as a unit:

*I put it **on the chair**.*
*Where did you put it? **On the chair**.*
*I put it **there**.*

and which did not contain a subject + predicate structure. Thus,
the unit in bold in:

*He arrived **at supper time**.*

is a phrase, whereas the unit in bold in:

*He arrived **while we were eating supper**.*

is a clause.

Five types of phrase are usually identified:
1 **noun phrases**: *The **man in the moon** is **a foolish myth**.*
2 adjective phrases: *She was **very pleasant**.*

3 verb phrases: *We **shall be arriving** by train*.
4 preposition phrases: *He is **in big trouble***.
5 adverb phrases: *I only set off **last week***.

Some modern linguists extend the term *phrase* to a word which functions in the same way as, or can replace, a phrase. Thus pronouns are often referred to as *noun phrases*:

All the children went to the fair.
They went to the fair.

and a **predicate** consisting of one word is often called a **verb phrase**:

We left.

See: **clause, rankshifting, transformational grammar**.

pidgins and creoles

Pidginisation refers to the processes of simplification and reduction that occur in languages when people who do not share the same language come into contact. The replacement in **Old English** of grammatical gender (where inanimate nouns could be either masculine, feminine or neuter) by natural gender (where males are masculine, females are feminine and inanimate objects are neuter) is an example of pidginisation and a direct result of the Viking invasions and the Norman Conquest.

Whilst pidginisation is widespread, the crystallising of a pidgin is less common. A *pidgin* is a simple, spoken language which evolves to permit communication between people who do not share a mother tongue. Pidgins, which are nobody's mother tongue, usually involve:

1 the exploitation of linguistic common denominators
2 a small vocabulary drawn almost exclusively from the socially dominant language
3 a relatively fixed word order
4 a reduced number of function words such as pronouns and prepositions
5 use of reduplication for emphasis
6 reinforcement by signs and body language

Rudimentary pidgins can be found where two language communities come into contact but do not need sustained or profound verbal interaction. The pidgin English which developed in Vietnam between GIs and non-English-speaking Vietnamese was a rudimentary pidgin which began to disappear as soon as US involvement in Vietnam ceased. Highly flexible pidgins have, however, developed in multilingual areas of the world, especially along trade routes. Since the European colonial expansion of the fifteenth century, flexible pidgins have evolved from Portuguese, Spanish, French, English and Dutch.

Many of these have become **creoles,** that is, the mother tongues of groups of speakers. A number of well-known creoles are Afrikaans (Dutch-related), Jamaican Creole (English-related) and Patois, the French-related creole of St Lucia.

The essential difference between a developed pidgin and a creole is sociological rather than linguistic: a pidgin tends to be learnt in conjunction with one or more mother tongues, whereas a creole tends to be the sole mother tongue of its speakers.

There are two large families of English-related pidgins and creoles in the world: the Atlantic varieties (all of which are influenced by West African languages) and the Pacific varieties, the best known of which is Papua New Guinea's Tok Pisin.

See: **Caribbean English, Cameroon English, creole, Nigerian English, Papua New Guinean English.**

place names

Place names can help to provide details of the history of a region, revealing the nature of earlier settlements. North-East England, for example, has many Norse-derived place names, reinforcing historical accounts of its being under Scandinavian rule from the ninth century. Among such names are: *Elsecar, Heckmondwike, Skelmanthorpe, Thurgoland* and *Wetwang.* In the midst of these, however, is the city of *Leeds*, which takes its name from a Celtic form, *Leodis*, thus revealing an earlier stage of settlement.

A study of US names and their pronunciation can reveal the patterns of settlement of different groups of Amerindians and Europeans. *Louisiana* was called after King Louis of France, *Virginia* after Queen Elizabeth of England (the 'Virgin' Queen), *Los Angeles* was named by the Spanish, and throughout the USA are names like *Mississippi* and *Susquehanna* which were taken over from the Indians by the European settlers.

Place names are sometimes extended into general usage as *toponyms*, deriving from Greek *topos* (place) + *onyma* (name). The word *bungalow*, for example, originally meant a house built in the Bengali style. Other widely-used toponyms are:

> *blarney* < Blarney, Co. Cork, Ireland
> *canary* < Canary Islands
> *denim* < de Nîmes, France
> *duffel* < Duffel, Holland
> *jeans* < Genoa, Italy
> *marathon* < Marathon, Greece
> *mascara* < Mascara, Algeria
> *tweed* < River Tweed, Scotland

See: **etymology, word formation.**

plagiarism

In theory, *plagiarism*, from Latin *plagiarus* (plunderer), is straightforward. It involves the theft and use of another's ideas, words or inventions and is thus unethical and, in certain circumstances, illegal. In practice, however, it is not always easy to draw a sharp dividing line between plagiarism and research that develops or depends on the work of others. As a matter of principle, it is desirable to give credit to all sources that have been consulted. The penalty for not doing so in a student essay may be failure; and the unacknowledged use in print of another's copyrighted material may lead to prosecution.

For unpublished student research, a **footnote** acknowledging the source is usually sufficient. For material to be published, an author needs permission from the original author or publisher if the quotation is:

1 over ten lines or 300/400 words in a single prose extract
2 over 800 words in a series of extracts
3 over 40 lines of poetry or an extract longer than one quarter of a poem
4 if the material consists of an illustration, photograph or table

In the UK the copyright period normally ceases to operate 50 years after publication. In the USA the copyright period is usually 56 years.

pleonasm

Pleonasm, from Greek *pleonazein* (to be excessive), is a term for the use of superfluous words:

The answer is ambiguous and its precise meaning is unclear.

Apleonastic is an adjective occasionally applied to a style where **redundancy** is kept to a minimum.

See: **circumlocution, periphrasis, redundancy, tautology, verbosity.**

plurals of nouns

Most nouns in English form their plural by the addition of *-s* or *-es*:

cat cats /kæts/
dog dogs /dɒgz/
horse horses /hɔsɪz, hɔrsɪz/
match matches /mætʃɪz/

although, as the phonetic equivalents illustrate, these two written endings comprehend three in the spoken medium /s, z, ɪz/.

The following rules comprehend the major difficulties and exceptions in *noun plurals* in English:

1 Nouns that end with a vowel + 'y' normally form their plurals by adding -*s*:

boy/boys   monkey/monkeys   trolley/trolleys

but we have:

money/moneys   monies (technical use)
storey/storeys (UK and US) *stories* (US)

2 Nouns that end with a vowel + 'o' form their plurals by adding -*s*:

cameo/cameos   folio/folios
radio/radios   video/videos

3 Nouns ending in a consonant + 'o' usually form their plurals by adding -*es*:

echo/echoes   hero/heroes   no/noes
potato/potatoes   veto/vetoes

The main exceptions to this rule are:

dynamo/dynamos   Eskimo/Eskimos   Filipino/Filipinos
photo/photos   piano/pianos   solo/solos   soprano/sopranos

Because of this variation, we have a number of nouns with two acceptable plurals:

banjo banjos/banjoes
cargo cargos/cargoes
domino dominos/dominoes

4 Nouns that end in 'ch', 's', 'sh', 'ss', 'x' or 'z' form their plurals with -*es*:

bunch/bunches   fez/fezes/fezzes   gas/gases/gasses
hoax/hoaxes   Jones/Joneses   loss/losses   wish/wishes

5 Nouns that end with a consonant + 'y' form their plurals with -*ies*:

berry/berries   fairy/fairies   hippy/hippies

6 Most nouns ending in 'f' form their plurals with -*ves*:

leaf/leaves   thief/thieves   wolf/wolves

Some words ending in 'f' have two acceptable plurals:

dwarf dwarves/dwarfs
hoof hooves/hoofs
scarf scarves/scarfs
wharf wharves/wharfs

7 The irregular nouns which occur most frequently are:

brother brethren (limited to religious language)
child children   *mouse mice*
foot feet   *ox oxen*
goose geese   *tooth teeth*
louse lice   *woman women*
man men

8 Certain plurals are taken over from other languages, including Latin:

datum data
fungus fungi (occasionally *funguses*)
genus genera
stimulus stimuli

Greek:

crisis crises
criterion criteria
phenomenon phenomena

Hebrew:

cherub cherubim
kibbutz kibbutzim
seraph seraphim

and French:

bureau bureaux
cheval chevaux
gateau gateaux

Because of the process of **analogy** with English words, some borrowed words have two plurals, often differentiated semantically or stylistically:

antenna	*antennae* (biology)	*antennas* (radio and TV)
appendix	*appendices* (formal)	*appendixes* (informal)
crocus	*croci* (formal)	*crocuses* (informal)
formula	*formulae* (science)	*formulas* (general)
medium	*media* (communication)	*mediums* (spiritualists)
nucleus	*nuclei* (science)	*nucleuses* (informal)
stigma	*stigmata* (religion)	*stigmas* (informal)

9 Some nouns, including many words for game and fish, do not change their form in the plural. The following are those that occur most frequently:

buck Chinese deer fish forceps
fowl grouse pike salmon series
sheep species trout

10 Plurals of compounds or fixed phrases usually take -*s* at the end:

bookcase bookcases
moneybag moneybags

Occasionally, however, the first element is pluralised:

fathers-in-law
passersby

or both parts are:

lords justices
trades unions

or sometimes two variants exist:

courts martial   court martials
spoonsful spoonfuls

See: **countable, foreign words in English, number.**

poetic diction

Poetic diction refers to the choice of vocabulary regarded as suitable for poetry. Words like:

beauteous
nymph
verdant

and archaisms like:

doth
'twas

are frequently considered poetic.

Writers in different periods have evolved their own characteristic **diction. Old English** poetry, for example, was marked by *kennings*, poetic **metaphors** such as *swan's bath* and *whale's road* for 'sea' and **circumlocutions** such as *giver of rings* for 'lord'. Most contemporary poets would probably subscribe to the view that there are no specifically 'poetic' words, only words which are either poetically appropriate or inappropriate.

See: **diction.**

polemic

A *polemic*, from Greek *polemikos* (warlike), is a controversial dispute, usually involving religious or social issues. It may be one-sided, constituting an aggressive attack on a person or principle:

*He launched into a **polemic** against Jones's pacifism.*

or it can involve closely-reasoned argument, as in Milton's polemic on the freedom of speech, *Areopagitica* (1644).

Occasionally, *polemic* is used to mean 'an agressive disputant' as well as a 'dispute'. Although *polemic* has occurred as both noun and adjective, there is a tendency for *polemical* to be preferred for adjectival uses.

polysemy

Polysemy, from Greek *poly* (many) + *sema* (sign), is the term used to denote that a **word** or **morpheme** can have several meanings. The word *fast*, for example, has five main meanings:

1 It is the equivalent of both 'quick' and 'quickly' in:

She has an extremely fast car.
She drives far too fast.

2 It occurs with the meaning of 'fully, completely' in the fixed phrase *fast asleep*:

In spite of all the noise, we found her fast asleep.

3 It is a colloquial equivalent of 'sexually promiscuous' or 'wild':

They have got in with a very fast crowd.

4 It can mean 'very tightly' in the collocation *stuck fast*:

The animals were stuck fast in the mud.

5 *Fast* can mean 'abstain from food' and can be used as both a noun and a verb:

Ramadan is a thirty-day fast.
People used to fast for forty days during Lent.

Morphemes, too, can be polysemous. *Un-*, for example, has three main meanings:

1 When it precedes a verb, it usually implies 'reverse the action of':

zip unzip

2 When it precedes a noun, it can change the word class and mean 'deprive of':

nerve unnerve

This usage is becoming archaic.

3 When it precedes an adjective, it can mean 'not':

true untrue

Polysemy is often exploited in crossword puzzles.

See: **ambiguity, pun, semantics, syllepsis.**

portmanteau word

A *portmanteau word*, from French *porter* (carry) + *manteau* (mantle) meaning 'a large travelling bag', is an older term for a **blend**. For example:

splurge—to spend extravagantly

is probably derived from a blend of:

splash + *surge*

See: **blend**.

possession

In English, *possession* can be indicated in four main ways:
1 by the use of the **genitive**:

John's success
the young girl's parents

2 by the use of **of**:

the six wives of Henry VIII
the tale of the Wife of Bath

3 by the juxtaposition of nouns:

man eater (eater of men)
table leg (leg of a table)

4 by the use of HAVE/GET/POSSESS and semantically related verbs:

*He **has** a lot of money.*
*They **possess** 45% of the country's wealth.*

The verb POSSESS and its related noun *possession* often co-occur with *of* in formal and legal language:

*He is **possessed of** enormous wealth.*
*She is in **possession of** those particular documents.*

The use of POSSESS meaning 'under the control of a devil':

*He was **possessed by** seven devils.*

is unusual outside biblical English, although a metaphorical extension of this usage survives in such structures as:

*What **possessed** you to do such an idiotic thing?*
*He drove like a man **possessed**.*

See: **apostrophe, case, genitive, of.**

précis

A *précis*, deriving from French *précis* (precise), is like a **paraphrase** in that it changes the form of a piece of language without altering its essential content. Unlike a paraphrase, a précis is always more condensed than the original and does not contain direct quotations from it. The length of a précis is usually predetermined at between one-third and one-fifth of the original.

The points to remember in précis-writing are:

1 Identify esssential information.
2 If possible, use your own words.
3 Ensure that the précis is coherent.
4 Retain the attitudes of the original piece.

See: **paraphrase**.

predicate

English **sentences** can be subdivided into **Subject** + *Predicate*:

Subject	Predicate
Robin	*died.*
Robin	*replied that they were sorry.*
Robin	*went on a spree.*

The predicate can consist of a verb alone or a verb plus all that follows it, as in the examples above. The verbal element of the predicate is often referred to as the *predicator*.

See: **verb phrase**.

prefix

A *prefix* is a **morpheme** that is added to the beginning of a stem in order to modify its meaning:

de + *mythologise*
mis + *understand*
retro + *rockets*

Prefixation is common in English, with prefixes coming from both native (e.g. *un-*) and Romance (e.g. *de-*) sources.

See: **affix, derivation, morpheme, suffix, word formation**.

prejudice

Prejudice, coming from Latin *prae* (before) + *judicium* (judgement), has undergone a process of semantic deterioration during the last two hundred years. Until the eighteenth century, *prejudice* was commendable in that it implied that a person had weighed up the evidence before reaching a conclusion about a person or idea.

In contemporary English, *prejudice* is applied to irrational attitudes formed without sufficient evidence or knowledge:

*He is **prejudiced** against strangers.*

Although it is possible to be prejudiced in favour of, as well as against, people and ideas, there is a tendency for it to be most commonly used for a hostile attitude against a person, a group of people or what they stand for:

*They are **prejudiced against** one-parent families.*

Certain prejudices are ingrained in the English language: professions usually imply men unless prefaced by *lady/woman*:

a lady doctor
a woman lawyer

and colour, race and religion are denigrated in such expressions as:

to black (a cargo, factory, ship)
to welsh

and in such nouns as:

nignog
wop

Consequently, attitudes (including prejudices) may be directly albeit unconsciously moulded by the languages we learn and speak.

See: **black, propaganda, racist language, sexist language.**

preposition

Prepositions are words like *at, in, with* which precede nouns, noun phrases and pronouns to form a unit:

*He was **at school**.*
*That's the man **in the moon**.*
*They came **with me**.*

The word *preposition* derives ultimately from Latin *praeponere* meaning 'to put in front of' and Latin prepositions always preceded and governed a noun phrase:

ad altare dei—to the altar of God

Because a Latin sentence could not end with a preposition scholars claimed that English sentences should not end with prepositions. This tenet would rule out such naturally-occurring utterances as:

*A preposition is a word you can't end a sentence **with**.*
*What did you put it **on**?*

and can result in such tortuous examples as:

*This is the sort of behaviour **up with which** I shall not put.*

Sentences ending in prepositions are perfectly acceptable in the spoken language but should be used sparingly in the written medium.

Prepositions belong to a closed set, the commonest being:

at by for from in of on to with

They can be simple (consisting of one word) or complex (consisting of two or three words):

because of
on account of

The units formed by prepositions and noun phrases are called *preposition(al) phrases* and they are most frequently used adjectivally:

*the boys **in blue***

adverbially:

*He went **to the country**.*

as complements:

*She was **in a hurry**.*

and to indicate possession:

*The Merry Wives **of Windsor**.*

See: **adjunct, parts of speech.**

preposition(al) verb

A *preposition(al) verb* is a unit consisting of a verb + a preposition:

*She **went into** labour.*

These units can be idiomatic:

*He **went into** the red.*

or literal:

*He **went into** the house.*

See: **phrasal verb.**

prescriptive grammar

A *prescriptive grammar* is one which provides its readers with rules telling them how the language *should* be used. These grammars instil such precepts as:

i before *e* except after *c*, thus *relieve* but *receive*
Nominative pronouns must follow BE, thus *It was I.*
Prepositions should not occur at the end of sentences, thus *To whom did you give it?* is preferable to *Who did you give it to?*

Prescriptive grammars often forbid certain uses:

Don't say *in actual fact. Actual* is redundant.
Don't use *less* with countable nouns: *less money* but *fewer women.*
Don't write abbreviations like *advert* in formal essays.

A grammar made up entirely of prohibitions is called a *proscriptive grammar.*

See: **grammar**.

presently

In the UK *presently* means 'in a little while' and it usually occurs in initial or final position:

*The doctor will see you **presently**.*

However, UK practice is increasingly following that of the USA in using *presently* in close proximity to the verb to mean 'at present':

*He is **presently** in New York.*

prime verbs

A *prime verb* is one that occurs very frequently in the language, can be shown to underlie many **synthetic** verbs:

He filed the document. ⇒ He put the document in a file.
She walks to work. ⇒ She goes to work on foot.

and is basic to much idiomatic language:

*I'll **bring** it off.*
*He'll **come** good.*
*She'll **go** bananas when she hears what you've done.*

The prime verbs in English are: **BE, BRING, COME, DO, GET, GIVE, GO, KEEP, MAKE,** PUT and TAKE.

See: **idioms, phrasal verb**.

principal, principle

Principal functions as an adjective meaning 'primary, most important':

> *It was hard to decide whether his **principal** motive was greed or fear.*

and as a noun with three main meanings:

1 a head teacher or director of a teaching institution:

> *She had only been at the school six years when she became **principal**.*

2 a person for whom someone else acts as representative:

> *He'll have to consult his **principal** before agreeing to the price.*

3 a sum of money invested:

> *It was impossible to live on the interest alone so they had to dip into the **principal**.*

Principle functions as a noun meaning 'rule, fundamental truth, basis of reasoning, ethic':

> *On **principle**, we're totally opposed to whaling.*
> *The 'Peter **Principle**' involves promoting people beyond the point where they can function efficiently.*

See: **problem pairs**.

pro forms

A *pro form* is any form which can substitute for other units or structures. The commonest pro forms in English are:

1 **pronouns** which can substitute for nouns and noun phrases:

> *That young man proposed to Mary.*
> ***He** proposed to **her**.*

2 **auxiliaries** (occasionally called 'pro-verbs'):

> *You can go and so **can** he.*
> *He wouldn't do that, **would** he?*
> *She ran away! **Did** she?*

3 **so**:

> *She wanted to run even though to do **so** was risky.*
> *Who said **so**?*

4 **adverbs**:

> *He went to Paris.*
> *He went **there**.*

See: **anaphora, cohesion**.

problem pairs

Problem pairs are pairs of words that give users difficulty because they are similar in form or function. A dictionary can help to disambiguate the pairs as long as a user is aware that a problem exists. The commonest pairs of problem words are listed below with brief exemplary sentences. The more complicated sets are also dealt with under separate headings. Where a difference of class occurs, this information is also provided.

accept (v) except (prep and v)

> *We'd like you to **accept** this small token of our esteem.*
> *Everyone went **except** me.*
> *Their policy was to **except** nobody. Everyone over eighteen was drafted.*

access excess

> *He was denied **access** to the children.*
> *She invariably had **excess** baggage.*

acetic ascetic

> *Table vinegar is made from **acetic** acid.*
> *His **ascetic** nature attracted him to a life of prayer and penance.*

adapt adopt

> *They **adapted** the appliances so that they would work on both voltages.*
> *The committee did not feel it could **adopt** your ideas as they stood. With certain changes, however, they may be acceptable.*

admission admittance

> *His **admission** that he had accepted bribes astonished everyone.*
> *Many museums now ask for an **admission** fee.*
> *It's impossible to gain **admittance** to his fortified mansion.*

adverse averse

> *She resented the **adverse** report she had received on her son's progress.*
> *I'm not **averse** to jogging. I'm just too lazy to get interested.*

affect (v) effect (n and v)

> *Such poor conditions are bound to **affect** the children's outlook.*
> *It's hard to know what **effect** the treatment will have on her.*
> *If you want to **effect** a significant improvement in sales, you'll have to work much harder.*

affectation affection

> *You've forgotten how to be natural. Your **affectation** is obvious in your speech, your manner, your clothes, everything.*

*The deep **affection** which the children had for their parents revealed itself in many acts of kindness.*

aggravate irritate

*The so-called medicines only **aggravated** his condition.*
*Your habit of saying 'hice' when you mean 'house' really **irritates** me.*

alive live

*After a five-day search they were found **alive** and well.*
*That wire is **live**! Don't touch it!*

all ready   already

*The children were **all ready** for the party.*
*They had **already** gone when we arrived.*

all together   altogether

*The children were **all together** in the one room.*
*He was an **altogether** different type.*

allude delude

*She often **alluded** to her first marriage.*
*She didn't try to **delude** us. The deception was unintentional.*

amend emend

*The constitution was **amended** to give all citizens equal rights.*
*He **emended** the texts, removing all inconsistent spellings.*

amiable amicable

*She was an **amiable**, well-intentioned person.*
*In spite of their row, they eventually reached an **amicable** arrangement.*

analogue analogy

*The lungs and gills may be described as **analogues**: they are similar in design and function.*
*The child produced the word 'goed', presumably on **analogy** with the past tense form of regular verbs.*

anticipate expect

*The doctor **anticipated** the next stage of the illness and was able to counteract it.*
*We **expected** you yesterday.*

apposite opposite

*She said very little at meetings but her comments were always **apposite** and pertinent.*

*You deliberately misinterpreted my statement. That's the **opposite** of what I intended.*

around round

*They had books lying **around** everywhere.*
*We walked **round** the lake.*

aural oral

*An '**aural**' examination relates to the ear and hearing.*
*An '**oral**' examination involves talking.*

beat win

*John **beat** Steve and Alan in the 400 metres hurdles.*
*Zara **won** the race.*

beside besides

*Why don't you sit down **beside** me?*
***Besides**, I've other things to do.*

biannual biennial

*It's worth checking whether the interest is **biannual**. If the interest is credited every six months, it can make quite a difference to your savings.*
*Their conferences are **biennial**. They meet every other year.*

born borne

*He was **born** in a stable.*
*They have **borne** their troubles with great patience.*

burst bust

*The winter was so severe that almost every household suffered from **burst** pipes.*
*That firm went **bust** five months ago.*

cannon canon

*They used those huge **cannons** for the twenty-one gun salute.*
*Such behaviour violates every **canon** of good taste.*

carat caret

*These rings are twenty-four **carat** gold.*
*A **caret** is a wedge-shaped character used to indicate that something has been omitted from a word or sentence.*

casual causal

*Many students look for **casual** employment during the vacation.*
*They looked in vain for the **causal** agent responsible for the rapid spread of the disease.*

censor censure

> He was one of a panel of **censors** responsible for commenting on the ethical content of soap operas.
> His **censure** of falling standards was severe.

cereal serial

> She has a different breakfast **cereal** every morning.
> My **serial** number is 01010101.

ceremonial ceremonious

> They were instructed to wear full **ceremonial** dress.
> He was inclined to be over formal and **ceremonious**.

childish childlike

> You're being **childish**! Why don't you grow up!
> He maintained a **childlike** innocence throughout his life.

complement compliment

> BE takes a **complement**, not an object.
> He paid her the **compliment** of listening carefully to everything she said.

comprehensible comprehensive

> It's just not **comprehensible**. It's gobbledygook!
> They undertook **comprehensive** reforms of the tax laws.

concession concessive

> After a strike lasting twelve months, the miners still could not wring any **concessions** from the Coal Board.
> **Concessive** clauses are usually introduced by 'although/as/but/though' and they involve a contrast.

contemptible contemptuous

> I find his lack of sensitivity **contemptible**.
> He was **contemptuous** of his opponent's skill.

continual continuous

> He had got used to the **continual** pain and hardly noticed the rare moments when it eased.
> We've had **continuous** rain for sixteen hours.

contort distort

> His eyes were evil, his face **contorted** and his mouth cruel.
> You have **distorted** the whole affair. It didn't happen like that.

council (n) counsel (n and v)

> He worked for the local **council** for thirty years.

*He often asked for **counsel** but only took the advice when it suited him.*
*When their marriage ran into trouble, they were **counselled** by the Marriage Advisory Bureau.*

defective deficient

*With my luck, even a new computer will be **defective**!*
*Their diet was **deficient** in calcium and iron.*

defensible defensive

*The general had blundered. Their position was not **defensible**.*
*He was always on the **defensive**, attacking before anyone could attack him.*

dependant dependent

*She has three **dependants**: her mother and two children.*
*Babies are completely **dependent** on their parents.*

deprecate depreciate

*She **deprecated** what she felt was the rapid decline of English.*
*If you don't invest wisely, your money will **depreciate**.*

desert (n and v) dessert (n)

*The Sahara is the biggest **desert** in the world.*
*He promised that he would never **desert** them and, in spite of problems, he stayed with them while they needed him.*
*They were allowed to have any **dessert** they wanted and they all chose apple pie and cream.*

device (n) devise (n and v)

*She invented the most wonderful **device**, a little contraption for magnifying the sun's rays.*
*'**Devise**' is a legal term referring to a clause in a will.*
*She **devised** a telephone-answering system of her own.*

discreet discrete

*She is the most **discreet** person I've ever met: she shows very good judgement in all she says and does.*
*The categories are absolutely **discrete** and do not overlap.*

eminent imminent

***Eminent** scientists often win the Nobel Prize.*
*By August 1939, war was clearly **imminent**, for those who could read the signs.*

equable equitable

> *They were too old to put up with the snow and ice of Alaska. They wanted to find a place with a more **equable** climate.*
> *We'll have to come to an **equitable** arrangement with them so let's avoid trouble and give everyone the same amount.*

exacerbate exasperate

> *Government action only seemed to **exacerbate** the suffering of the poor.*
> *He knows how to **exasperate** me. If he says that one more time I'll hit him.*

exceedingly excessively

> *It is running **exceedingly** well now.*
> *He was **excessively** and unnecessarily jealous.*

exercise exorcise

> *We'll have to **exercise** the dog. It's getting fat.*
> *If you don't believe in ghosts why are you looking for someone to **exorcise** that old house?*

explicit implicit

> *I'm not good at assembling gadgets. I make mistakes even when I try to follow **explicit** instructions.*
> *He had little education and no formal training, but his **implicit** faith seemed to need no external reinforcement.*

extant (adj) extent (n)

> *There are only about four manuscripts **extant**. The others were lost in an eighteenth-century fire.*
> *The **extent** of their losses became more apparent each day.*

fallacious fallible

> *That's a **fallacious** argument and you intended to deceive.*
> *We are all **fallible**, all capable of being wrong.*

foregone forgone

> *It was a **foregone** conclusion. Everyone could see that.*
> *He has **forgone** alcohol for the last twenty years.*

formally formerly

> *He will be **formally** introduced to the Ambassador tonight.*
> ***Formerly**, they had great wealth, but now they have nothing.*

gourmand gourmet

> *They call themselves '**gourmands**' but they are just gluttons.*
> *He was a **gourmet**, a connoisseur of good foods and wines.*

historic historical

The birth of a panda was an **historic** *event for the zoo.*
I've always wanted to write an **historical** *novel. The only trouble is that my knowledge of history is very limited.*

human humane

Yorkshire people sum up **human** *inconsistency by saying: 'There's nowt as queer as folk!'*
Surely there are more **humane** *ways of killing an animal?*

improvident imprudent

They were utterly **improvident,** *always behaving as if the future would look after itself.*
In spite of his apparent shrewdness, he made a number of **imprudent** *investments.*

industrial industrious

I believe he's a dealer in **industrial** *diamonds.*
She had the knack of finding conscientious, **industrious** *workers.*

ingenious ingenuous

We've found an **ingenious** *solution. It may not be legal but it is brilliant.*
It's hard to know if anyone of his age could be as innocent and **ingenuous** *as he appears.*

invaluable valueless

Your help has been **invaluable.** *We could have done nothing without you.*
They bought the painting hoping it might be a Goya but it turned out to be a **valueless** *imitation.*

its it's

The cat licked **its** *paws.*
It's *time to go home.*

judicial judicious

Everyone thought there should have been a **judicial** *enquiry into the disposal of those government contracts.*
I wonder if Solomon found it easy to be **judicious** *or if he too occasionally made unwise judgments?*

less fewer

We should probably eat **less** *meat and* **less** *sugar and drink* **less** *coffee.*
There were **fewer** *animals on show and* **fewer** *people looking at them.*

lightening (v)   lightning (n)

> *He wasn't exactly renowned for **lightening** other people's burdens!*
> *I'm afraid of thunder and **lightning**.*

loose lose

> *Don't let the animals **loose**.*
> *Don't **lose** your temper! Keep calm!*

luxuriant luxurious

> *Wherever we looked we could see **luxuriant** vegetation.*
> *They lived in a **luxurious** home. They had everything they could ever need or want.*

marshal (n and v)   martial (adj)

> *How many Field **Marshal(l)s** were there in France in 1945?*
> *He **marshalled** his family the way he had dragooned his troops.*
> *Do you know the 'Tin Soldier'? What comes after the line: 'With a **martial** tread through a storm of lead'?*

masterful masterly

> *He was **masterful**, domineering and imperious. He was good at giving orders but bad at taking them.*
> *Well done! That was a **masterly** achievement!*

material materiel

> *She bought eight yards of heavy **material** for her curtains.*
> *The USA gave the allies **materiel** support by supplying them with all the extra equipment they required.*

meretricious meritorious

> *Some people regarded the book highly, but he described it as tawdry, trashy and **meretricious**.*
> *His was a most **meritorious** action and he deserved the recognition he got.*

metal mettle

> *Tin and zinc are fairly common **metals**.*
> *You'll have to be on your **mettle** if you want to beat him!*

militate mitigate

> *Poor attendance could **militate** against you when it comes to promotions.*
> *The gifts of food **mitigated** the worst effects of the famine but did little to solve the underlying problem.*

momentary momentous

> *Don't throw away your career for what will eventually seem a **momentary** pleasure.*
> *It was a **momentous** occasion: the band played, the dignitaries arrived and everyone waited for the winner to be announced.*

monogram monograph

> *He always likes to have a **monogram** embroidered on his handkerchiefs.*
> *Her **monograph** was a detailed classification of rare blood groups.*

moral morale

> *African stories always have a **moral** because they were meant to teach as well as entertain.*
> *The **morale** in the group was poor because no one had any respect for or faith in their leader.*

notable noticeable

> *The discovery was all the more **notable** when you realise he had no formal education.*
> *Over the next few weeks the change in attitude became increasingly **noticeable**.*

observance observation

> *What sort of **observances** do you keep in Lent? Do you fast or abstain from meat?*
> *It was meant to be an **observation** post but I could see nothing because of the thick fog.*

obsolescent obsolete

> *Weapons have a relatively short useful life. These ones are **obsolescent** now and they will be totally **obsolete** in another five years.*

official officious

> *The government is expected to make an **official** announcement today.*
> *He was not well liked because he was an **officious** young man, always telling people the best way to do things.*

ordinance ordnance

> *There is an **ordinance** protecting grazing land.*
> *The **ordnance** section deals with military stores.*

permissible permissive

> *It's perfectly **permissible** to walk on the grass but you mustn't pick the flowers.*
> *He criticised our '**permissive** society' for failing to consider the long-term consequences of sexual freedom.*

practicable practical

> *It's just not* **practicable***. You'll have to come up with a different solution.*
> *I'm a* **practical** *person. I've never been interested in theory.*

precede proceed

> *The letter l* **precedes** *m in the alphabet.*
> *I don't think we should* **proceed***. It's getting dark and we don't know the area.*

prescribe proscribe

> *Doctors can only* **prescribe** *a limited number of drugs.*
> *Such marches should be* **proscribed***. They cause a great deal of trouble.*

prophecy (n) prophesy (v)

> *All the* **prophecies** *were fulfilled.*
> *He* **prophesied** *the end of the world.*

relative relevant

> *He compared their* **relative** *merits before deciding on the cheaper brand.*
> *I only want the* **relevant** *facts, not all the facts, just those that have a bearing on this matter.*

reverend (n) reverent (adj)

> *This is the* **Reverend** *John Smith.*
> *He was* **reverent** *in his attitude to all life forms.*

review revue

> *They both wrote very kind* **reviews** *of her last book.*
> ***Revues*** *aren't very popular with today's theatre-goers. They seem to prefer serious drama.*

role roll

> *I always fancied myself in the* **role** *of King Lear.*
> *His name should be included in a* **roll** *of honour.*

rout route

> *The* **rout** *of the second battalion led directly to their final defeat.*
> *We plan to take the scenic* **route** *through the mountains.*

sceptic (n) septic (adj)

> *Don't listen to that old* **sceptic***! He wouldn't believe it if he saw it with his own two eyes!*
> *The wound quickly turned* **septic** *because there were no antibiotics available.*

seasonable seasonal

> *Frost and snow are **seasonable** in Britain in January.*
> *The unemployment figures dropped because of the **seasonal** work in tourism and farming.*

seize siege

> *They **seized** his passport so that he couldn't leave the country.*
> *The **siege** eventually ended when the gunmen surrendered, freeing their hostage.*

sensual sensuous

> *Be careful how you use '**sensual**'. It tends to mean 'carnal' or 'licentious'.*
> *Every critic discusses his **sensuous** imagery, where all the senses, including the sense of smell, are gratified.*

sew sow

> *I hate **sewing**. My stitches are always crooked.*
> *The farmer **sowed** good seed.*

sewage sewerage

> *The Mediterranean has been polluted by the **sewage** of many countries.*
> *London's **sewerage** system was designed and built by the Victorians.*

sextant sexton

> *Navigators have used **sextants** for hundreds of years.*
> *The **sexton**'s sons usually help him to ring the bell and to dig graves.*

spacious specious

> *They lived in a **spacious** sixteenth-century abbey.*
> *That's a **specious** argument. It may sound attractive but it is false.*

stationary stationery

> *Passengers must wait until the bus is **stationary** before getting off.*
> *Their **stationery** is very distinctive: light blue paper and dark blue envelopes.*

superficial superfluous

> *There's no need to worry. The cut is only **superficial**, just a graze.*
> *Get rid of all **superfluous** gear. We keep only what is strictly necessary.*

temporal temporary

> *It is not always easy to draw a line between **temporal** and spiritual matters.*
> *We can only give you a **temporary** filling now but we'll do a permanent job when your abscess has cleared.*

usage use

> A 'raise in salary' is US **usage**; a 'rise' is more usual in the UK.
> This is of no **use** whatsoever. Get rid of it.

venal venial

> This post seems to attract **venal** politicians. Several have already been indicted for accepting bribes.
> It's only a **venial** sin. That means it's not as serious as a mortal sin.

veracious voracious

> George Washington is renowned for being **veracious**. He wouldn't tell a lie.
> He had the most **voracious** appetite! He ate as if he hadn't seen food for days.

See: **problem words**.

problem words

There are many words, usually latinate and polysyllabic, that are used vaguely or inaccurately because speakers are not certain of their meanings. Sometimes such misuse can lead to a change of meaning, (**aggravate**, for example, has taken on the meaning of 'irritate') but often it results in poor communication or the blurring of useful distinctions.

To restate that certain words should not be used in particular ways is unlikely to have much influence. Instead, we provide a list of the commonest problem words, citing their basic meanings and offering exemplary sentences:

anticipate—foresee and deal with in advance

> We **anticipated** the fluctuations in the market and so they did not adversely affect our trading.

bonus—something good in addition to what is due

> All staff members got a **bonus** of $100.

brutalise—make brutal or unfeeling

> Abject poverty tends to **brutalise** people. There is little scope for finer feelings when one has to struggle just to stay alive.

chronic—not acute, but long-term and recurrent

> About a quarter of the population suffers from **chronic** indigestion.

complex (n and adj)—1 a set of emotional desires and memories which may have been suppressed by the conscious mind but which continue to influence one's personality 2 a whole made up of interconnecting parts 3 not simple

An Oedipus complex can be defined as the sexual emotions and desires aroused in a male child by his mother. The equivalent emotions in a female child are referred to as the Electra complex.
He designed the new housing complex.
She never saw the easy solutions, only the complex ones.

crescendo—a gradual increase in volume in a piece of music

After the first crescendo we have a contrasting passage where we gradually play more and more quietly.

dilemma—a problem involving two (usually unattractive) alternatives

They were faced with a dilemma. If they agreed to the operation, she might not recover from the anaesthetic, but without the operation she would die.

echelon—a troop arrangement in which soldiers follow each other in such a way that each has a clear line of fire

Echelon arrangements continue to be used in modern warfare.

feasible—capable of being performed

It was the old man who suggested the only feasible plan.

forensic—used in courts of law

Forensic medicine involves the application of medical science to legal problems.

fulsome—abundant, copious, excessive

He described his own achievements in fulsome detail.

gracile—slender, slight, emaciated

The word gracile has gradually lost its association with 'starvation' because it has been confused with 'graceful'.

hoi polloi—the masses, the common people

He did not like general elections because he did not value the opinions of the hoi polloi, his usual term for the masses.

holocaust—a sacrifice consumed by fire, destruction by fire

Most people are frightened by the threat of a nuclear holocaust.

(*The Holocaust* is often used to refer to the slaughter of Jews during the Second World War.)

infamous—having a bad reputation

*Richard III was not nearly as **infamous** as Shakespeare suggests. Indeed, some historians believe he was a gentle and generous monarch.*

literally—in a non-metaphorical way

*He **literally** lost his shirt. Someone must have picked it up by mistake.*

myth—traditional story which attempts to explain beliefs or natural phenomena

*Many cultures have **myths** about how the human race began.*

panacea—a remedy for all ills

*Some people think that money is a universal **panacea**.*

pathetic—capable of evoking pity

*The '**Pathetic** Fallacy' suggests that Nature reflects human moods, by being sunny when we are happy and by raining when we are sad.*

peremptory—not admitting denial or contradiction

*He was disliked for his **peremptory** statements. People hated the fact that he knew he was always right.*

phobia—a deep and usually illogical fear

*Like many people she had a **phobia** about flying.*

potential—something that can develop

*Most of us seem to have a **potential** for violence.*

pristine—belonging to the earliest time or state, uncorrupted

*Adam and Eve lived in the Garden in a state of **pristine** innocence.*

protagonist—one who plays a leading role

*Many of the **protagonists** in the struggle for independence are unknown because no one took the early leaders seriously.*

quixotic—impractically and romantically devoted to chivalry

*Many people admired his **quixotic** attempts to establish a system of courtesy and gentleness among his pupils.*

rationalise—to explain by offering plausible reasons

*You can't **rationalise** everything. There are some reactions which are instinctive and not capable of logical explanation.*

schizophrenic—a person suffering from a phychotic disorder

> *Her mother was* **schizophrenic**. *Sometimes she was gentle and loving but at other times she behaved like someone demented.*

trauma—an injury, physical or mental

> *The* **trauma** *of the surgery sent her into shock.*

progressive

Structures containing BE + V$_{ing}$:

> *I am walking.*
> *She was walking.*
> *We have been walking.*
> *They had been walking.*
> *He will be walking.*

involve *progressive* or *continuous* **aspect** because they emphasise the continuity and duration of the action.

See: **aspect, verb phrase.**

pronoun

A *pronoun* is a word which can substitute for a noun or noun phrase:

> *The* **book** *is heavy.* → **It** *is heavy.*
> **John** *is here.* → **He** *is here.*
> **Mary Smith** *is tall.* → **She** *is tall.*

Pronouns can reflect **gender,** indicating in the third person singular whether a noun is masculine, feminine or neuter. They can also reflect **case.** The *nominative* occurs as the **subject** of a sentence, the *possessive* indicates possession and the *accusative* occurs after a preposition and as the **object** of a sentence:
Nominative:

> *I have talked to John.*
> **Who** *was singing?*

Possessive:

> *The teacher took* **his** *but not* **hers.**
> **Whose** *is it?*

Accusative:

> *John surprised* **me.**
> *To* **whom** *was the letter addressed?*

Pronouns belong to a closed set, which means we can list every single pronoun in the language. It is convenient to divide pronouns into eight sub-categories:

1 Personal Pronouns (12):

Person	Singular		Plural	
	Nom	Acc	Nom	Acc
1st	I	me	we	us
2nd	you	you	you	you
3rd Masc	he	him		
Fem	she	her	they	them
Neut	it	it		

2 Possessive Pronouns (6):

Person	Singular	Plural
1st	mine	ours
2nd	yours	yours
3rd Masc	his	
Fem	hers	theirs

3 Reflexive Pronouns (8):

Person	Singular	Plural
1st	myself	ourselves
2nd	yourself	yourselves
3rd Masc	himself	
Fem	herself	themselves
Neut	itself	

4 Demonstrative Pronouns (4):

Singular	Plural
this	these
that	those

5 Interrogative Pronouns (5):

Nom	Accusative	Possessive
who?	whom?	whose?
what?	what?	
which?	which?	

6 Relative Pronouns (5): these pronouns are used to introduce subordinate clauses.

that   *The hat **that** he sat on was mine.*
which *He kept all the letters **which** had been written.*
who   *She was the winner **who** resigned within two days.*
whom *They are the people on **whom** we all rely.*
whose *The child **whose** shoes were taken is waiting.*

7 Distributive Pronouns (5): these pronouns are often followed by
'of + pronoun':

all   *All (of them) went home.*
both   *Both (of you) should go.*
each   *Each (of us) received a present.*
either *Either (of them) might do.*
neither *Neither (of you) will play tomorrow.*

8 Indefinite Pronouns (3):

any   *He wouldn't have any.*
one   *One ought to try one's best.*
some   *Some like it hot.*

These pronouns often occur in compound forms such as *anyone*,
anybody, *somebody* and *something*. Occasionally, *so* and *such* function
like indefinite pronouns:

I think so.
Such is life!

See: **complement, noun phrase, object, parts of speech, pro forms, subject.**

pronunciation

There has never been an **Academy** for the English language and so
there has never been one form of *pronunciation* accepted as standard
for the entire English-speaking world. Most educated speakers approximate to the standard grammar and vocabulary of the written
language in their speech and pronounce the language according to
the accepted norms of their region. Increasingly, these norms are set
by regional radio and television announcers but because the media
are international as well as national in their influence, it seems
probable that people throughout the world are beginning to sound
more alike. There will probably always be individual and national
differences in the pronunciation of English, but the influence of the
media and the ease of international communication will ensure that
the differences will be outweighed by the similarities.

In spite of the fact that there is not and never has been *one*
acceptable way to pronounce English, people worry about pronunciation, and most letters to newspapers or radio and television com-
panies on the subject of **usage** relate to problems with or criticisms
of pronunciation.

It would in theory be possible to set up an international body to
monitor pronunciation, but any such body would find that pronunciation of all words changes with time and that logic has little to

do with preferences. Most English people at one time in the past pronounced post-vocalic *r*; now they do not although most Americans do. The *t* now frequently heard in the pronunciation of *often* is due to the influence of spelling and is acceptable whereas to pronounce the *t* in *castle* is not.

Speakers of English throughout the world agree more closely on the pronunciation of consonants than on that of vowels. Apart from the differences in vowels, however, General American English (GAE) and **Received Pronunciation** (RP) can be further differentiated as follows:

1 GAE is **rhotic**, RP is non-rhotic, that is, GAE pronounces post-vocalic *r* whereas RP has longer vowels.

2 In GAE, intervocalic (*t*)*t* in words such as *latter* and *biting* tends to sound like a *d*.

3 In GAE, the first vowel sound in words like *due*, *news* and *Tuesday* is /u/; in RP, it is /ju/.

4 In GAE, the words in each of the following sets tend to be **homophones**: *Mary, merry, marry, hairy, Harry, ant, aunt, can't, cant*, whereas such sets as *paw, poor, pour* are homophonous for many RP speakers.

5 In words of four or more syllables, GAE speakers tend to use more secondary and tertiary stresses than speakers of RP:

contemporary /kən'tɛmpəˌrɛrɪ/ (GAE) /kən'tɛmprɪ/ (RP)
laboratory /'læbərəˌtɔrɪ/ (GAE) /lə'bɒrɪtrɪ/ (RP)

6 Words ending in -*ile* tend to be pronounced /əl/ in GAE and /aɪl/ in RP:

fertile /fɜrtəl/ (GAE) /fɜtaɪl/ (RP)
missile /mɪsəl/ (GAE) /mɪsaɪl/ (RP)

7 A number of miscellaneous words are pronounced differently in the UK and the USA; the best-known of these are:

	USA	UK
ate	rhymes with *gate*	rhymes with *get*
figure	fig + yer	fig + er
lever	rhymes with *ever*	rhymes with *weaver*
processes	rhymes with *less + ease*	rhymes with *less + is*
route	rhymes with *bout*	rhymes with *boot*
shone	rhymes with *bone*	rhymes with *gone*

8 In both regions, the consonant cluster /kw/ in words such as *quart* and *quote* is being simplified to /k/. Many purists disapprove of the change especially in *quote* and related forms.

See: **accent, network norms, phonetics.**

propaganda

Propaganda is a clear example of a word whose meaning has been debased. It was originally a religious term derived from *Congregatio de Propaganda Fidei* (Congregation for the Spread of the Faith) and referred to the dissemination of Christian beliefs. Nowadays, the word implies:

1 the spreading of information for the purpose of hurting a cause, person or organisation and, less commonly,

2 the spreading of information with the intention of helping a cause, person or organisation.

Propaganda thus involves the transmission of information plus attitudes and values. Information, on its own, provides facts and figures (a weather forecast, populations) but propaganda packages the facts so as to produce a calculated response such as fear, dislike or distrust. Successful propaganda tends to use truths rather than lies, but selected truths often presented to reinforce a prejudice.

Like many successful communicators, propagandists tend to:

1 use emotive vocabulary: *patriotism*, *purity*

2 play on feelings of insecurity, pride, envy

3 emphasise the prestige of the speaker

4 aim to use devices, both linguistic (rhetoric, repetition) and non-linguistic (music, colour, crowds), to modify the attitudes of their audience.

See: **cliché, euphemism, semantic change.**

proper noun

Nouns can be subdivided into common (*cheese*) and proper (*China*), with *proper nouns* being signalled by the use of a capital letter. They can occur as **subjects**:

Wordsworth was a poet.

objects:

Who has read Virginia Woolf?

complements:

He thinks he is Hamlet!

and in preposition phrases:

I propose a toast to Robbie Burns.

Proper nouns cannot be modified as extensively as common nouns but the following patterns of modification are found:

1 the + descriptive adjective + person's name

the extraordinary Millie Milestone

When the structure 'a + (adjective) + proper noun' occurs, the reference is to one resembling the person named:

a new Jane Austen

or to a representative of a type:

a peeping Tom

2 possessive adjective (especially *our*) + proper noun. This is often used for family and pets:

our Henry
our Fido

3 NP + proper noun, or proper noun + NP:

the dramatist, Oscar Wilde
Pepe, our pedigree chihuahua

4 young/old + person/animal or ancient/modern + place:

poor old Joe
young Albert
ancient Egypt
modern Albania

5 proper noun + embedded sentence:

John Keats, who wrote 'Hyperion'

6 proper noun + preposition phrase:

Jeanie with the light brown hair

7 popular newspapers often use a considerable amount of pre-proper noun modification:

47-year-old father of two Martin Smith

A proper noun which is frequently used can become a common noun. This is particularly likely to happen with trade names:

cola
hoover

or with products from a place:

cashmere
denim

See: **noun, noun phrase, place names.**

prose

The word *prose* derives from the Latin phrase *prosa oratio* meaning 'straightforward speech'. Today, the term is applied to:

1 the normal language used in speech and writing
2 all written language that is not poetry
3 dull written or spoken discourse

Prose is usually thought to reflect the patterns of speech more closely than verse because of the variety and irregularity of its **rhythms**. Much prose **style**, however, utilises **parallelism** of sound, vocabulary and syntax, a fact that becomes clear whether we examine prose stylists of the sixteenth century like Francis Bacon:

> *Now I proceed to those errors and vanities which have*
> *intervened amongst the studies themselves of the learned,*
> *which is that which is principal and proper to the present*
> *argument...*
> *The Diseases and Humours of Learning*

or the oratory of the twentieth century:

> *I have a dream that one day this nation will rise up and*
> *live out the true meaning of its creed... I have a dream*
> *that on the red hills of Georgia the sons of former slaves*
> *and the sons of former slave owners will be able to sit down*
> *together at the table of brotherhood.*
> Martin Luther King, 28 August, 1963

It is probably true that good prose takes as much time and care as good poetry. It is probably also true that good poetry tends to be written by the young and good prose by the mature.

See: **parallelism, style.**

prosody

Prosody derives ultimately from Greek *prosoidia* (a song sung to musical accompaniment). Today, the word is most frequently applied to the study of verse form including such features as **rhyme, rhythm** and stanzaic patterns. In linguistics, *prosody* refers to the patterns of stress, rhythm, pitch and intonation in a language.

proverb

A *proverb* expresses a generally recognised truth in an easily remembered form. Unlike an **aphorism**, a proverb is usually anonymous:

> *Too many cooks spoil the broth.*

Each proverb is a self-contained sentence and the syntactic patterns tend to be fairly simple, allowing the saying to be easily retained and reproduced. Most of the verbs involved are in the simple present and affirmatives are more common than negatives or interrogatives. Proverbs are often centuries old and archaic in form :

Judge not, that ye be not judged.

Since proverbs are usually associated with oral cultures, they exploit such devices as **alliteration** :

Wilful waste makes woeful want.

rhyme :

Early to bed and early to rise
Makes a man healthy, wealthy and wise.

metre :

If you lie down with dogs
You'll get up with fleas.

and lexical and syntactic **parallelism** :

He who knows not and knows that he knows not is not so
bad ; but he who knows not and knows not that he knows
not is dangerous.

There seems to have been a gradual decline in the production of proverbs in English, coinciding with urbanisation and the growth of literacy.

Proverbs are the distilled wisdom of a group of people and their study can provide insights into the activities, interests and philosophy of the people who created them. Victorian England, with its emphasis on self-help, created :

God helps those who help themselves.

whereas speakers in West Africa found solace in :

God helps those who cannot help themselves.

See : **aphorism, maxim, oral tradition.**

psycholinguistics

Psycholinguistics is the branch of **linguistics** that studies the relationship between language and the mind. It may involve :

1 the study of language as it interacts with memory, perception and learning

2 the study of the psychological processes involved in acquiring, storing and remembering language

See : **aphasia, linguistics.**

psychologese

Psychologese is a type of jargon consisting of elements of technical vocabulary drawn from psychology and psychiatry. Often the terms are used inaccurately but many have been popularised by journalism, among them: *frustrate, neurotic, paranoid, phobia, psychotic, schizoid, schizophrenic, subliminal, traumatic.*

See: **jargon.**

pun

A *pun* is a humorous or witty use of a word or phrase to exploit its ambiguity:

She filed the papers and her nails.

or its similarity in sound to another word:

When is a door not a door? When it's ajar. (a jar)

Punning may be for comic effect or it may be for wit, as in the poetry of the metaphysicals:

The grave's a fine (i.e.'fine' + 'confined') *and private place
But none, I think, do there embrace.*
    Andrew Marvell, 'To his coy mistress'

or the epitaph attributed to John Donne on his inauspicious marriage:

*John Donne
Ann Donne
Undone*

The word *pun* was first recorded in English in the seventeenth century, but its etymology is uncertain.

See: **ambiguity, figurative language, polysemy, syllepsis.**

punctuation

Punctuation marks help to specify meaning, indicate emphasis, and signal the representation of speech, quotations and intonation. The conventions of punctuation are therefore not simply a useful addition to writing but an essential part of meaning. In English, the following thirteen items are the most commonly used features of punctuation:

apostrophe

The **apostrophe** which is represented by ' is used to indicate

1 possession:

> *the teacher's plan* (singular)
> *the teachers' plan* (plural)
> *the children's response*
> *someone's shoe*
> *a home of one's own*

The apostrophe is not used for possessive pronouns:

> *The house is his not hers.*
> *Whose is it? It is theirs.*

2 contractions:

> *there is* > *there's*
> *cannot* > *can't*
> *of the clock* > *o'clock*

3 omissions:

> *'86* (1986)
> *'alf* (half)
> *walkin'* (walking)

brackets

There are several types of brackets, parentheses ( ), square [ ], angle
< >, brace { }. Only the first two are regularly employed in writing.
Parentheses ( ) are used:

1 to isolate any information that is supplementary to the meaning
of a sentence, not essential to the syntax, and logically more remote
than an enclosure marked by commas or dashes:

> *The result (a 20% swing in favour of the ruling party) was conclusive.*

A whole sentence may be marked off:

> *The result was conclusive. (There was a 20% swing in favour of the
> ruling party.)*

2 to supply further information about a person or detail in a text:

> *John Fletcher (1887-1945) is still remembered in his village.*
> *Dialects (p.7ff) have already been discussed.*

3 to indicate options:

> *Any volunteer(s) will be welcome.*

4 for numbers within a sentence:

> *It was (1) well researched, (2) accurately documented and (3) clearly
> presented.*

Material within parentheses should be treated according to its status and position. A full sentence within parentheses should start with a capital letter and close with a full stop, exclamation or question mark when it can stand on its own:

Mary Ann Evans chose 'George Eliot' as her pseudonym.
(She may never have had her works published if she had used her own name.)

A full sentence should start with a lower case letter and have no full stop (though it may have a question or exclamation mark) when it is incorporated into another sentence:

Michael Finnegan (he was the thin one) was very versatile.

There is usually no punctuation before a parenthesis, although it may occur after the closing parenthesis:

It was a decisive vote (as you've seen), but feelings are still running high.

Square brackets [ ] are used:
1 to indicate that a letter, word or phrase is not part of the original text but has been inserted by the editor or someone quoting the original:

And sent it to Sir Patrick Spens
[who] *Was walking on the strand.*

2 with the word *sic* ('thus'), to signal that the writer quoting the passage has confirmed an unconventional or unexpected spelling, word or structure:

Eritrea should be annecksed [sic].
They presented her with a volume of poesy [sic] *written by her former students.*

Angle brackets < > are occasionally used to indicate graphemes, that is, the minimum contrastive unit in a system of writing. Thus <n> would represent all the various ways in which the letter *n* might be written.

Brace brackets { } are also called 'curly brackets' and they tend to be used to enclose alternative elements:

$$\text{he was} \begin{cases} \text{tired} \\ \text{angry} \\ \text{thirsty} \end{cases}$$

colon
The colon which is represented by : is used:
1 to introduce a word, phrase, sentence, list that explains, illustrates or rephrases the previous statement:

*The list was comprehensive: a compendium of bibliographical infor-
mation, recommended texts and required reading.*

2 to introduce a long quotation that is separated from the text,
indented and without quotation marks.
3 to separate a title from a subtitle, as in:

Beowulf: A New Translation

for ratios:

Common nouns outnumber proper nouns in the proportion 3:2 (i.e.
by three to two).

and for bibliographical references:

English World-Wide, V:1, 1984.

4 The colon follows the salutation in formal letters in the USA:

Dear Sir:

comma
The comma is represented by , and is one of the most widely used
marks of punctuation. Conventions for comma use vary slightly as
between language written to be read silently, where the commas
indicate logical subdivisions, and language written to be read aloud,
where the commas may indicate breath groups. Generally, however,
there is little ambiguity. The chief uses of the comma are:
1 to mark off clauses:

Since detailed descriptions are rare, this one is particularly welcome.

or phrases from clauses:

As a detailed description, it is particularly welcome.

2 to isolate interpolations (*in contrast, in addition*), sentence modifiers (*however, likewise, thus*) and phrases introducing examples (*for
example*):

*They received, in addition, a bonus every three months.
The stranger, however, was never seen again.
Take Freddie, for example.*

3 with words or phrases in a series but not before *and*:

*It was warm, sunny and cheerful.
They were in love, in harmony and in Paris in Spring!*

4 between adjectives modifying the same noun:

He was a tall, elegant man.

Again, if an *and* occurs between the adjectives, a comma does not precede *and*:

> *He was a tall and elegant man.*

5 to introduce a direct quotation:

> *She said, 'I can't see anything.'*

6 to isolate names, terms of address in speech and **tag questions**:

> *Hey, James, what's going on?*
> *I want to go home, you great big oaf!*
> *We went every year, didn't we?*

7 to indicate thousands, millions and billions:

> *There are, perhaps, 100,000 suns.*
> *His personal fortune was estimated at $10,000,000.*
> *They travelled 2,000,000,000 miles.*

8 to follow the salutation in all letters in the UK and in informal letters in the USA:

> *Dear Sir,* (UK)
> *Dear Joan,* (UK and USA)

dash

The dash which is represented by—is used:

1 as an alternative to parentheses or commas:

> *It was—on balance—a successful enterprise.*

Where the parenthesis occurs in the middle of a sentence, there must always be a closing as well as an opening dash.

2 as an alternative to a colon to indicate apposition or explanation:

> *The list was comprehensive—a compendium of bibliographical information, recommended books and required reading.*

3 together with the colon and usually at the end of a line to introduce an example, an illustration or direct speech:

> *He selected the following:—*
> *three turtle doves and a partridge*

Contemporary writers tend to use a colon alone instead of :—

4 in fiction to indicate disjointed or fragmented speech, as in the following passage from the speech of Miss Bates in Jane Austen's *Emma*:

> *I was reading it to Mrs. Cole, and since she went away, I*
> *was reading it again to my mother, for it is such a pleasure*
> *to her—a letter from Jane—that she can never hear it*

*often enough ; so I knew it could not be far off, and here
it is, only just under my huswife—and since you are so
kind as to wish to hear what she says ;—but, first of all,
I really must, in justice to Jane, apologise for her
writing so short a letter—only two pages you see—hardly
two—and in general she fills the whole paper and crosses
half.*

The dash is often overused. It is rarely an adequate substitute for a conjunction and whenever possible more precise vocabulary or punctuation should be used. In contemporary writing, the dash is seldom combined with another punctuation mark such as a comma or a question mark.

ellipsis
Ellipsis consists of three spaced dots . . . and indicates that something has been omitted from the original text or statement:

*Last night there were four Maries
Tonight there'll be but three.
There was Marie Seaton and Marie Beaton
And Marie Carmichael . . .*

Ellipsis may also be used to express tentativeness:

I may or I may not, who knows. . .

exclamation mark/point
The exclamation mark or exclamation point which is represented by ! is used:

1 to signal emphatic utterances:

You ran away!

2 to mark emphatic but often syntactically incomplete utterances:

*Not on your life!
Holy Toledo!
Not likely!*

full stop/period
The full stop or **period** which is represented by . is used:

1 at the end of a sentence that is not an exclamation or a question:

Suddenly, we reached the top.

2 with some **abbreviations**:

He loved his wife, i.e. the wife of the moment.

The use of the full stop to mark abbreviations is more common in the USA than in the UK but is gradually disappearing in international English.

hyphen

The hyphen which is represented by - is used:

1 at the end of a line to indicate that a word has been split. The division should take place between syllables, thus *per-mission* and not *perm-ission* (although the divisions often depend on house styles). In texts that are to be printed, a double hyphen is used at the end of a line if the hyphen should be retained irrespective of the position of the word:

Nobody knew her age or cared. She might have been twenty = one...

2 in some **compounds**: *twenty-two, mother-in-law, off-the-cuff remarks, a dyed-in-the-wool conservative*

3 after some **prefixes** (*co-occur*) but not others (*expel*). The more frequently such compounds are used, the less likely are they to retain the hyphen.

4 after the first part of a compound when two related compounds are mentioned:

first- and second-class tickets

5 for written fractions:

a two-thirds increase
one twenty-fifth of a mile

6 to abbreviate numbers and dates:

pages 125-27 (= 125 to 127)
the years 1916-18 (= 1916 to 1918)

A slightly longer line, but similar to the hyphen, is used between proper nouns that are not compounds but combinations:

the Spain–France match
the Kaylor–Sibson fight
the Washington–New York flight

oblique/slash

The *oblique* (UK) or *slash* (USA) / is used:

1 to juxtapose alternatives:

It could be for staff and/or students.
Tea/coffee will be served.

2 for a period passing from one calendar year to the next:

the academic year 1986/7

3 to mark off lines of poetry quoted as or in ordinary lines of prose:

In 'April Rise' Laurie Lee writes of 'Blown bubble-film of blue, the sky wraps round/ Weeds of warm light.'

4 two slashes indicate phonemic script:

The phonemes /p/ and /f/ were both realised as /p/.

question mark
The question mark which is represented by *?* is used:
1 to indicate a direct question:

Am I late?
I'm late?

Indirect questions are not followed by a question mark:

I asked if I was late.

2 within square brackets, to query a detail such as a date:

It was published in 1916 [?] by his brother.

3 in front of a linguistic example to indicate a structure which is only marginally acceptable:

?It had been being beaten.

quotation marks
Quotation marks may be single ' ' or double " ". Single quotation marks or *inverted commas* are more commonly used in the UK and double quotation marks are the norm in the USA. They are used:
1 for direct quotations:

'I'm hungry,' he complained. (UK)
"I'm hungry," he complained. (USA)

2 for the titles of short stories, short poems, chapters of books, radio and television programmes, songs and short musical works:

'From the Depths' was the name of my first story.
She sang 'Greensleeves' and several other traditional airs.

semicolon
The semicolon which is represented by *;* is used:
1 between clauses that are syntactically independent but semantically closely related:

He was an academic; he was a researcher of consummate skill; he was a skilled horseman; he was also a devoted husband.

2 to avoid over-using conjunctions:

In this passage, the kind of emotive emphasis carried in speech by stress and intonation is suggested by the exclamation marks; the attribution is marked ('complained' rather than 'said'); volume is indicated by the word 'loudly' in the narrative; and feeling is suggested by 'warmly'.

See: **abbreviations, apostrophe, ellipsis, quotation.**

purist

The term *purist* is applied to a person who:
  1 sets great store by correct **usage**
  2 objects to the use of foreign words
Purists tend to concentrate not on intelligibility or the pervasiveness of a form but on an item's **etymology**, on details of pronunciation, on grammatical precision and on **style**.

Many purists dislike semantic change (insisting, for example, that **aggravate** does not mean 'irritate'), recommend Latin-based structures (*It is I.*) and insist on logical usage ('since *due to* is a complement it cannot, logically, occur at the beginning of a sentence').

The idea of the 'purity' of the English language is discounted by any study of the history of English vocabulary, more than 30% of which derives from French and Latin. It is equally unrealistic to expect that word meanings will remain unchanged in a changing world.

Purists have been criticised by scholars who insist that a linguist's job is to 'describe and not prescribe'. This may be true, but purists are correct in claiming that rapid and uncontrolled change can lead to **ambiguity** and lack of precision. Most teachers realise that a touch of purist conservatism is necessary.

See: **'chestnuts'**.

qualifier

The term *qualifier* is applied to **adjectives** and **adverbs** which expand a headword such as a noun or verb. In traditional grammars, an adjective was said to *qualify* a noun whereas an adverb was said to *modify* a verb. Today, the terms are used interchangeably, with **modifier** being in wider use.

See: **modifier**.

quasi-modal

As well as the nine modals, *can, could, may, might, must, shall, should, will, would*, there are two sets of verbs which share some of the characteristics of modals and which can therefore be described as *quasi-modals*.

  1 *Dare, need, ought to* and *used to* share some of the formal properties of modals:
    (a) they can combine directly with 'not/n't':

  *You **daren't** say that again!*

(b) they can form questions directly:

Needn't I fill in this form?

They differ in the number of characteristics they share with the modals, but all the quasi-modals share at least two modal characteristics.

2 A number of verbs share the semantic characteristics of modals in being able to express attitudes concerning ability, compulsion, insistence, intention, obligation, permission, possibility and willingness. Below we list the most frequently occurring verbs in this set, together with exemplary sentences and parallel sentences involving modals:

BE to: *He is to sing tomorrow./He will sing tomorrow.*
BE able to: *She is able to walk now./She can walk now.*
BE about to: *I'm about to set out./I'll set out now.*
BE going to: *You're going to make it./You'll make it.*
GET to: *We didn't get to play./We couldn't play.*
HAVE to: *Has he to come?/Must he come?*
HAVE got to: *You've got to try./You must try.*
had better: *We'd better go./We should go.*
let: *Let me try./May I try?*
SEEM to: *They seem to be all right./They may be all right.*

See: **modality**.

question

Questions ask for information and they are signalled in the written medium by a question mark. Questions normally differ from statements in that they invert the order of the subject and the **auxiliary** verb:

He can dance well. → Can he dance well?

Where there is no auxiliary in the **verb phrase**, the dummy auxiliary **DO** is used:

He danced well. → Did he dance well?

There are five main types of question in English:
1 yes/no questions which demand the answer *yes* or *no*:

Are you tired?

2 Wh-questions involving the question words: *how?, what?, when?, where?, which?, why?*:

Why haven't they been told?

3 **tag questions,** involving auxiliaries:

*He isn't going, **is he***?

4 intonational questions which do not involve inversion of the subject and the predicate but indicate a query by rising **intonation**:

You won't have any?

5 rhetorical questions which are questions in form but not in meaning. A rhetorical question is often the semantic equivalent of an emphatic statement:

Am I hungry? = I'm very hungry.
Isn't it a shame? = It's a shame.

See: **auxiliary, interrogative, question tag, sentence.**

question tag

A *question tag* or *tag question* is an **interrogative** structure consisting of an **auxiliary** + pronoun and placed at the end of a statement:

*He's very cheerful, **isn't he***?

Tags can be both positive and negative. A positive tag follows a negative statement and a negative tag follows a positive one. Both types of tag can be used to request information:

*You posted it, **didn't you***? (Please tell me.)
*You didn't forget, **did you***? (Please tell me.)

to solicit agreement:

*He's a fool, **isn't he***? (I know you agree with me.)
*She's never on time, **is she***? (I'm sure we agree.)

or to soften an imperative:

*Sit down, **won't you***?

English is unusual in having so many tag questions: auxiliaries (including modals and **DO**) and the **quasi-modals** (*need, ought to*):

*I'm not on the committee, **am I***?
*You have seen her, **haven't you***?
*She doesn't smoke, **does she***?
*They needn't come, **need they***?

Many speakers of English as a second or foreign language find the proliferation of tags difficult to master and tend to use an invariant tag such as *isn't it?* or *not so?*

See: **questions, tags.**

quotation

The term *quotation* is used to indicate any phrase, verse, sentence or paragraph taken from another writer. A quotation should normally be an exact copy of the original, any alterations being clearly indicated and explained. The conventions for presenting quotations are as follows:

1 Quotation marks (or inverted commas) are double in the USA:

It has been called an "ynkehorne letter".

and single in the UK:

It has been called an 'ynkehorne letter'.

Quotations within quotations are signalled by the reverse of the above, thus single within double in the US and double within single in the UK:

It has been described as 'the "novel within a novel" technique'.

2 Any alteration to a quotation must be clearly indicated. Additions are marked by square brackets, omissions by **ellipsis**:

'For pronunciation, the best general rule is to consider
... as the most elegant speakers [those] who deviate least
from written words.'
    Samuel Johnson

If the original has an inaccurate or unusual spelling, an unexpected feature of vocabulary, unconventional syntax or a wrong date, the interpolation [sic] may be used to confirm that the quotation is accurate:

He called it 'a euphemistic [sic] style' and argued
that it 'shewed [sic] a strong sense of morality'.

An alteration, such as the italicisation of a word or phrase for special emphasis, should be recorded:

'Dictionaries are like watches; the worst is better than
none, and the best cannot be expected to go quite true.'
    Samuel Johnson (italics mine)

3 It is normal practice to place all punctuation marks belonging to the passage inside the quotation marks and those belonging to the writer outside:

He wrote, 'Men have become the slaves of their machines.'
I love the phrase 'paradoxical ratiocination'.

When a sentence ends with a quotation that ends with a full stop, the one full stop is sufficient.

4 Quotation marks are used for the titles of short poems, articles, stories and chapters in books. They may also be used for words cited as linguistic or lexical items rather than for their meaning:

She alternated between 'one' and 'I'.

(Italics may be used instead of quotation marks for this purpose but a writer should make consistent choices.) Quotation marks may also be used for a word that a writer disagrees with:

What he calls a 'dialect' is really an accent.

and for a word from a different language or a markedly different stylistic level:

She was always talking about her 'ambience'.
They were instructed to 'scram' and never return.

5 Prose quotations of up to ten typed lines or 100 words should be given within quotation marks and incorporated in the text. Longer quotations should not be given within quotation marks, should be separated from the text, be indented on the left-hand side, and be typed in single spacing for a **dissertation**, double for a **typescript**. A colon is normally used to introduce a longer quotation. (Some writers prefer to indent and separate from their text all quotations of more than ten words. Again, consistency is more important than dogma.)

6 Quotations of poetry consisting of a single line or less should be in quotation marks and incorporated in the text. Two lines are sometimes presented in this way, in which case the lines should be separated by a slash or oblique:

It is an echo of the poem 'The Second Coming' by W. B. Yeats,
in which he writes that 'Things fall apart; the centre
cannot hold;/Mere anarchy is loosed upon the world'.

Two or more lines of poetry are usually presented separate from the context without quotation marks, indented on the left-hand side and introduced by a colon. Quotation marks are retained if they occur in the original.

7 If a single paragraph is quoted, the first line is not usually indented further than a normal quotation, but if more than one paragraph is quoted consecutively then the first line of each is indented. When the paragraphs are a transcript of a speech, and so require quotation marks, the quotation marks are used at the beginning of each paragraph but at the end of the last paragraph only.

8 **Footnote** numbers, which give references for quotations, are typed slightly above the line, after the quotation and any punctuation. A series of quotations from one writer in a paragraph may be given a single footnote.

9 When quotations are set in a different type, quotation marks are unnecessary.

10 Quotation as part of scholarly **argument** is a way of providing evidence or illustration, and should therefore be used with discrimination. As part of a conversation, it may help to support an argument, perpetuate a tradition (such as the repetition of proverbial wisdom) or provide amusement. However, quotation can also be an unpleasant means of scoring points against someone who does not know a particular language (especially Latin or French) or who may not be as widely read as the speaker. This hostile use of quotation is evidence not of a cultured person but of one who uses knowledge (as others use gossip) for an ulterior motive.

See: **bibliography, ellipsis, footnote, plagiarism, punctuation, typescript.**

quotation, quote

These terms have slightly different uses in the UK and the USA, although the US usage is becoming increasingly common in the UK.

In the UK, *quotation* is a noun referring to something that is quoted:

*You shouldn't use such long **quotations**.*

and as part of the compound referring to the marks (or inverted commas) signalling it:

*Don't forget to close your **quotation marks**.*

The word *quote* is used as a verb:

*I must remember to **quote** that back at you.*

and as a noun meaning 'estimate':

*His **quote** for building the house was too high.*

In the USA, *quotation* is used for the matter quoted:

*Those **quotations** are very revealing.*

and *quote* is used as a verb:

*You must learn to **quote** accurately.*

as a noun for the punctuation marks:

*Put that in **quotes**.*

and, increasingly, as an alternative to *quotation*:

*Will **you** give us a **quote**?*

racialism, racism

For most speakers of English, these terms are used interchangeably to mean:

1 the belief that each race has distinctive physical (and perhaps mental) features which are determined by heredity

2 the belief that hereditary factors can cause one race to be superior to another

3 aggressive **prejudice** or discrimination based on race and the belief in racial inequality.

Some speakers try to reserve the word *racialism* for the first belief, which admits racial differences but not racial superiority or inferiority, and the word *racism* for a belief that implies inherent superiority of any race. This would be a useful distinction, but both terms have been so widely used for the second and third beliefs that it is simplest to regard the words as synonymous.

See: **racist language**.

racist language

Attitudes towards race and sex are relatively fixed in western society. For at least four centuries, the norm has been a white, Anglo-Saxon, Protestant male and anyone deviating from that norm has been at best 'different', at worst 'inferior'. The language reflects such prejudices.

White is equated with God, the angels, goodness; **black** with Satan, the damned, evil. And, in spite of the evidence of their eyes, to many people anyone who is not white is black. Speakers of English have had to make a special effort to stress that 'black is beautiful' and so counteract the negative impact of 'black' in such collocations as *blackguard*, *blackmail*, *black market*.

Non-Anglo-Saxons have been described as *Dagos*, *Frogs*, *Greasebacks*, *Gyppos*, *Micks*, *Polacks*, *Wogs* and *Wops* or, less offensively though no less racially, as *Ivans*, *Erics* and *Jocks*. Such attitudes are often enshrined in such children's verses as:

> *Taffy was a Welshman. Taffy was a thief.*
> *Taffy came to our house and stole a leg of beef.*

or:

> *My mother said I never should*
> *Play with the Gypsies in yonder wood.*

Religious prejudices, which often have a racial component, are less apparent in the language now than in the past but can still be found in words like *street urchin* (Muslim), *Tague* (Catholic), *Yid* (Jew).

Wherever differences exist in terms of class, money, race, religion or sex, prejudices have arisen and these prejudices find expression in our language and our stereotypes.

See: **black, Gypsy, racialism, sexist language**.

radio

Until the middle of the 1920s, people were exposed mainly to the language of their region, with the standard language being taught through school and the written medium. Increasingly, however, the *radio* impinged on the lives of most English speakers. At first, only the rich could afford sets but the radio rapidly became as normal an item of household furniture as a clock.

Radio has affected society in many ways but we shall limit our comments to its effect on language. First, most listeners assumed that the people broadcasting the news were speaking English the way it should be spoken, with the result that the **pronunciation** of newsreaders became equated with 'standard' pronunciation. Secondly, radio pronunciation was imitated, both consciously and unconsciously, with the result that regional differences in speech began to diminish.

From the early 1950s, the influence of the radio on language has been reinforced by television. People have become familiar with other varieties of English and US English, in particular, is well known and influential.

The popularity of radio and television programmes in English has helped to spread English throughout the world, making it possible for the first time in history for people to learn standard English chiefly through the spoken medium.

See: **network norms**.

raise, rear, rise

These words have different distributions in UK and US English, though US influence is increasingly evident in the UK.

Raise as a noun in the USA means an increase in pay or in a gambling stake:

*I didn't get the **raise** I was expecting.*
*Make it a **raise** of $10.*

As a verb in both the USA and the UK *raise* means 'lift, set/place in an upright position, bring up one's own children':

*He **raised** his eyes/family/hat/.*

In the USA *raise* can mean 'bring up a child':

> *She was **raised** by her aunt.*

Rear is used in the UK to mean 'bring up, foster':

> *He **reared** his family single-handed.*

Rise as a noun is the usual word in the UK for an increase in pay:

> *We've been limited to a 3% **rise**.*

It can also be used as a nominal equivalent of the verbs *raise* and *rise*:

> *There was a **rise** in the water level.* (cf. They raised the water level.)
> *There has been a **rise** in the number of people out of work.* (cf. The number of people out of work rose last month.)

See: **problem pairs, UK and US words**.

rankshifting

Certain models of **grammar** such as 'Scale and Category Grammar' (a model of grammar developed in Britain by Michael Halliday in the early 1960s) recognise such hierarchical arrangements of units as:

phoneme	/ʌ/
morpheme	*un-* as in *unfit*
word	*under*
phrase (group)	*under the trees*
clause	*which were under the trees*
sentence	*The plants which were under the trees were stunted.*

Such arrangements are referred to as *rank scales* because, usually, a sentence is composed of one or more clauses; the clauses are composed of one or more phrases; phrases are composed of words, words of morphemes and morphemes of phonemes.

The term *rankshifting* is applied to units that are 'shifted' down in 'rank' so that a clause may modify a phrase:

> *the title **which he gave it***

or a phrase a word:

> ***off-the-cuff** remarks*

or, on rare occasions, one word can be infixed into another:

> *abso**blooming**lutely*

See: **grammar**.

real, really

In very informal US English *real* is often used instead of *really* before adjectives and adverbs:

> *That's **real** nice.*
> *She drives **real** fast.*

Often, the entire adverb phrase consists of 'real + adjective':

> *Drive **real careful** now.*

Most **purists** disapprove of this **usage**.

See: **adjective, adverb**.

Received Pronunciation

Received Pronunciation, now usually referred to as *RP*, is a prestigious British **accent** which was and is associated with Oxford, Cambridge, the court, public schools, the BBC and with educated speakers whose regional origins are not apparent in their speech.

See: **accent, phonetics, pronunciation**.

redundancy

Redundancy has two main meanings in English:
  1 It can refer to the use of unnecessary words or phrases:

> *a **wee, small, tiny** child*
> *at this moment **in time***

  2 In linguistics, it refers to data which may be unnecessary but which may help our understanding. In a phrase such as:

> *those two dogs*

plurality is marked three times. Most speech contains redundancies and so we often understand utterances even if we miss part of what was said.

See: **circumlocution, pleonasm, tautology**.

reduplication

Reduplication refers to partial or complete repetition:

> *abracadabra*
> *puff puff*

It is used in some languages, such as Sierra Leone Krio, to indicate intensity:

> *tɔk* (talk)
> *tɔktɔk* (chatter)

plurality:

> *ston* (stone)
> *soso stonston* (stones everywhere)

and class change:

> *kɔna* (corner = noun)
> *kɔnakɔna* (secretive = adj)

In English, we find the following types of reduplication:
1 complete reduplications such as:

> *bye bye*
> *fifty fifty*
> *Hear! Hear!*
> *The* **Late Late** *Show*
> *tomtom*

2 complete reduplications with additional elements such as:

> *all in all*
> *by and by*
> *so and so*

3 identical stem reduplications such as:

> *hanky panky*
> *hocus pocus*
> *teeny weeny*

4 identical consonant pattern with a vowel change:

> *knick knack*
> *ping pong*
> *zig zag*

See: **pidgins and creoles.**

register

In **phonetics**, the term *register* refers to the voice quality, which is affected by the length, tension and thickness of the vocal cords. The vocal cords of a soprano, for example, are shorter and tenser than those of a baritone.

In **sociolinguistics**, *register* refers to varieties of language used in specific contexts. We can have, for example, a scientific register (a type of English characterised by the use of passives, by symbols and formulae, and by polysyllabic words); or the register of religion (characterised by archaisms such as *Thou*, literal translations such as *die the death* and an abstract vocabulary involving concepts such as *charity, eternity, faith, forgiveness*).

relative clause

A *relative clause* is an adjective clause. It is called a *relative clause* because it is often introduced by a relative pronoun or a preposition + relative pronoun:

> The meal **which you made** will be wasted.
> The women **whom we interviewed** refused the job.
> The parents **whose children we teach** have arrived.
> The horse **on which I put my money** is still running!

In speech and informal writing, object relative pronouns which introduce **clauses** can be omitted:

> The letter (**that**) I wrote must have been delayed.

See: **clause, defining and non-defining clauses, restrictive and nonrestrictive clauses.**

repetition

Repetition may occur at all levels of a language, including sound:

> *Coca Cola*

syllable:

> What have the words **deduct, defeat, defence** and **detail** got in common?

word:

> **Work, work, work**, that's all I ever seem to do.

and structure:

> If **you** drive carefully and if **you** avoid accidents you can get cheaper insurance.

Repetition can be both effective and impressive when used skilfully, but when it results from carelessness it can contribute to poor **style**:

> He had a **really great idea** and he was **really** glad that he had thought of it. He had never **really** had such a **great idea** before.

English can avoid nominal repetition by the use of pronouns and possessive adjectives, and verbal repetition by the use of auxiliaries and adverbs like *too* and *so*:

> *John Smith loved John Smith's wife and John Smith loved John Smith's children.* → *John Smith loved his wife and his children too.*

See: **elegant variation, parallelism, redundancy, tautology.**

reported speech

Reported (or *Indirect*) *Speech* is the term used to describe a set of conventions by which we express what someone is supposed to have said or thought. The temporal and spatial references, **word order**, degree of formality, as well as the pronouns and some adverbs, tend to differ from those in the postulated 'original' **direct speech**. However, as a study of the reported speech in any novel shows, there is often no one-to-one correlation between direct and reported speech:

Direct Speech	Reported Speech
'I love you,' she said.	She said that she loved him/her/them.
'Don't do it,' he cried.	He urged him/her/them not to do it.
'Hell! What's up now?'	He swore and asked what was happening then.

Some stylisticians have criticised the oversimplistic dichotomy and argued for a continuum between direct and reported speech.

See: **direct speech, speech in literature.**

rhetoric

The term *rhetoric* has two related meanings:

1 It can apply to the rhetoric practised and described in Classical Greek. This rhetoric was prescriptive, defining **formulas** for effective public speaking (and later, writing) in the form of rhetorical devices (such as **repetition**) or figures of speech (such as **litotes**). Aristotle claimed that rhetorical prose appealed to reason, whereas poetry appealed to the senses. Prescriptive rhetoric became popular in England in the sixteenth century. Modern examples of prescriptive rhetoric are the teaching of effective public speaking and instruction in the principles of composition.

2 It can apply to the devices used in literary language. Stylisticians examine rhetoric in their analysis of literary texts.

A person does not have to be trained in rhetoric to use rhetorical devices. Every effective speaker uses **parallelism** and repetition, often in threes:

> *I have come not to inform you, not to appeal to you, not to plead with you. I have come to* demand *your support.*
>   Trade Unionist speech

See: **figurative language, parallelism, style.**

rhotic

The word *rhotic* (occasionally *rotic*) is used to describe accents in which the *r* is pronounced in words such as *pair* and *park*. The degree of rhoticity can vary: in some accents of English, such as those of the eastern seaboard of the USA or the southeast of England, post-vocalic *r* is not pronounced; occasionally, in regionally-modified accents, it is barely perceptible; and in others, such as many Scottish accents, the *r* is rolled in all positions.

Rhotic accents are prestigious in the USA and Canada and non-prestigious in England, Australia and India.

See: **accent.**

rhyme

Rhyme is a form of **parallelism** in which there is a correspondence of sounds between syllables. The likeness depends on similar vowels (*pea, tea*) or similar vowels plus following consonant(s) (*jam, cram* or *bind, find*). Because rhyme depends on sound, similarity of spelling is not essential (*lamb, dram* or *head, red*).

The following types of rhyme are usually distinguished:

1 *masculine rhyme*, where we find correspondence between single stressed syllables:

crime and *rhyme*
delight and *sprite*

2 *feminine rhyme*, which has two consecutive rhyming syllables, the first being stressed, the second being unstressed and final:

breaking and *taking*
pleasure and *treasure*

3 *triple rhyme*, which has three consecutive rhyming syllables:

condition and *contrition*
happily and *snappily*

In English verse, feminine and triple rhymes tend to be limited to light or humorous verse.

4 *end rhyme*, where the corresponding syllables occur at the end of the line. The rhyming lines may be adjacent as in W.B. Yeats's 'There':

> *There all the gyres converge in **one**,*
> *There all the planets drop in the **sun**.*

or alternate, as in Shakespeare's sonnet 80:

> *O how I faint when I of you do **write**,*
> *Knowing a better spirit doth use your **name**,*
> *And in praise thereof spends all his **might**,*
> *To make me tongue-tied, speaking of your **fame**!*

or fit into a more unusual pattern, such as that used by Donne in 'The Sun Rising':

> *Busy old fool, unruly **Sun**,*
> *Why dost thou **thus**,*
> *Through windows, and through curtains call on **us**?*
> *Must to the motions lovers' seasons **run**?*

5 *internal rhyme*, where the rhyming syllables occur within a line as in the sonnet 'Carrion Comfort' by G.M. Hopkins:

> *O in turns of tempest, **me** heaped there; **me** frantic to avoid **thee** and*
> ***flee**?*

6 *eye rhyme* bases its parallelism not on sound but on spelling:

> *love* and *move*
> *key* and *survey*

7 *half rhyme* depends on a likeness (such as front vowel + consonant or diphthongs) rather than on perfect correspondence:

> *foot* and *goat*
> *bed* and *rid*
> *grow* and *shy*

8 *consonance*, when only the end consonants match:

> *good* and *played*
> *wife* and *if*

The term *rhyme scheme* is given to the sequence of end rhymes in a poem and is represented by a letter of the alphabet for each rhyme. Thus the rhyme scheme for a Petrarchan sonnet is abba abba cde cde (or cd cd cd) and the rhyme scheme for most traditional ballad stanzas is abab.

See: **parallelism**.

rhythm

Rhythm refers to regular auditory patterns in speech. In English, these patterns are associated with the amount of **stress** given to a particular syllable. In a word like *hospital,* for example, the first syllable receives more stress than the other two, whereas it is the second syllable which is stressed in *because.* Speech rhythms play a considerable part in intelligibility and so interference from a syllable-timed language such as French can create serious difficulties for a listener.

When the rhythm is systematically regulated as it is in verse it is known as **metre**.

See: **metre, parallelism, stress.**

satire

Satire, from Latin *satira* (medley), refers to an entertainment or work of literature that holds up to ridicule prevalent follies or vices. The *means* by which a satire is realised may vary but the intention is to cause amusement and through amusement to evoke protest or criticism.

Among the devices commonly used in satire are bathos, caricature, **irony**, ridicule, sarcasm and **wit**.

See: **irony, parody.**

scientific English

Since the end of World War II, more than 300,000 scientific words have been invented and accepted internationally. Many of these, such as *diethylcarbamazine* or *dimethyltryptamine* tend to be used only by scientists, doctors or students but others like *DNA* (deoxyribonucleic acid) or *vinyl/PVC* (polyvinylchloride) have been popularised by the media.

English has become an international language for scientists but, while scientists need to know **formulae** and the vocabulary and syntax necessary to classify, define, measure, quantify, explain, hypothesise and summarise, they may not need to know the technical vocabularies necessary for **linguistics, rhetoric** or **phatic communion**.

Scientific English tends to be marked by the following characteristics:

1 precise vocabulary, often polysyllabic and based on Greek and Latin roots

2 formulae interpretable throughout the world

3 complex premodification (*highly concentrated dye solution*)

4 simple or compound sentences preferred
5 when subordinate clauses occur, they are most frequently introduced by *if*, *when*, *that* and *which*
6 structures involving the **passive**
7 preference for present tense
8 preference for statements and avoidance of questions and exclamations
9 avoidance of the modals *may, might, must, shall, should, would*
10 avoidance of personal references

Scientists can, of course, write as parents and taxpayers as well as scientists. When they write as scientists, however, their aim is to communicate unequivocally and unemotionally with other scientists.

See: **jargon.**

Scotch, Scottish, Scots

The word *Scotch* should only be used as an adjective in fixed collocations associated with food, games, alcohol, animals and weather:

> *butterscotch* (candy)
> *Scotch broth* (thick soup)
> *Scotch egg* (hard-boiled egg encased in sausage meat)
> *hopscotch* (children's hopping game)
> *Scotch terrier*
> *Scotch whisky* (often referred to as *Scotch*)

In all human contexts, *Scots* or *Scottish* should be used.
Scots can be used as a noun referring to both the people:

> *There were two **Scots** in kilts.*

and the language:

> *I love English but I feel at home in **Scots**.*

and as an adjective, especially before *English*, *man*, *woman* or their equivalents:

> *Scots English*
> *a Scots lassie*

Scottish is used as an adjective only and is in free variation with *Scots*:

> *a Scottish tartan*
> *Scottish English*

Scottish English

Among the Germanic tribes that settled in Britain from the fifth century were the Angles, many of whom settled in southern *Scotland*.

Their language was Germanic; it was closely related to the dialects spoken by the Saxons and the Jutes; and it was described as *Inglis* until 1494, when Adam Loutful referred to it as both *Inglis* and *Scottis*.

Scots is the general term given to the dialect of English which developed in Scotland. It had its own orthographic conventions, its own translation of the Bible, and its standards were based on the court of Scotland, rather than that of England. The following extract from Nisbet's version of the Prodigal Son parable (1520) illustrates the conventions of early Scots:

> *Bot his eldar sonn was in the feeld; and quhen he com and*
> *nerit to the hous, he herde a symphony and a croude. And he*
> *callit aan of the servandis, and askit quhat thir thingis war.*
> *And he said to him, Thy bruther is cummin; and thi fadere has*
> *slayn a fat calf, for he resauet him saaf. And he was wrathe,*
> *and wald nocht cum in.*
>   Luke 15:25-8

Scots was and is a Germanic language which reached its peak in the sixteenth century and began to decline as a written language after the kingdoms were united in 1603 and James VI of Scotland (James I of England) moved his court to London. It received a further blow when the parliaments were united in 1707 and the united parliament met in London. Nevertheless, Scots continued to be used as a literary dialect by poets like Robert Burns and, to a lesser extent, by novelists like Walter Scott. It was also preserved by the people in their speech and folk traditions, including such proverbs as:

> *A dog winna yowl if ye strike him with a bane.*

and, apart from **Standard English**, Scots is the only English dialect with its own standardised orthographic conventions. In the twentieth century, Scottish writers created Lallans, a composite literary dialect of Scots illustrated by the following stanza from Hugh Mac-Diarmid's *Sic Transit Gloria Mundi*:

> *Forbye, the stuffie's no' the real Mackay,*
> *The sun's sel' since, as sune as ye began it,*
> *Riz in your vera saul; but what keeks in*
> *Noo is in truth the vilest "saxpenny planet".*

In Scotland today, as in many English-speaking regions, we find a number of class, urban and regional subdialects. We can, however, isolate the following main varieties:

1 Standard English spoken with an **RP** accent. This variety is limited to Scots, usually the landed gentry, who have been educated in England.

2 Standard English spoken with a Scottish accent

3 Southern Scots, similar to dialects in northern England

4 Central Scots, increasingly influenced by Glaswegian

5 Northern Scots, more strongly influenced by Norse dialects than other varieties of Scottish English

6 Highland English. Gaelic speakers were forced to accept English in their schools after the Jacobite rebellions of 1715 and 1745. This English was Standard English rather than Scots, and so Scottish people whose ancestral mother tongue was Gaelic often speak a variety of English closer to SE than to Scots.

Phonology

All varieties of Scottish English, with the exception of SE spoken with an RP accent, have the following phonological characteristics:

1 Scottish English is **rhotic**, with the *r* being rolled especially when it occurs in initial position or after *t* or *d*.

2 Because it is rhotic, Scottish English has a smaller vowel inventory than RP, having usually ten monophthongs /i, ɪ, e, ɛ, a, ɔ, o, u, ʌ, ə/ and four diphthongs /aɪ, aʊ, eɪ, ɔɪ/. It thus does not distinguish between the vowel sounds in *cap* and *psalm*, both of which are realised as /a/ or those in *pull* and *pool*, both of which are /u/. There is less difference in length between long and short vowels in Scottish English (such as between *beat* and *bit*) than in RP and the diphthongs are also shorter than their RP equivalents.

3 Because of the influence of education and the media, many words which were previously different in English and Scottish English are now coalescing, but the following differences are still widespread: the use of /eɪ/ in words like:

own—/eɪn/ (traditionally written *ain*)
home—/heɪm/ (written *hame*)
stone—/steɪn/ (written *stane*)

the use of /u/ rather than /aʊ/ in words like:

down—/dun/ (traditionally written *doon*)
round—/run/ (written *roon*)
town—/tun/

4 Scottish English uses two consonants more than RP: the velar fricative /x/ and the labio-velar fricative /ʍ/. /x/ occurs in words like *loch* /lɒx/ and place names like *Auchtermuchty* /ɒxtərmʌxti/. It is also regularly heard in words like *light* /lɪxt/ and *night* /nɪxt/, although this pronunciation is recessive. /ʍ/ is the usual Scottish pronunciation of *wh-* in words like *which* /ʍɪtʃ/ and *when* /ʍɛn/.

Vocabulary

1 Throughout the fifteenth and sixteenth centuries, there were very close ties between Scotland and France. The so-called 'Auld

Alliance' allowed Scots and French to have equal citizenship rights in Scotland and France. This close co-operation resulted in Scottish English absorbing many words from French, among them:

assiette > *ashet* (large plate)
fâcher > *fash* (angry)

2 Influence from Gaelic survives in words like:

clann > *clan* (extended family, tribe)
go leor > *galore* (a lot of)

as well as in place names involving *ard* (height), *blair* (plain) and *inver* (inlet).

3 Viking influence can be seen in such words as:

bryggja > *brig* (bridge)
kirkja > *kirk* (church)

4 A number of words are recognised throughout the world as Scottish, among them:

bairn (child)
bonny (fine)
burn (stream)
dram (drink)
sic (such)
wee (small)

Grammar

The grammar of Scottish English is increasingly influenced by that of the standard language but a number of differences remain, especially in intimate interactions. The commonest of these are:

1 The use of *nae* as a negator:

*He will **nae** go* (He won't go).
*You **cannae/canny** sing.*

2 The use of *aye* as an intensive:

*We're **aye** busy* (very busy).
*She was **aye** a bonny lassie* (always a pretty girl).

3 The use of *gar* meaning 'make, cause':

*It'd **gar** ye fash.*—It would make you angry.

4 The use of *maun* meaning 'must':

*Ye **maun** thole.*—You'll have to endure.

See: **Received Pronunciation.**

seaspeak

Seaspeak is a term coined on analogy with **Newspeak** to refer to a variety of English created to facilitate communication among people involved in navigation. English is the most widely-used maritime language in the world and confusion can arise when a master of a Greek supertanker, for example, talks to a Venezuelan harbour master. In 1980, a group of mariners and linguists analysed tape recordings of conversations between ships' officers and isolated the words and structures necessary for unambiguous communication. Thus, instead of a request such as 'Please meet us at the SB buoy at 2 o'clock', seaspeak users would give instruction, place and time like this: 'Meet pilot. Position SB buoy. Time 1400 GMT.'

See: **Newspeak**.

see, look, watch

The verb *see* implies perceiving something with the eyes; the verb *look* implies making an effort to see; and the verb *watch* implies both making an effort to see and observing an action or process for a purpose:

> *We **saw** them coming towards us.*
> *We **looked for** them but could not **see** them.*
> *We **watched** them for two weeks.*

When there is emphasis on conscious effort, *look* or *watch* should be selected. Thus, we may *see* a person, a play or a performance; but we *look at* a book because we are in control; and *watch* television because we are in control and also because a process is taking place.

See can be used in the simple present to imply a wider range of perceptions:

> *I **see** (i.e. I understand) what you mean.*

Hear is similar to *see* in that it has a related verb *listen* (*to*) which implies conscious effort:

> *I **listened** but I could **hear** nothing.*

and it can be used to imply 'believe, understand':

> *I **hear** he has left the company.*

semantic change

Semantic change refers to a process by which words alter their meanings. Thus *silly* meant 'holy' and the county of Suffolk was referred to as *Silly Suffolk* because of its many fine churches. There are several types of semantic change:

1 *amelioration*, when the associations of a word improve. *Minister* meant 'one who served or ministered to someone else' but now implies 'one in orders' or 'a high ranking government official'.

2 *deterioration*, when the meanings become less pleasant or lose some of their former glory. *Lust* used to mean 'pleasure' and not 'sexual desire'; *pretend* used to mean 'claim' rather than 'claim falsely' or 'make believe'; and *tart* (possibly from *sweetheart*) meant 'one who is loved' and not 'one who is promiscuous'.

3 *generalisation*, when the meaning of a word moves from the specific to the general. Thus *pow-wow* was extended in meaning from an Algonquian doctor, to the group around the doctor and to any group meeting for discussion.

4 *narrowing*, when a meaning becomes more specific. *Girl* originally meant 'a young person, either male or female'.

5 *radiation*, where a number of meanings develop from one central meaning. *Chip*, for example, can be a small piece of wood, potato or silicon.

6 *concretisation*, where an abstraction is concretised, as when *holiness, honour, majesty* or *worship* are used as terms of **address or reference**.

*This is for you, **your Holiness**.*

7 *euphemism*, when words for death, disease, bodily functions are avoided and replaced by idioms which are either pleasant circumlocutions:

go to one's eternal reward (die)

or humorous:

cash in one's chips (die)

8 *folk etymology*, where a false understanding can cause a shift of meaning. *Pantry*, for example, is derived from Latin *panis* meaning 'bread' but was associated with *pans* and so thought of as a place where pans were kept. And the US place name *Picketwire* is a folk etymology of *Purgatoire* (Purgatory).

Semantic change is inevitable in a language that is widely used, and puristic attempts to halt it are unrealistic.

See: **etymology, euphemism, folk etymology, propaganda, purist.**

semantics

Semantics is the branch of linguistics devoted to the study of meaning. The main areas studied are:

1 *polysemy*, that is, words can have more than one meaning. We

can have a *key* that opens doors, a piano key, a typewriter key and a key (i.e. a solution) to a mystery.

2 *synonymy*, that is, different words appear to have essentially the same meaning, thus *big* and *large*; *regal*, *royal* and *kingly*.

3 *antonymy*, that is, certain words appear to be opposites, thus *good* and *bad*; *high* and *low*.

4 *semantic features*, that is, certain words can be shown to contain identical information. Thus *cow* and *bull* are both nouns, both animate, both adult and both bovines. They differ essentially in that *cow* is female and *bull* male. Many words can be analysed into semantic features and such a technique is useful in explaining metaphor. If, for example, a man is described as *squeaking*, we notice that squeaking is appropriate to mice. A mouse shares many semantic features with a man, the essential difference being that a mouse is not human. Thus, the metaphor dehumanises the man. Linguists often refer to one unit of meaning (e.g. *adult*) as a *sememe*.

5 *hyponymy*, that is, the meanings of some words are included in the meanings of others, thus the meaning of *vegetable* is included in the meaning of *potato*.

6 *idioms*, that is, certain combinations of words have meanings which differ from the combination of their individual elements. Thus *take off* meaning 'imitate' cannot be deduced from the meanings of *take + off*.

See: **antonym, idioms, polysemy, synonym.**

sentence

The simplest definition of a *sentence* is that it begins with a capital letter and ends with a full stop:

Thanks.

Up we go.

A sentence is a grammatically independent unit which can express a statement, a command, a wish, an exclamation or a question. Sentences occur in the written medium and correspond loosely to speech utterances. An **utterance** is produced by a specific individual at a specific time and in specific circumstances. It can thus be affected by non-linguistic factors such as fatigue, interest or mood. A sentence, on the other hand, is an idealisation which linguists impose on language data. We can illustrate the relationship between an utterance and a sentence as:

utterance is to *performance* as *sentence* is to *competence*

Sentences can be subdivided in various ways:

1 A *major* sentence contains a finite verb:

Don't do that.

whereas a *minor* sentence does not:

Out.

Minor sentences are common in advertising and are spoken with the same intonation pattern as major sentences. Minor sentences are sometimes called *elliptical* or *incomplete* because we can usually supply a word or group of words to convert them into a major sentence:

[Get] out.

2 Sentences can occur as statements:

I like playing baseball.

questions:

Is he not coming?

commands or imperatives:

Come here at once.

exclamations:

You haven't lost again!

3 Sentences can be considered in terms of their syntactic simplicity. A *simple* sentence is one which contains only one verb phrase:

*The pound **has sunk** in value against all major currencies.*

A *compound* sentence consists of two or more simple sentences joined by co-ordinating conjunctions such as *and, but, or*:

*The pound has sunk in value **but** it is still worth 95% of its 1984 value.*

A *complex* sentence consists of two or more **clauses**, one of which is syntactically more important than the other(s). In other words, in a complex sentence we have one or more dependent clauses:

*The pound sank **because it was not supported**.*

A dependent clause is also referred to as a *subordinate clause* and an *embedded sentence*.

A minor sentence can be simple:

[Put it] Over here.

compound:

[Put it] Over here or [put it] over there.

or complex:

[Put it] Over here where everyone can see it.

See: **clause, speech and writing, utterance.**

serial verbs

Some languages, like English, can have several full verbs co-occurring in a sequence:

I want to try to learn to swim.
'Come kiss me, sweet and twenty.'

Such chains are known as *serial verbs*. They occur also in many African languages . In Yoruba, for example, we find:

Ra a fun mi. (Buy it for me. lit. Buy it give me).
Sare lo. (Run away. lit. Run go).

and English-related **pidgins and creoles** in the Atlantic region use serial verbs for several purposes such as:

1 to indicate location:

Bringam kam putam hia. (Bring it come put it here.)
I bin rɔn rich di haus. (He past run reach the house.)

2 to indicate when an action *almost* occurred (*inceptive aspect*):

A bin wan fɔl brok ma fut. (I almost fell and broke my leg.)

3 to stress the commencement of an activity:

Yu go bigin stat tren dat bif. (You shall begin to start and train that animal.)

See: **aspect, pidgins and creoles.**

sexist language

Sexist language refers to sexual **prejudice** made overt in language. All societies have prejudices. Western society tends to associate female beauty with slimness whereas until recently Nigerian Igbos associated it with fatness.

Many societies stereotype roles and relationships, often along sexist lines. In English-speaking communities, for example, the following stereotypes are frequently assumed:

1 that women talk more than men.
2 that women and men talk about different things, women discussing cooking, families, homes, men; men concentrating on business, sport, women and work.
3 that women are more phonologically correct than men.
4 that women use more intensifiers, such as *absolutely, quite.*
5 that women are good listeners.
6 that men can keep secrets.
7 that women are poor drivers.
8 that men are mechanically minded.

9 that women choose cars for their colour.

10 that men choose cars for their mechanical performance.

11 that girls are better at languages and subjects depending on memory.

12 that boys are better at mathematical and scientific subjects.

Some stereotypes are based at least partly on truth but many stereotypes are the result of prejudice, not fact.

Apart from stereotypes, there are a number of ways in which users of English are linguistically conditioned along sexist lines:

1 Except for words that by definition refer to females (*mare*, *mother*) and occupations traditionally held by females (*nurse*, *secretary*), English defines everyone as male. This is clear from an examination of early arithmetical problems:

> *If a man can walk ten miles in two hours, how many miles will four men walk in twelve hours?*

from terms for the average person:

> *John Doe*
> *the man in the street*

the personification of a country:

> *Uncle Sam*

and the fact that, unless prefixed by *lady/woman*, nouns such as:

> *beggar*
> *doctor*
> *writer*

tend to imply men.

2 Patriarchal assumptions are reinforced by encyclopaedias and schoolbooks which tell us, for example, that:

> *Man is the highest form of life on earth.*
>   *Britannica Junior Encyclopaedia*, 1971

and describe the activities of our *forefathers*. (The word *foremothers* does not exist.)

3 Women usually take on men's surnames and nationality after marriage with the result that history tends to be the story of men rather than both men and women.

4 Words with negative overtones which apply to both sexes as did:

> *courtesan harlot prostitute whore*

often lose their reference to men.

5 There are many names which reduce women in age, status or humanity:

> *babe bird broad chick doll dame*

and few male equivalents, although recently:

toy boy

has come into the language to refer to a young man 'adopted' as a successful older woman's companion.

6 Verbs of attribution in novels are often sexist. Women *chatter* and *scream*, men *thunder* or *roar*.

7 *He/his* are often used when *he or she*, *his or her* are implied:

*Everyone must do **his** best.*
*If a person works hard, **he** can achieve anything.*

8 *Man* is an extremely productive suffix:

chairman congressman

and, although *person* can be substituted for *man*, many people use *chairperson* to refer to a woman and *chairman* to refer to a man.

See: **prejudice, racist language**.

shibboleth

The word *shibboleth* derives from a Hebrew word *shibboleth* meaning 'stream'. In the Book of Judges 12:5ff. we learn how the Gileadites tested people to find out if they were Ephraimites:

Then said they unto him, Say now Shibboleth: and he said
Sibboleth: for he could not frame to pronounce it right.
Then they took him, and slew him at the passages of Jordan...

Today, *shibboleth* tends to refer to a linguistic usage regarded as capable of marking one group out from another. Thus, the pronunciation of the eighth letter of the alphabet is a shibboleth in Northern Ireland where Catholics say *haitch* and Protestants *aitch*; and the preference for *lift* as opposed to *elevator* could be enough to distinguish a Briton from an American.

Sierra Leone English

Sierra Leone (Lion Mountain) was named by the Portuguese in 1460. The British traded with the coastal Sierra Leoneans from the late sixteenth century and bought the land around modern Freetown as a home for ex-slaves. In 1787, 351 former slaves were shipped from Portsmouth and they were joined in Freetown by 1,131 Africans who had remained loyal to the British during the American War of Independence. Freetown became a Crown Colony in 1808 and gradually this status was extended to the rest of Sierra Leone. The country gained its independence in 1961 and today has a population of approximately 3.7 million.

English is the official language of Sierra Leone. It is used in education, government, commerce and international dealings. As well as English, however, Sierra Leone has another **lingua franca**, Krio. This is an English-related **creole** which is the mother tongue of the quarter of a million descendants of the Freetown settlers and is widely used throughout Sierra Leone. Krio has been used for religious instruction, song, drama, poetry and political persuasion and its status has been enhanced by the publication of a dictionary in 1980. The following text is a translation into Krio by Freddie Jones of a verse from Wilhelm Busch's *Max und Moritz*:

> *Dɛm kin se, ɛn misɛf gri,*
> It has frequently been stated
> *Man fɔ lan pas ABC.*
> People must be educated.
> *Wetin go pliz Gɔd insɛf*
> Not alone the A, B, C,
> *Na if wi bɛtɛ wisɛf.*
> Heightens man's humanity.
> *Rayt ɛn rid nɔto ɔl o,*
> Not just simple reading, writing
> *Pɔsin we gɛt sɛns fɔ no.*
> Makes a person more inviting.

The Krio people were of commercial and educational influence throughout West Africa from the late eighteenth century and may well have modified and reinforced the various English-related pidgins throughout West Africa.

In Sierra Leone we thus find a continuum of Englishes, from the standard language, through mother-tongue-influenced varieties and Krio-influenced forms, to Krio.

See: **African English, pidgins and creoles, West African English.**

simile

Simile comes from the Latin word *similis* (like). The word is applied to a figure of speech that overtly expresses a likeness between two beings, objects or ideas:

> *He's like a cat with two tails.*
> *The face was like a jail door with the bolts pulled out.*
> *Duty is as enduring as life.*

The comparison usually involves the words *as* or *like* and often combines unequal partners, such as 'human' + 'inanimate':

> **She** *was as fit as a* **fiddle**.

or 'human' + 'animal':

She's as crafty as a bee/fox.

There is often a play on the ambiguity of the shared word, so that in the following:

*He was as **game** as a **pheasant**.*
*She was as **nutty** as a **fruitcake**.*

game suggests both 'bird that is hunted' and 'resolute' and *nutty* implies both 'full of nuts' and 'crazy'.

There are regional preferences in similes. The following, for example, are characteristic of northern England:

as daft as a brush (crazy)
as thick as two short planks (unintelligent)

whereas Australians might use:

as awkward as a pig with a prayerbook
like a koala up a gum tree

West Africans:

as quickly as fire in a Harmattan wind
It passed like Christmas. (very quickly)

and Americans:

as corny as Kansas in August
as phoney as a three-dollar bill

When a comparison is implicit rather than overt, it is called a metaphor. Thus:

He bellowed like a bull.

is a simile, whereas:

John bellowed from morning until night.

is a metaphor.

See: **figurative language, imagery, metaphor.**

since

The word *since* can be used as an **adverb**:

*She joined the firm in 1970 and has worked there ever **since**.*

a subordinating **conjunction**, implying time or reason:

*He has wanted to be an astronaut **since** he was seven.*
*You weren't invited **since** you hate parties.*

and as a **preposition**:

We have been here since May 14.

In all uses of *since* except those where it is equivalent to *because*, *since* involves looking at a time from a point in the past.

When *since* functions as a subordinating conjunction, there are certain restrictions on its use. It can co-occur with:

1 the present perfect:

*She **has written** poetry **since** she was a child.*

2 the past perfect:

*They **had lived** there ever **since** they moved to town.*

3 the present tense in the pattern 'It is + length of time + since':

It's two years since we had a holiday.
It's ages since we went on a picnic.

4 the past tense in the pattern 'It was/had been + length of time + since':

It was almost six years since he had written.
It had been two days since they had heard from the climbers.

It does not normally co-occur with a negative:

*It's ages since we didn't get a morning paper.

See: **ago**.

Singapore English

Singapore, a former British colony and an independent republic since 1965, consists of a 570-square kilometre island and 60 smaller islands at the tip of the Malay Peninsula. Its population of 2.6 million (with a literacy rate of 86.8%) is made up chiefly of Chinese (76.1%), Malays (15.1%) and Indians (6.5%).

Of Singapore's four official languages (English, Mandarin, Malay and Tamil), English is predominant in both the official and private sectors. It is the medium of instruction in all schools (where students are also required to study their mother tongues as a second language) and in tertiary institutions. Because of the educational, social and ethnic diversity of the population (most of whom can speak some form of English), Singapore English exhibits a correspondingly wide range of linguistic features. The description here applies essentially to the English of young, educated Singaporeans.

Phonology

1 Singapore English is non-**rhotic**.

2 Rhythmically it is syllable-timed in that all syllables (stressed or unstressed) occur at equal intervals. Syllables that are marked by stress in mother-tongue English are distinguished by loudness and/or length rather than by pitch; unstressed syllables usually do not undergo vowel reduction; and liaison across words is rare. These features combine to produce the staccato effect many scholars have noticed in Singapore English.

3 The differences in both length and quality are largely neutralised in the pairs /i,ɪ/, /u,ʊ/, /æ,ɛ/,ɑ,ʌ/ and /ɔ,ɒ/ so that pairs of words such as *seat/sit, fool/full, pat/pet, cart/cut* and *port/pot* are virtually indistinguishable.

4 The RP diphthongs /eɪ/, /əʊ/, /ɛə/ and /ɔə/ are reduced to long monophthongs /e/, /o/, /ɛ/ and /ɔ/ respectively as in *day* /de/, *no* /no/, *dare* /dɛ/ and *door* /dɔ/.

5 The dental fricatives /θ/ and /ð/ are often replaced by /t,d/, so that *thin* becomes /tɪn/ and *this* /dɪs/.

6 There is little distinction between voiced and unvoiced consonants in word-final position, with the unvoiced consonants being preferred. Thus *shelve* sounds like *shelf*, *ridge* like *rich* and *cause* like *course*.

7 Word-initial /p,t,k/ are weakly aspirated. In word-final position, they are often replaced by a glottal stop, thus *sit* is often /sɪʔ/ and *pick* /pɪʔ/.

8 Consonant clusters tend to be simplified especially in word-final position, with *opt* becoming /ɒp/, *ask* /as/ and *sixth* /sɪks/.

Vocabulary

1 Words have been adapted from the indigenous languages:

makan (from Malay = to eat)
towkay (from Hokkien = shop-owner, businessman)

2 More widespread are English expressions which have acquired a local meaning:

fellow (person, not exclusively male)
follow (come/go with someone)
as such (therefore, as a result)
last time (formerly, in the past)

Grammar

1 There is a tendency to foreground the topic of the sentence:

This book I have read already.
My friend, he can speak five languages.

and for indirect or embedded questions to echo the word order of direct questions:

Do you know what is the problem?

2 Different tenses often co-occur in sequence:

If you miss the plane you would be sorry.
I think he would succeed.

3 Some speakers use progressive and perfective forms where the simple present or past form is expected:

I am having a terrible headache.
He is very rich. He had bought another house recently.

4 Some uncountable, especially concrete, nouns are treated as countable:

a chalk chalks
an equipment equipments
a luggage luggages

5 There are some differences in the use of prepositions:

They requested for more money.
He emphasised on the importance of hard work.

6 *Is it?/isn't it?* tend to be used as universal tags:

You're British, isn't it?
The show starts at 8, is it?

7 The -ed suffix is sometimes added or deleted from an adjective:

a matured person
a tensed feeling
a terrace house
ice water

See: **Chinese English, English in the Indian Sub-Continent, Malaysian English, stative and dynamic.**

slang

The etymology of the word *slang* is unknown but it refers to words and phrases peculiar to a particular group and often regarded as non-standard and inferior. There are two main kinds of slang:

1 items such as *bitch* (woman), *bite the dust* (die), *godfather* (one who pays the bills), *let the grass grow under your feet* (waste opportunities), *moll* (low-class female) which have existed for centuries.

2 items such as *amen wallah* (clergyman), *fab* (wonderful), *longshore lawyer* (unscrupulous lawyer), *pillshooter* (doctor), *wing* (penny) which are relatively ephemeral.

Slang is often witty and expressive but is usually inappropriate in writing and in formal speech.

There are many motives for using slang, including humour, originality, desire for exaggeration, euphemism and wish to identify with a particular sport, trade, school, religion or ethnic group.

ethnic group:

gaujo (Gypsy word for non-Gypsy)

The main subvarieties of slang are:
1 **abbreviations**:

sarky (sarcastic)
tranny (transistor radio)

2 back slang:

one > *no*
two > *oot*

3 **borrowings**:

imshee (go away/let's go, from Arabic)
plonk (cheap wine, from French)

4 **coinages**:

dingbat
thingamajig

5 **compounds**:

bees-knees (best)
bigshot (important person)

6 **euphemisms**:

blooming/ruddy (bloody)
darn (damn)

7 exaggeration:

fantabulous
mind-blowing

8 **onomatopoeia**:

kerplop
wham

9 phrases or sentences:

Get lost! (Off you go!)
take the mickey (tease)

10 rhyming slang/Cockney slang:

plates (*of meat*) = feet
titfer (*tit for tat*) = hat

11 suffixation, also known as 'Pig Latin'. Suffixes like *iggy/aggy* are attached to all words. This technique is favoured by children:

I'lliggy goiggy outiggy withiggy youiggy.

See: **colloquial English, jargon.**

SO

So can occur as:

1 an intensifying **adverb**:

I'm so tired.
He drives so slowly that even cyclists pass him!

2 a **conjunction** which can be used with and without *and*:

It was snowing heavily (and) so we went by train.

The sentence without *and* tends to be less formal. *So* also co-occurs with *that* to introduce clauses of purpose:

We saved hard so that they could have a good education.

and result:

We worked hard so that they could have everything they wanted.

That, like *and*, tends to be dropped in informal or colloquial styles.

3 a colloquial sentence modifier:

So there you are!

4 in spoken questions to belittle a statement:

He's very rich. So?/So what?

5 as a verb phrase substitute when combined with BE, DO, HAVE and the modal auxiliaries:

He wants to walk to the North Pole although to do so (i.e. to walk to the North Pole) *will use up all his resources.*
If you're going, then so am I.

6 as a clause substitute:

They'll be pleased to see us—at least, I hope so. (i.e. they'll be pleased to see us).

7 in the form *so-and-so* it occurs as a uncomplimentary noun phrase substitute:

That so-and-so has done it again!

8 *so-so* is used colloquially to mean 'not very well':

> *How is she today? Just* **so-so**.

See: **as, pro forms, substitution, such.**

sociolinguistics

Sociolinguistics concentrates on the study of language in society. It examines how and why people use particular languages or particular forms of language in their interactions with others. As well as studying the variety that exists in all languages, sociolinguistics also describes the information speakers may unwittingly provide with regard to their age, sex, education, regional and perhaps ethnic origins.

See: **linguistics, variable.**

solecism

Solecism is the term used to describe incorrect usage in grammar or idiom. It occurs in both speech and writing:

> *He gave it to* **John and I**. (John and me)
> *She* **don't** *want trouble*. (doesn't)

Poets occasionally deviate from the norms of grammar:

> *The world is charged with the glory of God.*
> *It will flame out, like* **shining from shook foil**...
>   G.M. Hopkins, 'God's Grandeur'

but poetic deviations are not regarded as solecisms.

See: **deviation.**

sound symbolism

Every language has a set of words in which there seems to be a direct link between the form of a word and its meaning. Such a link is known as *sound symbolism*. In English, for example, words like *cuckoo* and *peewit* imitate the call of the birds they represent; *bang, wallop* suggest the noises that are made when different objects collide; and certain sounds can suggest exertion or weight (the *-ump* in *lump, pump, thump*), light and movement (*fl-* and *gl-* in *flame, flicker, gleam, glimmer*), and repetitiveness (*-er* and *-le* in *stammer, twinkle*).

See: **onomatopoeia, synaesthesia, word formation.**

South African English

South Africa has a population of approximately 35 million, 67% 'Black', 19% 'White', 11% 'Coloured' (or 'Mixed Race') and 3% Indian. The White community is made up of Afrikaners and English speakers, and since South Africa ceased to be a member of the Commonwealth in 1961 the Afrikaner community has been increasingly dominant.

English is one of the two official languages of the country and the varieties of English used match the social, racial and political divisions in the country. Mother-tongue English, in both its standard and nonstandard forms, reflects the British origins of most speakers; Afrikaans English is the variety used by people whose mother tongue is Afrikaans and it is affected by Afrikaans in phonology, vocabulary and syntax; the English of the Black community reflects individual mother tongues and the influence of Afrikaans; the English of the Coloured people is also affected by Afrikaans and tends to show traces of Malay; and the English of the Indian community is similar to Indian English in other parts of the world but has absorbed a number of elements from Afrikaans. The variety of English described is the prestige form of mother-tongue English (SAE).

Phonology

1 SAE is non-**rhotic**.

2 There are the same number of **phonemes** in SAE and **RP** although there is a tendency for the vowel sounds /ɑ/ and /ɔ/ to converge thus making pairs like *par*, *paw*, and *cart*, *caught* homophones.

3 Diphthongs tend to be shorter than in RP with some speakers replacing /aɪ/ by /aː/ and /ɛə/ by /e/:

You can't /kɑnt/ *drive* /drɑːv/ *there* /ðe/.

4 The vowel /ɪ/ is usually replaced by schwa in unstressed syllables. Thus *villages* and *villagers* are homophones for many speakers.

5 The vowel sound /ɛ/ in *yes* is often replaced by /ɪ/ or by a diphthong /ɪə/.

6 The consonants /p,t,k/ are less strongly aspirated than in RP.

Vocabulary

Apart from the vocabulary common to all varieties of mother-tongue English, SAE has adopted words from Afrikaans:

boer (farmer)
stoep (veranda)

from African languages:

assegai (spear)
indaba (meeting)

from Malay:

> *babotie* (savoury minced meat)
> *sjambok* (hide whip)

from Portuguese:

> *mealie* (maize)
> *piccanin* (child)

and Indian languages have provided words for specifically Indian foods such as *biriani* and *tandoori*.

Grammar

1 *With* frequently occurs at the end of a sentence:

*Do you want it **with**?*

2 *Lend* seems to be replacing *borrow*:

*Can I **lend** that book, please?*

3 *Check you* is a colloquial equivalent of *I'll meet you*:

Check you *at Stuttaford's at 12.*

4 *Man* occurs as a general term of friendly address to both women and men:

*You should have seen me, **man**!*

5 *Shame* is widely used as an empathy formula:

*He broke his leg. **Shame**!*

See: **African English, Southern African English.**

Southern African English

In our account of *Southern African English*, we shall include nine countries, namely Angola, Zambia, Malawi, Lesotho, Zimbabwe, Mozambique, Namibia, Botswana and Swaziland, which together have an estimated population of over 40 million. (**South African English** is examined separately.) This area includes the following main varieties of English:

(a) mother-tongue English
(b) standard Southern African English
(c) Portuguese-influenced English
(d) Indian-influenced English.

Our description will focus on (b), which is the prestigious variety of the area.

Phonology

1 There are many similarities between the English of East and Southern Africa, the most marked of which is the tendency to raise the vowel sound in *back* so that *back* and *beg* differ mainly in terms of the final consonant.

2 Southern African English is non-**rhotic**.

3 There are fewer vowel contrasts than in **Received Pronunciation**. In particular, length distinctions are rarely preserved and so there is a tendency to merge:

/i/ and /ɪ/ so that *leave* and *live* are both /liv/
/æ/ and /ɛ/ so that *bat* and *bet* are both /bɛt/
/ɒ/ and /ʌ/ so that *cot* and *cut* are both /kɒt/
/u/ and /ʊ/ so that *fool* and *full* are both /ful/

4 Central vowels are avoided. Schwa is often replaced by /a/ and /ɜ/ by /e/ so that *Rita* is realised as /rita/ and *church* as /tʃetʃ/.

5 There is a tendency to devoice /b,d,g/ when they occur in word-final position. This tendency may have been reinforced by speakers exposed to Afrikaans- or German-influenced English.

6 /θ,ð/ are usually replaced by /t,d/ and, occasionally, by /s,z/.

7 Intrusive vowels tend to break up **consonant clusters** at the beginning and end of words:

/sⁱprɪŋ/ for *spring*
/tɛnɛts/ for *tenths*

Vocabulary

1 Words have been adopted from local languages:

mamba (snake)
shamba (farm)

2 Others have been given modified meanings. *borrow* can mean 'lend', *refuse* 'deny' and *touch* 'call at':

*He would not **borrow** me the money.*
*I told him he was guilty but he **refused** it.*
*I want to **touch** the hospital.*

Grammar

1 New **phrasal verbs** occur:

*I can't **cope up with** these problems.*
*We should **discuss about** this.*

2 There is a tendency to use *one* for the indefinite article:

*I stay in **one** lovely hostel.*
***One** lady told me.*

See: **African English, East African English, South African English.**

speaker orientation

Speaker orientation is a term used to indicate the fact that language choice often refers to **location** in terms of proximity or non-proximity to the speaker:

> *Take this book.* (i.e. the one close to the speaker)
> *Take that book.* (i.e. the one not close to the speaker)
> *Bring the book here.* (i.e. the book should be carried to the speaker)
> *Take the book away.* (i.e. the book should be carried away from the speaker).

Time is also expressed in terms of *now* (close in time to the speaker) and *then* (remote from the speaker):

> *We all have a comparatively easy life* **now**.
> *There was no electricity* **then**.

Often, when a speaker wishes to make a story more immediate, he shifts it from the past to the 'historic present':

> *Did you hear the one about Seamus O'Shaughnessy, the man who knew everybody? Well there was this Japanese and he's a millionaire, you see, and he wants to travel...*

There is also a rough correlation between the use of *come* (+ *into/to*) and pleasantness and the use of *go* (+ *from/off*) with unpleasantness:

> **come into** *money/one's own/***come** *good*
> **go into** *exile/retreat/***go** *grey*

See: **bring, location.**

speciality, specialty

There is considerable overlap in the meanings and uses of these words, with *speciality* being more widely used in the UK and *specialty* in the USA. In both countries *speciality* can mean:

1 a particular quality or skill
2 a branch of knowledge in which one specialises
3 in the UK, it can also mean a product for which a person or place is renowned, but this meaning is carried by *specialty* in the USA:

> *Chicken chasseur was the* **speciality** *of the house.* (UK)
> *Chicken chasseur was the* **specialty** *of the house.* (USA)

The related term *specialism* is used in both countries for both the act of specialising in a particular branch of learning and for the field of specialisation:

> *My own particular* **specialism** *is Icelandic sagas.*

but speakers of US English often use *specialty* with this meaning too:

> *Icelandic literature is my* **specialty**.

See: **UK and US words**.

speech and writing

Most speakers equate *language* with *speech* and this equation is no more harmful than the useful fallacy that the sun rises in the east and sets in the west. It is important to realise, however, that language is an abstract system which can be realised in a variety of mediums, the most frequently occurring of which are *speech and writing*. Mother-tongue speech and writing differ in a variety of ways:

Speech	Writing
involves sound	involves marks on a surface
produced by vocal organs	produced by hand + tool
perceived by ear	perceived by eye
organised in time	organised in space
usually spontaneous	usually prepared
usually transitory	usually more permanent
acquired effortlessly	acquired with effort
addressee usually present	addressee usually absent
message aided by gestures	message must be made explicit
marked by hesitations, slips	syntactically smoother
utterances linked by association	sentences linked by logical progression

Speech is the primary medium in the sense that it is acquired first and apparently without effort. It is also the most frequently used language medium throughout the world and the only medium in many communities. Writing develops in a society when speech is no longer adequate to fulfil all its linguistic needs. Writing permits easier and wider dissemination of knowledge and ideas.

speech in literature

The representation of speech has traditionally been a feature of literature. Drama, in particular, is heavily dependent on speech forms because it is intended to have an aural as well as a visual effect, but poetry, stories and the novel all use approximations to speech in an attempt to reflect and recreate life.

Drama, short stories and the novel often appear to use naturalistic speech involving hesitations, slips of the tongue, false starts, non-sequiturs, changes of direction in mid-sentence, and regional and dialectal forms. A close study of *speech in literature* will show, however, that a sensitive writer only uses enough features of speech to create an idiolectal illusion. An overuse of nonstandard forms or features of hesitation could result in confusion for the reader or viewer.

Writers know that readers understand the idiosyncrasies of speech. It is usually only necessary to indicate the background and nature of a character and to rely on the understanding and imagination of the reader. This may be done by the use of idiosyncratic words or phrases, a few spelling or syntactic modifications and by the use of attributive verbs such as *complained, enthused, rushed, stammered.* In live speech, conversation can often have little significance or value (other than **phatic communion**) but in literature speech must not only create the illusion of life, it must also reveal character, impart essential information to the reader and advance the narrative.

The language of literature is not limited to direct and indirect speech. Many stylisticians have drawn attention to the continuum from **narrative** to speech, a continuum which includes **stream of consciousness**, where thoughts, speech and narrative are interwoven.

See: **direct speech, reported speech, stream of consciousness.**

spelling

Spelling involves the forming of words with letters according to convention and accepted usage. Many people have commented on the fact that English spelling is often irregular. *Knight,* for example, sounds the same as *night,* and *read* can, depending on usage, rhyme with both *bead* and *bed.* George Bernard Shaw once pointed out that *ghoti* could spell *fish* if we took the sound *gh* has in *enough,* the sound *o* has in *women* and the sound *ti* has in *motion.* Many attempts have been made to reform English spelling. During the fifteenth and sixteenth centuries, English scholars changed spellings so as to make spelling conform to **etymology**. Thus *dette* became *debt* to show that it derived from Latin *debitum* and *dout* became *doubt* (Latin *dubitum*). Three centuries later, Noah Webster tried to reform US spelling. He ironed out many inconsistencies but many more remained.

Spelling and **pronunciation** diverge in three main ways:

1 Many words have silent letters:

dumb gnash knot honest ptarmigan psalm

2 There are many ways of spelling the same sound, /aɪ/ or /k/ for example:

aye guy high I my Thai rye
cat choler kettle khaki

3 Different sounds often have the same spelling, *-ough* or *s* for example:

bough cough though through tough
days sing sugar

Because of Webster's work and the prestige of his dictionaries, a number of differences exist between UK and US spellings. The most commonly-occurring differences are:

1 Common abstract nouns end in *-our* in the UK and *-or* in the USA. Both countries use *-or* for people and for medical/scientific nouns:

UK	USA	UK	USA
behaviour	*behavior*	*governor*	*governor*
colour	*color*	*pallor*	*pallor*
rumour	*rumor*	*tremor*	*tremor*
censor	*censor*		

2 Many nouns which end in *-re* in the UK have *-er* in the USA. Both countries use *-er* for people, for medical/scientific terms and for many verbs:

centre	*center*	*adviser/or*	*adviser/or*
litre	*liter*	*cater*	*cater*
metre	*meter*	*peter out*	*peter out*
theatre	*theater*		

3 *Many verbs end in -ise* in the UK and in *-ize* in the USA:

apologise	*apologize*	*realise*	*realize*
philosophise	*philosophize*		

Many users of UK English also use *-ize*, especially for **synthetic** verbs such as *colonize* and *transistorize*. In addition, both UK and US users have *-ise* in a number of verbs including *advertise, arise, chastise, circumcise* and *comprise*.

4 We often find consonants doubled before the morphological endings *-ed, -ing, -or/-er* in UK English:

councillor	*councilor*	*travelling*	*traveling*
kidnapped	*kidnaped*		

Usually, the doubling is optional in US English, although many Americans follow the rule that a consonant is doubled after stressed short vowels:

rebelling	*rebuffing*

5 US English prefers *-ense* where UK English has *-ence* although both forms occur in US English:

defence defense/defence	*pretence pretense/pretence*
licence license/licence	

Both countries have:

immense   incense   intense

6 Often, words or **morphemes** which end in *l* in UK English have *ll* in the USA:

fulfil/fulfilment fulfill/fulfillment	*skilful skillful*
instal/instalment install/installment	

although *fulfil*, *instal* and *skilful* are marginally acceptable in US English.

7 The UK causative morpheme *en-* is often replaced by *in-* in the USA:

enclose inclose/enclose	*ensure insure/ensure*
endorse indorse/endorse	

8 The UK spellings *-ae-/-oe-* are regularly replaced by *-e* in US English:

anaemia anemia	*diarrhoea diarrhea*
anaesthesia anesthesia	*foetus fetus*
haemorrhage hemorrhage	*manoeuvre maneuver*

9 A number of words ending in *-ogue* in the UK are regularly *-og* in the USA, although the *ogue* spelling is also found:

analogue analog	*dialogue dialog*
catalogue catalog	

10 The following miscellaneous list includes the words which normally have different spellings in the UK and the USA:

aluminium aluminum	*moult molt*
analyse analyze	*moustache mustache*
artefact artifact	*plough plow*
buses busses/buses	*programme program*
carcase carcass	*sulphur sulfur*
cheque check	*tyre tire*
draught draft	*waggon wagon*
mould mold	*woollen woolen*

11 UK English uses more hyphens in word compounding than is common in US English:

co-operate cooperate	*money-bags moneybags*

12 Some informal US spellings are popular, especially in advertising, but are not acceptable in formal contexts in either country:

donut tonite tho thru

13 The following words frequently cause spelling problems in both countries:

accommodation	nerve-racking (not *nerve-wracking)
biased (UK, US), biassed (US)	
bluish	parallel
Caribbean	pejorative
commitment	preferable
committee	preferred
desiccate	pronunciation
desperate	pus
diphthong	putrefy
duly (not *duely)	pygmy
ecstasy	questionnaire
embarrassment	queuing/queueing
exaggerate	rarefied (UK, US), rarified (US)
forebear (ancestor)	reconnaissance
forehead	seize
grievous	separate
hi(gh)jack	silhouette
honorary	soliloquy
humorous	stationary (still)
khaki	stationery (paper)
idiosyncrasy	supersede
liquefy/liquify	tying (not *tieing)
Massachusetts	vaccination
Mediterranean	weird
mortgage	wintry

See: -able, -ise, problem pairs, problem words, pronunciation, UK and US words, spelling pronunciation.

spelling pronunciation

Spelling pronunciation involves a change in pronunciation in response to a word's spelling. *Catholic* was once pronounced *Catolic*, *hotel* was *'otel* and *soldier* was *sojar*, but now such pronunciations would be regarded as nonstandard. More recently, words like *often* and *soften* or *castle* and *apostle* are having the *t* reintroduced. The *t* in *often* is perfectly acceptable and, in time, the others may also become standard.

Occasionally, pet forms of names can indicate earlier pronunciation:

Anthony pronounced *Antony* gave *Tony*
Elizabeth pronounced *Elizabet* gave *Betty*

Overseas learners of English often use spelling pronunciations including *mizzled* instead of *misled* and *Ex-mass* because of *Xmas*; and an increasing number of English users are pronouncing *porpoise* and *tortoise* to rhyme with *noise* instead of with the second syllable of *purpose*.

See: **speech and writing, spelling.**

split infinitive

A *split infinitive* involves the use of a modifier between the *to* and the verbal part of the **infinitive**:

to really like it

Infinitives in English are *often* but not *always* preceded by *to*:

I asked him to sing we listened to him sing
we wanted him to go we watched him go

and so the most useful definition of an English infinitive is as a verb form, identical with the imperative form of the verb:

Imperative   Infinitive
Be quiet!   *be*
Have a rest!   *have*

frequently co-occurring with *to* and capable of functioning as a nominal:

To feel is human.

although always maintaining certain characteristics of a verb:

To feel tired is human.
To feel a fool is human.

In many languages, the infinitive is marked morphologically and is usually translated by the infinitive including *to*:

Latin	French	English
amare	*aimer*	*to love*
amo	*j'aime*	*I love*
amamus	*nous aimons*	*we love*

The infinitive could not be split in Latin or French and so the belief grew that the English infinitive should not be split. This belief ignored two facts:

1 English infinitives are different from French infinitives in both form and usage:

French	English
*Je veux **aller** chez moi.*	*I want **to go** home.*
*Puis-je **aller** chez moi?*	*May I **go** home?*

2 English speakers and writers have been inserting modifiers between *to* and the infinitive since the fourteenth century.

Contemporary usage permits a modifier between the *to* and the infinitive:

> *to fully intend*

especially in speech and informal writing styles. There is still a lot of prejudice, however, against *split infinitives* and although this prejudice is illogical and grammatically unfounded, it is best to avoid *split infinitives* in formal contexts.

See: 'chestnuts', purist.

spoonerism

A *spoonerism* involves the unintentional transposition of the initial sounds of two (or occasionally more) words:

> *Tonight there will be widespread low-fying log.*

Unintentional spoonerisms are usually meaningless. The weather forecaster who made this slip actually claimed to have said *low flying log* and the term *spoonerism* is often applied to meaningful and usually humorous transpositions:

> *I love riding on a **well-boiled icicle**.* (well-oiled bicycle)
> *The film was full of **thud and blunder**.* (blood and thunder)

The term is derived from the name of the Reverend W.A. Spooner (1844-1930) who was well known for his eccentric behaviour. As well as producing sentences such as:

> *You have **tasted two worms**...* (wasted two terms)

he is also reported to have been so agitated at the beginning of a journey that he kissed the porter and gave his wife sixpence!

See: metathesis.

Sri Lankan English

Sri Lanka, formerly Ceylon, is a large island off the coast of southwest India with a population of just over 15 million. It was a British

Colony between 1802 and 1948, when it gained its independence, and for most of this time it was governed as part of the Indian Empire.

There are two large language groups in Sri Lanka. Approximately three-quarters of the population speak a variety of Sinhalese and 21% are Tamils, originally from the south of India. Apart from the linguistic differences, the Sinhalese are mostly Buddhist, the Tamils Hindu, and religious and political rivalry have exacerbated linguistic differences.

When Sri Lanka became independent in 1948 three languages were widely used (English, Sinhala and Tamil) with English being the preferred language of higher education. In 1972 Sri Lanka became a republic and attempted to replace English by Sinhala and Tamil in commerce, education and politics. The quality of English deteriorated, but recently Sri Lanka has stressed the value of English as a **lingua franca** and it is being reintroduced into higher education.

See: **English in the Indian Sub-Continent.**

Standard English

Standard or prestige varieties of language exist in most communities where one variety may be regarded as most expressive, most authoritative or most easily comprehended. *Standard English* is the term given to the spectrum of Englishes taught in schools, described in **grammars** and **dictionaries,** used by the media and written with relatively little variation throughout the English-speaking world. (Occasionally the term *General American English* is used as a synonym for standard US English.)

Standard English developed from a regional **dialect** spoken in and around London in the fifteenth century. Prestige varieties had existed before this time but from the fifteenth century people outside London began to write in a variety that approximated not to their own speech but to the norms of educated speakers in the London region.

This dialect was further enhanced by the establishment of printing houses in London towards the end of the fifteenth century and by the publishing of literature and the Bible in the London dialect. By the middle of the sixteenth century a written standard had emerged and the vocabulary and syntax of this standard were spread throughout England, and eventually the world, by education, travel and, more recently, by the media.

The existence of a standard written language did not entail a spoken standard. All educated speakers could write *caught* but some might pronounce it to rhyme with *short* while others rhymed it with *shot*. Standardised pronunciations only became widespread with the introduction of universal education and because of the influence of radio, films and television.

Standard English is not absolutely clearcut and discrete. It comprehends varieties which allow a speaker to indicate friendship or formality, casualness, intimacy or aloofness. Formal spoken styles are often close to written norms, with fewer reductions and weak forms than are found in colloquial speech.

See: **accent, dialect, network norms, pronunciation.**

stative and dynamic

Verbs in English are often subdivided into *stative* or *dynamic* depending on whether they can occur with the **progressive**. Dynamic verbs occur with the progressive; stative verbs do not:

> *I sing a lot. I'm singing in the rain.*
> *I know a lot. *I'm knowing you well.*

Stative verbs normally express states (BE, SEEM), senses (HEAR, SEE) and mental processes (KNOW, REMEMBER), whereas dynamic verbs tend to express action (DANCE, WALK). The majority of verbs in English are dynamic.

Although the terms *stative* and *dynamic* are usually applied to verbs, adjectives can be subdivided in a similar way:

1 stative verbs do not normally occur in imperative structures and certain adjectives appear to be similarly restricted:

> *Sing a song. * Resemble your father.*
> *Be happy. * Be short.*

2 stative verbs do not normally occur with the progressive, nor do certain adjectives:

> *He is dancing. *He is owning a house.*
> *He is being patient. *He is being drunk.*

The majority of adjectives in English are stative:

> *He is being fat/old/thin.*

See: **adjective, dynamic, verb.**

stream of consciousness

The term *stream of consciousness* was coined by William James in 1890. It refers to a representation of the continuous and controlled flow of thoughts and sensations. The term *stream of consciousness* is modern, but many of the techniques associated with it are to be found in soliloquies (in which a character attempts to express and explain his innermost thoughts) and in interior monologues (in which the mental processes of a character are presented).

Analyses of the writings of novelists such as James Joyce, Virginia Woolf and J.D. Salinger suggest that the linguistic features most commonly found in stream-of-consciousness novels are:

1 a preference for nominal sentences. Verbs reinforce time, and so:

the arrival of the train

is preferred to:

The train arrived.

2 use of short sentences, often minor sentences, with exclamations, free association and few linkage markers such as *because*, *thus*.

3 modification of usual word order, with **foregrounding** of objects, complements and adverbials:

A frightened man he saw.
Tired and weary he was.
On a night train to hell he sat.

4 reduction of subject pronouns:

Hits the bottom! Hard. Where to plant it? Over there in the corner.

5 reduced anaphoric references (pronominal references, auxiliary verbs) help to create the impression of disjointed thoughts.

6 use of untransformed **embeddings**:

Wondered will she come.

instead of:

He wondered if she would come.
'Will she come?' he wondered.

7 extensive use of features found in intimate speech: unfinished sentences, unexplained shifts in subject matter, reduced forms (*I'm*, *won't*), interrogatives and repetitions.

8 word play, including ambiguity, coinages and the revival of early meanings.

9 sound patterns, including **sound symbolism, onomatopoeia, alliteration** and **assonance**.

See: **speech in literature.**

stress

The term *stress* is used to indicate the degree of prominence given to a syllable. In English, certain syllables are produced with more force than others and these are called *stressed syllables*. Syllables which receive less stress are called *unstressed syllables*. In a word like *delight-ful*, for example, *-light-* receives more stress than either *de-* or *-ful*.

Stress can be used to differentiate meanings:

the 'White House   the 'white 'house

word classes:

'conduct (noun)   con'duct (verb)

and to highlight one part of the sentence:

Mary *ran the business*. (It was Mary and not someone else.)
Mary ran *the business*. (She didn't sell it.)

Structuralists postulated four degrees of stress for English, *primary*, *secondary*, *tertiary* and *weak*, illustrated by the compound:

elevator operator
1 4 3 4 2 4 3 4

but for most purposes the binary division of *stressed* and *unstressed* is adequate.

English has been described as a *stress-timed* language, whereas languages like French and Yoruba have been called *syllable-timed*. In syllable-timed languages, all syllables are produced at equal intervals of time, with the stresses occurring randomly. In stress-timed languages, however, the stresses occur at regular intervals with a random number of syllables occurring between stresses. This pattern of regular stresses and varying numbers of syllables can be illustrated from poetry:

The garden flew round with the angel, (x/x//xx/x)
The angel flew round with the clouds, (x/x//xx/)
And the clouds flew round and the clouds flew round (xx/x/xx/x/)
And the clouds flew round with the clouds. (xx///xx/)
    Wallace Stevens, 'The Pleasures of Merely Circulating'

The dichotomy between stress-timed and syllable-timed languages is not as absolute as has been suggested. Many Africans and Asians, for example, speak English as if it were a syllable-timed language.

See: **emphasis, metre, strong and weak forms, syllable.**

strong and weak forms

Many words in English have two pronunciations in connected speech, depending on whether they are stressed or not. Thus, the *and* in *bread and butter* would be pronounced strongly and in full /ænd/ if one wished to emphasise that both would be required, but reduced to /n/ in most contexts. The fully pronounced form is called *strong* and the reduced form *weak*.

Many grammatical words (articles, auxiliaries, conjunctions, pronouns, prepositions) have both strong (or accented or stressed) and weak (or unaccented or unstressed) forms. The following list comprehends the most frequently-used examples in the language. Non-rhotic and **rhotic** varieties are provided:

Word	Strong form	Weak form
a	/eɪ/	/ə/
am	/æm/	/əm,m/
and	/ænd/	/ənd,ən,n/
are	/ɑ/, /ɑr/	/ə/, /ər/
as	/æz/	/əz/
at	/æt/	/ət/
be	/bi/	/bɪ/
been	/bin/	/bɪn/
but	/bʌt/	/bət/
can	/kæn/	/kən,kn/
could	/kʊd/	/kəd,kd/
do	/du/	/dʊ,də,d/
does	/dʌz/	/dəz/
for	/fɔ/, /fɔr/	/fə/, /fər, fr/
from	/frɒm/	/frəm/
had	/hæd/	/həd,əd,d/
has	/hæz/	/həz,əz,z/
have	/hæv/	/həv,əv,v/
he	/hi/	/hɪ,i/
her	/hɜ/, /hər/	/hə,ə/, /ər,r/
him	/hɪm/	/ɪm/
his	/hɪz/	/ɪz/
is	/ɪz/	/z/
must	/mʌst/	/məst,məs/
not	/nɒt/	/nət, nt,n/
of	/ɒv/	/əv,v/
shall	/ʃæl/	/ʃəl,ʃl/
she	/ʃi/	/ʃɪ/
some	/sʌm/	/səm/
than	/ðæn/	/ðən,ðn/
the	/ði/	/ðɪ,ðə/
to	/tu/	/tʊ,tə/
us	/ʌs/	/əs,s/
was	/wɒz/	/wəz/
we	/wi/	/wɪ/
were	/wɜ/,/wər/	/wə/,/wr/
will	/wɪl/	/wəl,əl/
would	/wʊd/	/wəd,əd,d/
you	/ju/	/jʊ,jə/

The terms *strong* and *weak* are also applied to **verbs**. **Irregular verbs** such as DO and SEE, which form their past tense and past participles by means of vowel (and consonant) changes, are called *strong*:

> *do did done*
> *see saw seen*

Verbs which form their past tense and past participle by the addition of *-ed/-d/-t* are called *weak*:

> *look looked looked*
> *love loved loved*

All newly formed verbs (e.g. *computerise*) are weak and a number of strong verbs are becoming weak. THRIVE patterned like DRIVE:

> *thrive throve thriven*

but *thrived* is now acceptable for both the past tense and the past participle.

See: **stress, syllable, verb**.

structuralism

The term *structuralism* is usually applied to linguistic analyses which describe languages in terms of their *forms* (e.g. *boy, boys, boy's*) and *functions* (e.g. noun, subject). Often the classification is hierarchical, which means that one may organise English in terms of:

> phonemes e.g. /z/
> morphemes e.g. *-es*
> lexemes e.g. *match-es*
> phrases e.g. *with the matches*
> clauses e.g. *as he played with the matches*
> sentences e.g. *He talked as he played with the matches.*

Structuralist approaches to language flourished until the early 1960s. They were accurate and useful but were limited in that they concentrated on surface structure. Structuralists paid little attention to meaning and especially to the facts that structures which were superficially similar could have very different underlying meanings:

> *She advised me what to say* (i.e. I was to say it).
> *She asked me what to say* (i.e. she was to say it).

and that structures could look very different but have very similar underlying meanings:

> *John admired Mary.*
> *Mary was admired by John.*

Structuralism is also applied by scholars to the notion that all human behaviour, including friendship, religion and storytelling, can be analysed in terms of a network of recurring and interconnecting themes and relationships.

See: **grammar, transformational grammar**.

style

Style may be regarded as a distinctive method of writing or speaking. It thus involves selection from all the available options in a language. The selection may include choice of vocabulary (*calculation, estimation, sums, tally*), phrase (*absolutely delighted, as pleased as Punch, over the moon, very pleased*), sentence structure (simple, compound, complex, active or passive) as well as **imagery, punctuation** and rhetorical devices. Indeed, any linguistic choice is inevitably a stylistic choice since it affects the style of an utterance or a passage.

A person's style may be described as 'good' or 'bad' according to its effectiveness in achieving the purpose of the writer or speaker. If, for example, a speaker wishes to be friendly but uses formal structures and polysyllabic vocabulary, his intentions may well be misunderstood.

Stylistic choices may be deliberate and conscious (James Joyce once claimed that he spent an entire day working on the **word order** of two sentences) or automatic and unthinking (as in many everyday communications). Every speaker has a unique style or *idiolect* which may vary with time and circumstances. Similarly, many writers can be identified by their individual techniques. Keats, for example, often uses the verb *cloy* and juxtaposes the nouns *pleasure* and *pain*.

As well as individual styles, there are also *genre* styles such as those associated with journalism, advertising or **scientific English**. Subvarieties of English with their associated styles are studied and taught as *English for Specific Purposes*.

See: **journalese, scientific English, stylistics**.

stylistics

Stylistics is the branch of **linguistics** that studies the use of language in specific contexts and attempts to account for the regularities that mark language use by individuals and groups. For example, a stylistic analysis may reveal the characteristic features of popular journalism and explain the lexical and syntactic choices in terms of readership, conventions and the exigencies of time and space.

Literary stylistics is concerned with the linguistic choices that distinguish genres (poetry, drama and the novel, for example) and with the ways in which individual writers exploit language. This is both a linguistic and a literary exercise, since language is the medium of literature and **style** contributes to meaning. Literary stylistics serves as a bridge between linguistic and literary disciplines.

See: **deviation, rhetoric, style.**

subject

In English, the *subject* is a major constituent of a **sentence**. In finite sentences, it is the NP which:

1 normally precedes the predicate in declarative sentences:

The book was written in four days.

2 normally occurs within the predicate in interrogative sentences:

Was the book written in four days?

3 agrees with verbs in the present tense and with BE in both past and present:

The man sings well.
The men sing well.
The book was written quickly.
The books were written quickly.

The most frequently-occurring subjects are:
1 **noun phrases**:

The cars raced round and round.

2 pronouns:

They ran away.

3 proper names:

John Smith III arrived on time.

4 -ing forms:

Dancing is good for you.

5 to forms:

To err is human.

6 **nominalisations** (**nouns** derived from other parts of speech):

Their conversion surprised us all.
Ifs and buts are not enough.

7 finite clauses:

That Joan is a genius is obvious.

This sentence is less common than an equivalent using an anticipatory *it*:

It is obvious that Joan is a genius.

Subjects occur in active sentences:

*The **rat** ate the malt.*

in passive sentences:

*The **malt** was eaten.*

and in sentences with a copula:

***Rats** are rodents.*

So essential are subjects to declarative sentences that we have **dummy subjects** (i.e. subjects without much meaning) in sentences like:

It is raining/snowing. (What is *it*?)
There are three twos in six. (Where?)

Subject pronouns occur in **tag questions**:

*He was late, **wasn't he**?*

See: **noun, noun phrase, object.**

subjunctive

Grammars that were based on Latin models classified the **verb phrase** according to three categories:
1 declarative/**indicative**:

He eats fish.

2 **imperative**/command:

Eat that fish.

3 *subjunctive* (the verb form used in subordinate clauses).
 In English, there is usually no difference between the form of the **verb** used in main and subordinate clauses:

*I never **eat** fish.*
*I said that I never **eat** fish.*

However, there are three types of construction where the verb used may be classified as subjunctive:
1 in hypothetical statements:

*If I **were** you...*
*If this **be** proven...*

2 in a number of formulas:

Be that as it may
Long live the Queen!
So be it!

3 in formal statements involving *that* clauses:

I request that he be extradited.
We suggest that she be remanded in custody.

In English, the meaning that is carried in some languages by the subjunctive (doubt, suggestion, wishing) is often carried by modal verbs.

See: **modality, mood.**

subordination

When **clauses** or sentences are linked, they may be of equal syntactic status in which case they are co-ordinated:

John was tired but he carried on.

or one clause or sentence may be dependent on the other, in which case we say it is *subordinate* to the main clause:

Although John was tired, he carried on.

Subordinate (also called **dependent**) clauses are introduced by *subordinating conjunctions* (also called *subordinators*). These are function words like *although, if, since, when, until,* which introduce adverbial clauses:

I'll do it if he asks me.

that and *what,* which introduce noun clauses:

That he was honest was obvious.
She always said what she meant.

and *that, which, who, whom,* which introduce **relative** (adjectival) **clauses:**

The letter that I posted last week has still not arrived.

See: **clause, co-ordination, dependent, embedding.**

substantial, substantive

Substantial is an adjective meaning 'real, true, actually in existence, considerable in quantity or size or importance, most but not all':

a substantial house/part of the inheritance

Substantive can be used as an adjective and a noun. As an adjective, it means 'having a separate existence, real not apparent, enduring, relating to the essence of a thing':

*We need **substantive** and not just cosmetic improvements in sales.*

Recently, *substantive* has taken on the meaning of 'relating to matters of national or international concern':

*The East–West arms negotiators had **substantive** talks this morning.*

Substantive is used linguistically to refer to BE:

*The BE verb has been called the existential verb, the essive verb and the **substantive** verb.*

and as a synonym for *noun*:

*There are two **substantives** in the sentence 'Bears love honey'.*

The term *substantive universals* is applied to categories or features thought to occur in all natural languages. It is thus applied to:
1 units such as S (sentence), VP (verb phrase)
2 features such as ' + animate', ' + human'.

See: **problem pairs.**

substitution

When linguists postulate the existence of such classes as *nouns* and *prepositions*, or the relationships between classes, they attempt to support their hypotheses by offering evidence. Much of the evidence offered involves such operations as:
1 insertion:

I am fond of Tom. > *I am **very** fond of Tom.*

2 deletion:

*We **must** do our best.* > *We do our best.*

3 permutation (or transposition):

*I'll try again **soon**.* > ***Soon** I'll try again.*

4 substitution. This is the process of replacing one unit by another:

The big black cat sat on the mat. > ***It** sat on the mat.* > *It sat **there**.*

The ability to substitute 'it' for 'the big black cat' helps to illustrate the fact that **pronouns** can be substituted for noun phrases. The fact that 'there' can replace 'on the mat' supports the view that 'on the mat' is an adverbial phrase.

Substitution frames can be used to show the different types of units that can occur in certain roles. The object of a sentence, for example,

may be a pronoun, a noun phrase, a proper noun, a clause or a
non-finite verb form:

He wanted	this.
He wanted	all the food.
He wanted	Bonio.
He wanted	whatever he could get.
He wanted	to smoke.

All the units that can occur in a certain position in a structure form
a *substitution class*.

See: **anaphora, auxiliary, pronoun, question tag.**

such

Like **so,** *such* has a variety of functions, the chief of these being as
an intensifier and as a substitute for other units.

   1 *Such* frequently occurs as an intensifier. The form *such* occurs
before uncountable nouns and *such a* before countable nouns:

*We had **such** good fun!*
*You've never seen **such a** crowd!*

Such does not co-occur with the definite article or with demonstrative
or possessive adjectives:

*the/these/his such beautiful children

and the pattern for a countable noun in a negative construction is
often 'no + such + noun':

*We have **no such** passenger.*

   2 *Such* may be used as a pronoun in formal discourse:

*He was quixotic, witty and optimistic. **Such** was his disposition, but
his circumstances were in sombre contrast.*

   3 *Such-and-such* can occur in informal speech to avoid being
specific:

*He said **such-and-such** a thing often.*

   4 *Such as* may introduce examples:

*Nouns may be derived from place names, **such as** 'cashmere' (Kashmir), 'denim' (de Nîmes) or 'jersey' (Jersey Island).*

Such as is regarded as being more formal, and in the written medium
more correct, than **like**:

*Certain adjectives **such as** (**like**) 'mere' only occur before nouns and
not in constructions **such as** 'It was...'*

5 The term *suchlike* as in:

They may find drugs, smoking and **suchlike** *activities not only distracting but very easy to participate in.*

is generally regarded as colloquial or nonstandard. It should be avoided in writing or careful speech.

See: **as, pro forms, so.**

suffix

A *suffix* is a **morpheme** which is added to a stem or root:

rude + *ness* → *rudeness*

Suffixes can be used derivationally, that is, in the formation of new words which may belong to different classes:

grand (adj) + *eur* > *grandeur* (n)
subtract (v) + *ion* > *subtraction* (n)

They may also be used inflectionally, that is, in distinguishing between singular and plural nouns:

pencil pencil + *s*

between different verb forms:

look look + *s look* + *ed look* + *ing*

and in marking degrees in adjectives and adverbs:

great great + *er great* + *est*
fast fast + *er fast* + *est*

See: **affix, prefix, word formation.**

suprasegmental

A *suprasegmental* is a feature of speech which applies to more than one sound segment. Stress, nasality or loudness, for example, may affect an entire utterance.

See: **phonetics, stress.**

syllable

A *syllable* is a unit of language which can occur in isolation. In speech, it is often the equivalent of a **morpheme** in that it is usually larger than a sound but smaller than a word. Syllables in English may consist of:

1 a vowel alone (V): *a*, for example, in *alone*

2 a consonant + a vowel (CV): *de* in *delight*
3 two consonants + a vowel (CCV): *dry* in *drying*
4 three consonants + a vowel (CCCV): *scree* in *screeching*
5 a syllabic consonant, that is, nasals and laterals in words such as:

button /bʌtn̩/ *cattle* /kætl̩/

6 a consonant + a vowel + a consonant (CVC): *cat*
7 patterns involving CCVCC (*spurt*), CCCVC (*sprig*), CCCVCC (*sprint*), CCCVCCC (*sprints*) and CCCVCCCC (*strengths*) also occur.

In the written medium, we can hyphenate syllables and this is usually done by dividing words as follows:

beside be-side
betting bet-ting
costing cos-ting
loving lo-ving

It will be noticed that the syllable in the written medium does not exactly match the morpheme. Conventionally, we divide a word before a consonant when only one consonant occurs (bi-ting), between consonants when two occur (bat-ting, bas-ting) and after the second consonant when three or more occur (streng-then). Some linguists and publishers prefer to equate the syllable with the morpheme, producing *cost-ing*, *lov-ing*, *bit-ing*, *bast-ing* and *strength-en*. Such a method, however, runs into problems with words such as *batt-ing*.

Some languages are referred to as *syllable-timed* because syllables tend to occur at regular intervals of time whereas **stresses** occur randomly. English is a *stress-timed* language because stresses occur at regular intervals with a random number of syllables occurring between stresses.

See: **metre, morpheme, stress.**

syllepsis

Syllepsis, from Greek *syllepsis* (taking together), is a figure of speech with two overlapping uses:

1 It can refer to a syntactic relationship where a number of words depend on one word only but this word cannot agree with all of them in number:

It is doubtful if John or the children **know**.

or gender:

Janet and John each have **his/her/their** *responsibilities.*

2 It is often used as a synonym for *zeugma*, that is, the application

of a word to two or more other words, often with one meaning being literal and the other metaphorical:

*He **opened** his house and his heart to his new family.*

See: figurative language, polysemy.

synaesthesia

Synaesthesia comprehends the study of two linguistic phenomena:

1 the correlation between sounds and meaning. Certain sounds and sound combinations can evoke a particular reaction. Human nouns ending in *-ard*, for example, are often pejorative (*bastard, coward, laggard*); words involving high front vowels (/i/ and /ɪ/) often imply closeness or smallness (*here, this, bit, little*); colloquial adjectives ending in *-ky* can suggest criticism (*cocky, kinky, wonky*); and abstract nouns ending in *-ery* are often unfavourable (*flattery, mockery,* and *trickery*).

2 the transference of meanings from one sensory domain to another. Thus, the adjective *sharp* relates to the sense of touch but can be applied to sound (*flats and sharps*) and to taste (*a sharp sauce*); and sound adjectives like *loud* are frequently applied to colour (*a loud yellow*). Of all the senses, smell seems to have fewest descriptive adjectives directly relating to it (*acrid, pungent*) and tends to use taste adjectives instead (*a sweet smell*). There seem to be regular patterns in the transfer of adjectives from one sensory domain to another, with touch adjectives being most mobile and adjectives of smell being least mobile:

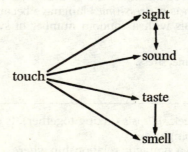

Meanings can, of course, be transferred from sensory domains to other fields:

*a **cold** nature*
*a **sharp** mind*
*a **blue** movie*

This phenomenon is a subdivision of **metaphor**.

See: **metaphor, onomatopoeia, sound symbolism.**

syncope

Syncope, pronounced /ˈsɪŋkəpɪ/, from Greek *synkope* (cutting short), refers to the loss of one or more sounds or letters from the middle of a word:

boatswain	is pronounced	*bosun*
coxswain	is pronounced	*coxun*

Syncope is frequent in British pronunciations of names:

Featherstonehaugh	is pronounced	*Fanshaw*
Worcester	is pronounced	*Wooster*

See: **aphesis, apocope, clipping, epenthesis.**

synecdoche

Synecdoche, pronounced /sɪˈnɛkdəkɪ/, is from Greek *synekdoche* (interpretation). It is a figure of speech in which a significant part is used to represent the whole:

The hand (the mother) *that rocks the cradle rules the world.*

or the whole is used to represent a part:

The union (some members) *voted to return to work.*

or the name of a material is used for the object it was used for:

He trod **the boards** (the stage) *for forty years.*

Many people confuse synecdoche and **metonymy** because they are both figures of speech in which one noun represents another. The difference is that with synecdoche the equated nouns bear a special relationship to each other:

A is part of B (as *hand* is of *human being*)
A includes B (as *union* does *members*)
A was used in making B (as *stage* is made of *boards*)

With metonymy, one noun (A) is used for another (B) when A is closely associated with B, thus *crown* for *monarch* in:

The Gambia was once a **crown** *colony.*

See: **figurative language, metonymy.**

synonym

Synonym derives from Greek *syn* + *onyma* (together + name) and refers to a sense relationship in which different words seem to have the same meaning and are in free variation with each other in all or most contexts:

> *Autumn Fall*
> *big large*
> *regal royal*

Close examination of words such as those above reveals that synonymy is always partial, rarely if ever absolute:

> *I love my **big** brother.* (*big* suggests *elder*)
> *I love my **large** brother.* (*large* suggests *fat*)

The nearest we come to total synonymy is when synonyms belong to different **dialects**, as with *Autumn* and *Fall*, although even here the choice of *Fall* would imply the region of origin of the speaker.

Words may be cognitively synonymous in that they have essentially the same reference:

> *die expire kick the bucket pass on/over*

but such words often differ stylistically in that they would be used on different occasions and in different contexts. Cognitively synonymous words may also differ in the emotional response they evoke. The A and B lists are often given as synonyms but the A words have more positive associations:

A	B
carpenter	*joiner*
statesman	*politician*
strongminded	*stubborn*

Absolute synonymy involving the identity of cognitive, emotive and stylistic implications is thus more of an ideal, or extreme, than a reality.

It has often been pointed out that the number of near synonyms for any object or phenonemon indicates its relative significance in a culture. English, for example, has many words for the use of excessive words (*circumlocution, periphrasis, pleonasm, tautology, redundancy, verbiage, verbosity*); Arabs distinguish many types of sand; Inuits have an extensive vocabulary for types of snow; and many dialect speakers in Ireland have a dozen different words for *potato*, including:

> *chat* (small, not very tasty)
> *cutling* (good for cutting and planting)
> *marley* (tiny but tasty)
> *poreen* (very tiny)

See: **antonym, connotation.**

syntax

Syntax, from Greek *syntassein* (to arrange together), refers to the study of the ways in which words are combined to form **sentences**. In many traditional accounts of language four levels of language were postulated:

1 Phonology: dealing with sounds and combinations of sounds

2 Morphology: dealing with word formation and including inflection (*cook/cooks/cooked*) and derivation (*amalgam/amalgamate*)

3 Syntax: dealing with the rules for combining words into acceptable sentences:

> *I saw the big brown cat yesterday.*
> **I the saw brown yesterday cat big.*
> *He can come.*
> **Come can he?*

4 Semantics: dealing with meaning.

Some linguists (especially from the UK) use the term **grammar** to comprehend both morphology and syntax; others, following Chomsky, describe language in terms of three major categories:

> Phonology
> Syntax
> Semantics

with syntax being the link between sound and meaning.

In all descriptions, however, syntax implies the rules governing acceptable arrangements of smaller units into larger ones.

See: **grammar**

synthetic

This word is used by linguists with two main references:

1 Languages are often subdivided into *synthetic languages*, where words consist of two or more **morphemes**, and *analytic languages*, where each word tends to be one morpheme.

2 Many causative sentences can occur in two forms:

(a) *Ojo makes your whole wash whiter.*
(b) *Ojo whitens your whole wash.*

The (a) forms, which are often more explicit, are called *analytic* sentences and the (b) forms, where two or more words are combined, are called *synthetic*.

Many synthetic verbs are related to adjectives:

> *activate* < *active* + *ate*
> *legalise* < *legal* + *ise*

and others to nouns:

beautify < beauty
hospitalise < hospital

See: **analytic, ergative.**

taboo words

All languages have words and expressions that are regarded as unsuitable for general use either because they deserve particular reverence or because they are felt to be 'unclean' or vulgar. In English there are six main areas associated with linguistic taboos. (The word *taboo* derives from the Polynesian word *tabu* which referred to a prohibition forbidding certain actions, contacts, relationships or words.)

1 *Religion*—Words associated with God and religion are only fully acceptable in religious contexts. Even then, many orthodox Jews avoid the use of the word *God*. In colloquial speech, terms like *God, Jesus, damn* and *hell* occur frequently but can still give offence and should be avoided. **Euphemisms** for these words, such as *Gosh, Jeepers Creepers, dash* and *heck*, are usually considered inoffensive but tend to be limited to colloquial speech. Latinisms, often abbreviated to initials, are acceptable but such forms as *DG < Deo Gratias* (Thanks be to God) and *DV < Deo Volente* (God willing) are rarely used now.

2 *Sex*—Words relating to sex or the sex organs are only fully acceptable in intimate relationships or in medical contexts. The most frequently used of the so-called 'four letter words' has been reduced to an emphasiser in such contexts as:

He's fucking stupid!
She fucking well did!

Four letter words can be extremely offensive.

3 *Bodily excretions*—All bodily excretions with the exception of tears and perhaps sweat can have taboo associations.

4 *Disease and Death*—Many people avoid discussing serious illnesses like *cancer*, often preferring to use a euphemism such as *terminally ill*. The subject of death is not so much avoided as dealt with in euphemistic or idiomatic terms:

if anything should happen to me (when I die)
casket (coffin)
pass on/away (die)
earthly remains (dead body).

Mental illness or handicap is also a taboo subject and is often dealt with in terms of euphemisms:

He's not all there.
She's a little eccentric/a little confused.

or 'humorous' idioms:

> *a screw loose/missing*
> *off his rocker*

Abbreviations are frequently used so that speakers may avoid overt reference to illness:

> *AIDS* (Acquired Immune Deficiency Syndrome)
> *Big C* (cancer)
> *DTs* (delirium tremens)

5 *Social stratification*—Some people are embarrassed by talk of wealth or poverty, preferring understatement or idiom:

> *He's well off/rolling in it.*
> *They're down on their luck.*

Classifications occur but euphemisms are preferred:

> *upper class, middle class and working* (not 'lower') *class*
> *the rich countries and the third world* (not 'poor' world)

Some occupations are judged less prestigious than others and re-named:

> *garbage/refuse collector* > *sanitation officer*
> *electrician/machine worker* > *engineer*

6 *Age and weight*—The fear of growing old or of being obese has engendered such euphemisms as:

> *evergreen clubs* (clubs for people who are 60 +)
> *senior citizens* (people over 60)
> *fuller figure* (fat)
> *Junoesque* (tall and fat—women)
> *High and Mighty* (tall and fat—men)

In the British parliament, certain 'unparliamentary expressions' are taboo. Among the terms which may not be used are: *cad*, *cheeky young pup*, *dog*, *jackass*, *liar*, *prevaricating*, *rat*. This list is extended from time to time. In June, 1984, *fascist* was judged 'unparliamentary' and added to the list.

See: **euphemism.**

tags

There are three types of *tags* in English:

1 **question tags**, involving an **auxiliary** verb + (negative) + pronoun which are attached to statements in order to elicit agreement:

> *He's tired, isn't he?* (expected answer 'Yes')
> *He isn't tired, is he?* (expected answer 'No')

2 reinforcement tags, which tend to be a feature of colloquial English and more widespread in the UK than in America:

You're an idiot, you are.
Lovely people, the French.

3 speech **fillers**, especially *you know, you see*:

I knew him, you see.
It's getting late, you know.

See: **auxiliary, fillers, question tags, speech and writing.**

Tanzanian English

The United Republic of Tanzania (with a present population of 20 million) came into existence in 1964 with the merging of Tanganyika and Zanzibar. Tanganyika was part of German East Africa until after the First World War, when it began to be administered by Britain until it achieved independence in 1961. Zanzibar was a British Protectorate from 1890 until 1963.

When the Republic of Tanzania was formed, English was the official language, the chief medium of education, government and international activities. Swahili was, however, more widely understood by the masses and less obviously a marker of privilege. Gradually, it has replaced English in primary and early secondary education, in internal commerce and in government. Swahili has an advantage over English in being widely spoken, even by uneducated Africans, in several countries in East and Central Africa, but it lacks international currency. English continues to be widely used in secondary and tertiary education, in literature and in international dealings.

See: **African English, East African English.**

tautology

Tautology, from Greek *tautologus* (saying the same thing), involves the repetition of the same idea, often using different words:

*Little Willie's **dead and gone** and now he **is no more**;*
For what he thought was H_2O was H_2SO_4.

Many orators and writers use tautology for effect:

He was a riddle, a mystery, an enigma.

and such repetition, even with slight semantic modification, is acceptable. It is less acceptable when used to avoid answering questions:

> *Our defence policy on nuclear arms is to have nuclear arms for our defence.*

a statement which is as informative as the mathematical tautology that:

> $2 = 2$

See: **circumlocution, pleonasm, redundancy, repetition.**

telegraphese

Telegraphese is a term given to the elliptical style used in telegrams, diaries, headlines, slogans and in **stream-of-consciousness** novels. It is characterised by a brevity resulting from the omission of inessential words. A six-word headline in *The Times* (London), for example:

> *Veto call on gifts to parties*

is explained in a nineteen-word sentence:

> *The council voted to call for a law requiring companies to ballot share-holders before making donations to political parties.*

A telegram such as:

> *Arriving Dallas noon. Meet Flight AA129.*

costs considerably less than the longer equivalent:

> *I shall be arriving in Dallas at noon. Please meet Flight number AA129.*

Conjunctions and prepositions tend to be omitted and pronouns and auxiliary verbs are either omitted or reduced in number.

See: **paraphrase, précis, stream of consciousness.**

tense

Tense is the term applied to distinctions of **time** which are made overt in the **verb phrase**:

> *I like him because he is kind.* (time = now)
> *I liked him because he was kind.* (time = before now)

Often, tense and **aspect** co-occur:

> *I am trying to fix it.* (time = now + continuity)
> *I have tried to fix it.* (time = before now + completion)

but whereas the marking of aspect always presupposes the marking of tense:

I was listening intently. (tense + aspect)

tense may occur without aspect:

I listened intently. (tense)

Traditionally, three main tenses, present, past and **future,** have been described but there is not a one-to-one relation between tense and time:

1 The so-called *present tense* is frequently used for the expression of scientific or sociological truths:

Water boils at 100 degrees centigrade.
A stitch in time saves nine.

for oral narratives (sometimes called the 'narrative aspect' or the 'historic present'):

There was this man. He walks up to me and says...

and, with an adverb, to mark future time:

I leave tomorrow.

2 The so-called *past tense* is frequently used to mark hypothetical or unreal meaning:

I wish I knew (at this moment).
It's time we stopped (now) *quarrelling.*

It is also used in reported speech:

'I'm tired.' → *He said that he was tired.*

3 *Future* time can be marked in a variety of ways in English:

I set out next week.
I'm setting out next week.
I'm going to set out next week.

none of them by means of a morphological change in the verb.

Many contemporary linguists suggest that English has two tenses: a past tense and a non-past tense and that futurity can be expressed in many ways:

1 by modal + verb:

I shall go.
I could go if you babysat for us.

2 by a variety of verbal forms, alone or in combination with adverbials:

He leaves at noon.
He is about to leave.

Tense usage throughout the English-speaking world is virtually identical. The one marked difference is that some speakers of US English tend to use the conditional modals in consecutive clauses:

*I **would** have gone if I **would** have seen him.*

whereas other speakers of English prefer:

*I **would** have gone if I **had** seen him.*

See: **aspect, modality, time, verb phrase.**

than I, than me

Purists insist that *than* should be followed by the subject pronoun:

*He is taller **than I**.*

assuming that such a sentence is a reduced form of:

*He is taller **than I am** (tall).*

Such a contention ignores the parallel structures:

*He went in **before me**.*
*He went in **before I did**.*

Contemporary usage:
1 allows the use of 'than + object pronoun' in speech and informal writing:

*She's got more money **than us**.*

2 prefers 'than + subject pronoun' in formal contexts:

*She has more money **than we**.*

3 demands 'than + subject pronoun' in all contexts where the pronoun is followed by a verb:

*She's got more money **than we have**.*
*They are faster **than we are**.*

See: **as, case.**

their, there, they're

These words are sometimes confused.
Their is a possessive adjective:

*They lost **their** dog.*

The possessive pronoun is *theirs*:

*It was **theirs**. I've often seen it in their house.*

In informal contexts, *their* often serves as the equivalent of *his or her*:

> *Everyone should do **their** best.*

There can occur as a pronoun:

> *There was once a wise old owl.*

as an adverb of place:

> *I was sure I had put it **there**.*

and as an exclamation, often implying satisfaction:

> ***There**! I told you it would work.*

They're is a pronoun + verb, a reduced form of *they* + *are*:

> *They're older than I thought.*
> *They're cheap at the price.*

till, to, until

Till and *until* have the same meaning and are both acceptable in all styles of speech and writing, although *till* is more widely used in the UK, especially in conversation, and *until* in the USA. Both forms are used in **time** references for a period ending at a specific time:

> *We waited **till/until** the plane was out of sight.*

and they may both occur as **conjunctions**:

> *She pleaded with him **till/until** he relented.*

and as **prepositions**:

> *We have booked it **till/until** Friday.*

'Til, the clipped form of *until*, is nonstandard.

To can also be used in time references, in contexts where the length of time is specified:

> *It's two weeks **to/till** midsummer.*
> *We work from nine **to** five.*

See: **conjunction, preposition, time words**.

time

Time is often equated with **tense** and, although time references can be carried in the verb, they are not limited to it. Futurity is often expressed in English by means of a non-past verb + an adverbial:

> *I fly out tomorrow.*

or by a combination of the non-past tense, **progressive aspect** and an adverbial:

I am flying out tomorrow.

Many nouns also incorporate a time reference:

*His **past** caught up with him.*
*'**Youth** is wasted on the young.'*

and kinship terms give information on generation as well as (occasionally) sex:

ancestors
grandparents   great-aunts/uncles
parents   aunts/uncles
children   cousins
descendants

See: **family tree, tense, time words**.

time words

There are three conventional ways of expressing **time** and although all three are used throughout the world, there are differences between preferred uses in the UK and the USA.
1 Minute(s) + hour (twelve-hour clock)
According to this spoken method, the minutes are given before the hour. In the UK, the prepositions *past* and *to* are used, whereas US usage prefers *after* and *of*. Both varieties can use *quarter* and *half* when referring to 15, 30 and 45 minutes:

Time	UK	USA
5.05	five past five	five after five
5.15	quarter past five	quarter after five
5.30	half past five/half five	half after five
5.45	quarter to six	quarter of/to/till six
5.55	five to six	five of six

but *half after five* is less common than *5.30* in the USA, and the UK form *half five* is never used by US speakers.

The word *minutes* must be used with numbers which cannot be divided exactly by five:

*It's two **minutes** past/after five.*
*It's twenty-two **minutes** to/of six.*

Times on the hour are given with *o'clock*:

*It's just four **o'clock**.*

Colloquially, however, many speakers say:

It's just four.

Where it is necessary to distinguish between day and night, the **abbreviations** *a.m.* (*ante meridiem* = before noon) and *p.m.* (*post meridiem* = after noon) are employed:

They will arrive at 3.p.m. (= 15.00)
She didn't leave until 3 a.m. (= 03.00)

2 Hour + minute(s) (twelve-hour clock)
This method uses figures only and occurs mainly in formal announcements and in writing:

It's 4.30 not 4.25.
The train arrives at 6.06.

3 Hour + minute(s) (twenty-four-hour clock)
This method has become increasingly popular, even in speech, since the advent of digital clocks and watches and of international travel. The cycle is from midnight (00.00) to midnight and all times are given as figures:

At the third stroke, it will be 9.27 and 30 seconds.
The flight has been delayed until 13.30.
Depart 07.45 Arrive 14.30.

Where precision is essential, the words *hundred hours* are added to times on the hour:

We set out at eighteen hundred hours. (= 18.00)

Some of the terms used in English to express time illustrate both the semantic changes that can affect all words and a human tendency towards procrastination. Thus, *anon, by and by, in a moment/minute, just now* and *soon* all meant 'immediately' but changed to 'in a little while'.

See: **dates, time.**

to forms

Verb forms such as *to see* are referred to as **infinitives**, *to infinitives, to forms* and V_{to}. The *to form* has the following characteristics:
1 It can be either simple:

to follow

or complex:

to be following
to have been following
to have been followed

or clipped:

I didn't go because I didn't want to.

2 It can be used as a **noun phrase**:

To err is human.
I want to sing.

as a **complement** to intransitive verbs:

He will come to see you tomorrow.

and as a complement to adjectives:

I'm very happy to meet you.

3 There is often little semantic difference between an active and a passive *to form*:

There's a lot to do.
There's a lot to be done.

4 The *to form* often occurs in the construction 'verb + object pronoun + to form':

Do you want us to stay?
We expect them to do their best.

In these and similar examples, the pronoun looks as if it is the object of the verb it follows but it functions as the subject of the *to form*:

Do you want us to stay? Shall we stay?
We expect them to do their best. They'll do their best.

See: **infinitive, verb phrase**.

tone languages

In many languages, words and grammatical categories are often distinguished by tone, thus in Lamnso, a Cameroon language, *lum* can, depending on tone, mean 'man' or 'rat' or 'bite'. Languages which use tone in such a way are known as *tone languages*.

A number of English-related **pidgins and creoles** utilise tone to differentiate meaning. In Krio, the English-related **creole** of Sierra Leone:

ɛn (with a high level tone) means 'and'
ɛn (with a high falling tone) means 'hen'

English is not regarded as a tone language although a number of distinctions seem to be carried by tone changes:

It rained some.

can mean both:

> It rained a little.

and:

> It rained a lot.

Similarly, the sentence:

> She's quite beautiful.

can, with different degrees of stress and pitch, mean:

> She's fairly beautiful.

and:

> She's extremely beautiful.

See: intonation, stress.

transformational grammar

A *transformational grammar* (often referred to as *TG*) is a grammar which recognises different levels in language and attempts to relate these levels systematically. Sentences such as:

> She advised me what to do.

and:

> She asked me what to do.

look alike but the first implies:

> She advised me about what I should do.

whereas the second implies:

> She asked me about what she should do.

Similarly, pairs of sentences such as:

> John saw Mary.
> Mary was seen by John.

may look different but they are similar in meaning and can be shown to be related. The underlying pattern of the active sentence is:

$$NP_1 \ past + V \ NP_2$$

and this can be transformed into the passive sentence by the rule:

$$NP_1 \ past + V \ NP_2 \Rightarrow NP_2 \ past + BE + past \ participle \ of \ V \ (by \ NP_1)$$

Noam Chomsky first described a transformational grammar in

Syntactic Structures (1957). There have been many changes of model since then but all models attempt:

1 to make explicit what the native speaker implicitly knows

2 to assign a structure to a potentially infinite set of sentences belonging to a specific language

3 to describe *competence*, that is, the perfect storehouse of linguistic knowledge rather than *performance*, that is, actual language data with all its imperfections.

Since native speakers can associate noise with meanings and meanings with noise, TG models have three components:

1 a phonological component, to deal with sounds and sound patterns

2 a semantic component, to deal with meaning

3 a syntactic component, to explain how strings of noises are matched with specific meanings. Most native speakers recognise two levels of structure, a surface level where very different meanings may be carried by similar patterns:

John is delightful.
John is delighted.

and a deeper level where similar meanings are carried by similar patterns. The syntactic component is therefore subdivided into a base subcomponent and a transformational subcomponent. The base subcomponent assigns structures of the following kind (called 'phrase markers'):

S → NP + VP
(Sentence can be rewritten as noun phrase + verb phrase)
NP → det + N (determiner + noun)
VP → V + NP

which can also be represented as a tree diagram:

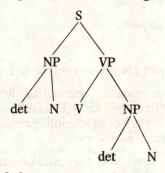

providing a simplified representation for such sentences as:

The boy loves the girl.
The dog ate the bone.

The transformational subcomponent operates on phrase markers showing how surface structure forms like:

The woman followed the man.
The man was followed (by the woman).
The following of the man (by the woman)

are all derived from such an underlying structure as:

NP_1 past + V NP_2

where NP_1 = 'the woman', V = 'follow' and NP_2 = 'the man'.

The account above is, of necessity, superficial, but it stresses the essential point that the TG model attempts to parallel the native speaker's linguistic abilities. TG models also emphasise the underlying similarities in all human languages.

See: **active voice, competence and performance, deep structure, grammar, passive voice, transformations, universals of language.**

transformations

Transformations (also called *transforms* and *T-rules*) are the rules which occur in the transformational subcomponent of a transformational model of grammar. Transformations allow a grammarian to explain:

1 insertion:

Pour some coffee. ⇒ *Pour yourself some coffee.*

2 deletion:

Mary ran away and John ran away. ⇒ *Mary and John ran away.*

3 permutation:

Call John up. ⇒ *Call up John.*

4 substitution:

They arrived and the party began. ⇒ *On their arrival the party began.*

Transformations can be either optional or obligatory. Optional transformations help to account for stylistic differences, such as the preference for passive sentences in scientific prose. Obligatory transformations are of two main kinds:

1 obligatory in the sense that they must be used. Most native speakers can use both:

Call Jane up.
Call up Jane.

but must use:

Call her up.
*Call up her.

2 obligatory in the sense that they must not be used. The passive transformation, for example, can only apply to transitive verbs such as DRIVE and not to intransitive verbs such as ARRIVE:

She drove the car. ⇒ *The car was driven by her.*
He arrived home. ⇒ **Home was arrived by him.*

See: **transformational grammar**.

transitive

A *transitive* **verb** is one which can take a direct **object**:

I saw him.
He attracts me.

Verbs which can take two objects are often called *ditransitive*:

I gave her the money.
She made them a lovely cake.
He wrote me a letter.

Many verbs in English can occur both transitively and intransitively:

The child opened the window.
The window opened.

See: **active voice, ergative, passive voice, verb**.

travel

There are some differences in the terminology for travel in the UK and the USA, although the increase in international travel and exchanged television programmes has made many speakers of English familiar with both varieties.

UK	USA
articulated lorry	trailer truck
bonnet	hood
book (holiday)	make a reservation
boot	trunk
caravan	trailer
car park	parking lot

central reservation	median strip/divider
cloakroom (restaurant)	checkroom
coach	(long-distance) bus
cul-de-sac	dead-end
diversion	detour
dual carriageway	divided highway
dynamo	generator
estate car	station wagon
gear lever	gear shift
guard (railway)	conductor (railroad)
jack-knife	fishtail
junction	intersection
lay-by	pull-off
left luggage room	baggage room
level crossing	grade crossing
milometer	odometer
motorway	freeway, superhighway, express way
mudguard, wing	fender
number plate	license plate
pavement, footpath	sidewalk
petrol	gasoline, gas
public convenience/toilet	restroom/washroom
railway	railroad
receptionist	desk clerk
return ticket	round-trip ticket
reversing lights	back-up lights
silencer	muffler
single ticket	one-way ticket
sleeping car, pullman	pullman, sleeping car
subway	underpass
sump	oil pan
timetable	schedule
tube, underground	subway

See: **Americanism, Anglicism, UK and US words.**

Trinidadian English

The islands of *Trinidad and Tobago*, with a population of 1.2 million, have been united since 1889 and won their independence from Britain in 1962. The islands have known many inhabitants, Arawaks, Africans, Spanish, French, Dutch, British and Indians. The official language is English, but many people speak a local variety known as *Trinibagianese* and large numbers use **creole** English.

The English in Trinidad and Tobago is non-**rhotic** and has been

influenced in vocabulary by Hindi and other Indian languages (about 37% of the population being of Indian origin).

See: **Caribbean English, West Indian English.**

typescript

The entire *typescript* (TS) of a text intended for publication, including **footnotes** or endnotes, **bibliography** and **quotations,** should be typed with double spacing. The format for a **dissertation** or photo-ready copy differs in having single spacing for the notes, bibliography and indented quotations.

Where possible A4 paper (approximately 12×8.5 inches) should be used and margins should be wide, 1 to 1.5 inches at the top, bottom and sides. There should be about 28 lines to the page and the script should be numbered consecutively from the first page to the last, not chapter by chapter. To guard against loss, it is advisable to type the author's surname before the number on each page. Name and academic address may be required at the beginning or end of the TS but the conventions of individual journals should always be checked.

The title of the article or chapter should be typed at the top of the first page of text in capitals. Neither underlining nor a full stop should be used. The first **paragraph** should not be indented but other paragraphs should be indicated either by indenting the first line five spaces or by doubling the normal space between lines and not indenting. Prose quotations of up to 100 words should be incorporated in the text within quotation marks. Longer quotations should not have quotation marks but should be indented five spaces at the left margin. Spaces should be left after most **punctuation** marks: one after a comma, two after a colon, semi-colon, exclamation mark, question mark and full stop. Two hyphens can be used to indicate a dash and lower case *l* can be used for the figure *1*.

Italics can be indicated by underlining. Titles of books, plays, journals and long poems should be underlined and quotation marks should be used for the titles of other works.

Texts may be organised according to a system of numbered sections and subsections. This method allows references to be inserted immediately as it does not depend on page numbers.

Small corrections may be written or typed in above the line involved but margins should not be used for this purpose. All quotations, notes and references should be checked and an exact copy of the TS should always be kept.

See: **bibliography, dissertation, footnotes, italics, paragraph, quotation.**

U and non-U

U and *non-U* are terms invented in 1954 by the British writer A.S.C. Ross. *U* refers to *upper-class speech* and *non-U* to all the rest. Ross wrote a number of books and articles distinguishing prestigious U forms from stigmatised non-U equivalents. He claimed, for example, that U speakers invariably put the stress on the first syllable of *lamentable*, say *rich* and not *wealthy* and avoid **clichés** (*leave no stone unturned*) and **jargon** (*pilot project*), but he insisted that it was possible to be too affected in speech. For example, he would rule out the use of such a phrase as:

> *beyond a peradventure*

Ross was correct in believing that speakers often reveal their class origins in their speech. His comments are, however, markedly class-ist, although they still carry weight in parts of British society.

If speakers of English are to communicate freely, then certain standards of **pronunciation**, vocabulary and syntax are clearly desir-able. Today, however, these standards are more likely to be advanced by films, radio and television than by a privileged minority.

See: **Received Pronunciation, shibboleth.**

Ugandan English

Uganda was a British protectorate from 1894 until 1962, when it was granted independence. English is the official language of Uganda's 14 million inhabitants and widely used in education, in the media and as a link language between Ugandans of different linguistic back-grounds. English is not widely used among the poor, for whom Swahili is the most useful **lingua franca.**

See: **African English, East African English.**

UK and US grammar

The overlap between the two main varieties of world English is large and increasing. Nevertheless, differences occur in **pronunciation, spelling**, vocabulary and grammar. The main grammatical differ-ences are to be found in the use of adjectives and adverbs, articles, auxiliaries, noun forms, prepositions, pronouns and verb forms.

1 Adjectives and adverbs
(a) Colloquial US **English** frequently uses adjectives where col-loquial UK **English** requires an adverb:

> *He drives **real** fast.*
> *We had a **real** good time.*

(b) *Different* tends to be followed by *from* in UK English and *than* in US English:

This pen is different from that one. (UK)
This pen is different than that one. (US)

(c) Adverbs ending in *-wise* occur more frequently in US English, often with the meaning 'concerning this noun' or 'as far as this noun is concerned':

Foodwise, he's easy to please.
How are we fixed timewise?

The *-wise* adverbs tend to be criticised in both communities.

(d) Speakers of UK English use the present perfect affirmative with the adverbs *already* and *yet*. Many US speakers prefer the simple past:

Have you finished it already/yet? (UK)
Did you finish it already/yet? (US)
I've seen it already. (UK)
I saw it already. (US)

(e) *Momentarily* and *presently* can be used by US speakers to mean 'in a moment' and 'at present':

I'll finish it momentarily.
He is presently in China.

2 Articles
Speakers of both varieties use articles in very similar ways but the following phrases tend to differ:

UK English	US English
be at table	be at the table
be in hospital	be in the hospital
go to university	go to a university
in future	in the future

This is only a tendency, however, and many Irish and Scots speakers also prefer the US forms.

3 Auxiliaries and quasi-modals
(a) *Dare* and *need* are less commonly used as quasi-modals in US English:

UK English	US English
I daren't do it.	I don't dare do it.
You needn't go.	You don't have to go.

(b) The dummy auxiliary *DO* tends to be used differently:

UK English	US English
Have you any wool?	Do you have any wool?
Yes, I have.	Yes, I do.

(*c*) *Ought to* and *used to* tend not to be used as quasi-modals in US English:

UK English	US English
Ought I to go?	Should I go?
I **oughtn't** to have gone.	I shouldn't have gone.
He **usedn't** to be cross.	He didn't use to be cross.

It should be added that many young UK speakers no longer accept *usedn't to* but are unhappy with *didn't use to*.

(*d*) *Shall* is less common than *will* in US English, tending to be limited to proclamations (*There shall be...*) and *Shall we?* suggestions:

UK English	US English
I **shan't** go.	I **won't** go.
We **shall** have to leave.	We **will** have to leave.

(*e*) *Would* is used to denote regular past actions in US English:

We **went** there every day. (UK)
We **would go** there every day. (US)

4 Noun forms

(*a*) Collective nouns are more likely to take a singular verb and singular pronoun substitution in US English:

The government **have** made up **their** mind, **haven't they**? (UK)
The government **has** made up **its** mind, **hasn't it**? (US)

(*b*) Nouns such as *inning(s)*, *math(s)* and *sport(s)* tend to have different forms in the UK and the USA:

It was the best **innings** I've seen all year. (UK)
It was the best **inning** I've seen all year. (US)
He has decided to study **maths**. (UK)
He has decided to study **math**. (US)
She is excellent at **sport**. (UK)
She is excellent at **sports**. (US)

(*c*) The morphemes *-ee* and *-ery* are more productive in US English, providing forms such as:

advisee retiree
crookery fakery

(*d*) Speakers of US English regularly transform phrasal verbs into nouns, producing:

a cook-out   a fly-over   a turn-off

Such nouns are quickly absorbed into UK English.

5 Prepositions

Occasionally, different prepositions are preferred in UK and US English or one variety requires a preposition where the other does not:

UK English	US English
He hid it **behind** the house.	He hid it **in back of** the house.
I haven't seen her **for** weeks.	I haven't seen her **in** weeks.
I live **in** River Street.	I live **on** River Street.
I've tried talking **to** her.	I've tried talking **with** her.
It's five **past** four.	It's five **after** four.
Let's do it **on** Sunday.	Let's do it Sunday.
She threw it **out of** the door.	She threw it **out** the door.
Please fill **in** this form.	Please fill **out** this form.
We'll have to check it.	We'll have to check it **out**.
They were **in** a sale.	They were **on** sale.
Rows A **up to and including** D are reserved for non-smokers.	Rows A **through** D are reserved for non-smokers.
The plane departed **from** Austin.	The plane departed Austin.
They protested **against** the war.	They protested the war.

6 Pronouns

(a) *One* tends to be used more frequently in speech in the UK:

One instinctively knows what to say.

Many Americans would prefer to use *you* in such contexts. When Americans select *one* they can use *he/she* in subsequent clauses. UK speakers are taught to use *one* for all references:

*One should always do what **one** knows is right.* (UK)
*One should always do what **he/she** knows to be right.* (US)

(b) *One another* is much less formal in UK English:

*They really loved **one another** deeply.* (UK)
*They really loved **each other** deeply.* (US)

7 Verb forms

(a) US speakers are less likely to use *to infinitives* after COME, GO, HELP and ORDER:

*Come **to see** me tomorrow.* (UK)
*Come **and see** me tomorrow.* (US)
*She went **to get** it.* (UK)
*She went **and got** it.* (US)

You should help to clean the car. (UK)
You should help clean the car. (US)
We ordered him to be followed. (UK)
We ordered him followed. (US)

(b) US English uses more subjunctive constructions in formal English:

He advised that we should be set free. (UK)
He advised that we be set free. (US)
It is necessary for you to be punished. (UK)
It is necessary that you be punished. (US)

(c) Verb morphology is sometimes different:

dived (UK) *dived/dove* (US)
got (UK) *got/gotten* (US)
learnt (UK) *learned* (US)

The differences highlighted above are not absolute. Many young speakers in the UK now use constructions that their parents would have considered **Americanisms**.

See: **GET, pronunciation, quasi-modal, spelling, UK and US words, UK English, US English, yet.**

UK and US words

The many vocabulary differences between UK and US English can be categorised under three main headings:
1 Words which are known only in one country:

Oxbridge (pertaining to Oxford and Cambridge Universities) (UK)
panda car (police patrol car) (UK)
odometer (milometer) (US)
Phi Beta Kappa (academic fraternity) (US)

2 Words that have different meanings in the two countries:

chaps (UK men, US leggings)
vest (UK undergarment, US sleeveless garment)

3 Words that are widely recognised as being equivalent:

Autumn and *Fall*
candidature and *candidacy*
centenary and *centennial*
entitled and *titled*
firework and *firecracker*

The major semantic fields in which differences occur are: **Business and Finance, Clothes, Education, Food and Drink, Household and Accommodation** and **Travel**. Each of these has a separate entry.

UK English

The term *United Kingdom* comprehends England, Scotland, Wales, Northern Ireland, the Isle of Man and the Channel Islands. It is preferred in this book to *Great Britain*, which denotes the political union of England, Scotland and Wales only. The population of just over 56 million is more multicultural and multilingual than it has ever been, but, because the census forms do not ask questions about race, it is impossible to estimate how many ethnic minorities exist in Britain. There are, however, large settled communities (1% and above) of **Gypsies**, Indians, Pakistanis, Southern Irish and West Indians, as well as smaller communities of Chinese, Cypriots, Maltese and Poles.

There are more regional and social **dialects** in the UK than in any other part of the English-speaking world. Although education and the media are exerting a levelling influence on the language of all, it is still possible with the majority of people to estimate their regional origin and their social standing from the way they speak. Each region has a spectrum of dialects. In Yorkshire, for example, *thou/thee* can occur as a marker of intimacy and as a means of indicating one's superiority:

If thou thees me, I'll thee thou and see how thou likest it.

the regular past progressive is:

I/you/he/she/it/they were stood

and vocabulary items such as:

anyroads (anyway)
bits and bobs (bits and pieces)
leyk (play)

are still widely used.

UK English is one of the two main varieties of world English. The standard language is the medium of education throughout the country and, although there is no standard pronunciation, RP (**Received Pronunciation**) is the most prestigious **accent** and the one that is used for national broadcasts and official announcements. RP is also a prestige **norm** in many countries which were previously part of the British Empire.

See: **accent, Anglo-English, Anglo-Romani, Irish English, pronunciation, Scottish English, spelling, UK and US words, Welsh English, West Indian English**.

Ulster Scots

Ulster Scots is a variety of **Scottish English** spoken in Northern Ireland. It is the mother tongue of many of the Ulster people whose ancestors came from Scotland. Like Scottish English, it is **rhotic**, uses fewer vowel contrasts than RP and uses /x/, a palatal fricative, in such words as *Augher* /ɔxər/ and *lough* /lɔx/. The vocabulary of Ulster Scots is still recognisably Scottish:

> *chookie* (chicken)
> *dunt* (thump)
> *forby* (as well as)
> *hallion* (a clumsy fool)
> *neb* (beak, nose and mouth)

The features that distinguish the grammar of Scottish English from other British varieties are found also in Ulster Scots. These include the use of the negator *na/nae* after the auxiliary:

> He **diznae** *know a parlour from a midden.*

and the use of *aye* as an intensive:

> *She's* **aye** *throughother.* (She's very untidy.)

The term *Scotch Irish* is used in the USA for people from Ulster.

See: **Hiberno-English, Irish English, Scottish English.**

understatement

Understatement is a type of **irony** in which something is deliberately described as being less than it really is. It is common in colloquial contexts:

> *It's not half cold.* (It's extremely cold.)
> *I can live with it.* (I like it a lot.)

In literary contexts, understatement is formally known as the rhetorical device of **meiosis**. Shakespeare uses it in *Romeo and Juliet* when Mercutio (Act 3 Scene 1) describes his wound:

> ... *'tis not so deep as a well, nor so wide as a churchdoor,*
> *but 'tis enough, 'twill serve...*

See: **irony, litotes, meiosis.**

unique

Unique, from Latin *unicus* (*unus* = one), is not a **gradable adjective**. Logically, something cannot be more or less unequalled, and therefore expressions such as:

rather unique
more unique
most unique
very unique

are absurd. However, logic is not always adhered to in usage, and the increased occurrence of forms such as *more unique* suggests that its meaning is changing from 'unequalled' to 'remarkable' or 'notable'. (A similar change affected *singular*.) Such a semantic shift could rob us of a useful distinction. We have many words for 'notable', few for 'having no like or equal', and consequently there is resistance to the change.

See: **adjective, gradable**.

universals of language

The fact that all languages are capable of being translated into all others suggests that, at some level, all human languages are similar. These similarities may be accounted for in terms of biology: all human beings seem to be predisposed to acquire a specific type of communication system. Support for a 'biological blueprint' may be found in the regularity of the onset of language and the speed with which mother tongues are acquired. All children of whatever background pass through a number of maturational stages as they learn the language of their environment.

Human languages all share certain phonological, syntactic and semantic characteristics. They make use of vowels and consonants and of word order; they all allow discussion of past, present and future events; they all have methods of indicating singularity and plurality, location, possession and pronominal reference; they all have rules for deriving certain structures from others; and they all evince creativity.

Other types of linguistic universals have been suggested, including the notions that all languages have noun phrases and verb phrases, and that within languages there are certain types of probabilities. For example, if a language has the surface order:

Predicate + Subject + Object

it is likely that the adjective will follow the noun. Thus, in Gaelic, we find:

Chuala mé Seán.—I heard John. (Heard I John)

and:

Seán mór—Big John (John big)

If, however, the language patterns like English:

Subject + Predicate + Object

then it is likely that the adjective will precede the noun.

Most linguists agree that there are linguistic universals, but there is still debate as to their extent and exact specification.

See: **acquisition of language, Behaviourism, transformational grammar.**

US English

The *United States of America* is made up of 50 states and the District of Columbia. Its population of over 232 million makes it the largest English-speaking country in the world. As in the UK, there are many regional and social **dialects**, but a regional **accent** is less of a social stigma in the USA than in the UK and there is no accent which is as unmarked for regional origin as RP is in the UK.

There are three main speech areas in the USA:

1 *eastern*, which includes New England and New York

2 *southern*, which includes Alabama, Arkansas, the Carolinas, Florida, Georgia, Kentucky, Louisiana, Mississippi and Virginia

3 *General American*, which includes the rest

Such divisions are to some extent arbitrary and oversimplified (many speakers from Texas, for example, have much more in common with speakers from Kentucky than they do with speakers from Hawaii), but they reflect patterns of settlement in the USA.

The most widely described accent is GAE (General American English) and this implies the accents of educated speakers throughout the USA, the accents used by national newscasters.

US English is one of the main varieties of English in the world. It is the most influential variety in parts of Central America and the Caribbean, South America, the Philippines, Liberia and Japan and its influence is being felt by most countries which watch US films or television, listen to Voice of America radio or read American publications.

See: **Black English, pronunciation, spelling, UK and US grammar, UK and US words.**

usage

As long as people continue to speak English, users will continue to worry about which *usages* are correct and which are not. Often there is a simple answer:

between you and I

is incorrect because prepositions take the accusative form of the pronoun, thus:

between us between you and me between him and me
from us from you and me from him and me

Occasionally, there is nothing *linguistically* wrong with an expression but it may be unacceptable because it is stylistically inappropriate. The idiom:

snuffed it

is as grammatically correct as:

died

but would not be acceptable in an expression of sympathy.

Words and phrases can come into the language because there is a need for them. An *ummer* is a useful term for a hesitant speaker, and most adults have been involved in *a catch 22 situation*. Such words and phrases are often criticised because they can be overused and reduced to the status of **cliché**.

Other items of language, borrowed phrases such as:

comme il faut (as it should be done)
infra dig (beneath one's dignity)
verb sap (a word is enough to the wise)

are rarely criticised as 'poor usage' but when they are deliberately used to stress one's educational background, they can be as unacceptable as slang.

See: **'chestnuts', cliché, purist, slang.**

utterance

A distinction is frequently made between an *utterance* and a **sentence**. An *utterance* is a speech event. It is produced by a specific individual at a specific time and in certain circumstances. It is often defined as 'a stretch of speech before and after which there is silence', a definition that encompasses monosyllabic morphemes such as *Sh!* and lengthy monologues. It also includes language use such as the following:

I'm a not too clear a clear about you didn't actually a specify you didn't and I'm not clear what you said a meant really

which was uttered by an educated speaker without appreciable pause. Such utterances are often hard to transcribe because they do not follow the norms of the written language.

See: **competence and performance, sentence, speech and writing.**

Vanuatuan English

Vanuatu (formerly New Hebrides) is a group of small islands in the southwest Pacific. Between 1897 and 1980 the islands were governed jointly by Britain and France, and English and French were the official languages. In 1980 Vanuatu with its population of 100,000 became the 44th member of the Commonwealth.

Although English and French were the official languages for over eighty years, the effective language of wider communication among islanders and expatriate settlers was *Bislama*, an English-related pidgin, similar in origin and form to Tok Pisin, the **lingua franca** of Papua New Guinea. Since independence, the three languages—English, French and Bislama—have been given official status and Bislama is widely used in commerce, government and international dealings. The norm for standard English is set by the local anglophone settlers, many of whom have been educated in Australia or New Zealand. Bislama is being expanded lexically and syntactically and is used for one-third of the items in the most widely-read local paper, *Tam Tam*:

Bill i pas blong mekim jenis	*Bill passed to make changes*
Paliamen hemi appruvum finis Bill	*Parliament has just approved a Bill*
blong jenisim samfala wod mo	*to change some of the wording*
toktok insaed long Konstitusem.	*in the constitution.*

See: **Papua New Guinean English, pidgins and creoles.**

variable

The word *variable* is used in three main ways in language studies:

1 Word **classes** in English are occasionally subdivided into those which are *variable*, that is, capable of expressing distinctions by a change of form:

bad worse worst
boy boys
build builds building built
I me mine

and those which are *invariable*:

and but
in on

2 Words are occasionally described as being *free variables* when they can substitute for each other in all or almost all contexts. *Till* and *until* are free variables:

Wait till/until I arrive.

3 William Labov used the term to apply to phonological, lexical and syntactic variation that correlated with class, style, age, sex, regional or religious background. For example, most speakers vary in their pronunciation of -*ing* forms. In rapid colloquial speech, many say *walkin'* although they would use the more correct pronunciation if they were reading or talking formally. Equally, most speakers have a set of vocabulary items which would only be used in intimate circles and which might provide information on the user's background. A New Yorker, for example, who spoke of *boychik* (lad) or *kiddush* (blessing) would be likely to be Jewish. Syntactic variables are also widespread. In a formal situation, speakers approximate to the standard norms:

*I would have **gone**...*

but the same speakers may use:

*I would have **went**...*

when they are not exercising conscious control over their performance.

The variability which is found at all levels of language and which usually corresponds to social differences can also help explain how and why languages change.

See: **shibboleth, sociolinguistics.**

variety

The term *variety* is used to mean a subdivision of a language. This subdivision may be regional (e.g. Appalachian English), occupational (e.g. medical English), sex-related (e.g. women's language), stylistic (e.g. religious English) or may reflect the age of the speaker (a seventeen-year-old girl rarely sounds like a middle-aged woman). Because *variety* can comprehend such different subdivisions, from an entire **dialect** to occupationally-influenced vocabulary, many scholars avoid the term, preferring to use *dialect* for regional usage, **register** for socially-motivated styles and *field* for distinct subject matter.

See: **dialect, register, style.**

verb

A *verb* has traditionally been defined as a 'doing' word and, although this definition does not comprehend **copula** verbs:

*She **is** a teacher.*
*He **seemed** tired.*

it is often useful. A more adequate definition can be based on formal criteria. Verbs can change their form in response to subjects:

I/you/we/they sing
he/she/it sings

time:

He sings every day.
He sang yesterday.

aspect:

He is singing.
He has sung.

voice:

He was singing.
It was sung.

and **mood**:

Sing!
If he sang tomorrow, he'd miss his flight.

Verbs can be subdivided in various ways:
1 They can be described in terms of the number of nominals with which they habitually occur. Verbs like *ARRIVE, DIE, DISAPPEAR* require only one nominal, in the subject slot:

John *arrived.*
Mary *died.*

These are called 'one-place' verbs and they are **intransitive**, that is, they do not take an object nor can they occur in a passive construction. Other verbs like *ADD, KILL, SEE* tend to require two nominals, a subject and an object:

The chef *added* **the flour.**
John *killed* **Peter.**

These are called 'two-place' verbs; they are **transitive** and can occur in passive constructions:

The flour was added (by the chef).
Peter was killed (by John).

A number of other verbs such as *GIVE, MAKE, WRITE* can require three nominals, a subject, a direct object and an indirect object:

John *gave* **him the packet.**
Mary *made* **him his favourite meal.**

These are called 'three-place' verbs; they are transitive and can occur in passive **transformations**:

> *The packet was given to him (by John).*
> *His favourite meal was made for him (by Mary).*

Three-place verbs do not always need three nominals. WRITE, for example, frequently occurs with both one and two nominals:

> *John writes.*
> *Mary writes stories.*

although it might be argued that a direct and indirect object are always implicit.

2 A number of verbs such as *BOIL, RING* and *OPEN* appear to occur equally often with one and two nominals:

> *The water boiled. John boiled the water.*
> *The bell rang. John rang the bell.*

The term **ergative** (from a Greek verb meaning 'cause') is applied to the **causative** relationship that exists between such pairs of sentences as:

> *The plate broke.*
> *She broke the plate* (i.e. caused the plate to break).

where the subject of an intransitive verb becomes the object of the same verb and a new subject is introduced as the agent or cause of the action.

3 Verbs may be either **main** (or lexical):

> *She **sang** and **danced** and **had** a wonderful time.*

or **auxiliary**:

> *She **can** sing and **should** dance but she **won't**.*

4 Verbs may be either **finite** (requiring a subject) or non-finite (not taking a subject). The non-finite forms are the to **infinitive**, the present **participle** and the past participle:

> *to go*
> *going*
> *gone*

All other forms are finite:

> *(they) go*
> *(he) goes*
> *(she) went*

5 Verbs that take complements and not objects are known as copulas:

She is a teacher.
She felt a fool.
She looks nice.
She seems angry.

See: **auxiliary, copula, dummy subject, ergative, gerund, modality, verb phrase.**

verb phrase

The term *verb phrase* is used in three main ways in English:
  1 It can refer to a **main verb** preceded by one or more **auxiliaries**:

(he) may watch
(he) may have been being watched

The pattern for such verb phrases is:

Modal + HAVE + BE_1 + BE_2 + Headverb

a formula which may be interpreted as follows:

First position: Modal + base form of the following verb:

(he) may watch

Second position: HAVE + past participle of the following verb:

(he) has/had watched

Third position: BE + present participle of the following verb:

(he) is/was watching

Fourth position: BE + past participle of the following verb:

(he) is/was watched

with the maximum verb phrase containing four auxiliaries and one lexical verb.
  Verb phrases may be finite:

(he) may have been watching

or non-finite:

having gone
to be seen

2 It can refer to the verb + all that follows it in a sentence:

She sang.
She will sing a song.

She will attempt to sing that song tomorrow morning at nine o'clock.

This usage is particularly widespread in transformational accounts where 'Sentence' is defined as 'Noun Phrase + Verb Phrase'.

3 It is often applied to **phrasal verbs** where a group of words functions like a single verb:

You won't believe what he got up to (did) *this time.*
We ran into (met) *each other yesterday.*

See: **auxiliary, transformational grammar, verb.**

verbosity

Verbosity, from Latin *verbum* (word), implies the use of more words than are necessary:

He crawled like a child on his hands and knees.

Verbosity is a common feature of speech but is less acceptable in writing. It is perhaps a comment on users of the language that we have many more terms for styles involving too many words than we have for styles that are spare.

See: **circumlocution, periphrasis, pleonasm, redundancy, tautology.**

vernacular

The term *vernacular* derives from Latin *verna* (slave). It is used to refer to:
    1 the native language or nonstandard **dialect** of an area
    2 languages without a writing system or written tradition
    3 local varieties of a language, such as 'the Liverpool vernacular'

vocabulary

The *vocabulary* of a language is a comprehensive list of the **words** that occur in it. Often, these words are arranged alphabetically in **dictionaries,** where **definitions** and **etymologies** are also supplied. The term is also applied to the stock of words used by a specific writer or group of speakers in a particular period. When applied to an individual, a distinction is usually made between:
    1 an *active vocabulary,* that is, the words actually used

2 a *passive vocabulary*, which contains words that are understood but rarely used. Many language users would never say *contumely* or *desuetude*, for example (and may not even be certain of their pronunciation), but would recognise such words and might use them in writing.

See: dictionary, lexicography, lexicon.

voice

The word *voice* is used in two ways in descriptions of language.
  1 It occurs in descriptions of **verbs** and sentences where a distinction is made between **active voice**:

She bought the farm.

and **passive voice**:

The farm was bought (by her).

2 In **phonetics**, a distinction is made between:
  (a) voiced sounds such as vowels
  (b) voiced consonants such as /b,n,z/, which are produced while the vocal cords are vibrating
  (c) voiceless sounds such as /f,p,s/, which are produced without vibration of the vocal cords.

See: active voice, passive voice, phoneme, verb.

vulgarism

A *vulgarism*, from Latin *vulgus* (common people), is a word, phrase or expression that is stigmatised as coarse or substandard. These may vary with time: *kid* (child), *sheila* (female) and *whatever* (whatever) have been classified as *vulgarisms* although many speakers would now classify *kid* as colloquial.
  The term *vulgarism*, as its etymology suggests, has frequently been associated with class distinctions and nonstandard usages such as:

I seen him.
You shoulda went.

Today, however, it is most frequently applied to any usage that is coarse, offensive or stylistically too colloquial for its context. The items in bold in the following sentences may be regarded as *vulgarisms*:

She told him to f— off.

*They were determined to exclude **yobbos** and vandals.*
*Both the definition and the etymology were **way off beam**.*

See: **barbarism, colloquial English, slang, taboo words.**

wake

Many speakers are uncertain about which form of *WAKE* to use, mainly because there are four verbs (*WAKE, AWAKE, WAKEN, AWAKEN*) which have overlapping uses and meanings.

In UK and UK-influenced **English,** *WAKE* is an **irregular verb** with the past time form *woke* and the past participle *woken*:

I woke up suddenly.
He was woken by the noise.

In **US English,** the verb can be irregular, as in the UK, but there is a growing tendency for it to be regularised:

They waked us at noon.

The forms *wake, woke* and *woken* are still, however, the preferred forms throughout the world. WAKE can be used in both transitive and intransitive constructions:

I woke her (up) immediately.
He woke (up) at nine.

AWAKE is usually treated as an irregular verb (*awoke, awoken*) although some US speakers regularise it (*awaked*). It can also be used in transitive and intransitive constructions:

It awoke old, forgotten memories.
She awoke to find that he had gone.

As a verb, AWAKE is most frequently used in the past tense, but it also occurs as a predicative adjective:

It's no use. I'm wide awake now!
They're bound to be awake at this time.

WAKEN is a regular verb and shares with WAKE the meanings of 'rouse someone from sleep' and 'be in an alert state':

I tried to waken him.

WAKEN is often thought to be more literary than WAKE.

AWAKEN is a regular verb and is much less frequently used than the other verbs:

That noise would awaken the dead.

Like WAKEN it is often thought to be literary.

In certain parts of the world, WAKE can mean 'keep a vigil over the dead' and this WAKE is regular and transitive:

He was waked in his own home.

although the noun is probably more widely used than the verb, as in the following adage:

The sleep that knows no waking is followed by the wake that knows no sleeping.

See: **a- words.**

-ward, -wards

The use of final *s* with adjectives and adverbs ending in -*ward* is declining:

a backward glance
He looked forward not backward.

It is now more usual to use the forms without *s* as in:

backward   forward
homeward   inward
outward   toward

Although the forms in -*s* are still acceptable, it seems likely that preference for -*wards* will become a marker of region and/or age.

See: **among, while.**

well

The word *well* has many uses in English. It can be:
1 a noun:

*They need to build artesian **wells**.*

2 a verb:

*The tears **welled** up.*

3 a **discourse marker**:

Well, I just stood there.

4 an interjection often indicating disapproval:

Well! I wouldn't have expected this.

or surprise:

> *Well! Well! Well! So that's what you've been up to!*

5 an **adverb**, with *better* and *best* as comparative and superlative forms:

> *He is **well** dressed now but he used to be the **best** dressed man in town.*

6 an **adjective**, with *better* and as its comparative form:

> *He's not **well** today but may be **better** tomorrow.*

Well is widely used as a predicative adjective:

> *I'm very **well**, thank you.*

but is quite rare in attributive position:

> *He's not a **well** man.*

See: **adjective, adverb.**

Welsh English

The Celts now known as the *Welsh* (*Wealh* is an **Old English** word meaning 'Celt, Briton, foreigner') occupy an area in the south-west of Britain, although Welsh-derived place names are found to the south in Cornwall, and to the north in Cumbria and Scotland, suggesting that Welsh speakers were once more widespread throughout the UK. Almost all of the 2.75 million people in Wales have a good command of English, although as many as half a million have Welsh as a mother tongue and so speak English as a second language. As one might expect, therefore, the English spoken by many in Wales is strongly influenced by Welsh.

Phonology
1 The intonation of Welsh, where the voice often rises for the second syllable of a disyllabic word, is carried over into *Welsh English* (WE), causing lilting, sing-song patterns.
2 **Assimilation** and **elision** are frequent with *his song* being realised as /hɪs sɒŋ/ and with *That's wrong, then* being heard as /æts rɒŋ ɛn/.
3 WE has fewer diphthongs and more monophthongs than RP. In particular, /eɪ/ is often realised as /e/ and /oʊ/ as /o/.
4 The sound /jʊ/ as in *situation* /sɪtjʊeɪʃən/ is often realised as /u/, thus /sɪtueʃən/.
5 WE is non-**rhotic**.
6 The consonants /t,d,n,l,s,z/ are often dental and not alveolar.
7 The voiceless plosives /p,t,k/ are strongly aspirated and the

fricatives /f,s/ are also aspirated when they occur at the beginning of a word.

8 WE has a voiceless alveolar lateral fricative /ɬ/ which occurs in words such as *Llangollen*. (Non-Welsh speakers can approximate to this sound by saying *hlan + goh + hlin*.)

9 WE has a voiceless alveolar roll /r̥/ in place names beginning with *Rh* such as *Rhondda*. (To approximate to the pronunciation, one can say *hron + dha*.)

10 Unvoiced medial vowels tend to be lengthened so that *chapel* sounds like *chap + pel* and *pity* like *pit + ty*.

Vocabulary

The influence of Welsh on the vocabulary of English has not been fully explored. Among the well-known borrowings are:

> *bard*
> *cog* (part of a wheel)
> *cromlech* (megalithic tomb)
> *eisteddfod* (festival, plural *eisteddfodau*)
> *penguin* (head + white)

More pervasive than borrowings is the use of Welsh names, such as *Bronwen, Gladys, Glyn, Gwen(llian), Gwyn, Megan, Olwyn, Owen*, and the Welsh formula for surnames *ap + father's name* has produced *Bevan* (ap Evan), *Powell* (ap Howell), *Price* (ap Rees) and *Pugh* (ap Hugh).

Influence from Welsh can be seen also in the use of the address term *bach*:

> *Need your rest, **bach**.*

which is sometimes replaced by *boy*:

> *Need your rest, **boy**.*

and in informal or intimate contexts by *boyo*:

> *Need your rest, **boyo**!*

Again, as in Welsh, the term *stranger* can be used for any outsider, even one from the next village:

> *You're like us, boy—don't like **strangers**.*

Grammar

The ways in which the syntax of WE differs from other types of UK English depends on the degree of influence from Welsh. Nevertheless, the following characteristics are found in the English of the majority of people in Wales.

1 An extensive use of *well* as a preface to an answer:

> ***Well***, *beats me.*

2 In informal speech the subject pronoun and the auxiliary are often deleted:

[I] *Could manage it with you, Parry. Couldn't do it without help.*
[Do you] *Need help, boy?*
[You have] *Earned it, boy.*

3 The filler *look you* occurs frequently in conversations and explanations:

It's hard work, look you.
Everyone stayed out, look you, because miners got to stick together.

4 The structure 'There's + adjective + now' often occurs:

There's happy now. (We/they/you are content now.)

See: **Celtic influences.**

West African English

West Africa comprises fourteen countries, Senegal, Gambia, Guinea-Bissau, Guinea, Sierra Leone, Liberia, Ivory Coast, Ghana, Togo, Benin, Nigeria, Cameroon, Equatorial Guinea and Gabon, and has a population approaching 140 million. English is an official language in Gambia, Sierra Leone, Liberia, Ghana, Nigeria and Cameroon and is the most widely-taught second language of the other eight countries. In spite of the multilingualism of the area (with over 1,000 indigenous languages) and five different colonial legacies (British, French, German, Portuguese and Spanish), there is a homogeneity about all the varieties used. This is because the mother tongues of West Africa have many phonological and syntactic similarities, and because there is a chain of mutually-intelligible coastal **pidgins and creoles** from Gambia to Gabon which influences the English of the region.

The main types of English spoken in the region are:

(a) the English of expatriates (mainly American, British, Dutch, Indian and Lebanese)

(b) Standard *West African English* (always a second language)

(c) the mother-tongue **creoles** of Liberia (Merico) and Sierra Leone (Krio) and of the Krio-speaking settlers in Gambia, Nigeria, Cameroon and Equatorial Guinea

(d) the pidgin Englishes of the coastal regions and of many urban communities

(e) broken English

The variety described here is (b) because it is the language of prestige and advancement and the variety most frequently used by the media.

Phonology

1 Standard West African English (SWAE) is non-**rhotic.**
2 There are no central vowels or centring diphthongs:

better is realised as /beta/
bird is realised as /bed/
but is realised as /bet/
here is realised as /hia/
fire is realised as /faia/
glare is realised as /glea/

3 There are fewer vowel contrasts than in RP with a strong tendency to realise:

beat and *bit* as /bit/
hat and *heart* as /hat/

4 The narrow diphthongs in *gate* and *goat* tend to be monophthongised to /get/ and /got/.
5 /θ, ð/ tend to be replaced by /t,d/:

thief is frequently /tif/ and *father* is /fada/

6 Intrusive vowels are introduced into word-initial **consonant clusters:**

straight is frequently /setret/

and word-final clusters are often reduced:

sand is frequently /san/

Vocabulary

1 Each area has its own set of lexical items, especially those drawn from local languages, but the following words are widely used throughout the region:

akara (beancake)
balance (small change)
branch at (stop off at, go via)
bush (remote place, outlandish, primitive)
chop (food, eat)
danshiki (type of shirt)
dash (tip, something for nothing)
fufu (pounded yam/corn)
juju (magic, witchcraft)

2 Many local idioms occur:

be in state (be pregnant)
enstool (instal a chief)
have long legs (have influence)

3 In francophone zones, many French words are adapted into English including:

dossier (CV, file)
mission (trip)
titularize (confirm, establish)

Grammar

Many West Africans speak and write standard international English but many also use constructions which are common to many non-native users of English. These include:

1 problems with articles:

*I bought **one** fine car.*
There was series of rehearsals.

2 the tendency to use uncountable nouns as countable:

***Furnitures** are now being manufactured in Accra.*

3 problems with tense and modals:

*I **have gone** to Jos two years ago.*
*You **would** (i.e. will) please buy this book for me.*

4 nonstandard phrasal verbs:

*She **has taken in**.* (become pregnant)
*I can't **voice out** my real opinion.*

5 the use of *is it/isn't it/not so* as universal **tags**:

*You are tired, **isn't it**?*
*You did your best, **not so**?*

In all the anglophone countries of West Africa, the indigenous languages are being studied and described, but English is the chosen language for advertising, the civil service, education, government, the media and much local literature.

See: **African English, Cameroon English, Nigerian English, pidgins and creoles.**

West Indian English

The term *West Indian English* is used to refer to two related phenomena:

1 the spectrum of Englishes found in the Caribbean
2 a similar spectrum found in Britain and, to a lesser extent, in Canada, among people of West Indian origin

The spectrum ranges from creole English, through creole-influenced English to standard English with regional accents. West Indians in the Caribbean and Canada are increasingly influenced by US norms, whereas West Indians in Britain reflect British standards and conventions.

Many West Indians speak and write standard English but working-class communities still show influences from Caribbean creoles. Among such influences are the tendencies to:

1 substitute *t* and *d* for /θ, ð/ producing:

tin for *thin* and *den* for *then*

2 palatalise *g* and *k* producing:

gyaadin for *garden* and *kyat* for *cat*

3 substitute *n* for *ng* in present participles:

dancin' singin' waitin'

4 simplify **consonant clusters** at the end of syllables:

yesterday > *yesaday*
band > *ban*

This tendency frequently results in the past tense of regular verbs sounding like the unmarked verb form:

banned > *ban*
laughed > *laugh*
screamed > *scream*

5 use vocabulary items which refer specifically to West Indian food:

calalu (green vegetable)

or culture:

nancy (spider hero of many tale cycles)

or which indicate the influence of African languages:

nyam (eat)

6 use **intonation** to distinguish between statements and questions:

You got trouble?

and between *can* and *can't*:

Di teacher doan seem to know dat di chile kyaan unnastan. (can't understand)

7 do without BE as both **copula** and **auxiliary**:

She a fine scholar.
We happy most of the time.

8 use **serial verbs**:

Take de ting go now.

West Indians, like other groups, reflect the speech patterns of their environment and their peers. In Britain, many West Indians continue to live in mainly West Indian communities, thus reinforcing West Indian speech patterns.

See: **Caribbean English, creole, pidgins and creoles.**

while, whilst

There is no semantic distinction in the UK between *while* and *whilst*:

*You can use the house **while/whilst** we're on holiday.*

but many young speakers regard *whilst* as archaic or literary:

They strayed and played and had no cares
***Whilst** all the world was young.*

Whilst is very rare in US English.
While can function as a noun:

*Wait a little **while**.*

and as a subordinating **conjunction** meaning 'during the time that':

*Sit down **while** I read the instructions.*

and 'although, whereas':

***While** sunshine is good for everyone, too much can be harmful.*

See: **among, conjunction.**

who, whom

The uses of these pronouns differ according to syntax and style. *Who* is a subject pronoun:

***Who** is that?*
*I couldn't see **who** was talking.*

and *whom* an object pronoun, that is, the form which functions as the object of a verb or which follows a preposition:

***Whom** did you see?*
*To **whom** did you give it?*

In theory, therefore, *who* and *whom* are variants which reflect case and parallel the usage of *they* and *them*:

> *Who did it? They did it.*
> *Whom did you see? Did you see them?*
> *With whom will you go? Will you go with them?*

(It will be noted, however, that *whom* is normally fronted.)
In colloquial speech, *who* is frequently substituted for *whom*:

> *Who did you go with?*

but this is still not fully acceptable in the written medium.

See: **case, pronoun, relative clause.**

who's, whose

These forms are sometimes confused although the rules that control their use are simple:
Who's is the reduced form of *who is*:

> *Who's that?*

Whose can be used as a possessive adjective:

> *Whose coat is that?*

and as a pronoun:

> *Tell me whose it is.*

See: **apostrophe.**

with

With is a **preposition** which has varied uses in English. It can mean 'in the company of':

> *I went there with Bob.*

'in opposition to':

> *He often fights with his brother.*

'in agreement with':

> *She's with us on the subject of pollution.*

and 'in the direction of':

> *The visiting team played with the wind.*

With can also be used to indicate the instrument involved in, or the cause of, an action:

You hit me **with** *a stone.*
Jay was numb **with** *grief.*

to imply that actions or events occurred at the same time:

She drove off **with** *the radio blaring.*

and to indicate cause:

With *the children in school, she found that she had a lot of free time.*

See: **case grammar, preposition.**

word

Although most speakers have an intuitive awareness of what a *word* is, it is not an easy concept to define. We would all agree that *book* and *case* are words but there might well be disagreement as to whether *bookcase* is one word or two. And although *a* and *computer* are both words, they function differently in that the former is unlikely to occur in isolation.

No definition of *word* is entirely satisfactory but the following subdivisions help:

1 An *orthographic* word is a group of letters with a space on either side. Thus, there are fourteen orthographic words in the previous sentence. Orthographic words can only occur in writing. The equivalent in speech is a *phonological* word, that is, a sound or group of sounds which can be spoken in isolation. In science fiction films, robots frequently insert pauses between words:

The...task...is...finished.

2 A *morphological* word relies only on form. Thus *take* and *takes* are two morphological words because they have different forms. Alternatively, *key* is one morphological word, whether it means a 'metal object for opening a door' or a 'solution to a problem'.

3 A *lexical* word or *lexeme* comprehends all the morphological variants of nouns, verbs, adjectives and adverbs. Thus:

book books
buy buys buying bought
big bigger biggest

would be regarded as three lexical words.

4 A *semantic* word is defined in terms of meaning. Thus *ear* mean-

ing 'organ of hearing' and *ear* meaning 'segment of grain' can be regarded as different semantic words.

The term *weasel word* implies the use of a word or words to avoid making a forthright statement about an issue. Politicians are often adept at using weasel words:

Q. *What is your opinion of the recent massacre in Beirut?*
A. *That's a very interesting question. It would appear that the full evidence is not available. Of course, no one can condone violence, violence perpetrated for the wrong reasons...*

See: **doublespeak, euphemism, morpheme.**

word formation

Word formation is a collective term for the processes by which new words are introduced into the language. The main processes (which are described in separate entries) are:

1 **acronyms** (*SALT* < Strategic Arms Limitations Talks)
2 **back formation** (*gatecrash* < gatecrasher)
3 **blending** (*aggrovoke* < aggravate + provoke)
4 **borrowing** (*ersatz* < German *ersatz* meaning 'substitute')
5 **calquing** (*superman* < German *Übermensch*)
6 **clipping** (*zoo* < zoological garden)
7 **coining** (*jabberwocky* created by Lewis Carroll)
8 **compounding** (*bankrate*)
9 **derivation** (*unwisely*)
10 **folk etymology** (*Welsh rabbit* < Welsh rarebit)
11 **functional shift** (*a high*)
12 **sound symbolism** (*bang, crash, wallop*)
13 toponyms—from **place names** (*cashmere* < Kashmir, *nylon* < N(ew) Y(ork) + Lon(don)).

word order

Word order implies arranging words into larger units. In highly inflected languages such as Latin, word order can be flexible because case endings indicate relationships. Thus, irrespective of the order of the words *nauta, puellam* and *amat*:

Puellam nauta amat.
Nauta puellam amat.
Amat puellam nauta.

we know that:

The sailor loves the girl.

In languages which have little or no **inflection,** word order is essential
for distinguishing between:

The sailor loves the girl.

and:

The girl loves the sailor.

In English, the normal **sentence** order is:

(S) P (O) (C) (A)

where the P(redicate) unit is essential, but S(ubject), O(bject), C(om-
plement) and A(djunct) are optional, and where A is the most mobile
of the units involved. Thus we can have such sentences as:

Try! —P
We try. —S P
We try everything. —S P O
We always try everything. —S A P O
I made him happy. —S P O C
I made him happy for a while. —S P O C A

Normal word order can be changed for stylistic or poetic effect:

Him I made happy. —O S P C
We three kings of orient are. —S C P

Such changes often involve a change of focus, emphasising the item
which has been moved from its regular position.
    Different word order can often signal different meanings:

*I **still** don't drink* (implication 'I never have').
*I don't **still** drink* (implication 'I used to').

and such differences are apparent in the following headline:

His mind was strong but his body weak.

from which the reader can correctly deduce:

He died.

If the headline had been:

His body was weak but his mind strong.

the implication would be:

He lived.

See: **foregrounding, sentence.**

yes/no questions

There are two types of **questions** in English, questions such as:

Are you there?
He told you?

which require the answer *yes* or *no* and are known as *yes/no questions* and questions such as:

When did they arrive?

which require answers other than *yes/no* and which are called *Wh-questions*.

In parts of the world where English is not a native language *yes/no* questions involving negatives often cause problems. Many speakers in Fiji, Papua New Guinea, India and parts of Africa use *yes* to imply:

What you have said is correct.

and *no* to imply:

What you have said is not correct.

Thus, if A breaks a plate and B exclaims:

You didn't break another plate?

A may truthfully reply:

No.

See: **question**.

yet

Yet usually functions as an **adverb**. When used in sentence-final position, it is approximately equivalent to 'up to now':

I haven't found it yet.

In more formal circumstances *yet* occurs after *not*:

*I have **not yet** found it.*

When *yet* occurs medially in an affirmative statement it can have negative implications:

*I've **yet** to discover a satisfactory solution.* (i.e. So far I have not discovered a satisfactory solution.)

In formal styles, *yet* can occur as a **conjunction** with the meaning of 'but' or 'nevertheless':

We have tried. Yet, in spite of trying, we have failed.

Some speakers experience difficulty in distinguishing the adverbs *yet*, *still* and *already*. *Yet* is used when we talk about something we expect to happen:

He hasn't arrived yet (but he is expected).

Still is used to imply that the action is continuing:

They are still talking.

Already implies that something has happened earlier than might have been expected and often implies surprise:

Have you finished it already? That was quick.

See: **UK and US English.**

Yiddish influences

Yiddish is an abbreviation for *yidish daytsh* (Jewish German). It is a **creole** derived from Hebrew and German and was widely used in Jewish communities in Eastern Europe. Yiddish has been carried to America, Australia, Britain and South Africa by Jews who migrated from Eastern Europe, and it is one of the official languages of Israel.

Yiddish influences were originally limited to the English of people who had spoken Yiddish as a mother tongue but it can now be detected in the English of New Yorkers (approximately 25% of New York's population is of Jewish origin), of US speakers generally and in other parts of the world with sizable Jewish communities.

Yiddish influences are most apparent in:

1 vocabulary. Among the words borrowed are items relating to culture:

bar mitzvah (ceremony marking the religious coming-of-age of a boy)
bris (circumcision ceremony)
kiddush (blessing over bread and wine)

to food:

bagel (type of bread roll)
gefilte fish (chopped fish, often served as fish cakes)
matzo (unleavened bread)

to people:

goy (non-Jew)
klutz (clumsy person)
shiksa (non-Jewish girl)

to characteristics, expressions and exclamations:

chutzpah (cheek)
kosher (genuine)
schmaltz (sentimentality)
Mazel tov! (Good luck!)
Shalom! (Peace!)
Oy veh! (Heavens above!)
Shtoom! (Say nothing!)

2 in syntax, including a change in word order:

A fool I have for a son!

use of noun phrases in apposition:

My son the doctor

use of:

Enjoy!

and the use of *already* and *yet* as the English equivalents of *shoyn* and *noch*:

Already he's tired/He's tired already! (criticism not description)
Yet he doesn't come?/He doesn't come yet?

See: **foregrounding**.

your, you're

Your and *you're* are occasionally confused, as in the following printed sign in a hospital X-ray department:

*Ladies, if there is any possibility of **you're** being pregnant, please tell the radiographer before treatment.*

Your is a possessive adjective which precedes a noun or noun phrase:

*I couldn't forget **your** birthday.*

It also precedes a present **participle** which is used as a noun:

*What are the chances of **your** staying?*

In informal speech, *you* is often used before present participles:

*What are the chances of **you** staying?*

You're is a contraction of *you are*:

*Watch where **you're** going.*

See: **apostrophe, gerund, participle**.

Zambian English

The Republic of Zambia was explored by Livingstone in the 1850s and, because of its pleasant climate, it attracted a number of British settlers. It became the British Protectorate of Northern Rhodesia in 1911, was part of the Federation of Rhodesia and Nyasaland from 1953 to 1963 and became independent in 1964.

English is an official language for Zambia's 6 million people and it is widely used in education, government, the media and in intertribal and international dealings.

See: **East African English, Southern African English.**

zero forms

The term *zero* is widely used in linguistic analyses of English in dealing with patterns which are not altogether regular. It is used, for example, to help explain:

1 words which change their classes without any affixation. Thus:

high (adj) → *high* (noun) (*high* + ∅)
up (prep) → *up* (verb) (*up* + ∅)

The new word classes resemble words which change their **class** by means of affixation:

nice (adj) → *nicety* (noun) (*nice* + *ity*)
up (prep) → *uproot* (verb) (*up* + *root*)

This phenomenon where a word changes its class without affixation is known as *zero affixation*.

2 words which can imply plurality without a change in form:

Singular	Plural
deer	*deer* + ∅
sheep	*sheep* + ∅

This phenomenon is often referred to as *zero plural*. Zero plurals are frequently used in expressing **age, measurements, money** and **weights:**

a sixty-year-old man
It's three foot wide.
That was two pound fifty.
It weighed four hundredweight.

3 the fact that **conjunctions** may be omitted:

He said (that) he was tired.
The man (whom) we saw was young.

This phenomenon is sometimes referred to as *zero connectors* or *zero conjunctions*.

See: affix, age, conjunction, measurements, money, plurals of nouns.

Zimbabwean English

Zimbabwe, earlier *Southern Rhodesia*, became a British colony in 1898. By 1923 it gained a measure of self-government and was part of the Federation of Rhodesia and Nyasaland from 1953 to 1963. Like South Africa, Southern Rhodesia had a settled white population, the leaders of whom opposed the notion of 'one man, one vote'. In 1965, the white minority broke away from Britain but its Unilateral Declaration of Independence (UDI) was declared illegal. In 1980, general elections were held and Zimbabwe came into existence.

English is an official language for Zimbabwe's population of 8 million. It is the language of education, government, much of the media and virtually all intertribal and international discussion.

See: East African English, Southern African English.

Index